Lecture Notes in Computer Science   11864

More information about this series at http://www.springer.com/series/7409

Ingmar Weber · Kareem M. Darwish ·
Claudia Wagner · Emilio Zagheni ·
Laura Nelson · Samin Aref ·
Fabian Flöck (Eds.)

Social Informatics

11th International Conference, SocInfo 2019
Doha, Qatar, November 18–21, 2019
Proceedings

 Springer

Editors
Ingmar Weber
Qatar Computing
Research Institute
Doha, Qatar

Claudia Wagner
University of Koblenz-Landau
Koblenz, Germany

GESIS - Leibniz Institute
for the Social Sciences
Cologne, Germany

Laura Nelson
Northeastern University
Boston, MA, USA

Fabian Flöck
GESIS-Leibniz Institute
for the Social Sciences
Cologne, Germany

Kareem M. Darwish
Qatar Computing
Research Institute
Doha, Qatar

Emilio Zagheni
Max Planck Institute
for Demographic Research
Rostock, Germany

Samin Aref
Max Planck Institute
for Demographic Research
Rostock, Germany

ISSN 0302-9743   ISSN 1611-3349   (electronic)
Lecture Notes in Computer Science
ISBN 978-3-030-34970-7   ISBN 978-3-030-34971-4   (eBook)
https://doi.org/10.1007/978-3-030-34971-4

LNCS Sublibrary: SL3 – Information Systems and Applications, incl. Internet/Web, and HCI

This Springer imprint is published by the registered company Springer Nature Switzerland AG
The registered company address is: Gewerbestrasse 11, 6330 Cham, Switzerland

Preface

This volume contains the proceedings of the 11th Conference on Social Informatics (SocInfo 2019), held in Doha, Qatar, during November 18–21, 2019. Continuing the tradition of this conference series, SocInfo 2019 brought together researchers from the computational and social sciences with the intent of closing the gap that has traditionally separated the two communities. The goal of the conference was to provide a forum for academics from many disciplines to define common research objectives and explore new methodological advances in their fields. The organizers welcomed a broad range of contributions, ranging from those that apply the methods of the social sciences in the study of socio-technical systems, to those that employ computer science methods to analyze complex social processes, as well as those that make use of social concepts in the design of information systems. The most welcomed were the papers that belonged to more than one discipline.

This year SocInfo received 86 submitted papers from a total of 183 distinct authors, located in 30 different countries. We were glad to have a broad and diverse committee of 46 Senior Program Committee members and 131 Program Committee members with a strong interdisciplinary background from all over the world. The Program Committee reviewed all submissions and provided the authors with in-depth feedback on how to improve their work. As last year, SocInfo 2019 employed a double-blind peer-review process involving a two-tiered Program Committee. Papers received an average of four to five reviews by the Program Committee, as well as a meta review from the Senior Program Committee. Based on their input, the program chairs selected 17 full and 5 short papers for oral presentation, and 21 submissions for poster presentations.

In addition to posters and paper presentations, SocInfo 2019 hosted three great keynotes and four invited talks delivered by Franceso Billari (Bocconi University), Emre Kiciman (Microsoft Research AI), Katy Börner (Indiana University in Bloomington), Yelena Mejova (ISI Foundation), Luca Maria Aiello (Nokia Bell Labs), Aniko Hannak (Vienna University of Economics and Business), and Giovanni Luca Ciampaglia (University of South Florida).

We would like to congratulate and thank all the authors and attendees for selecting this venue to present and discuss their research. We would like to thank everybody involved in the conference organization that helped us in making this event successful. We owe special thanks to the Steering Committee of this conference for their input and support, particularly the chair of the Steering Committee, Adam Wierzbicki, and Luca Maria Aiello, who is another active member of the committee. The organizers are extremely grateful to all the reviewers and the members of the Program Committee for their efforts in making sure that the contributions adhered to the highest standards of scientific rigor and originality. We are also grateful to Ridhi Kashyap and Minsu Park as workshop chairs, to Rumi Chunara and Bogdan State as tutorial chairs, to Jisun An as web chair, to Sofiane Abbar as sponsorship chair, and to Kholoud Aldous as registration chair. We are very thankful to our sponsors, the Qatar National Research

Fund, Qatar Computing Research Institute, Northwestern University in Qatar, Carnegie Mellon University in Qatar, and Springer for providing generous support. A special thanks to Qanect for their help in logistics and planning.

Finally, we hope you will enjoy reading through the proceedings and that you will continue to engage with the SocInfo community.

November 2019

Samin Aref
Kareem Darwish
Fabian Flöck
Laura Nelson
Claudia Wagner
Ingmar Weber
Emilio Zagheni

Organization

General Chairs

Ingmar Weber   Qatar Computing Research Institute, Hamad Bin Khalifa University, Qatar

Kareem M. Darwish   Qatar Computing Research Institute, Hamad Bin Khalifa University, Qatar

Program Committee Chairs

Claudia Wagner   GESIS - Leibniz Institute for the Social Sciences, Germany

Emilio Zagheni   Max Planck Institute for Demographic Research, Germany

Laura K. Nelson   Northeastern University, USA

Workshop Chairs

Ridhi Kashyap   University of Oxford, UK

Minsu Park   Cornell University, USA

Tutorial Chairs

Rumi Chunara   New York University, USA

Bogdan State   Facebook, USA

Proceedings Chair

Fabian Flöck   GESIS - Leibniz Institute for the Social Sciences, Germany

Submission Chair

Samin Aref   Max Planck Institute for Demographic Research, Germany

Web Chair

Jisun An   Qatar Computing Research Institute, Hamad Bin Khalifa University, Qatar

Sponsorship Chair

Sofiane Abbar   Qatar Computing Research Institute, Hamad Bin
                               Khalifa University, Qatar

Registration Chair

Kholoud Aldous   Qatar Computing Research Institute, Hamad Bin
                               Khalifa University, Qatar

Steering Committee

Adam Wierzbicki   PJIIT, Poland
Karl Aberer   EPFL, Switzerland
Katsumi Tanaka   Kyoto University, Japan
Anwitaman Datta   Nanyang Technological University, Singapore
Ee-Peng Lim   Singapore Management University, Singapore
Noshir Contractor   Northwestern University, USA
Michael Macy   Cornell University, USA
Hsinchun Chen   University of Arizona, USA
Sue B. Moon   KAIST, South Korea
Andreas Ernst   University of Kassel, Germany
Andreas Flache   University of Groningen, The Netherlands
Dirk Helbing   ETH, Switzerland
Luca Maria Aiello   Nokia Bell Labs, UK
Daniel Anthony McFarland   University of Stanford, USA
Irwin King   The Chinese University of Hong Kong, Hong Kong,
                               China

Senior Program Committee

Luca Maria Aiello   Nokia Bell Labs, USA
Samin Aref   Max Planck Institute for Demographic Research,
                               Germany
Ciro Cattuto   ISI Foundation, Italy
Daniel Ciganda   Max Planck Institute for Demographic Research,
                               Germany
Dennis Feehan   University of California, Berkeley, USA
Miriam Fernandez   Knowledge Media Institute, UK
Fabian Flöck   GESIS Cologne, Germany
Kiran Garimella   Massachusetts Institute of Technology, USA
André Grow   Max Planck Institute for Demographic Research,
                               Germany
Alex Hanna   Google Cloud, USA
Denis Helic   Graz University of Technology, Austria
Kenneth Joseph   University at Buffalo, USA

Fariba Karimi	GESIS - Leibniz Institute for the Social Sciences, Germany
Ridhi Kashyap	University of Oxford, UK
Emre Kiciman	Microsoft Research AI, USA
Katharina Kinder-Kurlanda	GESIS - Leibniz Institute for the Social Sciences, Germany
Ryota Kobayashi	National Institute of Informatics, Japan
Kiran Lakkaraju	Sandia National Laboratories, USA
Florian Lemmerich	RWTH Aachen University, Germany
Bruno Lepri	MobS Lab, Fondazione Bruno Kessler, Italy
Kristina Lerman	University of Southern California, USA
Elisabeth Lex	Graz University of Technology, Austria
Walid Magdy	The University of Edinburgh, UK
Eric Malmi	Google, Switzerland
Afra Mashhadi	UN Global Pulse, USA
Yelena Mejova	ISI Foundation, Italy
Kevin Munger	Princeton Center for the Study of Democratic Politics, USA
Zachary Neal	Michigan State University, USA
Wolfgang Nejdl	Leibniz University Hannover, Germany
Weike Pan	Shenzhen University, China
Marco Pellegrini	Institute for Informatics and Telematics of CNR, Italy
Jason Radford	University of Chicago, USA
Miriam Redi	Wikimedia Foundation, UK
Timothy Riffe	Max Planck Institute for Demographic Research, Germany
Blaine Robbins	New York University Abu Dhabi, UAE
Daniel Romero	University of Michigan, USA
Alex Rutherford	Scalable Cooperation (MIT Media Lab), USA
Diego Saez-Trumper	Wikimedia, Spain
Kavé Salamatian	Polytech'Annecy Chambéry, France
Michael Schultz	Northwestern University, USA
Steffen Staab	Institut WeST, University Koblenz-Landau, Germany
Bogdan State	Stanford University, USA
Rochelle Terman	University of Chicago, USA
Devesh Tiwari	Northeastern University, USA
Christoph Trattner	University of Bergen, Norway
Katrin Weller	GESIS - Leibniz Institute for the Social Sciences, Germany

Program Committee

Palakorn Achananuparp	Living Analytics Research Centre, Singapore Management University
Thomas Ågotnes	University of Bergen
Wei Ai	University of Michigan

Diego Alburez-Gutierrez	Max Planck Institute of Demographic Research
Hamed Alhoori	Northern Illinois University
Kristen Altenburger	Stanford University
Tawfiq Ammari	University of Michigan
Pablo Aragón	Universitat Pompeu Fabra
Mossaab Bagdouri	Walmart eCommerce
Ebrahim Bagheri	Ryerson University
Vladimir Barash	Graphika, Inc.
Dominik Batorski	University of Warsaw
Martin Becker	University of Würzburg
George Berry	Cornell University
Ginestra Bianconi	Queen Mary University of London
Livio Bioglio	University of Turin
Jim Blomo	SigOpt
Svetlana Bodrunova	St. Petersburg State University
Ludovico Boratto	Eurecat
Ulrik Brandes	ETH Zurich
Cody Buntain	SMaPP Lab, New York University
Colin Campbell	Washington College
Leslie Carr	University of Southampton
Claudio Castellano	ISC-CNR, Sapienza Universita' di Roma
Fabio Celli	Gruppo Maggioli
Nina Cesare	Institute for Health Metrics and Evaluation, University of Washington
Stevie Chancellor	Georgia Institute of Technology
Charalampos Chelmis	University at Albany State University of New York
Yi-Shin Chen	National Tsing Hua University
Dimitris Christopoulos	Modul University Vienna and The University of Edinburgh
Taejoong Chung	Rochester Institute of Technology
David Corney	Full Fact
Denzil Correa	Bayer Pharma R&D
Michele Coscia	IT University of Copenhagen
Andrew Crooks	George Mason University
Ángel Cuevas	Universidad Carlos III de Madrid
Rubn Cuevas	Universidad Carlos III de Madrid
Tiago Cunha	University of Michigan
Thomas Davidson	Cornell University
Emiliano De Cristofaro	University College London
Emanuele Del Fava	Max Planck Institute for Demographic Research
Jana Diesner	University of Illinois at Urbana-Champaign
Djellel Difallah	New York University Center for Data Science
Sofia Dokuka	National Research University Higher School of Economics
Victor M. Eguiluz	Institute for Cross-Disciplinary Physics and Complex Systems, Universitat de les Illes Balears

Motahhare Eslami	University of Illinois at Urbana-Champaign
Reza Farahbakhsh	Institut Mines-Télécom, Télécom SudParis
Katayoun Farrahi	University of Southampton
Vanessa Frias-Martinez	University of Maryland
Gerhard Fuchs	University of Stuttgart
Sabrina Gaito	University of Milan
Peng Gao	University of California, Berkeley
Floriana Gargiulo	GEMASS-CNRS, University of Paris Sorbonne
Sofia Gil-Clavel	Max Planck Institute for Demographic Research
Maria Glenski	University of Notre Dame
Jessica Godwin	Max Planck Institute for Demographic Research
Kwang-Il Goh	Korea University
Christophe Guéret	Accenture Labs
Francesco Gullo	UniCredit
Pritam Gundecha	IBM Research Almaden
Mohammed Hasanuzzaman	ADAPT Centre Dublin
Tuan-Anh Hoang	L3S Research Center, Leibniz University of Hanover
Kim Holmberg	University of Turku
Christopher Homan	Rochester Institute of Technology
Geert-Jan Houben	Delft University of Technology
Yuheng Hu	University of Illinois at Chicago
Dmitry Ignatov	National Research University Higher School of Economics
Adam Jatowt	Kyoto University
Marco Alberto Javarone	School of Computing, Electronics and Mathematics, Coventry University
Hang-Hyun Jo	Asia Pacific Center for Theoretical Physics
Kazuhiro Kazama	Wakayama University
Styliani Kleanthous	University of Cyprus
Andreas Koch	University of Salzburg
Sergei Koltcov	National Research University Higher School of Economics
Hemank Lamba	Carnegie Mellon University
Renaud Lambiotte	University of Oxford
Walter Lamendola	University of Denver
Georgios Lappas	Technological Educational Institute (TEI) of Western Macedonia
Yanina Ledovaya	Saint Petersburg University
Deok-Sun Lee	Inha University
Xiao Ma	Cornell Tech
Matteo Magnani	Uppsala University
Matteo Manca	Eurecat (Technological Center of Catalunya)
Lydia Manikonda	Arizona State University
Gianluca Manzo	Centre National de la Recherche Scientifique
Emanuele Massaro	École polytechnique fédérale de Lausanne
Naoki Masuda	University of Bristol

Hisashi Miyamori	Kyoto Sangyo University
Jose Moreno	Institut de Recherche en Informatique de Toulouse
Tsuyoshi Murata	Tokyo Institute of Technology
Shinsuke Nakajima	Kyoto Sangyo University
Keiichi Nakata	University of Reading
Mirco Nanni	KDD-Lab, The Alessandro Faedo Institute of Information Science and Technologies
Daniela Negraia	Max Planck Institute of Demographic Research
Alexandra Nenko	National Research University Higher School of Economics
Finn Årup Nielsen	Technical University of Denmark
Carlos Nunes Silva	Universidade de Lisboa
Jason Nurse	University of Kent
Symeon Papadopoulos	Information Technologies Institute
Luca Pappalardo	University of Pisa, KDD-Lab, and The Alessandro Faedo Institute of Information Science and Technologies
Sergei Pashakhin	National Research University Higher School of Economics
Leto Peel	Universite Catholique de Louvain
María Pereda	Universidad Politcnica de Madrid
Hemant Purohit	George Mason University
Muhammad Atif Qureshi	ADAPT Centre Dublin
Giancarlo Ruffo	Universita' di Torino
Mostafa Salehi	University of Tehran
Piotr Sapiezynski	Northeastern University
Kazutoshi Sasahara	Nagoya University
Michael Schaub	Massachusetts Institute of Technology
Rossano Schifanella	University of Turin
Frank Schweitzer	ETH Zurich
Rok Sosic	Stanford University
Srinath Srinivasa	International Institute of Information Technology Bangalore
Pål Sundsøy	Norges Bank Investment Management
Xian Teng	University of Pittsburgh
Michele Tizzoni	ISI Foundation
Klaus G. Troitzsch	University of Koblenz-Landau
Charalampos Tsourakakis	Harvard University
Onur Varol	Northeastern University
Wenbo Wang	Kno.e.sis Center, Wright State University
Sanjaya Wijeratne	Kno.e.sis Center, Wright State University
Joss Wright	Oxford Internet Institute, University of Oxford
Kevin S. Xu	University of Toledo
Elena Yagunova	St. Petersburg State University
Hirozumi Yamaguchi	Osaka University
Jie Yang	Amazon Research

Arjumand Younus	Insight Center for Data Analytics, University College Dublin
Nicholas Jing Yuan	Huawei Technologies
Yang Zhang	CISPA Helmholtz Center for Information Security
Arkaitz Zubiaga	Queen Mary University of London

Additional Reviewers

Makan Arastuie	The University of Toledo, USA
Ly Dinh	University of Illinois at Urbana-Champaign, USA
Xinlei He	Fudan University, China
Ming Jiang	University of Illinois at Urbana-Champaign, USA
Minglei Li	The Hong Kong Polytechnic University, Hong Kong, China
Polyvios Pratikakis	Foundation for Research and Technology – Hellas, Greece
Janina Sarol	University of Illinois at Urbana-Champaign, USA
Konstantinos Sotiropoulos	Boston University, USA
Raksha Pavagada Subbanarasimha	International Institute of Information Technology Bangalore, India
Bartlomiej Surma	Helmholtz Center for Information Security, Germany
Amalia Triantafillidou	Technological Educational Institute of Western Macedonia, Greece
Eirini Tsichla	Technological Educational Institute of Western Macedonia, Greece
Zhefeng Wang	Huawei, China
Cyril Weerasooriya	Rochester Institute of Technology, USA
Rui Wen	University of Science and Technology of China, China
Zhiqiang Zhong	University of Luxembourg, Luxembourg

Sponsors

Qatar National Research Fund (QNRF)
Qatar Computing Research Institute (QCRI)
Northwestern University in Qatar (NU-Q)
Carnegie Mellon University in Qatar (CMU-Q)
Springer

Contents

Full Papers

Airbnb's Reputation System and Gender Differences Among Guests: Evidence from Large-Scale Data Analysis and a Controlled Experiment

Eunseo Choi and Emőke-Ágnes Horvát[(✉)]

Northwestern University, Evanston, IL 60208, USA
eunseochoi2019@u.northwestern.edu, a-horvat@northwestern.edu

Abstract. Sharing economy platforms are rapidly scaling up by reaching increasingly diverse demographics. However, this expansion comes with great difficulties in adequately identifying and responding to everyone's needs. In this paper, we study gender-related behaviors of guests on the currently most prominent home-sharing platform, Airbnb. While our results confirm the efficacy of Airbnb's reputation system, we also find that the level of trust and participation on the platform varies by gender. In particular, female solo travelers are more likely to be conscious of review sentiment and choose more often female hosts than male solo travelers. Our findings are obtained by combining exploratory data analysis with large-scale experiments and call for further studies on the usage of sharing economy platforms among subpopulations, informing and improving both policy and practice in these growing online environments.

Keywords: Sharing economy · Reputation systems · Trust · Gender bias

1 Introduction

Airbnb provides both small entrepreneurs the chance to thrive and travelers to secure cost-efficient housing options. Despite the economic benefits that the platform presents, the interplay between guests making booking requests and hosts choosing to selectively accept requests might facilitate discrimination based on demographic characteristics. For instance, previous research has uncovered racial bias on Airbnb [12,13]. To counter such biases, Airbnb provides a reputation system based on user reviews, has a damage protection and insurance program, publicizes anti-discrimination policies, and promotes an instant booking option that does not require hosts' approval. Recent research has shown that this reputation system is effectively mitigating some social biases [3,21]. However, it remains unclear how in particular men and women use the information provided by the reputation system and how this influences their choices as guests to book

© Springer Nature Switzerland AG 2019
I. Weber et al. (Eds.): SocInfo 2019, LNCS 11864, pp. 3–17, 2019.
https://doi.org/10.1007/978-3-030-34971-4_1

with a host or not. This study addresses thus the question of *whether male and female travelers exhibit differential information processing and decision-making on Airbnb to increase and facilitate their usage of the platform.*

With an analysis of large-scale Airbnb data and human subject experiments, we focus on people who travel alone, as multiple travel websites have seen a surge of demand from this understudied market segment [4,14,19]. Our study makes the following contributions:

1. It identifies large-scale trends in the structural underpinnings of the reviewing process by studying patterns in host–guest networks built from Airbnb data.
2. It uncovers guests' safety-concerns on the platform using simple linguistic analyses of over 150,000 Airbnb reviews.
3. It studies experimentally the different role of review sentiment for men and women.
4. It examines the effect of the preference to interact with other users of one's own gender (i.e., homophily) on booking rates.

The results are aligned with and extend previous findings in social computing [3,16,21,25,26,33,34]. The paper is structured as follows: we summarize relevant work in Sect. 2 and detail the used methodologies and obtained findings in Sects. 3 and 4. Finally, we discuss results in light of existing literature proposing directions for further research in Sect. 5.

2   Related Work

Social Biases. Recent research has started to explore biases in online rental marketplaces and showed that hosts exhibit different acceptance rates for guests with certain racial characteristics. Specifically, Edelman, Luca, and Svirsky conducted a field experiment in which they created fictitious guest profiles with distinctively white or African-American names and sent booking requests to actual hosts on Airbnb. This experiment showed that African-American guests were 16% less likely to be accepted compared to white guests [13]. In a separate experiment that tested for digital discrimination against Airbnb hosts, Edelman and Luca found African-American hosts to be at a disadvantage as well, making less money than white hosts [12]. Based on this literature, *it is unclear whether and how gender bias would manifest itself on Airbnb.* More broadly, there is evidence that women are perceived as more trustworthy than men in an artificial investment setting [5], which suggests that female hosts could have an advantage over male hosts. Additionally, there is evidence that the preference for females is more pronounced among other females [30]. To accurately assess the implications of a potential preference for one's own gender on Airbnb, we need systematic comparisons about the participation rates of men and women. If there would be a strong imbalance in participation on top of a considerable in-group preference, the smaller group's growth could be limited.

Gender-Based Risk Aversion. Since participation rates may be closely associated with perceived risks, this research is also informed by previous literature on gender-based risk aversion. An extensive body of literature reported that women are in general more risk-averse than men (e.g., see [6]). In the context of the sharing economy, a study on online freelance work found that while workers of both genders considered crime and distance when accepting tasks to complete, female taskers were less likely to accept tasks than males in the presence of safety concerns [34]. The difference in willingness to perform tasks was close to 20%. Again, *it is not well understood how risk is perceived and dealt with on Airbnb.* If we were to find female users to be more concerned about their safety when using the platform and thus be more sensitive to negative signals about hosts than male users, this would have implications for policies imposing universal non-discrimination rules under the assumption of uniform attitudes towards risk.

Reputation Systems. Various studies have also investigated the effect of similar reputation systems. Favorable reputation and trust are positively correlated, and high trust can affect consumer decision-making [11,14,15,20,23,25,26]. A study involving field experiments found that both positive and negative reviews significantly increase the acceptance rate for Airbnb guests with an African-American-sounding name [8]. These results suggest that information provided by the reputation system about service quality reduces the risks perceived by consumers. Ert et al. compared specific features of the reputation system with evaluations of trustworthiness: After measuring the effect of star ratings and number of reviews, they showed that the latter has a stronger effect on engendering trust than average ratings [15]. None of these studies, however, have explicitly considered demographic characteristics of reviewers contributing to the reputation system nor how these reviews might be evaluated differently by guests from the same vs other demographic groups. *We are thus lacking an understanding of the potential differences between male and female guest's use of Airbnb's reputation system.*

3   Exploratory Data Analysis of User Activity on Airbnb

3.1   Data and Methods

To first gain a macro-level understanding of Airbnb users' behavior, we use large-scale data available on *InsideAirbnb.com* [17,29]. To ensure representativeness and sample sizes that lend themselves to statistical analysis, we picked listings associated with three large cities from across the U.S.: New York City (25,636 listings recorded between March 12th, 2009 and March 4th, 2018), Los Angeles (18,405 listings recorded between January 10th, 2009 and May 10th, 2017), and Chicago (3,610 listings recorded between July 3rd, 2009 and May 10th, 2017). For each city, we manually picked 100 listings and verified that the available data is consistent with the real information provided on Airbnb's website. This sample contained details about 47,651 listings that accumulated in total 1,014,134 reviews.

We assigned gender to each unique host and reviewer using U.S. census data [2], applying a procedure similar to [18,35]. Additionally, we validated each person's gender with the GenderChecker database [1]. In total, 84.2% of the reviewers and hosts were gender-identifiable. To restrict our sample to solo travelers, we filtered out reviews that used collective group words like "us", "we", and "our". We further limited the data to listings that are commonly chosen by individuals traveling alone, i.e., private or shared rooms. By doing so, we focus on the concerns of solo travelers who are unlikely to have had the resources to opt for a whole house or apartment and were thus only left with the option to share space with strangers on Airbnb. These data processing steps restricted our sample to 18,123 listings and 169,632 reviews.

To uncover systematic trends, we performed both structural and linguistic analyses. First, we explored preferences in choosing one gender over the other in the Airbnb context with a structural mapping of the reviewing process to a host–guest bipartite network [24]. Essentially, we built a network for every city by connecting each host having a listing in the considered region with every guest who left a review on their profile. Since we have extensive longitudinal data for over six years, the resulting networks can be assumed to reflect stable gender-related patterns. Second, we studied the content of the reviews. We used a common dictionary-based approach known as LIWC [31] to match stemmed words from the reviews with a large human-curated dictionary. LIWC was only used to annotate reviews with their overall sentiment. To also investigate user concerns about security, we identified and counted the occurrence of safety-related words (i.e. "safe", "secure", "lock", "safety", "dangerous", "crime"). Note that while not every Airbnb guest writes reviews, we used reviewers as a proxy for Airbnb guests throughout both types of analyses.

3.2   Results

Structural Analysis. Table 2 in Appendix shows the number of hosts and solo traveling guests of both genders in the three networks. Although in NYC and LA, female hosts outnumber male hosts, across the board there are less female guests who write reviews. In total, 44.0% of the 149,112 unique gender-identifiable reviewers were women. To better understand the link between roles (guest vs host), gender, and prevalence of activity on Airbnb, we show the distribution of users with a given number of activities (i.e., having written a review as a guest and having had a review written for them as a host) in the studied time frame (see Fig. 3 in Appendix). For each city, we find typical right-skewed distributions indicating that most activity is generated by a few users, while the majority of people utilize Airbnb only occasionally. While it is unsurprising that guests have systematically less activity than hosts, the gender differences are interesting. In terms of the number of reviews written, which is a proxy for the number of stays of a guest on Airbnb, male guests write significantly more reviews than female guests (Mann-Whitney U tests: $p < 0.001$ for all three cities). Male hosts also receive significantly more reviews (i.e., proxy for the number of visitors a host has) in NYC and Chicago (Mann-Whitney U tests: $p < 0.001$ and $p = 0.03$). The fact that male hosts receive more reviews in NYC is especially noteworthy given that, in absolute numbers, there are fewer male hosts than female hosts.

In addition to differences between male and female users' presence and frequency of activity on the platform, we study how gender-homophily could penetrate Airbnb's booking system. Homophily is the tendency to prefer others within one's own gender group, which is a fundamental and wide-spread social process in the formation of social ties [22]. We compute a homophily index [9] that captures the fraction of female reviewers (guests) among prior reviewers on a listing when the current reviewer (guest) chooses it. We find that female guests choose listings reviewed previously by more females than males, while male guests choose listings reviewed by more males. The difference between male and female guests is consistently significant (Chi-squared tests: $p < 0.001$) across all three cities (see Fig. 1).

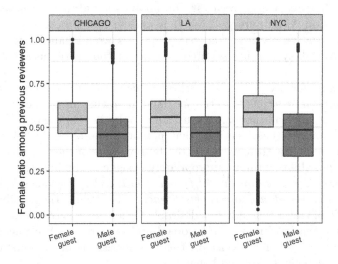

Fig. 1. The fraction of females among the reviewers seen by female vs male guests when considering a listing indicates that female guests choose listings reviewed by more females.

Linguistic Analysis. The overall sentiment of review texts was strongly skewed towards positive reviews (98.6% positive). This wide-spread positivity is in agreement with trends identified on Airbnb five years ago [36]. Next we explore basic differences in the text of male and female users' reviews. To examine whether safety concerns vary by gender, we compared female and male reviewers' explicit mentions of safety-related words. The frequency of safety-related words mentioned by female and male reviewers was measured by listing words that are generally associated to security and counting the instances. Among female solo reviewers, 6.6% mentioned concerns or satisfactions related to safety, while only 5.3% of male solo reviewers talked about safety. This difference is statistically significant ($p < 0.001$).

Summary and Unanswered Questions. Our analysis of large-scale Airbnb data resulted in four main findings. First, although there tend to be more female hosts, male hosts have more reviews and, by extension, more guests. Second, there are fewer female than male reviewers (guests) and they write less reviews. Third, female guests choose listings reviewed by more females. Finally, female guests' reviews mention safety-concerns more frequently. While the first two findings represent observations about patterns created over more than six years on Airbnb around the LA, Chicago, and NYC area, the last finding lends itself to experimental study. To strengthen thus the validity of these findings and further explore potential explanations behind them, in what followed we conducted an experiment that tackles the following questions:

1. *How effective are positive reviews?* Our analysis found that essentially nearly all reviews on Airbnb are positive. It is unclear how potential guests would react to negative reviews. Understanding this would indicate whether the current Airbnb system has selected an efficient tool in the usage of positive reviews.
2. *Is there a preference for hosts of either gender and do reviewers of a specific gender have more weight?* On the one hand, literature about the link between trust and gender indicates more trust for females [5]. On the other hand, our empirical analysis has identified that potential guests on Airbnb might be drawn to listings with reviews written by reviewers of their own gender. We test this possibility with an appropriately designed experiment.
3. *Is the lower participation rate of female solo travelers explained by gendered response and sensitivity to review sentiment?* To exclude the possibility that this mode of travel is simply less desirable for female solo travelers, we create identical scenarios for men and women and explore which elements of the situation influence their decisions, this way increasing our understanding of a key factor behind observed behaviors.

4   Experimental Study

Given existing evidence for the effectiveness of Airbnb's reputation system [3,8], we anticipate that reviews influence decision-making for both genders. However, literature on women's risk-aversion [6] suggests that they might be more sensitive to review sentiment than men. We thus test whether review sentiment impacts guests differently based on their gender. To better understand differences in participation on Airbnb and to more directly address the different risk-attitudes in the face of safety concerns, we also test whether guest gender itself is associated with booking decision after accounting for factors related to review sentiment, host and reviewer gender. Additionally, we consider insights from the large-scale data analysis related to gender-based homophily and different levels of concern about safety for men and women. To assess the effect of homophily, we first examine whether the gender of reviewers on a certain host's profile acts as a significant decision factor for guests, for instance as a strategy to better assess risk with the help of reviews from others of the same gender. Second, we investigate the possibility that guests have preference with regard to host gender. To this end, we explicitly test for an interaction effect between guest and host gender. Our hypotheses are as follows:

H1.1 *There is an interaction effect between the sentiment of review text and guest gender.*
H1.2 *Guest gender affects booking decision.*
H1.3 *Reviewer gender affects guests' booking decisions.*
H1.4 *There is an interaction effect between host and guest gender.*

For the experiment, we created a set of fictitious profiles such that each profile had a gender-revealing host name, reviewer name, and one review (either positive or negative). Reviews used in each profile were randomly drawn from *InsideAirbnb* data by sentiment category. Both positive and negative reviews had similar word counts. Reviews only discussed sentiment towards the host without mentioning any physical attributes of the listed property to avoid confounding. Additionally, we inserted star ratings into a random sample of profiles to better replicate the effects of the reputation system. Selected profiles with a negative review were given 3 stars, while profiles with a positive review were given 5 stars.

We recruited 1,041 Mechanical Turk workers who had completed more than 1,000 tasks, had above 97% acceptance rate, were residents of the U.S., and were current Airbnb users. Participants were shown one of sixteen randomly assigned host profiles that were simplified mock-ups of real Airbnb profiles. To avoid confounding, host profile photos were replaced with scenery images and fictitious hosts were assigned race-neutral names. Participants were then asked whether or not they would send a booking request if they were to travel alone and only had enough budget to book a shared/private room on Airbnb. One attention checker was included that asked participants halfway through the questions which type of room they were opting for in this study. We retained only those participants' answers who stated to be making decisions as solo travelers looking to book shared/private rooms. For each combination of variables, we measured the percentage of participants who decided to book with the host. The randomization of host profiles and participants acted as a valid instrument for the estimation of causal relationships.

4.1   Results

As shown in Fig. 2, we examined the difference in booking rate by review sentiment and guest gender using non-parametric proportion tests. We stratified the data by the sentiment of the review text. When one negative review was presented in a host's profile, female participants (guests) had a 1.3% probability of booking, while male participants (guests) booked in 6.2% of the cases;

this difference is statistically significant ($p = 0.006$). However, the difference in the booking rate between male and female participants was *in*significant in the presence of a positive review ($p = 0.784$). Similarly, without further controls, the overall difference in the probability of deciding to book between male and female participants (i.e., 32.4% vs 27.3%) was not significant ($p = 0.08$). We also stratified the data by host gender. Female participants had a 33.3% probability of booking with female hosts and a 21.5% probability of booking with male hosts, a difference that is statistically significant ($p = 0.002$). In the absence of other controls, the difference in male participants' probability of booking with female vs male hosts was 28.6% vs 36.3%, $p = 0.09$. Finally, participants did not show statistically significant booking differences based on the gender of reviewer when we stratified the data by reviewer gender.

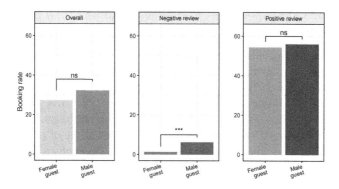

Fig. 2. Booking rates as percentages in the experimental study. The difference in the overall booking rate between male and female guests is insignificant, but it becomes significant in the presence of a negative review.

We formally tested these findings with a logistic regression model whose dependent variable was the decision to book or not. Key independent variables were guest gender, host gender, reviewer gender, and review sentiment (i.e., either positive or negative review about a host). Our model explicitly tested for interaction effects between these variables. Additionally, we controlled for guest age, income, frequency of activity on Airbnb, as well as star rating of host. Table 1 shows the results. Positive reviews are a highly significant indicator of booking. One positive review played a significant role in increasing the chances that a female guest would book with a host of any gender. Holding other variables constant, the odds of a female guest choosing a host with a positive review was 115 times higher than the odds of a female participant choosing a host with a negative review. In a similar scenario, the odds of a male participant (guest) choosing a host with a positive review was 21 times higher than the odds of a male participant (guest) choosing a host with a negative review. Positive review sentiment plays thus a role among both genders, although female guests are more

Table 1. Results of logistic regression models for our experimental study. The model emphasizes the role of positive reviews. Above and beyond that, the model also indicates that on the one hand there is a significant gender-homophily between guests and hosts with whom they book and on the other hand female guests book overall less. Note that guests in this table correspond to study participants, hosts and reviewers are deduced from the fictitious profiles.

Variable	Coeff	SD
Female host	-0.28	0.24
Positive review	3.07^{***}	0.31
Female guest	-2.12^{***}	0.64
Female guest x Female host	1.03^{**}	0.34
Female reviewer	0.10	0.24
Female guest x Female reviewer	-0.18	0.34
Female guest x Positive review	1.67^{**}	0.61
Stars	0.40^{*}	0.17
Constant	0.14	1.45
Deviance = 809.95		
Penalized Deviance = 781.76		
McFadden's pseudo R^2 = 0.36		

Note: $^{*}p < 0.05$; $^{**}p < 0.01$; $^{***}p < 0.001$.

sensitive to the sentiment of review text than male guests, supporting hypothesis H1.1.

Although the lower overall booking rate for women was not significant in the direct comparison, the odds of female guests booking are 88% less than the odds of male guests booking, confirming hypothesis H1.2. In contrast, hypothesis H1.3 is not supported: Reviewer gender and its interaction with guest gender are insignificant, suggesting that positive reviews are efficient regardless of the gender of the reviewer. Finally, we studied the effect of guest gender and its interaction with host gender. Both female and male participants (guests) in our experiment demonstrated their preference for hosts of their own gender. Holding other variables constant, the odds that a male guest booked a male host were 25% greater than the odds of them booking with a female host. Female guests displayed an even stronger homophily: The odds of a female guest booking with a female host were twice the odds of them booking with a male host. This finding supports hypothesis H1.4 and concludes our regression analysis.

To further unpack the finding that solo female guests were more sensitive to negative reviews than male participants, in a post-experiment questionnaire, we asked about accommodation preferences and safety-concerns. 1,275 of our experimental study participants (631 females and 644 males) responded to this questionnaire. 70% of the participants indicated that they would rather stay at a hotel than book a room on Airbnb if they had to travel alone. 80% of the respondents who preferred hotels selected "security" as one of their reasons.

Broken down by gender, 73.3% of females preferred hotels over Airbnb and 89.2% of them mentioned security as a reason. In contrast, only 65.9% of males preferred hotels over Airbnb, and a lower percentage of them (i.e., 69.6%) referred to security as a reason. The questionnaire encapsulated the perceived association between risk and staying at an Airbnb and implied that safety is a key involved risk. According to participants' responses, users (especially female solo travelers) opt for hotels instead of Airbnb listings because of the safety of hotels. This observation is aligned with previous research indicating that women are more risk-averse than men in the presence of safety concerns in the sharing economy and beyond [6,34].

5   Discussion and Conclusion

This paper extends previous studies on the role of front-end features in signaling trustworthiness of a user [8] by initiating questions about gender-related differences in solo travelers' usage of Airbnb. Specifically, the paper studies the effect of the reputation system on male versus female guest's trust judgments. Our study created new knowledge about how male and female solo travelers utilize Airbnb's reputation system and its (gender-related) features designed to give guests the opportunity to leave reviews and have more information about their choices. We examined whether and how informational elements available in this reputation system acted as a security blanket.

Given our finding that one positive review leads to a sizeable increase in booking rates for both male and female guests compared to one negative review, it is extremely important for new hosts with no prior hosting experience to receive positive reviews from their first guests. Our results also show gender-homophily among guests of both gender. This result explains why male hosts had a higher number of reviews in our structural analysis of *InsideAirbnb* data. *InsideAirbnb* data had a greater number of male than female reviewers (96,726 vs 72,906). Male guests preferring male hosts led to a greater number of bookings for male hosts. This effect was overcoming a larger absolute number of female hosts and a potentially higher trust in them. The result implies that simply having a high percentage of female hosts does not necessarily mean that Airbnb is a hospitable ecosystem for female hosts to thrive.

InsideAirbnb data indicated that female reviewers explicitly stated more safety-related words than male reviewers. Additionally, in our experiment solo female guests were more sensitive to negative reviews than male participants. Given that Airbnb (a peer-to-peer platform) has a different business structure from, and provides different service than hotels (business-to-peer institutions), women traveling solo require stronger signals of safety. The lower number of female reviewers in *InsideAirbnb* data suggests that more risk-averse solo travelers had effectively opted out of using the platform. Participants in our study, especially females, appealed to gender-homophily as a strategy to deal with uncertainty [10]. While homophily is effective in this respect, it can also have considerable drawbacks. Most importantly, the imbalance in male vs female guests' participation on top of a considerable in-group preference can be assumed to further restrain the expansion of the platform's female user base.

With this dilemma in mind, Airbnb could potentially carefully leverage the features in its reputation system that enable homophily to lower the barrier to participation. For example, Airbnb could offer its users personalized recommendation of hosts with an eye for exposing guests to a variety of host options, but also encouraging connections within subpopulations when the risk-aversion of the guest is high. Airbnb can potentially provide (female) solo travelers with more equitable access to its sharing economy platform. For our specific recommendation to be valid, however, further research is required to test and measure its impact.

5.1 Limitations of Exploratory Data Analyses

InsideAirbnb Data. There are some intrinsic limitations to the dataset that utilized public information compiled from the Airbnb website. The group that verified, processed, and analyzed aggregate data is unaffiliated with Airbnb [17], but the accuracy and completeness of the entire information cannot be guaranteed. More importantly, while findings from real Airbnb profiles provided some insights about actual Airbnb hosts and guests who travel alone, the data comprised only the sample of guests who left reviews and did make the choice to book a shared/private room. Finally, we acknowledge that gender is not binary [28] and use in this study name-based gender assignment approaches to approximate salient categories that display gendered behavior.

Structural and Linguistic Analysis. In the linguistic analysis, the frequency of safety-related words mentioned by female and male reviewers was measured by listing words that are generally associated to security and counting the instances. We did not consider reviews that are less explicit and more descriptive about safety-related situations during reviewers' stay. For example, we did not consider reviews such as "It was really dark at night and I heard someone knocking on my door multiple times" or "My host installed and hid a camera in my room."

We also did not consider or measure the distribution of key safety concerns expressed by reviewers on Airbnb. Although this does not significantly influence our current findings, in the future, we could expand on how guests connect Airbnb with safety issues and better specify their concerns, which could involve issues about hosts, location, electronic transaction process, and more. In addition to analyzing review content, future studies should explore the linguistic characteristics of the positive reviews and their relation with booking decisions. In other words, given that most reviews are positive, whether certain distinctive linguistic characteristics within positive reviews make readers convinced to book a place is still a question to be explored. Future studies could also explore how emotional tone and linguistic style differ by reviewer gender.

5.2 Limitations of the Experimental Study

Absence of Host Decision. Inside Airbnb data, on which we conducted our EDA, accounts for successful transactions between guests and hosts. In our experiments, however, we take Airbnb hosts decision making into account only indirectly. Female hosts having less reviews than male hosts may not solely be attributed to guests favoring same gender host. If female hosts also exhibit gender-homophily favoring same gender guests, more so than male hosts, there will be a surplus of female hosts in the market given the relatively large number of female hosts and small number of female guests. This may provide additional explanation as to why female hosts had less reviews and, by extension, less guests in our structural analysis.

Number of Reviews. In our experimental study, we only included one review for each of our fictitious host profiles to avoid confounding. We found that the host profile with a positive review attracts more booking. However, in reality, listings can have multiple reviews. It may be that the fraction, not the existence of positive reviews matters the most in solo guests' decision making. The results of our study call for further investigations using multiple reviews in a host profile. Those studies could also verify the effect of reviewer gender on booking. In our exploratory data analysis, we saw that female guests book listings with greater fraction of females than males. In our experiment, however, we found reviewer gender to be statistically insignificant. If the reviewer gender only becomes significant after a certain number of reviewers, such discrepancy in results may be reconciled.

Atypical Motivation. Participants in our studies knew that they were put in a hypothetical situation and it is difficult to know whether each participant was fully engaged and made their truest possible decisions involving trust. If participants lacked the motivation to evaluate the provided host profiles, this could have affected our findings. Future studies should consider conducting a field experiment to explore solo guests' decision outcomes in real settings. For example, one possible study could collaborate with current Airbnb hosts in a specific geographic area (controlling for other attributes of hosts and listing characteristics) and analyze booking requests they received to more accurately estimate the effect of variables explored in this study.

Altogether, our findings provide a better understanding of male vs female solo travelers' usage of Airbnb's reputation system. These results have implications for designing an open and safe space on the platform for the growing market segment of solo travelers. Above all, our study highlights the value of not assuming uniform attitudes towards risk, but breaking down the user population into subpopulations with differing behaviors and needs. We thus encourage future research examining Airbnb's reputation system and policies to consider perspectives across different subpopulations. Our approach relying on both insights from large-scale user activity data and controlled experiments produced knowledge that can potentially lead to a more personalized and thoughtful service experience that will ultimately embrace and satisfy a more diverse population on the platform.

Acknowledgments. The authors would like to thank Joshua Becker and Johannes Wachs for their feedback. We are also grateful to all the anonymous Mechanical Turk participants for their input to the presented experimental studies (IRB: STU00207726). This work was supported in part by a Northwestern Undergraduate Summer Research grant and the U.S. National Science Foundation (IIS-1755873).

A   Appendix

Table 2. Basic statistics of host–reviewer networks built for NYC, LA, and Chicago.

	NYC	LA	Chicago
Female hosts	5,445	3,483	627
Male hosts	4,898	2,908	690
Female reviewers	35,167	24,584	6,336
Male reviewers	43,706	31,749	8,884
Total reviews	87,241	65,339	16,271

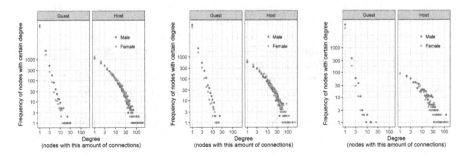

Fig. 3. Degree distributions of networks built for NYC, LA, and Chicago. Bipartite networks connect each host having a listing in the considered region with every guest who left a review on their profile. The number of reviews written by guests and the number of reviews obtained by hosts show that, in all but one case, male guests write and male hosts receive significantly more reviews.

References

1. Name checking database: Gender checker. https://www.genderchecker.com/
2. Baby names from social security card applications national leveldata (2016). https://catalog.data.gov/dataset/baby-names-from-social-security-card-applicati ons-nationallevel-data

3. Abrahao, B., Parigi, P., Gupta, A., Cook, K.S.: Reputation offsets trust judgments based on social biases among airbnb users. Proc. Nat. Acad. Sci. **114**(37), 9848–9853 (2017). https://doi.org/10.1073/pnas.1604234114
4. Booking.com: Holidays with me, myself and I give women a self esteem boost, August 2014. https://news.booking.com/holidays-with-me-myself-and-i-give-women-a-self-esteem-boost
5. Buchan, N.R., Croson, R.T., Solnick, S.: Trust and gender: an examination of behavior and beliefs in the investment game. J. Econ. Behav. Organ. **68**(3), 466–476 (2008). https://doi.org/10.1016/j.jebo.2007.10.006
6. Byrnes, J.P., Miller, D.C., Schafer, W.D.: Gender differences in risk taking: a meta-analysis. Psychol. Bull. **125**(3), 367–383 (1999). https://doi.org/10.1037//0033-2909.125.3.367
7. Cheng, M., Foley, C.: The sharing economy and digital discrimination: the case of Airbnb. Int. J. Hosp. Manag. **70**, 95–98 (2018). https://doi.org/10.1016/j.ijhm.2017.11.002
8. Cui, R., Li, J., Zhang, D.: Discrimination with incomplete information in the sharing economy: evidence from field experiments on Airbnb (2016). https://doi.org/10.2139/ssrn.2882982
9. Currarini, S., Jackson, M.O., Pin, P.: An economic model of friendship: homophily, minorities, and segregation. Econometrica **77**(4), 1003–1045. https://doi.org/10.3982/ECTA7528.
10. Currarini, S., Mengel, F.: Identity, homophily and in-group bias. Eur. Econ. Rev. **90**, 40–55 (2016). https://doi.org/10.1016/j.euroecorev.2016.02.015
11. Diekmann, A., Jann, B., Przepiorka, W., Wehrli, S.: Reputation formation and the evolution of cooperation in anonymous online markets. Am. Sociol. Rev. **79**(1), 65–85 (2013). https://doi.org/10.1177/0003122413512316
12. Edelman, B., Luca, M.: Digital discrimination: the case of Airbnb.com. Harvard Business School Working Paper, no. 14–054 (2014)
13. Edelman, B., Luca, M., Svirsky, D.: Racial discrimination in the sharing economy: evidence from a field experiment. Am. Econ. J.: Appl. Econ. **9**(2), 1–22 (2017). https://doi.org/10.1257/app.20160213
14. Elliott, A.F.: Why are so many of us now choosing to travel alone? May 2018. https://www.telegraph.co.uk/travel/comment/whats-behind-the-rise-in-solo-travel
15. Ert, E., Fleischer, A., Magen, N.: Trust and reputation in the sharing economy: the role of personal photos in Airbnb. Tour. Manag. **55**, 62–73 (2016). https://doi.org/10.1016/j.tourman.2016.01.013
16. Hannák, A., Wagner, C., Garcia, D., Mislove, A., Strohmaier, M., Wilson, C.: Bias in online freelance marketplaces: evidence from Taskrabbit and Fiverr. In: Proceedings of the 2017 ACM Conference on Computer Supported Cooperative Work and Social Computing, pp. 1914–1933 (2017). https://doi.org/10.1145/2998181.2998327
17. InsideAirbnb: Get the data. http://insideairbnb.com/get-the-data.html
18. Karimi, F., Wagner, C., Lemmerich, F., Jadidi, M., Strohmaier, M.: Inferring gender from names on the web: a comparative evaluation of gender detection methods. In: Proceedings of the 25th International Conference Companion on World Wide Web. pp. 53–54. International World Wide Web Conferences Steering Committee (2016). https://doi.org/10.1145/2872518.2889385
19. Lazer, D., Kennedy, R., King, G., Vespignani, A.: The parable of Google Flu: traps in big data analysis. Am. Assoc. Adv. Sci. **343**(6176), 1203–1205 (2014). https://doi.org/10.1126/science.1248506

20. Livingston, J.A.: How valuable is a good reputation? a sample selection model of internet auctions. Rev. Econ. Stat. **87**(3), 453–465 (2005). https://doi.org/10.1162/0034653054638391

21. Ma, X., Hancock, J.T., Lim Mingjie, K., Naaman, M.: Self-disclosure and perceived trustworthiness of Airbnb host profiles. In: Proceedings of the 2017 ACM Conference on Computer Supported Cooperative Work and Social Computing, pp. 2397–2409. ACM, New York (2017). https://doi.org/10.1145/2998181.2998269

22. McPherson, M., Smith-Lovin, L., Cook, J.M.: Birds of a feather: homophily in social networks. Ann. Rev. Sociol. **27**(1), 415–444 (2001). https://doi.org/10.1146/annurev.soc.27.1.415

23. Melnik, M.I., Alm, J.: Does a seller's ecommerce reputation matter? evidence from eBay auctions. J. Ind. Econ. **50**(3), 337–349 (2003). https://doi.org/10.1111/1467-6451.00180

24. Newman, M.: Networks: An Introduction. Oxford University Press Inc., New York (2010)

25. Resnick, P., Zeckhauser, R.: Trust among strangers in Internet transactions: empirical analysis of eBay's reputation system. In: The Economics of the Internet and E-commerce Advances in Applied Microeconomics, pp. 127–157 (2002). https://doi.org/10.1016/s0278-0984(02)11030-3

26. Resnick, P., Zeckhauser, R.J., Swanson, J., Lockwood, K.: The value of reputation on eBay: a controlled experiment. Exp. Econ. **9**, 79–101 (2006). https://doi.org/10.1007/s10683-006-4309-2

27. Ridgeway, C.L.: Why status matters for inequality. Am. Sociol. Rev. **79**(1), 1–16 (2014). https://doi.org/10.1177/0003122413515997

28. Rode, J.A.: A theoretical agenda for feminist HCI. Interact. Comput. **23**(5), 393–400 (2011). https://doi.org/10.1016/j.intcom.2011.04.005

29. Rosenbloom, S.: New tools and tours for solo travelers, December 2017. https://www.nytimes.com/2017/12/15/travel/getaway-solo-travel.html

30. Rudman, L.A., Goodwin, S.A.: Gender differences in automatic in-group bias: why do women like women more than men like men? J. Pers. Soc. Psychol. **87**(4), 494–509 (2004). https://doi.org/10.1037/0022-3514.87.4.494

31. Tausczik, Y.R., Pennebaker, J.W.: The psychological meaning of words: LIWC and computerized text analysis methods. J. Lang. Soc. Psychol. **29**(1), 24–54 (2010). https://doi.org/10.1177/0261927X09351676

32. Thebault-Spieker, J., et al.: Simulation experiments on (the absence of) ratings bias in reputation systems. In: Proceedings of the ACM on Human-Computer Interaction, vol. 1, pp. 101:1–101:25, December 2017. https://doi.org/10.1145/3134736

33. Thebault-Spieker, J., Terveen, L.G., Hecht, B.: Avoiding the south side and the suburbs: the geography of mobile crowdsourcing markets. In: Proceedings of the 18th ACM Conference on Computer Supported Cooperative Work & #38; Social Computing, CSCW 2015, pp. 265–275. ACM, New York (2015). https://doi.org/10.1145/2675133.2675278

34. Thebault-Spieker, J., Terveen, L.G., Hecht, B.J.: Toward a geographic understanding of the sharing economy: systemic biases in uberx and taskrabbit. ACM Trans. Comput.-Hum. Interact. **24**, 21:1–21:40 (2017)

35. Wachs, J., Hannák, A., Vörös, A., Daróczy, B.: Why Do Men Get More Attention? Exploring Factors Behind Success in an Online Design Community. arXiv e-prints arXiv:1705.02972 May 2017

36. Zervas, G., Proserpio, D., Byers, J.: A first look at online reputation on Airbnb, where every stay is above average. Social Science Research Network (2015)

Arabs and Atheism: Religious Discussions in the Arab Twittersphere

Youssef Al Hariri[✉], Walid Magdy, and Maria Wolters

School of Informatics, The University of Edinburgh, Edinburgh, UK
{y.alhariri,wmagdy,maria.wolters}@ed.ac.uk

Abstract. Most previous research on online discussions of atheism has focused on atheism within a Christian context. In contrast, discussions about atheism in the Arab world and from Islamic background are relatively poorly studied. An added complication is that open atheism is against the law in some Arab countries, which may further restrict atheist activity on social media. In this work, we explore atheistic discussion in the Arab Twittersphere. We identify four relevant categories of Twitter users according to the content they post: atheistic, theistic, tanweeri (religious renewal), and other. We characterise the typical content posted by these four sets of users and their social networks, paying particular attention to the topics discussed and the interaction among them. Our findings have implication for the study of religious and spiritual discourse on social media and provide a better cross-cultural understanding of relevant aspects.

Keywords: Atheism · Arabic · Religion · Islam · Twitter

1 Introduction

Several reports show that the number of Arab atheists is growing[1] in a region that is often intolerant to atheists [4,11,14,23]. The limited existing studies analysing discussions about atheism online [7,20] focused on Western and Christian societies.

In this work, we investigate how atheists in the Arab societies leverage Twitter to discuss their disengagement from religion, mainly Islam, which is the dominant religion in the Arabic region, and the interactions by different users around this topic. We characterise relevant types of user accounts by distinguishing between four main groups: Arab atheists, who do not believe in a deity; Arab theists, who believe in a religion; Arab Tanweeri's, who believe in Islam but also accept other beliefs and promote religious reform; and Other, who do not openly discuss their religious views. We focus on the main topics discussed online by

---

[1] Sources: https://newhumanist.org.uk/articles/4898/the-rise-of-arab-atheism https://www.washingtontimes.com/news/2017/aug/1/atheists-in-muslim-world-growing-silent-minority/.

© Springer Nature Switzerland AG 2019
I. Weber et al. (Eds.): SocInfo 2019, LNCS 11864, pp. 18–34, 2019.
https://doi.org/10.1007/978-3-030-34971-4_2

each of these user groups, and the way in which their opponents engage with them through replies and retweets.

For our analysis, we collected and analysed the tweet timelines of around 450 user accounts who were heavily engaged in discussions concerning atheism. Our study investigates the following research questions:

- RQ1: What are the common topics and features that Arab Atheists share that distinguish them from Theists, Tanweeris, and Others?
- RQ2: How do Arab Atheists interact with the other three groups?

Our analysis shows that there are active online discussions between Arabs from across the religious spectrum. Most of the discussions are related to local and regional topics and mainly topics related to the oppression of women. The vast majority of Arabs who believe in a deity are from Saudi Arabia and they show solidarity with their government. Arab Christians are more likely to argue against Islam than to argue against Atheism.

We believe that this study sheds the light on one of the most interesting and sensitive topics in the Arab world that has been relatively neglected in the literature. Our findings should promote research in this direction to have further in-depth analysis to the topic of atheism and religion in the Arab world.

2 Background

2.1 Religions vs. Atheism, Globally and in the Arab Societies

Religion is still a force to be reckoned with in today's world [5]. Both religiosity and non-religiosity are highly complex and multifaceted. In this paper, we will adopt concepts that are particularly well suited to the context of discussing Islam. In general, religions consist of a community of believers who share tenets of faith and practices of worship, some of which may require separation from others [8,9,17]. Within a religion, there are often many branches which may or may not coexist peacefully with each other. For example, Islam has two major denominations, Sunni and Shia, which in turn are split into many branches and sub-denominations [22].

Non-religiosity is also highly diverse. It includes wider groups such as humanism, indifferentism, secularism, agnosticism, irreligion, anti-religions and atheism [6,16]. Around 16% of the world's population identify as atheist or non-religious [18]. While atheists are minority in Arab countries [3,18,24], the number of Arab atheists appears to have increased noticeably recently despite the harsh penalties for atheism in several Arab countries [4,15,23]. A poll conducted in 2012 shows that an average of 22% of Arabs expresses atheist views, or at least some measure of religious doubts by using their social media accounts [4,15].

2.2 Social Media, Globally and in the Arab Societies

Twitter has 336 million active users per month [25] and its data has been used before to study religions on social media. In [7] the authors analysed more than

250k Twitter accounts to understand the main features of religiosity on Twitter for users from the US. The work found a reasonable positive correlation between Twitter data, i.e. declared religions, and offline surveys data for geographic distribution of religious people. The study includes analysing the tweets and networks for each user to identify discriminative features of each religious group and to study the linkage preference. It shows that the networks dynamics, mainly followers, friends, retweets and mentions, tell more about the religious users and provide more effective features than the tweets contents. They also observe that Twitter users tend to interact more with users within the same religion.

Arabs have positive views about social media and its influence on their societies. According to [13], Arabs are influenced positively towards other cultures, opinions, views and religions after their involvement in social media. Social media has many different functions. It facilitates the revolutions spread during the Arab Spring in 2011 [13], but it also serves as a propaganda and recruitment venue for extremist groups around the world [2,10,12,19]. It also serves as a platform for underrepresented groups, such as Arab atheists, to communicate and show their existence.

There is surprisingly little work on online atheist communities within the Arab or Muslim societies. A notable exception is [21]. In her study of Indonesian atheists, she found that social media helped atheists activists to safely highlight their existence in a religious country, Indonesia, show their positive side, and build a thriving community. However, they risked exposure through contact with human rights activists around the world through social media.

Far more attention has been paid to radical theists in the Arab world. Magdy et al. [12] sought to understand the origins and motivations of ISIS Arab supporters by comparing data for about 57,000 Arab Twitter accounts before and after the emergence of ISIS. They find that historical data can be used to train a classifier to predict a user's future position on ISIS with an average F1-score of 87%. There are also clear differences in the topics discussed. ISIS opponents are linked to the position of Arab regimes, rebel groups, and Shia sects; while ISIS supporters talk more about the failed Arab Spring. [12]. Interestinly, the most widely used distinctive hashtag used by ISIS supporters "#Million_Atheist_Arab" which was part of a campaign by Arab atheists. This indicates that the topic of atheism is well known and discussed in the Arab world, despite the lack of studies.

A particular facet of religious discussion on Arab social media is hate speech about both religion and atheism [1]. The study by Albadi et al. shows that 42% of the studied tweets ($n = 6000$) that cross-reference religions contain hate-speech.

We conclude that there is a clear gap in our knowledge of religious discourse and dialogue between atheists and theists on the Arab social media. We propose to address this gap by applying a quantitative analysis to characterise the Arab online theist and atheist communities.

3   Data Collection

3.1   Collecting Active Users Discussing Atheism

For retrieving relevant accounts, we received a list of 200 Arabic Twitter accounts from Bridge Foundation[2], a non-profit organisation based in London that aims to build bridges between Islam and other religions. These accounts had been labelled by their volunteers as promoting atheism content. We manually reviewed these accounts by inspecting their description and shared content. We only kept those that (1) explicitly mentioned that they are atheists and (2) promote atheism or clearly criticise religions in the majority of their tweets. Thus, we ended up with only 80 accounts that met our criteria. We used these 80 accounts as our seeding accounts. We used the Twitter streaming API to collect all the tweets that interacted with these accounts for 4 months between Feb and May 2018. We collected over 100 K tweets during that period and limited our analysis to those 434 user accounts interacted with the seed accounts over 200 times, either by retweeting, replying, or mentioning them. We consider these to be the most active users on the topic of atheism on Arab social media at that time. For these 434 accounts, we collected their entire Twitter timeline to study their network interactions and the content they discuss in their tweets. In total, we collected a set of 1.3M tweets for these accounts.

3.2   Data Annotation

After careful inspection of the data, we labelled the accounts based on the contents of their tweets and the beliefs they promote in their timelines. The four labels we devised according to the content are:

- **Atheistic** content that promotes content denying the existence of God (or gods) or explicitly rejects a religion (or religions) without any sign of religious affiliation.
- **Theistic** content that shows belief in God or disclose a religious affiliation and defends it.
- **Tanweeri** content that shows affiliation to Islam (or another religion), but promotes religious reform and accepts other beliefs.
- **Other** none of the above.

Three native Arabic speakers, from three different Arab countries, received a workshop training for labelling the accounts. The main purpose of the training was to ensure clear understanding of the annotation guidelines and isolating any personal beliefs while annotating the data. Each annotator was instructed to inspect most of the collected tweets for each of the accounts before making a judgement. They also had access to the user description and link to their online profile to assist them making decisions if needed. Judgements were based both on the Twitter users' own tweets and on frequent retweets of a particular stance.

---

[2] https://bridges-foundation.org/.

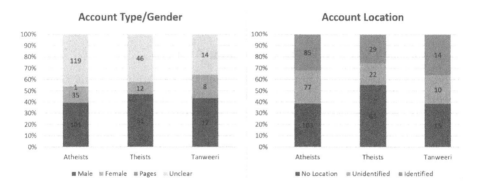

Fig. 1. Type, Gender, and Location of Accounts

Initially, 50 accounts were labelled by all three annotators. Cohen's Kappa values between each annotator pair were 0.732, 0.592, and 0.634, which reflects the subjective nature of interpreting statements of belief. The main confusion was found between the 'Atheistic' and 'Tanweeri' labels. After discussion of sources of disagreement, the annotators proceeded to label the remaining 383 accounts. The average time for labelling one account ranged between 15–30 min.

In addition, the annotators tried to identify if the account belongs to an individual person or a formal entity that promotes certain stances. For individual accounts, we also recorded gender, if it was identifiable.

3.3 Data Statistics

Since the seed list consisted of atheist accounts, it is not surprising that most of the accounts we labelled belong to atheistic class ($N = 256, 59\%$). 109 accounts (25%) are labelled as theistic, 39 (9%) as tanweeri, and 30 (7%) as Other.

Regarding the type of the accounts, only one atheist account is a page, while all the others are personal accounts for Twitter users. Figure 1 shows the distribution of accounts gender for each of the categories. In addition, it shows which of these accounts has an identifiable location listed in their profile. As shown, there are more males than females in the collected accounts, while for around 40% of the accounts gender was not clear. Tanweeri users have the largest percentage of females among other groups and they tend to declare their gender more than other groups. For location, theistic users have more identifiable locations than the atheists and tanweeris. This might be for security reasons of atheists to protect themselves against laws in some of the Arab countries. Most of the identifiable locations are from Saudi Arabia for all accounts, followed by USA for atheist and theist accounts. Details on identified location of users in each group is shown in Appendix in Fig. 2.

4   Analysis of Atheism Discussions on Twitter

For each account, we apply our analysis on both the content and the network interactions of the accounts. This includes the accounts they retweet their tweets (**retweets**), the accounts they reply to (**replies**), the accounts they mention in their tweets (**mentions**), the hashtags used by the account (**hashtags**), and the Web domains linked in their tweets (**domains**). In the following discussion, all tweets are rephrased to protect the original posters.

4.1   Top Discussed Topics

In this section, we analyse the topics that are most frequently discussed within the 1.3M tweets in the timelines of all the 434 accounts. This should highlight the discussion topics by the most active Arab users on atheism. We used hashtags to describe the topics that users talked about. Tweets will not be quoted, so that they cannot be traced back to their authors. However, we provide example English translations of those tweets.

As shown in Table 1 (more details in Appendix Table 3), almost all classes talk about similar topics such as rationalists, Middle-East countries, ISIS, women's oppression, Saudi women's rights, regional conflicts, and topics related to atheism and reformation, such as tanweer, ex-Muslims, atheists and atheism. Table 2 gives few example tweets of the usage of these hashtags in context.

The hashtag CreatingAlmohawer (training the interlocutor) refers to an online program designed to train Muslims to rebut unfounded claims about Islam. Most of Arab atheists do not only argue against Islam, but against all religion, specifically the Abrahamic religions (Judaism, Christianity and Islam). However, Islam is the most discussed religion as most of them were Muslims. Relevant hashtags include Abrahamic dice and Former_scriptures; relevant tweets argue that since archaeology provides counterevidence to the Jewish Bible, this makes all Abrahamic religions invalid. Other tweets questioned the existence of Moses, a prophet in Abrahamic religions, and claimed that there is no evidence to prove his existence. Interestingly, the hashtag Former_scriptures is also used by some non-Muslim theists to argue against Islam.

Topics related to the oppression of women attract users from all groups. The hashtags 'SaudiWomenDemandDroppingGuardianship' and 'StopEnslavingSaudiWomen' come from a long-term online campaign led by Saudi women who want freedom from social restrictions and supported by feminists from the region and around the world. Atheist users claim that the Saudi women must have their freedom of choice without the guardian system. For example, they will explicitly demand dropping restrictions on travelling, obtaining a passport, and driving. While some theist users show sympathy with the cause, most of them reject it. For example, one tweet claims that travelling on a passport is already possible with the guardian's electronic permission, and another claims that the campaign for dropping guardianship is managed by men. Similar polarisation are found around the hashtags talk about different cases of oppression against women

Table 1. Top 25 hashtags from each class translated into English. Full details of hashtags shown in Appendix

---

All: Rationalists, SaudiArabia, CreatingAlmohawer (interlocutor training), ISIS, Islam, StephenHawking, Israel, Egypt, Iran, Truth, Yemen, Syria, Friday, CEDAWSaudi, SaudiWomenDemandDroppingGuardianship, Qatar, Kuwait, DroppingGuardianship, AForgottenWomenPrisoners

---

Atheistic: DelusionTrade, ExMuslim, Atheism[*], EvolutionFact, Atheist[*], Tunisie, SaveDinaAli, TweetAPicture, RaifBadawy, Science, BlessedFriday, QuranInPictures, Trump, YouthTalk, Sweden, WomenCarDriving, FreeSherifGaber, Woman, ALogicalQuestion, DontSayIAmDisbeliever, WhereIsAminah, OsamaAljamaa, UnveilingIsNotMoralBreakdown, WomenInternationalDay, ViolenceAgainstSaudiWomen

---

Theistic: Atheist, Atheism, ChildrensMassacreInAfghanistan, Pray, SpreadOfIslam, ChristianityFact, Jesus, Palestine, Bible, AlAzharIsComing, Quran, Atheists, LegalizationOfZionization, Urgent, Continued, DefenceQuranAndSunnahByProofs, AssadBombardDomaChemicalWeapons, Christianity, MesharyAlAradah, Jesus, NaizakTranslation, Gaza, Aleppo, Turkey, IranProtests

---

Tanweeri HashemiteOccupation, OAyedDoNotSteal, WeakHadithEmployedBySahwa, CleaningSchoolsFromSururiWomen, FlutesRevelation, CrownPrince, Al-NassrFc, CrownPrinceOnCBC, SlaveryAllowanceForSaudiWomen, HowISurviveFromSahwa, RefusedToReleaseHisDaughter, IDecidedToWearItOnMyHead, AlmutlaqAbayaIsNotObligatory, Brothers, Yemen, SaudiWomenProudOfGuardianship, SaveMeFromViolence, CompassWithIslamBahiri, NoClouserShopsDuringPrayTime, MyFaceVeilIsHonor, SaudiCinema, MajidaElRoumi, CinemaInSaudiArabia, OffendedWomenOnly-GymClosed, MBSInterviewsTheAtlantic

---

such as WhereIsAmna, AbusedWomanInAbha, SaveDinaAli, RefusedToRelease-HisDaughter and MajedManaOmairOppresseHisWife. All of these hashtags are related to cases of women in Saudi Arabia. Tweets number 5, 7, 9 and 10 in Table 2 shows some tweets related to these hashtags. Some theists support the victim, but others try to find excuse for the case. For instance, some theists in the latter hashtag claim that the wife is benefiting from the accusations and accuse her of treason.

All groups intensively discussed terrorism and terrorist groups. While atheists blame Islam for terrorist groups, such as ISIS, theists claim that ISIS is used by Islamophobes to equate Islam with terror. It is noticeable to see that Atheists prefer to mention ISIS by using its English acronym, Arabic name (The Islamic State الدولة الإسلامية), or the acronym Da'esh (داعش) within hashtags such as Da'esh_is_an_Islamic_Product. On the other hand, theists prefer to mention ISIS by its Arabic acronym. While some Tanweeris argue that ISIS is not the real Islam, others blame the religion for the spread of terrorist groups.

Table 2. Sample (translated) tweets with Significant Hashtags. A: Atheistic, T: Theistic, and W: Tanweeri timeline

1	A	Religious drugs generate huge profits for delusion traders and dealers and more poverty for the people #Rationalist
2	A	#Delusion_traders successfully make simple minds fools, mindless and inhuman
3	A	I am going to publish a simple introduction to Palaeontology Which is an overwhelming proof to the #EvolutionFact; Follow me
4	A	Anyone benefited from the diffusion would promote myths and delusions #DelusionTrade
5	A	@user: #ViolenceAgainstSaudiWomen #SaveDinaAli where is Dina Ali? she was disappeared since a year
6	A	@hrw_ar you need to prove credibility to protect that girl from being killed by her family
7	A	@user: #ViolenceAgainstSaudiWomen Religions shouldn't be a law
8	A	We are living in 2018 and still there are people being arrested for expressing their political views and religious beliefs. We should have legal codes to protect the freedom of speech. #freeSherifGaber #FreeSherifGaber
9	A	#ViolenceAgainstSaudiWomen #SaudiWomenDemandDropGuardian640 #StopEnslavingSaudiWomen We demand justice for female victims of domestic violence
10	T	A A Darwinian Atheist says please help Dina. Why we don't consider her story as a natural selection or an evolutionary development? #SaveDinaAli
11	T	Atheists did not support Muslims to liberate lands or to defend themselves, but they believe that they have the right to live between them. #rationalists
12	T	The Gravity theory Scientist believes in God and says atheists are the most stupid
13	T	Some atheists talk about the capital punishments for atheists in Islam; However, they ignore that it is applied through a justice body. #rationalists
14	T	#FreeSherifGaber This is the penalty for any beggar who trades in atheism and asks for funding to produce rotten mould
15	T	#FreeSherifGaber he worked for months to prepare a storytelling with full of lies, ignorance and fabrication but the response is quickly found
16	T	RT @user Anyone claims that violence against women and children is allowed in Islam is a liar #Al-AzharIsComing
17	T	@hrw_ar We will stay protected by our families and you should stop attacking our religious and cultural heritages. It is a crime against us
18	T	#ChildrensMassacreInAfghanistan USA has problem with the Holy Quran not with Muslims. #Rationalists
19	W	Yes, the cost is prohibitive; there will be mass destruction, killing and displacement. But it is less costly than governing the Iranian criminal gangs #HashemiteOccupation
20	W	#OAyedDoNotSteal, what are we did not discover yet from the Sahwa era?
21	W	Lots of Hadiths were fabricated by Sahwa scholars and it is time to execute them WeakHadithEmployedBySahwa
22	W	#WeakHadithEmployedBySahwa Assassinating #Sahwa is a national duty
23	W	#CleaningSchoolsFromSururiWomen The school is an educational body. It shouldn't be part of a religious party and it is unacceptable to be used for the interests of some!
24	W	Schools are the most places to spread Sahwa thoughts specifically women teachers of schools in Riyadh. #CleaningSchoolsFromSururiWomen
25	W	#CleaningSchoolsFromSururiWomen Obligating students to wear veil with the face cover enforces them to follow a certain jurisprudential
26	W	Soon women will travel and enjoy their full rights the same as men. May Allah prolong the life of this leader #CrownPrinceOnCBC
27	W	Soon there will be Shia members in the Council of Ministers and in the government. Also, the president of the most important university in KSA is Shiite. We have a mix of Islamic schools and sects #MBSInterviewsTheAtlantic

In addition, the data set shows interactions with international organisations conducted from both atheists and theists. Atheists are willing to contact international organisations to seek protection or to promote their opinions (example: Tweet 6, Table 2), while theists also actively discuss their point of view on similar topics.

For instance, in Spring 2017, Human Rights Watch (HRW) tweeted that "An emergency case resulted from guardianship law in KSA #SaveDinaAli". A theistic account denied that and argued that she might have escaped after committing a crime or there is a hidden information. Another tweet published by HRW argues that while allowing women to drive is a step forward, but the guardianship law in Saudi should be abolished. A female theist replied with tweet number 17 in Table 2. Another theist wrote: "@hrw_ar it is not your business". In another tweet, HRW quoted a claim of prisoner abuse in Saudi Arabia that was made by the New York Times. A theist denied that news and wrote: "You should have truth, most of these news are fabricated". These samples show that Arab theist society actively engages with reports by other organisations.

Theists are more likely to talk about Arab countries and Middle East countries, such as Iran and Turkey, than atheists and tanweeris, whereas these two groups are more interested in topics relating to Saudi Arabia. All classes are divided in their opinion about conflict regions in the Middle East. For example, the majority of atheists look forward to dramatic changes in relationships of Arab countries with Israel while some of them refuse any rapprochement. However, most of theists claim that news of such changes, especially regarding the relationship between Israel and Saudi Arabia, are fabricated.

4.2   Distinctive Topic Discussion by Groups

To have a clear understanding about the trends that are mostly used, we ran a logistic regression analysis for each of the three main groups (Atheist, Theist, Tanweeri) with the top 50 hash tags as features. The hashtags with the highest weight are considered to be particularly distinctive. A sample of the top hashtags used by Atheists, Theists and Tanweer groups are shown in the Appendix Table 4. Notice that the table shows the frequencies of each hashtag from the three groups.

The most frequent hashtags mentioned by atheists are related to evolution theory, delusion trade, atheism and leaving Islam. The data set shows that Arab atheists strongly support evolution theory, and provide evidence to convince others. Most theists are not interested in discussing the theory, while others respond with the hashtag (خرافة_التطور - "Evolution is a myth"). Atheists also show solidarity with other atheists or activists. That is clear from hashtags such as FreeSherifGaber, RaifBadawy, AbdullahAlQasimi (one of the most controversial Saudi writers), and OsamaAljamaa (Saudi Psychologist), which are cited and retweeted by atheists. Abdullah Al Qasimi, as described in tweets, changed his position from being an Islamic Salafi scholar to defending atheism and tanweer, while Aljamaa has written about personal development and self-awareness, and his works are cited widely by Arab atheists. Finally, atheists talk more about atheism and leaving Islam. Relevant hashtags include ExMuslim, Atheism, Atheist, TheReasonWhyILeftIslam, and ExMuslimBecause.

Table 4 shows samples of the 15 most frequent hashtags that theists used in their tweets. Most of the accounts in this category are located in Saudi Arabia, which can be inferred from country-specific hashtags such as MohammadBin-Salman, TurkiAlSheikhThePrideOfPeople. Arab theists widely discuss atheism and atheist by using their Arabic names (الحاد - atheism) and (ملحد - atheist). Also, it is clear that most of theistic content either discusses or criticises Christianity. This is shown by hashtags such as Truth about Christianity, Jesus, Christianity, Contradictions of the Bible, and Books about Christianity. In addition, hashtags that talk about terrorism are specifically used by this class of authors. Theists talked about ISIS by using its short Arabic name الدولة (the state) and its leader (Al-Baghdadi). Theists also talk about Al-Qaeda, its Syrian branch (Al Nosra front and Hayat Tahrir Al-Sham), and their leader (Algolani and Al-Zawahiri), as well as conflict regions such as Al-Raqqah, Afghanistan, Syria, Palestine, Gaza, Aleppo, Iran and Yemen. One of the most significant hsahtags used by theists is #Al-AzharIsComing. It is published by a famous Egyptian Islamic scholar. His tweets are widely retweeted by theists, and as described in his tweets, Al-Azhar is one of the oldest academic bodies in the Islamic countries.

The typical hashtags that are used by Tanweeris are a mix of different cultures and opinions. One of the most discussed topics between tanweeris is the Hashemite Occupation, which talks about Islamic sects that took control over Yemen. Some of tweets show refusal of the existence of Islam as a religion in Yemen, but most of them talk about the conflict in Yemen and rejection of Houthis. Also, Tanweeris discussed a wider spectrum of Islamic parties and movements. However, most of their discussions show solidarity with their governments against different Islamic parties and scholars. In addition, they show a clear rejection of the opinions of scholars and sheikhs. In fact these tweets are also evidence for their solidarity with the government in KSA. This is reflected in tweets related to the Crown Prince of KSA Mohammad bin Salman interviews as shown in tweets 26 and 27.

Interestingly, the most frequent hashtags are related to Saudi football, in particular to a club from the Capital city 'Riyadh'. Most of the accounts with tanweeri contents are fans of this club. The hashtag Urawaian Proverbs is used by Al-Nassr FC fans to mock another team from the same city after it was defeated by Urawa Reds FC.

4.3   Network Interactions Around Atheism

Analysing the social network is an important step towards understanding the motivation of Arab atheists to declare their beliefs online. Here, three types of interaction network are analysed, user mentions in self-written tweets, mentions in replies, and accounts that they retweet. Due to potential repercussions for the Twitter users mentioned, especially since some Arab countries criminalise atheism, we will not list the names of the accounts, unless they are official news sources, but instead characterise their content. Account names are available on request from the authors after signing a confidentiality agreement.

Interestingly, as shown in Fig. 3 Atheists are more likely to mention, reply and retweet to members from their groups. Also, they are the most mentioned accounts by users of different beliefs. This is aligned with the previous findings that Arab societies openly discuss their beliefs online. It might be good to investigate more the tweets that both Atheists and Tanweeris reacted to, especially given that Tanweeris are less likely to be mentioned by atheists. Atheists are also very active in publishing replies to members from all groups. A sample of these tweets show that they support each other, defend their opinions, convince others, and discuss others' beliefs. Arab Theists are more likely to retweet each other than to retweet other groups. They amplify significant tweets, such as tweets published to explain a phenomenon and link it to religious belief or to support their opinions.

Even though many of the accounts mentioned in Atheist tweets are self-described atheists, the most frequent mentioned account belongs to a well known supporter of the measures taken by the new Saudi leadership. The accounts mentioned most frequently by theists are mostly belong to a famous religious figure or to an active theist who defend Islam. Most of the Muslim believers argue against atheism and promote Islam in their timelines. There are some Christian believers who argue against Islam but not against atheism.

4.4   Domains Analysis

Web domains might give information about the source of information each group prefer. Hence, we analyse the most frequent domains used by each class that are shown in Appendix Table 5.

The most frequent websites used in tweets by atheists are related to social media platforms such as instagram.com, facebook.com, pscp.tv, curiouscat.me and ask.fm. The reason for this might be that these websites help them link to and reach out to other atheists in their societies, and share posts with atheism relevant content. The domain "wearesaudis.net", also frequently mentioned by atheists, is an online forum that provides suggestions and guidance on how to seek asylum in different countries including Israel. Atheists are also more interested in online resources about science, such as ibelieveinsci, and they often interact with non-Arabic news websites such as dw.com, bbc.com, arabic.rt.com, theguardian.com, independent.co.uk, f24.com, dailymail.co.uk, and nytimes.com. Atheists also widely share online campaign posts from change.org, which hosts many human rights petitions, and the domain of the organisation Human Rights Watch, hrw.org. This organisation covers human rights in the Middle East, especially the Arab Spring countries, and Saudi Arabia.

On the other hand, the most frequent domains used by the theists are du3a.org, d3waapp.org, alathkar.org and 7asnat.com. These sites are auto-post services for Islamic supplications, duas, and notifications. In addition, qurani.tv and quran.ksu.edu.sa are frequently used, but we were unable to determine if they are used as auto-post services or cited actively. The news sources preferred by believers are those written in Arabic, such as the Arabic service of Russia Today (arabic.rt.com), Saudi Press Agency (spa.gov.sa) and Sabq News (sabq.org). The most referenced non-arabic news source by Arab theists is cnsnews.com. However, most of theists believe that it not a trusted source; it is regared as a "liar" and "a conservative and right wing American source".

Like Atheists, Tanweeris often share content from other online social media platforms on Twitter. Relevant URLs include curiouscat.me, instagram.com, facebook.com, and pscp.tv. They also uses the tools to track and report the changes on their followers. Similar to atheists, they are interested in scientific sources such as n-scientific.org. Tanweeris prefer to access and interact with mix of official and non-official, Arabic and non-Arabic news sources. However, they prefer sources related to traditional newspaper such as alqabas.com, thenewkhalij.news, alghadeer.tv, aljarida.com and alhudood.net. Also, they use Iranian news sources such as mojahedin.org, Iraqi news source such as alsumaria.tv and alghadeer.tv, and one non-arabic source ansa.it. This supports our observation that Tanweeri are interested in challenging cultural restrictions in Arab societies and interacting with other cultures as inspiration for reform.

5   Discussion, Conclusion and Future Work

In this study, we shed some light on a neglected, but important topic, online discussion of Atheism in the Arab world. While our analysis is mostly descriptive and quantitative, we believe that it provides valuable insights about the atheist community in the Arab world and how they interact with other online users, which should provide a solid baseline for future work. Our analysis to the most active 434 Arab users on Twitter discussing atheism shows that there is a large discussion of the topic online between mainly three groups: (1) users promoting atheism and argue against religion; (2) users who are refuting atheism and its arguments, and (3) users who does not explicitly deny religions but asking for reform of them. Our findings shows that a lot of the discussion about atheism in the Arab world includes the situation in the Middle East. Atheists focus more on the rights of some groups in the Arab world, such as violence against women. Theists discuss more the national challenges facing the society. Tanweeris were found to show more solidarity with their governments while criticising Islamic groups and their interpretation of Islam. We observed that Arab atheists are willing to communicate with foreign cultures such as Western news sources, TV shows, and world wide organisations. Tanweeris interact more with traditional news sources such as newspapers, and discuss non-religious content. Theists were found to reference a lot of Islamic content in their tweets.

In future work, we hope to replicate this study with Theist and Tanweeri seed lists, in order to obtain a more rounded picture of Arab religious discourse online. We also plan to investigate the network dynamics and the directions of interaction and links in more depth. Finally, we may consider building a classifier that determines the current position of a given Twitter account and tracks potential changes over time, but that requires being mindful of potential ethical implications, given that atheism is illegal in several Arab countries.

We hope that this study will motivate applying much deeper analysis to this sensitive topic in the future.

Acknowledgement. We would like to thank Bridges Foundation for their support by providing the initial seeding list of accounts that we later reviewed and filtered. In addition, we are highly thankful for Dr. Jacob Copeman, an expert anthropologist in Atheism and non-religion, for his valuable feedback and suggestions for our study.

Appendix

Table 3. The highest occurrence of hashtags used by all groups

Hashtag (Translation)	Atheistic	Theistic	Tanweeri
عقلانيون (Rationalists)	28048	16743	2377
السعوديه (Saudi Arabia)	2274	1018	453
داعش (ISIS)	972	2001	86
صناعه المحاور (Creating Almohawer (interlocutor))	938	1159	123
الاسلام (Islam)	888	716	75
ايران (Iran)	514	648	96
سوريا (Syria)	543	611	67
مصر (Egypt)	663	464	81
اليمن (Yemen)	690	347	71
تنوير (Tanweer)	836	50	117
قطر (Qatar)	351	362	103
عقلانيون جدد (New rationalists)	437	678	19
نظريه التطور (The theory of evolution)	613	454	41
ستيفن هوكينج (Stephen Hawking)	625	194	94
ماجد مانع عمير معنف زوجته (Majed Mana' Omair oppress his wife)	606	69	123
اسرائيل (Israel)	552	191	99
العراق (Iraq)	460	446	47
حقيقه (Truth)	527	382	52
محمد بن سلمان (MBS)	264	88	129
CEDAWSaudi	251	105	122
الصحوه (Sahwa)	293	47	114
النرد الابراهيمي (Abrahamic dice)	319	3	120
الكويت (Kuwait)	271	197	80
FreeRaif	427	49	84
القدس (Jerusalem)	279	358	28
نقد الموروث (Criticise ancestral)	418	58	72
رمضان (Ramadan)	471	128	47
القدس عاصمه فلسطين الابديه (Jerusalem is the eternal capital of Palestine)	226	352	23
Free Sherif Gaber	529	10	54
سعوديات نطلب اسقاط الولايه (Saudi women demand dropping of guardianship)	258	83	66
الرياض (Riyadh)	206	112	64
اسقاط الولايه (Dropping of guardianship)	235	149	51

Table 4. The most frequent hashtags used by each group

Hashtag (Translation)	Atheistic	Theistic	Tanweeri
تجاره الوهم (Trades of illusion)	859	5	40
ExMuslim	719	60	51
Atheism	614	72	27
حقيقه التطور (Evolution is a fact)	609	8	29
الحريه لشريف جابر (Free Sharif Jaber)	533	66	88
Atheist	481	23	29
Tunisie	474	5	0
SaveDinaAli	430	5	18
غرد بصوره (Tweet a picture)	369	46	29
نطالب بحريه الاعتقاد (We demand freedom of belief)	369	0	112
رائف بدوي (Raif Badawy)	361	16	8
علوم (Science)	316	19	30
جمعه مباركه (Blessed Friday)	313	106	43
القران بالصور (Quran in pictures)	293	1	3
ترامب (Trump)	281	103	12
ملحد (Atheist)	166	1214	6
الالحاد (atheism)	129	473	6
مذبحه الاطفال في افغانستان (Afgan children's massacre)	16	449	9
دعاء (Pray)	2	403	0
انتشارالاسلام (Spread of Islam)	0	348	0
حقيقه النصرانيه (The fact of Christianity)	7	345	0
يسوع (Jesus)	30	316	1
فلسطين (Palestine)	165	312	35
الكتاب المقدس (Bible)	10	297	0
الازهر قادم (Al-Azhar is coming)	11	280	1
Quran	42	266	2
الملاحده (Atheists)	10	262	0
شرعنه التصهين (Legalization of zionization)	0	230	0
حساب الدفاع عن الوحيين بالحجج والبراهين (Defence of Quran and Sunnah by arguments and proofs)	0	201	0
الاحتلال الهاشمي (Hashemite occupation -over Yemen-)	1	0	236
لا تسرق يا عايض (O Ayed, Do not steal)	43	3	140
احاديث ضعيفه استغلتها الصحوه (Weak Hadith employed by sahwa)	142	32	85
تنظيف المدارس من السروريات (Cleaning schools from Sururi women)	64	33	84
بوح ناي (Flute's revelation)	13	1	78
ولي العهد (Crown prince)	103	35	75
النصر (Al-Nassr FC)	18	21	65
ولي العهد علي قناه CBS (Crown prince on CBS)	110	29	64
بدل عبوديه للمرأه السعوديه (Slavery allowance for Saudi women)	26	8	63
كيف نجوت من الصحوه (How I survive from Sahwa)	122	35	59
اب يرفض خروج ابنته من السجن (Refused to release his daughter)	114	66	54
قررت البس عبايه علي الراس (I decided to wear it on my head)	85	40	54
المطلق العبايه غير الزاميه (Almutlaq Abaya is not obligatory)	137	48	52
الاخوان (Brothers)	57	21	49
اليمن (Yemen)	136	40	47

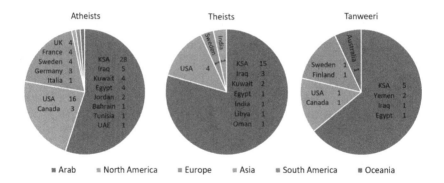

Fig. 2. Identified Locations for Atheist Group

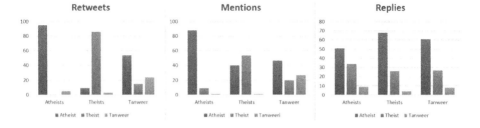

Fig. 3. Interaction Network of Each Group

Table 5. The 20 most frequent Domains that are used by Each class.

Atheists		Theists		Tanweer	
Domain	Freq.	Domain	Freq.	Domain	Freq.
ask.fm	901	du3a.org	11768	fllwrs.com	323
wearesaudis.net	596	d3waapp.org	2807	crowdfireapp.com	134
goodreads.com	439	alathkar.org	1402	eremnews.com	63
ibelieveinsci.com	273	kaheel7.com	375	alqabas.com	59
dw.com	213	almohawer.com	327	thenewkhalij.news	57
al-eman.com	198	sabq.org	175	8bp.co	43
atheistrepublic.com	170	unfollowspy.com	151	n-scientific.org	35
ahewar.org	163	bayanelislam.net	139	alghadeer.tv	21
atheistdoctor.com	154	antishobhat.blogspot	129	maktaba-amma.com	21
dorar.net	135	kutub-pdf.net	122	alarab.co.uk	15
imdb.com	86	spa.gov.sa	109	telegra.ph	12
libral.org	62	i.imgur.com	108	aljarida.com	12
linkis.com	61	ncbi.nlm.nih.gov	97	alhudood.net	11
arabatheistbroadcasting	59	justpaste.it	96	dr-alawni.com	9
dkhlak.com	58	7asnat.com	90	alsumaria.tv	9
iqtp.org	57	quran.to	82	ansa.it	8
syr-res.com	50	survey-smiles.com	82	arabic.mojahedin.org	6
bassam.nu	45	cnsnews.com	75	arabketab4u.blogspot	6
friendlyatheist.patheos	33	alkulify.blogspot	68	marebpress.net	5
mustafaris.com	28	estigfar.co	56	emaratalyoum.com	5

References

1. Albadi, N., Kurdi, M., Mishra, S.: Are they our brothers? Analysis and detection of religious hate speech in the Arabic Twittersphere. In: 2018 IEEE/ACM International Conference on Advances in Social Networks Analysis and Mining (ASONAM), pp. 69–76, August 2018. https://doi.org/10.1109/ASONAM.2018.8508247
2. Awan, I.: Society cyber-extremism: ISIS and the power of social media. Society **54**(2), 138–149 (2017)
3. Banks, J.A.: Citizenship Education and Global Migration: Implications for Theory, Research, and Teaching. American Educational Research Association, Washington DC (2017). https://books.google.co.uk/books?id=IYQwDwAAQBAJ
4. Benchemsi, A.: Invisible atheists (freedom of speech and atheist views in Arab countries). New Repub. **246**(4), 24–31 (2015)
5. Berger, P.L. (ed.): The Desecularization of the World: Resurgent Religion and World Politics. Ethics and Public Policy Center, Washington, D.C. (1999)
6. Blanes, R.L., Oustinova-Stjepanovic, G. (eds.): Being Godless: Ethnographies of Atheism and Non-religion. Berghahn Books, Incorporated, New York (2017)
7. Chen, L., Weber, I., Okulicz-Kozaryn, A.: U.S. religious landscape on Twitter. In: Aiello, L.M., McFarland, D. (eds.) SocInfo 2014. LNCS, vol. 8851, pp. 544–560. Springer, Cham (2014). https://doi.org/10.1007/978-3-319-13734-6_38
8. Croucher, S.M., Zeng, C., Rahmani, D., Sommier, M.: Religion, culture, and communication. Oxford Research Encyclopedia of Communication (2017). https://doi.org/10.1093/acrefore/9780190228613.013.166
9. Durkheim, É.: The Elementary Forms of the Religious Life. Allen and Unwin (1976). https://books.google.co.uk/books?id=rFwVAAAAIAAJ
10. Fisher, A.: How Jihadist networks maintain a persistent online presence. Perspect. Terrorism **9**(3) (2015). http://www.terrorismanalysts.com/pt/index.php/pot/article/view/426
11. Kingsley, P.: Egypt has the highest number of atheists in the Arab world - 866; Figure is according to Dar al-Ifta, an official government wing, which says the number of atheists is a dangerous development. The Guardian, London, England, December 2014
12. Magdy, W., Darwish, K., Weber, I.: FailedRevolutions: using Twitter to study the antecedents of ISIS support. First Monday **21**(2) (2016). https://doi.org/10.5210/fm.v21i2.6372
13. Mourtada, R., Salem, F.: Social Media in the Arab World: Influencing Societal and Cultural Change? Governance and Innovation Program, Dubai School of Government, January 2012
14. Nabeel, G.: Atheists in Muslim world: growing silent minority (2017). https://www.washingtontimes.com/news/2017/aug/1/atheists-in-muslim-world-growing-silent-minority/
15. Pew Research Center's Religion & Public Life Project: Religious composition by country, 2010–2050 (2015). http://www.pewforum.org/2015/04/02/religious-projection-table/2010/number/all/
16. Quack, J., Schuh, C.: Conceptualising religious indifferences in relation to religion and nonreligion. In: Quack, J., Schuh, C. (eds.) Religious Indifference, pp. 1–23. Springer, Cham (2017). https://doi.org/10.1007/978-3-319-48476-1_1
17. Rees, J.: Religion and culture (2018). https://www.e-ir.info/2017/01/08/religion-and-culture/

18. Religion & Public Life Project: Global religious diversity (2014). http://www.pewforum.org/2014/04/04/global-religious-diversity/
19. Richey, M.K., Binz, M.: Open source collection methods for identifying radical extremists using social media. Int. J. Intell. CounterIntell. **28**(2), 347–364 (2015). https://doi.org/10.1080/08850607.2014.962374
20. Ritter, R.S., Preston, J.L., Hernandez, I.: Happy tweets: christians are happier, more socially connected, and less analytical than atheists on Twitter. Soc. Psychol. Pers. Sci. **5**(2), 243–249 (2014)
21. Schfer, S.: Forming 'forbidden' identities online: atheism in Indonesia. ASEAS - Austrian J. South-East Asian Stud. **9**(2), 253–268 (2016)
22. Shahrastānī, M.i.A.a.K.: Muslim sects and divisions : the section on Muslim sects in Kitāb al-Milal Wa 'I-Nihal. Kegan Paul International, London (1984)
23. Stuart, H.: The hard lives of non-believers in the middle east. Miller-McCune.com (2016
24. The Global Religious Landscape: Social science and the public interest (brief article). Society **50**(2), 99 (2013)
25. We Are Social, Hootsuite, DataReportal: Most popular social networks worldwide as of July 2019, ranked by number of active users (in millions) (2019). https://www.statista.com/statistics/272014/global-social-networks-ranked-by-number-of-users/

Deep Dive into Anonymity: Large Scale Analysis of Quora Questions

Binny Mathew[1(✉)], Ritam Dutt[1], Suman Kalyan Maity[2], Pawan Goyal[1], and Animesh Mukherjee[1]

[1] Indian Institute of Technology Kharagpur, Kharagpur, India
binnymathew@iitkgp.ac.in, ritam.dutt@gmail.com, pawang@cse.iitkgp.ac.in,
animeshm@gmail.com
[2] Northwestern University, Evanston, USA
suman.maity@kellogg.northwestern.edu

Abstract. Anonymity forms an integral and important part of our digital life. It enables us to express our true selves without the fear of judgment. In this paper, we investigate the different aspects of anonymity in the social Q&A site Quora. Quora allows users to explicitly post anonymous questions and such activity in this forum has become normative rather than a taboo. Through an analysis of millions of questions, we observe that at a global scale *almost no difference* manifests between the linguistic structure of the anonymous and the non-anonymous questions posted on Quora. We find that topical mixing at the global scale to be the primary reason for the absence. However, the differences start to feature once we "deep dive" and (topically) cluster the questions and compare them. In particular, we observe that the choice to post the question as anonymous is dependent on the user's perception of anonymity and they often choose to speak about *depression, anxiety, social ties* and *personal issues* under the guise of anonymity. Subsequently, to gain further insights, we build an *anonymity grid* to identify the differences in the perception on anonymity of the user posting the question and the community of users answering it. We also look into the *first response time* of the questions and observe that it is lowest for topics which talk about personal and sensitive issues, which hints toward a higher degree of community support.

Keywords: Quora · Q&A · Anonymity · Response rate

1 Introduction

Anonymity in Q&A Sites: Question answering sites are one of the primary sources on the Internet that attempt to meet this huge information need of the users. Q&A sites like Yahoo! Answers, Quora, Stack Exchange are community

---

B. Mathew and R. Dutt—Contributed equally to this paper.

© Springer Nature Switzerland AG 2019
I. Weber et al. (Eds.): SocInfo 2019, LNCS 11864, pp. 35–49, 2019.
https://doi.org/10.1007/978-3-030-34971-4_3

efforts that provide answers to questions on a wide range of topics. Some of these sites like Yahoo! Answers and Quora have a unique feature that allows users to post questions anonymously which enables them to ask judgmental or controversial questions freely. Quora, in addition, has two interesting and very rich features – (i) the questions can be organized topically that allows the users to search for relevant answers easily and the moderators to manage and route/promote questions to appropriate communities for garnering better answers and (ii) there is an underlying social network that allows user to follow other users, questions and topics. Over the years these have immensely enriched the interactions within the forum thus improving both the question and the answer quality.

Anonymity in Quora Contrasts Other Online Forums: In the Quora ecosystem, asking questions anonymously is as much acceptable to the community as asking non-anonymously; as high as 38.7% questions are asked anonymously on Quora. Further, the acceptance of a question from the community is dependent on the responses it has received. Consequently, we observe that the mean number of responses for the anonymous and non-anonymous questions on a global scale is approximately 2.86 and 2.99 which shows a high level of acceptance. Users resort to asking questions anonymously because they feel that it has various benefits like revealing the "truth"[1] or asking sensitive questions like "I am depressed. How do I hide it at school?" without the fear of its repercussions. The practice has become normative and no longer a taboo or something to be looked down upon.

Key Contributions and Observations of this Paper: Analysis of a dataset of as large as 5.1 million Quora questions reveals that around 38.7% of them are posted anonymously. This observation forms the primary motivation of the current paper where we present a detailed and extensive measurement study characterizing the anonymous questions on Quora. We summarize our main contributions and observations in this paper in the following.

- We observe that at a global scale there is *almost no difference* between the linguistic structure of the questions posted anonymously and those posted non-anonymously.
- We identify that at the global scale there is a lot of topical mixing, i.e., those questions that should be apparently posted as anonymous are sometimes posted as non-anonymous and vice versa.
- As a next step, we "deep dive" into the data, whereby, we (topically) cluster the questions and individually inspect the clusters containing large volumes of anonymous questions and compare them with those that predominantly contain non-anonymous questions. Nuanced linguistic differences start becoming apparent revealing that users extensively query about *depression, anxiety, social ties* and *personal issues* within the guise of anonymity.

---

[1] www.quora.com/Why-did-Quora-add-the-anonymous-option-for-answers-and-ques tions.

- To gain further insights, we propose an anonymity grid to identify the differences in the perception of anonymity between the user posting the question and the user community answering the same.
- We also introduce the concept of First Response Time (FRT) to quantify the time taken for a question to receive the first response.

2 Related Work

There have been several research in the past to study anonymity in the online and offline settings. In this section, we present a short review of the different aspects of anonymity research.

Anonymity in Social Media: Several social media sites allow options to post content anonymously. Facebook provides 'confession pages' while Yahoo! Answers and Quora allow users to post questions and answers as anonymous. There are several mobile services that allow anonymous sharing like Whisper and Secret. In Correa et al. [4], authors study the sensitivity and types of content posted on Whisper and Twitter. They find that the anonymity of 'whispers' is not binary, implying that the same question text exhibit different levels of anonymity, depending on the user's perception. In addition, they find significant linguistic differences between whispers and tweets. In Birnholtz [2], the authors study the questions that are posted on Facebook confession boards (FCBs). They find that users ask about taboo and stigmatized topics and tend to receive relevant responses that are potentially useful and contain less negativity. In Bernstein et al. [1], the authors study online ephemerality and anonymity on /b/ board in 4chan. They find that over 90% of the posts in /b/ board are made anonymously. In De Choudhury and De [5], the authors study the impact of anonymity on sharing of information related to stigmatic health topics.

Research on Quora: In Wang et al. [15], the authors perform a detailed analysis of Quora. They show that heterogeneity in the user and question graphs are significant contributors to the quality of Quora's knowledge base. They show that the user-topic follow graph generates user interest in browsing and answering general questions, while the related question graph helps concentrate user attention on the most relevant topics. Finally, the user-to-user social network attracts views, and leverages social ties to encourage votes and additional high quality answers. Maity et al. [12] study the dynamics of temporal growth of topics in Quora and propose a regression model to predict the popularity of a topic. In Patil and Lee [14], the authors analyze the behavior of experts and non-experts in five popular topics and extract several features to develop a statistical model which automatically detect experts. In Maity et al. [10,11], the authors find that the use of language while writing the question text can be a very effective means to characterize answerability and it can help in predicting early if a question would eventually be answered. There have been very few studies on anonymity in Quora. In Paskude and Lewkowicz [13], the authors analyze the anonymous and non-anonymous answers in the health category of Quora and found that anonymous answers and social appreciation correlates with the answer's length. Our work is different from this as we primarily focus on questions instead of answers.

3   Dataset Description

We obtain the Quora dataset from the authors of Maity et al. [12] and build on it to have a massive set of 5,160,765 questions and 488,122 topics (along with the topic logs). The questions contain information regarding the date of creation, the user[2] who has posted the questions and also answered them, the topics assigned to the question etc. Table 1 lists some of the numbers related to the dataset.

Table 1. Properties of the dataset.

Dataset properties	Number
#Questions extracted	5,160,765
#Anonymous questions	1,997,474
#Non-anonymous questions	3,163,291
#Answers of anonymous questions	5,727,278
#Answers of non-anonymous questions	9,464,554
#Anonymous answers of anonymous questions	589,569
#Anonymous answers of non-anonymous questions	727,088
#Deleted answers of anonymous questions	570,285
#Deleted answers of non-anonymous questions	873,365

4   Rise of Anonymity in Quora

As a first experiment, we measure the prevalence of the usage of the anonymity feature by the Quora users for asking questions. We find from our dataset that approximately 38.7% of the questions have been posted as anonymous. In Fig. 1, we plot the ratio of the questions posted as anonymous to the total number of questions posted over time. Clearly, there is sharp increase in this ratio over time. Further, we note that the fraction of anonymous answers garnered by the anonymous questions is 10.29% as opposed to 7.68% by the non-anonymous questions.

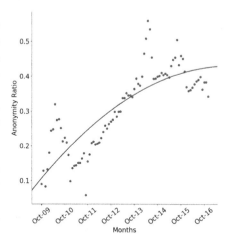

Fig. 1. Ratio of anonymous questions to the total number of questions over time.

---

[2] We did not remove the users whose accounts were deleted. On deletion, the username is simply replaced with "user" placeholder and does not make it anonymous. For more details please visit: https://www.quora.com/What-happens-when-I-deactivate-or-delete-my-Quora-account.

For a detailed understanding of the differences between the questions tagged as anonymous (henceforth 'Anon') and those tagged as non-anonymous (henceforth 'Known'), we start with simply understanding the type of questions that are posted as Anon and Known.

Question Types: We observe that majority of the questions posted on Quora are interrogative sentences. The head word of a question, i.e., words like "what", "why" are a key feature used in traditional question classification [7,9]. We selected a set of common interrogative English pronouns[3] that we treat as head words, namely – "what", "how", "which", "where", "who", "when" – and check their frequency of occurrence.

5   Analysis at the Global Scale

In Fig. 2a, we illustrate the proportion of these head words in the two question groups – Anon and Known. From the figure, we observe that Anon group tends to feature more "how" type questions than the Known group. This could indicate that the Anon questions are asking for detailed reasons. The Known group tends to feature more "which", "where" and "what" type questions. This indicates that Known group tends to ask for specific information that are open-ended or restricted range of possibilities, or regarding 'some place'.

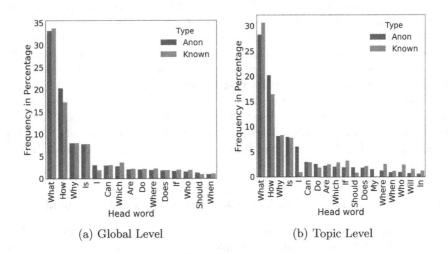

(a) Global Level   (b) Topic Level

Fig. 2. Distribution of different types of head words

Linguistic Analysis: Previous literature on anonymity [2,4] have noted that there are significant differences between the text posted as Anon and those posted as Known. We thus attempt to verify whether this claim holds for Quora

---

[3] https://goo.gl/EFXQJx.

Table 2. Mildly significant linguistic differences between the questions of the Anon and the Known group at the global scale

Category	Cohen's d	Anon	Known	Diff. (%)
PRON (Pronoun)	0.1413	0.0395	0.0325	21.476
Negative	0.0611	0.0442	0.0383	15.349
Positive	−0.0310	0.0984	0.1026	−4.119
Family	0.0552	0.0019	0.0012	55.429
Sexual	0.0892	0.0032	0.0016	89.284
Friends	0.0648	0.0023	0.0014	68.024
I	0.1404	0.0265	0.0195	36.330
We	−0.055	0.0024	0.0034	−28.931

as well. To this purpose, we consider two groups of question text – one comprising all questions tagged as Anon while the other comprising all questions tagged as Known. For each group we perform standard POS tag analysis (i.e., the fraction of different parts-of-speech in the text), named entity analysis (i.e., the fraction of different types of named entities in the text)[4], sentiment analysis[5] (i.e., the fraction of positive, negative and neutral sentiment words in the text) and LIWC analysis[6] (i.e., the fraction of words in different linguistic and cognitive dimensions identified by the LIWC tool) on the text. Finally, we look for statistically significant differences between these two groups with respect to the above analysis. As the size of our sample is very large, standard t-test would be very ineffective as it will transform small differences into statistically significant differences - even when they are practically insignificant [6]. Therefore, we use Cohen's d [3] to find differences that are practically significant. We do not find evidence of strong differences between the two groups. These findings are in agreement with the previous research done on Quora [13]. In Table 2 we note those fractions that are mildly significant (as per the Cohen's d-test). We also use the metric $Diff(\%)$ in a way similar to Correa et al. [4] to quantify the difference[7].

5.1 Absence of Significant Linguistic Differences at the Global Scale

Correa et al. [4] acknowledges that anonymity is not a binary concept and it is perceived differently by different people. The veracity of the above claim is established upon closer examination of the Anon and Known questions in our dataset. We note instances of common Known questions that talk about topics

---

[4] We use the POS (Parts of Speech) tagger and NER (Named Entity Recognizer) of SpaCy: https://spacy.io.

[5] We use VADER [8].

[6] http://liwc.wpengine.com/.

[7] Definition available in Appendix.

prevalently associated with some form of stigma or taboo. Many Anon questions, on the other hand, seem to be very general in nature.

Table 3. Ambiguously tagged questions – Known questions pertain to topics corresponding to some stigma or taboo while Anon questions are more general.

Anon	Known
What building is similar to the taj Mahal in form?	How do I get rid of mental depression?
How would you describe a river?	I am 17 and still single. Is it normal?
What are the best google summer of code projects	I missed my period. Am I pregnant?
What is the best camera ever?	I am currently facing abuse at home
	I am only 17, what should I do?

Table 3 shows some examples of such 'ambiguously' tagged questions. We quantify this ambiguity by observing and illustrating the phenomenon of a 'global scale topic mixing'. We note that this forms the prime reason for the absence of any clear division of the anonymous and the non-anonymous questions at the global scale.

5.2   Topical Mixing at Global Scale

In order to get a better understanding of the topical mixing that takes place at the global scale, we look into the distribution of *anonymity score* associated with the questions. First, we assign a 'topical anonymity score (TAS)' to each topic based on the fraction of anonymous questions in the topic. So, each topic will have a TAS between zero and one with a one meaning that all the questions posted in this topic are anonymous. Next, we use TAS to the check the anonymity of a question. The anonymity score for a question, which we term the 'Question Anonymity Score (QAS)' is defined as the mean TAS of all the topics that the question is tagged with. Thus, if a question is tagged with topics that have high TAS, the question will also receive a high QAS. To check for the topical mixing, we divide the questions into two sets based on whether the question was posted as anonymous or non-anonymous. Figure 3 shows the distribution of QAS associated with the Anon and the Known groups. As seen from the figure, there is a huge overlap between the Anon and the Known questions. This is the primary reason why we do not observe a significant difference between the Anon and the Known groups at the global scale.

6   Topical Anonymity

The lack of significant difference between the Known and the Anon group at the global scale further motivated us in making more granular investigations.

One way to make such fine-grained investigation would be to analyze a group of questions together. We, therefore, attempt to group the questions in topical clusters and study their characteristics. We make use of the topics assigned to the questions for this purpose.

6.1 Anonymity Ratio

Topics assigned by users impose one such natural grouping on the questions. We consider only those topics which have at least 20 questions to ensure that the topic is sufficiently represented. The topic based clustering (TC) aims at segregating the Quora questions into three major types of clusters – (i) those that contain predominantly anonymous questions which we call *anonymous clusters* (ii) those that contain predominantly non-anonymous questions which we call *non-anonymous clusters* and (iii) those that we call *neutral clusters* and are somewhere in between (i) and (ii).

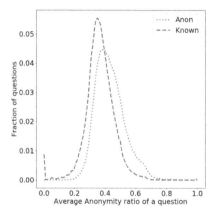

Fig. 3. Anonymity ratio of questions.

Table 4. Basic statistics of the clusters obtained.

Cluster property	TC
μ_{a_r}	0.3903
σ_{a_r}	0.1528
#Anonymous clusters	7617
#Non-anonymous clusters	6881
#Neutral clusters	36241

We define the *anonymity ratio* (a_r) of a cluster as the ratio of the anonymous questions to the total questions in that cluster. Let the mean a_r across all the clusters be denoted by μ_{a_r}; similarly, let the standard deviation be denoted by σ_{a_r}. We define a cluster as anonymous (Anon) if its $a_r \geq \mu_{a_r} + \sigma_{a_r}$. Similarly, we call a cluster non-anonymous (Known) if $a_r \leq \mu_{a_r} - \sigma_{a_r}$. The clusters having a_r values in between these two extremes are the neutral ones. Table 4 lists some of the properties of the clusters generated. Figure 4 plots the distribution of a_r for the clusters.

In the following, we repeat the analysis earlier reported at the global scale for each of the Anon and the Known clusters.

Question Types: We observe that the differences in the head word distribution becomes more prominent in topical clusters as shown in Fig. 2b. Specifically questions that start with 'I' are more prominent among the Anon group than the Known ones.

Structural Analysis: We perform simple structural analysis on the question-texts of the Anon and Known group such as word distribution, question length and POS (Parts-of-Speech) analysis.

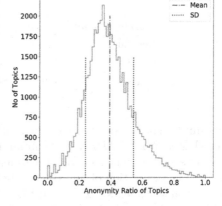

Fig. 4. Anonymity ratio (a_r) across the different clusters for topic based clusters.

Word Usage: We observe that the average word count for the Anon clusters is 15.17, while for Known clusters it is 13.81. This is due to the questions being more expressive in the Anon clusters.

POS Analysis: To find if there are any linguistic differences in the framing of question texts, we analyze the usage of POS tags in the question texts. We compute the distribution of different POS tags the POS tags follow the Universal Dependency Scheme[8] for both the Anon and the Known topics. Some of the striking observations from Table 5 are that the tags like verbs and pronouns strongly prevail in the Anon topics, while nouns seem to be in higher usage in Known topics. The questions in Anon cluster use more pronouns indicating that people use anonymity to ask more personal questions. The lower presence of nouns in Anon cluster is unsurprising since anonymous users would prefer not to disclose their identities by referring to persons, facilities, locations etc.

Table 5. Fraction of different POS tags across the Anon and the Known clusters. Only cases with significant difference are shown

Part-of-speech tag (simple)			
POS category	Cohen's d	Anon	Known	Diff. (%)
Noun	−0.402	0.276	0.3245	−14.826
Verb	0.236	0.220	0.199	10.549
Pronoun	0.569	0.065	0.029	124.966

---

[8] http://universaldependencies.org/u/pos/.

Table 6. Sentiment score of VADER across the Anon and the Known topics.

Sentiment score	Cohen's d	Anon	Known	Diff. (%)
Neutral	−0.298	0.826	0.874	−5.496
Positive	0.157	0.112	0.091	23.869
Negative	0.248	0.061	0.035	75.286

Sentiment Analysis: We perform sentiment analysis of the question text across clusters using VADER [8] to obtain the distribution of the positive, negative and neutral sentiments across the different clusters. We observe from Table 6 that a major proportion of questions in both the Anon and the Known clusters have neutral sentiments (82.6% and 87.4% respectively). However, questions in the Anon clusters have relatively higher (75.28%, Cohen's $d \sim 0.25$) negative sentiments as compared to the Known clusters. These results are in correspondence with past observations that anonymous content generally bear more negative sentiments [4].

Psycholinguistic Analysis: In this section, we first perform LIWC analysis of the question text across the Known and the Anon clusters. We report the significantly different categories in Table 7. Note how the extremely personal categories like 'sexual', 'family', 'friends', 'body', 'feel', 'shehe', 'I' feature in exorbitantly high fractions across the Anon clusters. These results are in agreement with the previous observations that the Anon clusters talk more about personal questions whereas the Known clusters talk more about general questions.

Table 7. Fraction of different lexical categories across the Anon and the Known clusters. Only cases with significant difference are shown.

LIWC category	Cohen's d	Anon	Known	Diff. (%)
Leisure	−0.273	0.009	0.018	−51.468
Space	−0.252	0.052	0.068	−24.306
Negemo	0.194	0.024	0.015	60.408
Body	0.228	0.013	0.005	168.218
SheHe	0.237	0.007	0.002	287.416
Family	0.247	0.006	0.001	749.53
Friends	0.297	0.011	0.001	1224.947
Sexual	0.357	0.013	0.001	1644.211
Humans	0.359	0.019	0.005	310.755
I	0.511	0.045	0.012	274.765
Ppron	0.585	0.069	0.027	160.326

7   More Insights

7.1   Anonymity of Answers

Thus far we have been designating a question as anonymous if the user posting the question would tag it as anonymous. This is therefore the user's perception about the question. In this discussion, we would like to point out that there could be a community perception about the same question and this might well be different from the individual's perception. One way to quantify the perception of the community could be to observe the *level of anonymity in the answers* garnered by a question. Next we define this concept precisely.

For every question posted by a user, we compute the number of answers garnered by it. We note that it is possible that a question actually posted as anonymous can have a larger proportion of answers that are non-anonymous. The individual perception of the user asking the question therefore, in this case, is different from the community (i.e., users answering the question) perception. Based on these differences, one can easily conceive of an anonymity grid as follows.

Anonymity Grid. To better understand this, we combine the user and the community perspective of anonymity. The four groups so formed – (i) (question Anon, answer Anon), (ii) (question Anon, answer Known), (iii) (question Known, answer Anon) and (iv) (question Known, answer Known) constitute a 2 × 2 table which we refer to as the anonymity grid. In Table 8, we report some of the representative Quora topics in each of these four classes. We observe that most of the taboo and sensitive topics correspond to the class (i) while the most general topics correspond to the class (iv).

In order to find topics which belong to the different groups in the anonymity grid, we first filter out all the topics which have less than 1000 questions. Then, for each topic we find the fraction of questions in each of the cell in the anonymity grid. We then simply rank the topics in each cell based on the this fraction. Table 8 shows the top 15 topics in each cell of the grid. The topics obtained as a result of the ranking algorithm resonate well with our expectations.

- The category (question Anon, answer Anon) has a large proportion of topics pertaining to relationships, sex, dating etc. which are highly sensitive and thus justifiably anonymous in terms of both questions and answers.
- The category (question Anon, answer Known) contains topics related to health, jobs, careers, personal grooming, pets etc. It has questions which are highly personal to the user (e.g., 'How do you overcome depression') who wish to seek advice anonymously. The thriving userbase of Quora which has many domain experts and the desire for social recognition drives the answers in this category to be predominantly non-anonymous.
- The category (question Known, answer Anon) contains topics like politics, religion and experience/advice. Answers in such topics might often lead to controversy and could generate backlash for the user. Thus, these questions

Table 8. Representative topics in the anonymity grid

	Question Anon	Question Known
Answer Anon	Advice about love, adult dating advice, love and relationship advice, breaking up, romantic relationships, girlfriends, relationships and sex, dating and friendship, love life advice, marriage advice, boyfriends dating advice, relationships and dating of young people, love	Experiences in life, bharatiya janata party bjp, narendra modi, god, culture of india, life and living, politics of india, humor, advice for everyday life, muslims, bollywood, people, philosophy of everyday life, islam, indian ethnicity and people, spirituality, hinduism
Answer Known	Dog breeds, obstetrics and gynecology, acne, womens health, menstruation, programming interviews, hairstyles, dermatology, english sentences, purpose, phrase definitions, pregnancy, skin care, teeth, pets, google recruiting, phrases, emotional advice, makeup cosmetics, hair care	Major league baseball, international space station, seo tools, black holes, solar panels, aircraft, military technology, general relativity, camera lenses, ipad applications, spacetime, virtual reality, military aircraft, solar energy, nuclear energy, satellites, national football league nfl

are often answered anonymously although the question itself is posted as non-anonymous, since the main target of the backlash and controversy are the answerers and not the user posting the question.
– The category (question Known, answer Known) contains very general topics like sports, science and technology etc. where both the answers and questions in these topics are posted non-anonymously.

7.2   First Response Time for Questions and Topics

In addition to observing the number of responses garnered by a question, it is also interesting to note the *first response time* (henceforth FRT). We define FRT of a question as the amount of time elapsed (in hours) between posting the question and receiving the first response. We can then compare the FRT of the anonymous questions and non-anonymous questions within a topic by observing their corresponding median FRT. We consider the median FRT to prevent the skewness arising from unanswered questions or questions answered after a long period of time (1–2 years).

We present a comparison of the FRT for the anonymous and non-anonymous questions on the global, topical and extremes level in Table 9. We observe that while on a global scale, there is not much difference in the FRT for the Anon and the Known questions, the questions in the Known topics require 66% more time to receive their first response as compared to the Anon Topics.

Table 9. Comparision of the median first response time (FRT) of the anonymous questions and non-anonymous questions at different levels.

Category	Anon questions	Known questions	Diff (in %)
Global	10.267	10.0	2.667
Anon topics	5.45	5.733	−4.942
Known topics	9.25	9.35	−1.07
Anon-Anon	1.35	2.033	−33.607
Anon-Known	10.55	8.433	25.099
Known-Anon	2.917	3.4	−14.216
Known-Known	5.367	4.417	21.509

We consider the top 50 representative topics of each cell in the anonymity grid (described in earlier section). We then observe the differences in FRT of the anonymous and non-anonymous questions (of the representative topics) for each cell, as shown in Table 9. The categories in Table 9 correspond to Anon question and Anon answer (Anon-Anon), Anon question and Known answer (Anon-Known), Known question and Anon answer (Known-Anon) and Known question and Known answer (Known-Known). It is interesting to note that the cells which have a comparatively higher proportion of anonymous answers have a lower median FRT for the anonymous questions than the non-anonymous ones and vice-versa. Also, another interesting insight is that the median FRT for the Anon-Anon category is 1.35 h, which is significantly small as opposed to the others. This illustrates that topics with higher proportion of anonymous answers tend to receive faster response to the anonymous questions. This can be a very crucial point in designing a predictor that can automatically suggest how to post an anonymous question to receive quick answers.

8   Conclusions and Future Works

In this paper, we performed a large scale anonymity analysis on the popular Q&A site Quora and found that on a global scale, there are no significant differences between the anonymous and non-anonymous questions. This happens because of the differences in the users' perspective in choosing to post the question as anonymous or not. In order to understand the nuances of anonymity in Quora, we then topically clustered the questions. We found that several linguistic and psycho-linguistic features become prominent here. Finally, we introduced the idea of an anonymity grid and studied how the perception of anonymity of the user posting the question differs from the community that answers it.

As a part of future work, we would investigate the temporal aspects of anonymity. Specifically, we would like to ask what kind of changes does a topic undergo from the perspective of anonymity. There would be some topics which would have been predominantly anonymous initially, but as the society progresses and social norms change, people might start to post questions/answers non-anonymously in that topic causing a gradual shift in the anonymity ratio of the topic.

A   Appendix

Cohen's d: The Cohen's d test is primarily used to measure the effect size, which is an estimate of the strength of the relationship of two variables. Given the mean and standard deviation of two populations, denoted by μ_1 and σ_1 and μ_2 and σ_2 respectively, the Cohen's d-test is the ratio of the difference of their means to their pooled standard deviation, more succinctly represented by the following expression

$$d = \frac{\mu_2 - \mu_1}{\sqrt{\frac{\sigma_1^2 + \sigma_2^2}{2}}}$$

A Cohen's d-value of magnitude 0.2 indicates small effect, 0.5 indicates medium effect while 0.8 signifies large effect.

Diff(%): We use the metric $Diff(\%)$ in a way similar to Correa et al. [4] to quantify the difference in features between the Anon and the Known Group. The Diff(%) metric is simply the percentage mean difference of a feature between the Anon and Known group and is represented as

$$Diff = \frac{Anon - Known}{Known} \times 100\%$$

References

1. Bernstein, M.S., Monroy-Hernández, A., Harry, D., André, P., Panovich, K., Vargas, G.G.: 4chan and/b: an analysis of anonymity and ephemerality in a large online community. In: ICWSM, pp. 50–57 (2011)
2. Birnholtz, J., Merola, N.A.R., Paul, A.: Is it weird to still be a virgin: anonymous, locally targeted questions on facebook confession boards. In: CHI, pp. 2613–2622. ACM (2015)
3. Cohen, J.: Statistical Power Analysis for the Behavioral Sciences, 2nd edn. Routledge, Abingdon (1988)
4. Correa, D., Silva, L.A., Mondal, M., Benevenuto, F., Gummadi, K.P.: The many shades of anonymity: characterizing anonymous social media content. In: ICWSM, pp. 71–80 (2015)
5. De Choudhury, M., De, S.: Mental health discourse on reddit: self-disclosure, social support, and anonymity. In: ICWSM, pp. 71–80 (2014)
6. Faber, J., Fonseca, L.M.: How sample size influences research outcomes. Dent. Press J. Orthod. **19**(4), 27–29 (2014)

7. Huang, Z., Thint, M., Qin, Z.: Question classification using head words and their hypernyms. In: EMNLP, pp. 927–936. ACL (2008)

8. Hutto, C.J., Gilbert, E.: Vader: a parsimonious rule-based model for sentiment analysis of social media text. In: ICWSM (2014)

9. Li, F., Zhang, X., Yuan, J., Zhu, X.: Classifying what-type questions by head noun tagging. In: ACL, pp. 481–488 (2008)

10. Maity, S.K., Kharb, A., Mukherjee, A.: Language use matters: analysis of the linguistic structure of question texts can characterize answerability in Quora. In: ICWSM, pp. 612–615 (2017)

11. Maity, S.K., Kharb, A., Mukherjee, A.: Analyzing the linguistic structure of question texts to characterize answerability in Quora. IEEE Trans. Comput. Soc. Syst. 5(3), 816–828 (2018)

12. Maity, S.K., Sahni, J.S.S., Mukherjee, A.: Analysis and prediction of question topic popularity in community Q&A sites: a case study of Quora. In: ICWSM, pp. 238–247 (2015)

13. Paskuda, M., Lewkowicz, M.: Anonymous Quorans are still Quorans, just anonymous. In: 7th International Conference on Communities and Technologies, pp. 9–18. ACM (2015)

14. Patil, S., Lee, K.: Detecting experts on Quora: by their activity, quality of answers, linguistic characteristics and temporal behaviors. Soc. Netw. Anal. Min. 6(1), 5 (2016)

15. Wang, G., Gill, K., Mohanlal, M., Zheng, H., Zhao, B.Y.: Wisdom in the social crowd: an analysis of Quora. In: WWW, pp. 1341–1352. ACM (2013)

The Demography of the Peripatetic Researcher: Evidence on Highly Mobile Scholars from the Web of Science

Samin Aref[1]([✉]) [iD], Emilio Zagheni[1] [iD], and Jevin West[2] [iD]

[1] Max Planck Institute for Demographic Research,
Konrad-Zuse-Str. 1, 18057 Rostock, Germany
{aref,zagheni}@demogr.mpg.de
[2] Information School, University of Washington, Seattle, WA 98195, USA
jevinw@uw.edu

Abstract. The policy debate around researchers' geographic mobility has been moving away from a theorized zero-sum game in which countries can be winners ("brain gain") or losers ("brain drain"), and toward the concept of "brain circulation," which implies that researchers move in and out of countries and everyone benefits. Quantifying trends in researchers' movements is key to understanding the drivers of the mobility of talent, as well as the implications of these patterns for the global system of science, and for the competitive advantages of individual countries. Existing studies have investigated bilateral flows of researchers. However, in order to understand migration systems, determining the extent to which researchers have worked in more than two countries is essential. This study focuses on the subgroup of highly mobile researchers whom we refer to as "peripatetic researchers" or "super-movers."

More specifically, our aim is to track the international movements of researchers who have published in more than two countries through changes in the main affiliation addresses of over 62 million publications indexed in the Web of Science database over the 1956–2016 period. Using this approach, we have established a longitudinal dataset on the international movements of highly mobile researchers across all subject categories, and in all disciplines of scholarship. This article contributes to the literature by offering for the first time a snapshot of the key features of highly mobile researchers, including their patterns of migration and return migration by academic age, the relative frequency of their disciplines, and the relative frequency of their countries of origin and destination. Among other findings, the results point to the emergence of a global system that includes the USA and China as two large hubs, and England and Germany as two smaller hubs for highly mobile researchers.

Keywords: High-skilled migration · Big data · Bibliometric data · Web of Science · Science of science

© Springer Nature Switzerland AG 2019
I. Weber et al. (Eds.): SocInfo 2019, LNCS 11864, pp. 50–65, 2019.
https://doi.org/10.1007/978-3-030-34971-4_4

1   Introduction

In the global economy, highly skilled migration [9] and the mobility of researchers [4] have become central issues for research and policy. The interest in these issues is reflected in numerous studies that have investigated the mobility of researchers across countries [6,10,17,19–22,26,30]. In this article, we focus on the movements of researchers as a subcategory of mobility processes among highly educated people, which have far-reaching consequences for the exchange of knowledge and the development of new ideas, as well as for the emergence of competitive advantages for the countries involved in the resulting circulation of knowledge.

Studying migration among the highly skilled (and researchers in particular) at the global level is difficult using classic demographic methods, in part because a world migration survey does not exist [33]. Recent studies that have examined international mobility among researchers have used bibliometric data as a complementary approach [10,20]. This method involves tracking the international movements of researchers through the changes in the affiliation addresses on their publications. By generating the equivalent of a census of publications, the application of this method makes it possible to assess the mobility of scholars.

The feasibility of this method has been tested in previous studies that estimated migration flows [19,20]. As most of the existing studies on this topic limited their focus to specific disciplines [11,15], or to comparisons of a few countries [8,11,17,19,21] or of mobile vs. non-mobile scholars [17,26], more in-depth analysis is needed to provide us with a better understanding of international mobility in academia. That is the objective of this study.

The issue of the mobility of researchers is similar to the issue of migration, as a survey of 17,000 researchers showed that among the factors researchers consider when weighing an international move include the opportunity to achieve a better quality of life and a higher salary, and the desire to discover another culture [12,13,24]. The idea of using the affiliations of researchers to analyze their mobility patterns can be traced back to Rosenfeld and Jones in 1987 [23], who used biographical information from the American Psychology Association directory to study the mobility patterns of psychologists by gender. Another pioneering study [16] tested the suitability of bibliometric data in the biomedical field for studying the international mobility of elite researchers, and for investigating phenomena such as brain drain. Several studies have shown that internationally mobile scholars have a substantially greater research impact than non-mobile scholars when measured by citation-based indicators [22,26]. More comprehensive studies on this topic investigated return migration among scholars using a 10-year worth of bibliometric data for 17 countries [20], and combined bibliometric data with other data sources to examine the relationship between return mobility and scientific impact in the context of Europe [5]. Other recent studies have investigated the directional flows of researchers using bibliometric data over a 60-year period ending in 2009 [30], and have used networks to model and analyze geographical career paths over time [31].

Our focus here is on researchers who have published with main affiliation addresses from at least three distinct countries, according to Web of Science data over the 1956–2016 period. We refer to these researchers as "peripatetic researchers" or "super-movers" and provide analyses of their common features, mobility paths, and return migration.

2 Methods and Materials

A key advantage of using bibliometric data for studying the mobility of researchers is the availability of millions of publications in bibliometric databases, such as Web of Science [22], Scopus [2], and Dimensions [27]. Each publication serves as a data point that indicates the addresses of the authors on a certain publication date. These data points provide proxies not only on the geographic locations of researchers, but on their fields of research and the disciplines of the publication venues. We track the international movements of researchers through the changes in the main affiliation addresses listed in more than 62 million publications indexed in the Web of Science database. This is the initial step in establishing a longitudinal dataset on the mobility of researchers across all research fields, and in different disciplines. Observing, consistent with the literature [22], that more than 90% of the researchers showed no signs of international mobility, we focus on the small fraction of scholars whose main affiliation track indicates that they moved across international borders. In particular, we focus on researchers whose Web of Science publication data show that they have published with main affiliation addresses from at least three distinct countries, which we consider an indication that they made more than one international move.

With a nod to Aristotle's Peripatetic school, we refer to this small group of highly mobile scholars as "*peripatetic researchers.*" The term "peripatetic" means "moving from place to place." Derived etymologically from the Greek, peripatetic literally means "of walking," as Aristotle required his students to walk alongside him as he lectured. Using our dataset of "peripatetic researchers" (whom we also call "*super-movers*"), we provide several in-depth statistics related to mobility and return migration, disaggregated by new variables involving age and origin. Similar methodologies have been deployed in the past, but a longitudinal global-level study that includes all highly mobile scholars has not previously been undertaken. Our aim in conducting such a study is to shed some light on the common characteristics of peripatetic researchers and their mobility patterns. We do so by tracking the international paths of these researchers over the 1956–2016 period. While there are a number of methodological challenges associated with studying scientific mobility and collaboration using bibliometric data that should be taken into consideration [1,3,7,10,20], we believe that the novel approach we propose and the results we obtain will prove timely and relevant, and will provide a foundation for future research in this field.

3   Results

In this section, we present the main results of our analysis of Web of Science authorship records from 1956 to 2016. An authorship record is the linkage between a publication and an author of that publication. We extracted all of the authorship records of the super-movers (the individuals whose publications had main affiliation addresses in at least three distinct countries). This extraction resulted in nearly 1.7 million authorship records, which make up the main dataset that we describe and analyze in the following subsections.

An initial look at the most common countries in the dataset shows that the USA, China, Japan, Germany, England, and South Korea are the six countries with the highest number of authorship records. Of the total 1.7 million authorship records of peripatetic researchers in our dataset, almost 68% refers to one of these six countries which all have more than 100,000 authorship records.

3.1   Common Characteristics of Peripatetic Researchers

We define *the country of academic origin (destination)* as the country that appears in the earliest (latest) publication of an individual researcher. Figure 1 illustrates the most common countries of main affiliation associated with the earliest publications of the super-movers (in Fig. 1a), and with their latest publications (in Fig. 1b) over the 1956–2016 period. Figure 1 shows that the USA and China were the most common and the second-most common countries of academic origin, while this order was reversed for the destinations of the super-movers. When we take the relationship between mobility and scientific impact into account [22, 26], we find that our observations for the USA and China are consistent with a *Nature* survey of 2,300 respondents [32], which showed that although the USA has historically been the country with the greatest scientific impact, China is expected to have the greatest impact in 2020.

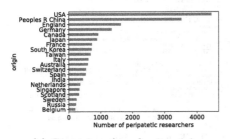
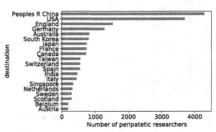

     (a) Countries of academic origin   (b) Countries of academic destination

Fig. 1. Twenty most common countries of academic origin (a) and academic destination (b) among the super-movers

Also in Fig. 1, we can see that England and Germany were, respectively, the third- and fourth-most common countries of origin and countries of destination. Countries such as Canada and Italy were more likely to be the country of academic origin (ranked several steps higher as the country of origin) than the country of destination, while the opposite pattern (ranked several steps higher as the country of destination) is observed for South Korea and Australia.

We divide the number of super-movers for each country of academic origin by the country's population (in 2016 [29]) to obtain a measure of super-movers per capita. This allows us to make a different comparison across countries. Of the 20 countries included in Fig. 1a, Switzerland, Singapore, Scotland, England, Taiwan, Canada, and Australia were ranked 1, 2, 3, 6, 7, 9, and 10, respectively, in terms of the number of super-movers per capita. It should be noted that neither the USA nor China were in the top 20 countries based on the per capita measurement.

We also investigate the question of whether the scientific output of the peripatetic researchers was homogeneous across disciplines using the titles and subject categories of the publication venues in our dataset of 1.7 million authorship records. Figure 2 shows the subject categories and titles of the publication venues that appeared most frequently. Looking at Fig. 2a, we can see that multidisciplinary chemistry was by far the most common subject among the authorship records of the super-movers. Among the other subjects that appeared most frequently were multidisciplinary sciences, oncology, and multidisciplinary physics, followed by several other fields of chemistry, physics, and medicine that were ranked in the top 10. An analysis of the most common publication venue titles show a fairly similar pattern, with *Plos One* being ranked first followed by several physics journals, alongside *European Heart Journal*, *Blood*, and *Chemical Communications* which were ranked in the top ten. Meanwhile, several chemistry and physics journals, *Circulation*, and *Journal of Alloys and Compounds* appeared in the lower ranks of the top 20 list displayed in Fig. 2b.

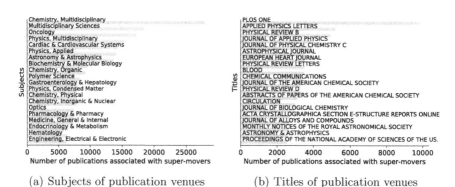

(a) Subjects of publication venues   (b) Titles of publication venues

Fig. 2. Twenty most common subject categories (a) and titles (b) of publication venues among the publications of the super-movers

In Appendix A, we compare the mobility patterns of peripatetic researchers from different countries of academic origin by individually plotting the international paths of the super-movers from China, England, Germany, Japan, and the

USA. The sizes of the nodes in Figs. 6, 7, 8, 9 and 10 are proportional to their in-degrees, which equal the number of moves to that country. The out-degrees of the nodes, represented by darker shades, equal the number of moves out of a country. The direction of the curved edges is clockwise.

Looking at Figs. 6, 7, 8 and 9, we can see that the USA was the country that the super-movers from China, England, Germany, and Japan moved in and out of second-most frequently. We list the countries that the super-movers moved in and out of third- to fifth-most frequently in decreasing order of frequency. The super-movers from China also frequently moved in and out of Taiwan, Canada, and Singapore. The super-movers from England were especially likely to move in and out of China, Switzerland, and Germany. We also observe that the super-movers from Germany frequently moved in and out of Switzerland, England, and France. The super-movers with an academic origin in Japan had frequent moves to and from China, South Korea, and Australia. Figure 10 shows the four countries that the super-movers from the USA most frequently moved in and out of to be China, England, Germany, and South Korea.

We use betweenness centrality (which measures how often a specific node appears in the shortest path between two other nodes of the network [14]) to rank the countries in a network of all super-movers' paths. Countries with the highest betweenness centrality were the USA, England, France, Germany, and Australia respectively. It should be noted that China was ranked 18 which seems to suggest that while China is an important node in the global system of science, it has limited influence as a connector in the paths of highly mobile scholars.

The data show that most of the peripatetic researchers had three countries of main affiliation in their international mobility paths. However, some have been affiliated with even more countries as shown in Fig. 3a.

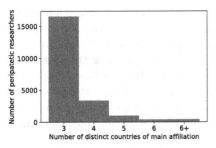
(a) Super-movers by number of countries

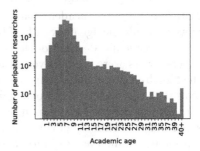
(b) Super-movers by academic age

Fig. 3. Number of super-movers by their number of countries (a) and academic age (b)

We define the real-valued variable *academic age* as the duration in years between the publication dates of the earliest and the latest authorship records of an individual scholar. Figur 3b shows the academic ages of the peripatetic researchers. Note that the y-axis in Fig. 3b is on a logarithmic scale. The mode of academic age is in $[6, 7]$ (similar to the findings of [30] for mobile scholars), but academic ages up to 10 are also very frequent. Two major reductions in frequency are observed in the academic age brackets 10–11 and 30–31, the latter being possibly attributable to retirement.

The results displayed in Fig. 3b therefore suggest that the levels of experience among the peripatetic researchers in our data varies substantially. Based on the peaks and valleys of academic age observed in Fig. 3b, we continue our investigation by categorizing the authorship data into three brackets based on academic age: $[0, 7)$ for early-career, $[7, 14)$ intermediate-level, and $[14, +\infty)$ senior super-movers. We observe in our data that most of the super-movers (49%) belong to the early-career group. A slightly smaller but still substantial fraction (44%) of the super-movers belong to the intermediate group, while a much smaller share (6%) of the super-movers belong to the senior group. Given these observations, we provide in Subsect. 3.2 several individual-level statistics with respect to academic age and country of academic origin, as the two main factors for disaggregating the authorship records of peripatetic researchers.

3.2   Destinations and Return Migration

In this subsection, we take the heterogeneity in levels of experience into consideration and accordingly provide an individual-level analysis of destinations and return migration.

Figure 4 shows the most common countries of academic destination for the three academic age brackets. Figure 4a shows that the USA was the most common country of destination for the early-career super-movers (academic age up to seven) by a small margin, while Fig. 4b and c show that China was, by a large margin, the most common country of destination for both the intermediate super-movers (academic age between seven and 14) and the senior super-movers (academic age above 14). The third- and the fourth-most common countries of academic destination for both the early-career and the intermediate super-movers were, respectively, England and Germany; while the third- and the fourth-most common countries of academic destination for the senior super-movers were, respectively, Japan and England. As Fig. 4 shows, certain countries, such as South Korea and Japan, were popular destinations for the more senior super-movers; while other countries, such as Australia, Canada, and Spain, were especially common as destinations for more early-career super-movers.

We use the international mobility paths of each peripatetic researcher to check whether they had returned to their country of academic origin. For each country of academic origin X, we quantify *return migration* as a simple fraction of the number of super-movers who had country X in both their earliest and their latest publications to the total number of super-movers from country of academic origin X.

Note that return migration aggregated for all countries equals 0.28, 0.49, and 0.45 for the age brackets $[0, 7)$, $[7, 14)$, and $[14, +\infty)$, respectively; which seems to suggest that the intermediate and the senior super-movers were more inclined

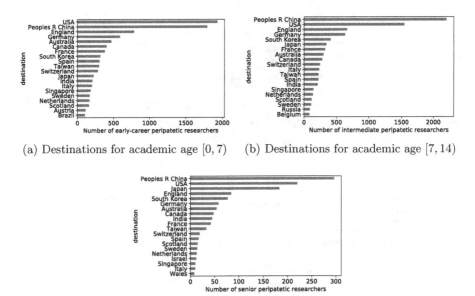

(a) Destinations for academic age $[0, 7)$ (b) Destinations for academic age $[7, 14)$

(c) Destinations for academic age $[14, +\infty)$

Fig. 4. Most common countries of academic destination among super-movers by academic age within the ranges of (a) $[0, 7)$, (b) $[7, 14)$, and (c) $[14, +\infty)$

to return to the country where they first published than the early-career super-movers, who may have been visiting several countries as part of their professional development.

Figure 5 shows the fractions of return migration among the early-career and the intermediate super-movers for different countries of academic origin, with larger circles and darker shades representing a larger value of return migration. In this analysis, we have omitted all of the countries for which the number of super-movers within the respective academic age bracket was less than five. The exact numeric values for return migration are provided next to the names of the countries in Fig. 5. Figure 5a shows that no early-career super-mover from Cameroon, Saudi Arabia, or Vietnam had returned to his/her country of academic origin.

Looking at Fig. 5, we can see that for both the early-career and the intermediate super-movers, levels of return migration were relatively low in Iran, Singapore, Ukraine, and Venezuela; and were medium-low in countries such as Australia, Austria, Canada, Egypt, Finland, Hungary, Ireland, the Netherlands, Scotland, Switzerland, and the USA. Levels of return migration were medium in Denmark, England, France, Germany, Israel, Italy, Norway, Pakistan, Spain, and Taiwan. The countries with medium-high levels of return migration were Brazil,

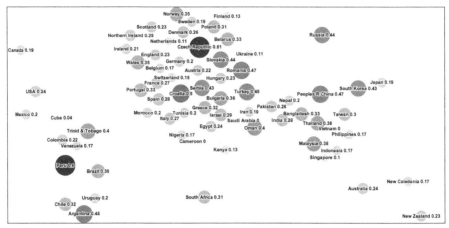

(a) Return migration for academic age up to 7 (early-career)

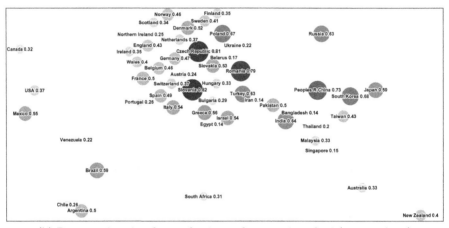

(b) Return migration for academic age between 7 and 14 (intermediate)

Fig. 5. Fraction of return migration by country of academic origin and academic age bracket: (a) early-career and (b) intermediate (high-resolution version online)

Greece, Poland, and Slovakia; while the countries with high levels of return migration were the Czech Republic, China, Romania, Russia, South Korea, and Turkey.

Comparing to the average values, we observe that for seven countries – Bangladesh, Bulgaria, Belarus, Malaysia, Portugal, Thailand, and Wales – levels of return migration were relatively high among the early-career researchers, but were relatively low among the intermediate super-movers. For Japan and Mexico, the opposite pattern is observed: levels of return migration were relatively low among the early-career and relatively high among the intermediate super-movers.

Our results can be combined with country-specific fractions of researchers working abroad. For instance, the early-career return migration value for India becomes particularly informative when combined with the existing knowledge that 40% of India-born researchers below 37 years of age have been employed outside of India [28].

4   Limitations and Advantages of Using Bibliometric Data

While using new data sources for studying mobility of researchers seems promising [22,30], we would like to remind the reader that there are some well-known challenges associated with relying on bibliometric data that our study does not resolve [2,22]. For example, the time it takes to conduct research and publish papers is an essential factor that should not be neglected. This time lag prevents us from observing mobility events at the exact point in time when they occurred. Our analysis and results were solely based on main affiliation (as opposed to considering multiple affiliations [22]) which does not always represent the actual geographic location of a researcher. Furthermore, we are unable to observe and track international mobility not represented in Web of Science publication data, which are known to be biased toward certain languages, and to underrepresent certain countries [25]. We should, therefore, stress that our analysis is based on the underestimate of mobility that is currently achievable within the limits of bibliometric data. Future methodological research on scientometrics and complementary data sources could, perhaps, address these issues.

An important technical limitation of the data is related to author disambiguation. We used the author IDs that Web of Science offers and performed sensitivity analyses based on a set of 7,000 manually disambiguated authorship records. Although the substantive results of our paper did not change, we observed that author disambiguation represents an important challenge to the validity of the dataset. Thus, we believe that new and innovative methods of algorithmic author name disambiguation are needed to improve the overall quality of bibliometric data.

Despite these limitations, it is also important to point out that by using bibliometric data, we have been able to conduct an analysis of mobility that is more cross-disciplinary, longitudinal, globally scaled, and contemporary [1,10, 22] than studies that use classic data sources, such as registries, surveys, and censuses. Most of the studies that use bibliometric data, including this one, have the advantage of being easily replicable at different levels of analysis. For instance, our framework can be adopted for investigating scientific mobility at a national or a regional level, across scientific fields, and across research institutes and universities.

5   Discussion and Future Directions

In this paper, we provided for the first time (to the best of our knowledge) a snapshot of the characteristics of highly mobile scholars (super-movers), whom we define as those researchers who have had main affiliations in at least three distinct countries. Our goal was to identify the common features that distinguish a highly selected group of researchers who are in some ways still "outliers," but who also serve as the oil that lubricates the global system of brain circulation in science. We have witnessed the emergence of a system that includes the USA and China as two large hubs, and England and Germany as two smaller hubs for highly mobile scholars. It is important to note that, despite the bias toward English-speaking journals in the Web of Science, China was the top country of destination among the super-movers in the dataset. This may be an indication of the progress China has made in reaching its goal of becoming a major science powerhouse.

Demographic perspectives have seldom been considered in previous bibliometric research. With this study, we add a demographic flavor to the science of science literature by also accounting for the age patterns of mobility, and by considering metrics (like return migration) that are common in demographic studies, but are not typically considered in the science of science literature. Accounting for the age distribution of scholars is essential to avoid obtaining spurious results that are affected by compositional changes in the underlying population. Among the aims of this article is to foster the development of bridges between demographic and scientometric research. We expect that fruitful interdisciplinary collaborations will emerge and evolve in the future.

This study represents the initial step in a continuing effort to construct a longitudinal dataset on the mobility of researchers and on the geographical trajectories of their career paths. The data on these trajectories could be used to generate migration estimates that facilitate the investigation of phenomena such as brain drain and brain circulation. In addition, by leveraging the networked structure of the data, it may be possible to test and advance network theories of international migration [18].

We developed a panel of fine-grained data on the geographic trajectories of highly mobile scholars, which are intended to stimulate further research at the intersection of migration research and scientometrics. On the one hand, the data can be used to address the question of to what extent countries' shares of brain circulation depend on factors such as the diversity of their science system and national-level measures of research quality. On the other hand, the data can be used to study the effects of international mobility on measures of research quality and impact for individuals, organizations, and countries.

Acknowledgements. The authors thank the anonymous referees for their comments, and Chowdhury Majedur Rahman for assistance with the data quality checks. SA and EZ designed and conducted the research and wrote the paper. JW contributed in extracting the data.

A   International Paths of the Peripatetic Researchers

(see Figs 6, 7, 8, 9 and 10)

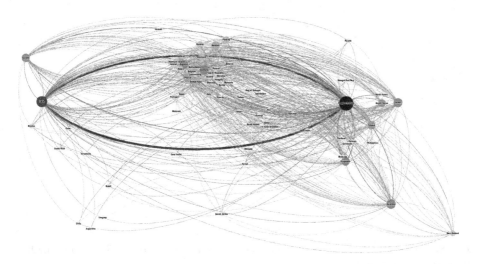

Fig. 6. Paths for super-movers from country of academic origin China (high-resolution version online)

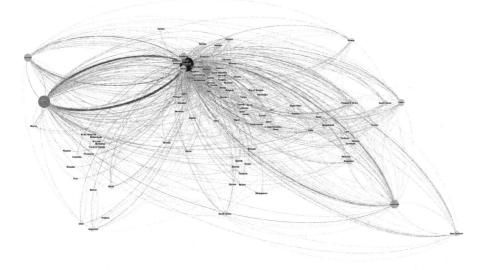

Fig. 7. Paths for super-movers from country of academic origin England (high-resolution version online)

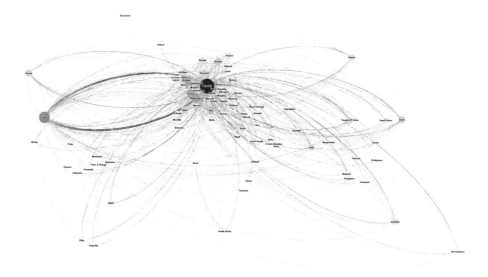

Fig. 8. Paths for super-movers from country of academic origin Germany (high-resolution version online)

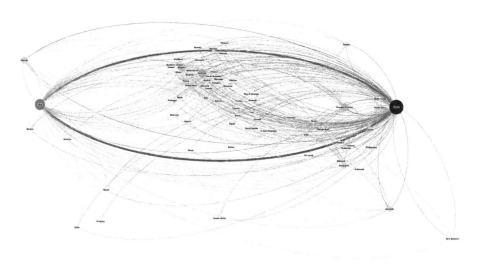

Fig. 9. Paths for super-movers from country of academic origin Japan (high-resolution version online)

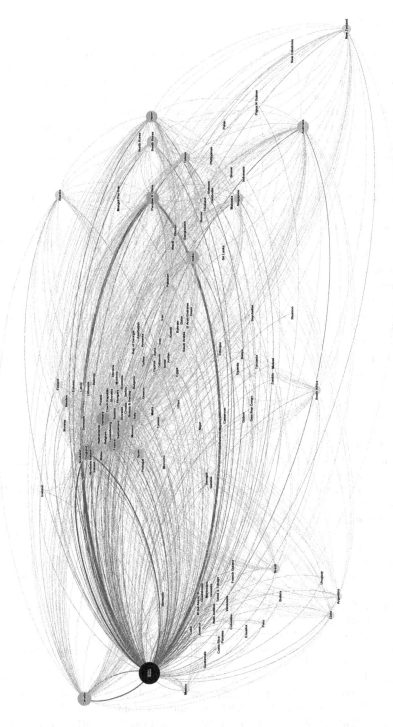

Fig. 10. Paths for super-movers from country of academic origin USA

References

1. Alburez-Gutierrez, D., Aref, S., Gil-Clavel, S., Grow, A., Negraia, D., Zagheni, E.: Demography in the digital era: new data sources for population research. In: Arbia, G., Peluso, S., Pini, A., Rivellini, G. (eds.) Book of Short Papers SIS2019, pp. 23–30. Pearson (2019). https://doi.org/10.31235/osf.io/24jp7
2. Appelt, S., van Beuzekom, B., Galindo-Rueda, F., de Pinho, R.: Which factors influence the international mobility of research scientists? In: Geuna, A. (ed.) Global Mobility of Research Scientists, pp. 177–213. Academic Press, San Diego (2015). https://doi.org/10.1016/B978-0-12-801396-0.00007-7
3. Aref, S., Friggens, D., Hendy, S.: Analysing scientific collaborations of New Zealand institutions using Scopus bibliometric data. In: Proceedings of the Australasian Computer Science Week Multiconference, p. 49. ACM, New York (2018). https://doi.org/10.1145/3167918.3167920
4. Arrieta, O.A.D., Pammolli, F., Petersen, A.M.: Quantifying the negative impact of brain drain on the integration of European science. Sci. Adv. **3**(4), e1602232 (2017). https://doi.org/10.1126/sciadv.1602232
5. Cañibano, C., Vértesy, D., Vezzulli, A.: An inquiry into the return mobility of scientific researchers in Europe. JRC Technical reports (2017). https://doi.org/10.2760/54633
6. Cañibano, C., Otamendi, F.J., Solís, F.: International temporary mobility of researchers: a cross-discipline study. Scientometrics **89**(2), 653–675 (2011). https://doi.org/10.1007/s11192-011-0462-2
7. Chinchilla-Rodríguez, Z., Miao, L., Murray, D., Robinson-García, N., Costas, R., Sugimoto, C.R.: Networks of international collaboration and mobility: a comparative study. In: Proceedings of the 16th International Conference on Scientometrics & Informetrics, pp. 270–280 (2017). 10261/170060
8. Conchi, S., Michels, C.: Scientific mobility: an analysis of Germany, Austria, France and Great Britain. Fraunhofer ISI Discussion Papers (2014). http://hdl.handle.net/10419/94371
9. Czaika, M.: High-skilled Migration: Drivers and Policies. Oxford University Press, New York (2018). https://doi.org/10.1093/oso/9780198815273.001.0001
10. Czaika, M., Orazbayev, S.: The globalisation of scientific mobility, 1970–2014. Appl. Geogr. **96**, 1–10 (2018). https://doi.org/10.1016/j.apgeog.2018.04.017
11. Dyachenko, E.L.: Internal migration of scientists in Russia and the USA: the case of physicists. Scientometrics **113**(1), 105–122 (2017). https://doi.org/10.1007/s11192-017-2478-8
12. Franzoni, C., Scellato, G., Stephan, P.: The mover's advantage: the superior performance of migrant scientists. Econ. Lett. **122**(1), 89–93 (2014). https://doi.org/10.1016/j.econlet.2013.10.040
13. Franzoni, C., Scellato, G., Stephan, P.: International mobility of research scientists: lessons from GlobSci. In: Global Mobility of Research Scientists, pp. 35–65. Elsevier (2015). https://doi.org/10.1016/B978-0-12-801396-0.00002-8
14. Freeman, L.C.: Centrality in social networks conceptual clarification. Soc. Netw. **1**(3), 215–239 (1978)
15. Hadiji, F., Mladenov, M., Bauckhage, C., Kersting, K.: Computer science on the move: inferring migration regularities from the web via compressed label propagation. In: Proceedings of the 24th International Conference on Artificial Intelligence, IJCAI 2015, pp. 171–177. AAAI Press, Palo Alto (2015). http://dl.acm.org/citation.cfm?id=2832249.2832273

16. Laudel, G.: Studying the brain drain: can bibliometric methods help? Scientometrics **57**(2), 215–237 (2003). https://doi.org/10.1023/A:1024137718393
17. Marmolejo-Leyva, R., Perez-Angon, M.A., Russell, J.M.: Mobility and international collaboration: case of the Mexican scientific diaspora. PLoS One **10**(6), e0126720 (2015). https://doi.org/10.1371/journal.pone.0126720
18. Massey, D.S., Arango, J., Hugo, G., Kouaouci, A., Pellegrino, A., Taylor, J.E.: Theories of international migration: a review and appraisal. Popul. Dev. Rev. **19**(3), 431–466 (1993)
19. Moed, H.F., Aisati, M., Plume, A.: Studying scientific migration in Scopus. Scientometrics **94**(3), 929–942 (2013). https://doi.org/10.1007/s11192-012-0783-9
20. Moed, H.F., Halevi, G.: A bibliometric approach to tracking international scientific migration. Scientometrics **101**(3), 1987–2001 (2014). https://doi.org/10.1007/s11192-014-1307-6
21. Robinson-García, N., Cañibano, C., Woolley, R., Costas, R.: Scientific mobility of early career researchers in Spain and the Netherlands through their publications. In: 21st International Conference on Science and Technology Indicators-STI 2016, Book of Proceedings, Valencia, Spain (2016). https://doi.org/10.4995/STI2016.2016.4543
22. Robinson-García, N., Sugimoto, C.R., Murray, D., Yegros-Yegros, A., Larivière, V., Costas, R.: The many faces of mobility: using bibliometric data to measure the movement of scientists. J. Inf. **13**(1), 50–63 (2019). https://doi.org/10.1016/j.joi.2018.11.002
23. Rosenfeld, R.A., Jones, J.A.: Patterns and effects of geographic mobility for academic women and men. J. High. Educ. **58**(5), 493–515 (1987). https://doi.org/10.1080/00221546.1987.11778276
24. Scellato, G., Franzoni, C., Stephan, P.: Migrant scientists and international networks. Res. Policy **44**(1), 108–120 (2015). https://doi.org/10.1016/j.respol.2014.07.014
25. Sugimoto, C.R., Larivière, V.: Measuring Research: What Everyone Needs to Know. Oxford University Press, New York (2018)
26. Sugimoto, C.R., Robinson-García, N., Murray, D.S., Yegros-Yegros, A., Costas, R., Larivière, V.: Scientists have most impact when they're free to move. Nat. News **550**(7674), 29 (2017). https://doi.org/10.1038/550029a
27. Thelwall, M.: Dimensions: a competitor to scopus and the web of science? J. Inf. **12**(2), 430–435 (2018). https://doi.org/10.1016/j.joi.2018.03.006
28. Toma, S., Villares-Varela, M.: Internationalization and diversification of academic careers. In: High-Skilled Migration: Drivers and Policies. Oxford University Press, New York (2018). https://doi.org/10.1093/oso/9780198815273.003.0012
29. United Nations, Department of Economic and Social Affairs, Population Division: World population prospects 2019 (2019). http://population.un.org/wpp/. Accessed 1 July 2019
30. Vaccario, G., Verginer, L., Schweitzer, F.: Reproducing scientists' mobility: a data-driven model. arXiv preprint arXiv:1811.07229 (2018)
31. Vaccario, G., Verginer, L., Schweitzer, F.: The mobility network of scientists: analyzing temporal correlations in scientific careers. arXiv preprint arXiv:1905.06142 (2019)
32. Van Noorden, R.: Global mobility: science on the move. Nat. News **490**(7420), 326 (2012). https://doi.org/10.1038/490326a
33. Willekens, F., Massey, D., Raymer, J., Beauchemin, C.: International migration under the microscope. Science **352**(6288), 897–899 (2016). https://doi.org/10.1126/science.aaf6545

Did the Black Panther Movie Make Blacks Blacker? Examining Black Racial Identity on Twitter Before and After the Black Panther Movie Release

Firman M. Firmansyah$^{(\boxtimes)}$ and Jason J. Jones

Stony Brook University, Stony Brook, NY 11794, USA
{manda.firmansyah, jason.j.jones}@stonybrook.edu

Abstract. The Black Panther movie release in early 2018 has been a phenomenon not only in the entertainment industry but also in American society. Film critics and major media have claimed that this award-winning movie has played significant roles in the African American community. Nevertheless, little research has been done to confirm such effects. Using publicly available data from Twitter as a proxy to measure black racial identity, we found that there were significant differences in the prevalence of Twitter users having black identifiers (i.e., African/Afro American, black, woke) in their bios before and after the Black Panther movie release, $F(2, 858) = 92.097$, $p < .001$, and between black male and female users, $F(1, 858) = 19,239, p < .001$. How these findings illuminate the association between the Black Panther movie and black racial identity, which may then shed more light on how the former may affect the latter through the lens of social identity theory is discussed.

Keywords: Black racial identity · Black Panther movie · Twitter · Social identity

1 Introduction

1.1 The Black Panther Movie

The release of the Black Panther movie in early 2018 in the United States has been a phenomenon not only in the entertainment industry but also in American society. It tells a story of T'Challa, a young king of a technologically advanced and yet hidden African fictional nation named Wakanda, in defending his throne from formidable threats [1]. T'Challa uses a heart-shaped herb mutated by *vibranium*, a precious fictional metal, to become the Black Panther and defeat his enemies. Black Panther is unlike most superhero movies in that the production team was led by black artists. The film had a predominately black cast, was written by two black screenwriters and directed by a black director. At the time of writing, Black Panther has been the highest-grossing domestic movie in 2018, even beating the most anticipated Marvel movie, "Avenger: Infinity War" [2]. It has received many prestigious awards and numerous impressive nominations in various categories including the Best Motion Picture in the

© Springer Nature Switzerland AG 2019
I. Weber et al. (Eds.): SocInfo 2019, LNCS 11864, pp. 66–78, 2019.
https://doi.org/10.1007/978-3-030-34971-4_5

76th Golden Globe Awards [3] and the Best Production Design in the 91st Academy Awards (the Oscars) [4].

Film critics and major media have claimed that the Black Panther movie has played significant roles in the African American community[1]. Its storytelling has arguably changed the depiction of black people in the entertainment industry [5]. The Black Panther movie has been labeled as a defining moment, which embraces blackness and attracts many African Americans to feel Wakanda as the "promised land" [6]. This movie has been also praised as a breakthrough in black cultural representation, which brings 500-year dreams of freedom, land, and autonomy into a "reality." In that regard, it has been argued that the Black Panther movie would help African Americans strengthen their identity and reduce negative stereotypes associated with the race [7].

1.2 Twitter Bio and Black Racial Identity

Apart from its achievements and proclaimed results, little research has been done in investigating the extent to which the Black Panther movie has affected African Americans both as individuals and community. In this study, we sought empirical evidence for change in racial identity. We used publicly available social media content to do so. Specifically, we examined Twitter users' self-descriptions to observe changes over time. We consider this method a rough analog to the Twenty Statements Test (TST) [8] – an established method to measure self-perceived identity. In TST, individuals are instructed to write twenty answers to a simple question, *"Who am I?"* in the blanks on a paper. On Twitter, users are prompted to write a bio about themselves in fewer than 160 characters when they create an account. This bio appears on the users' profile page along with their name, username, profile picture, and self-reported location. Users may change their bios at any time. Whether users set their accounts private or not, information on their profile page is still visible to the public – including those who do not have a Twitter account.

Given that users have very limited space to describe themselves to the public on Twitter and considering that race is less salient on the online environment than it is on the offline environment, we argue that having words in the bio that reveals one's race (race identifiers) is a bold decision. It may indicate that race is indeed central to the user's identities. For example, should users write black or African American in their bios, they presumably perceive race as an important part of their identities. Should users not write any black identifiers in their bios, even though they are African Americans, it may indicate that race, for some reasons, is less central to their identities. This logic corresponds with validated items used to measure centrality dimension, the extent to which individuals normatively define themselves regarding race, in the Multidimensional Inventory of Black Identity – Teen (MIBI-T) and in the Multidimensional Model of Racial Identity (MMRI) [9, 10]. Some of the items are as follows.

"If I were to describe myself to someone, one of the first things that I would say is that I'm Black" (MIBI-T)
"Being Black is an important reflection of who I am" (MMRI)

---

[1] In this study, African American is used interchangeably with Black.

1.3   Present Study

This current study aimed to investigate the prevalence of Twitter users having black identifiers in their bios (or black prevalence for short), before and after the Black Panther movie release. Prevalence itself was defined as the number of observed users having certain identifiers in their bios per one million observed users in the specific period.[2] For example, hypothetically, the black prevalence in 2018 is 150. It means that 150 out of 1 million users observed in 2018 have black identifiers in their bios. By comparing black prevalence in 2017 and 2018, the findings of this study illustrate the association between the Black Panther movie release and racial identity among African Americans, which might reflect an effect of the former upon the latter. It should be noted, however, that this study does not claim to reveal a causal relationship between the Black Panther movie release and black racial identity. Rather, it gives preliminary evidence highlighting their association, which then can serve as a point of departure for further analysis, including causal inference.

This study used January 1st, 2018 as the cutoff in investigating ways in which the Black Panther movie release might affect black prevalence. Days prior to the cutoff were subsumed under before-the-movie-release period, while days on and after it were subsumed under after-the-movie-release period. Indeed, the Black Panther movie was not premiered until January 29th, 2018 and was not in theaters in the United States until February 16th, 2018. However, as of early January 2018, its movie trailers had been broadcasted massively through national television, YouTube channels, and other means. Furthermore, this cutoff corresponds with the cutoff of the two datasets used in this study. Using any date other than January 1st, 2018 to compare the two datasets might confound the results. It is the case because the algorithms used the cutoff as the anchor to filter distinct users. More detailed explanation about this issue can be found in the methods section.

This study examined the association between the Black Panther movie release and black racial identity through the social identity theory, which posits that social identity, self-image derived from group memberships, depends on group's stereotypes [11]. When a social group such as race has positive stereotypes, individuals tend to reveal their membership; when it has negative stereotypes, individuals tend to conceal it. Since the Black Panther movie arguably succeeded in redefining black stereotypes in the United States, from negative to positive, we predicted that the black prevalence in 2018 would be significantly higher than the prevalence in 2017. Furthermore, since the lead actor in the Black Panther movie is male, we predicted that the movie would affect black female and male differently. That said the hypotheses in this study were:

1. Black prevalence in 2018 will be significantly higher than in 2017.
2. Black male prevalence will be significantly higher than Black female prevalence.

---

[2] It should be noted that one million is an arbitrary multiplier. Its advantage is to provide whole numbers for analysis rather than discussing fractional percentages with multiple decimal points.

2 Methods

2.1 Datasets

This research used two datasets of 1% random sample of publicly visible Twitter bios collected continuously using a computer program from January 2017 through December 2017 (the first dataset), and from January 2018 through May 2018 (the second dataset). Each dataset consists of users' Twitter IDs (a unique number generated when creating a Twitter account), timestamps (details of the time when Twitter bios were sampled in Unix format), and Twitter bios as at the timestamps. The program filtered in Twitters users whose accounts were in US time zones and used English as the interface language. The algorithms also removed duplicated users so that each dataset consists of distinct users only. Due to the randomization process, the same users might be observed in both 2017 and 2018. This condition, however, would not affect the analysis since this study used prevalence as the standardized measure. It focused on changes in the samples that arguably represent changes in the population level. Moreover, this study used the same cutoff as the datasets did. Doing so would eliminate confounding effects due to sorting and filtering processes.

The second dataset ends on May 24th, 2018 due to a technical change implemented by Twitter in reaction to the European Union General Data Protection Regulation (GDPR). Specifically, on that date, the Twitter API ceased to provide users' time zones. This change makes our filtering process unworkable beyond that date, because we specifically filter users to those who have chosen US time zones for their profile. There are alternative methods to filter users by location. For one, we might filter based on the text that users enter in their profile "location" field. There are many methods to translate these user-entered strings to geolocations, and it will take some time to evaluate the options and implement this alternative method of filtering. Hence, for the moment, we restrict our analysis to tweets collected from January 1st, 2017 through December 31st, 2017 and from January 1st, 2018 through May 24th, 2018.

2.2 Measure

As mentioned earlier, this study used prevalence as a standardized measure of Twitter users having black identifiers in their bios. Let bP_t be the black prevalence at t time, bN_t be the numbers of observed Twitter users having black identifiers at t time, and T_t be the total numbers of observed Twitter users at t time, the formula to calculate black prevalence at a given time is as follows.

$$bP_t = \frac{bN_t}{T_t} \times 1 \, \text{million} \tag{1}$$

It should be noted that the black prevalence in yearly basis would give a big picture regarding the yearly trend while its daily basis would give it in more details. Furthermore, since the daily prevalence would have more data points and variances, it allows performing further analyses such as analysis of variance (ANOVA) and Tukey's honest significant difference (Tukey's HSD) test.

2.3   Procedure

Sorting. In this step, we run SQL queries on each dataset with the following key-words: African American, Afro American, black, and woke as the black identifiers. Woke is a slang term derived from the African American Vernacular English that is used to raise awareness of injustice or racial tension among the black community [12]. Out of 11,496,613 observed Twitter users in 2017, there were 85,635 using black identifiers on their bios. While in 2018, out of 7,203,444 observed Twitters users, there were 60,006 using black identifiers. Note that these are raw counts before the validation step and transformation to standardized measure step described below.

Validating. Using users' Twitter IDs sorted from the previous step, we retrieved users' display names with the help of R package, 'rtweet' [13]. This process also sorted out users who deleted their accounts prior to the date of analysis. Following this process, we employed 'wru' package to predict users' race utilizing Bayesian inference [14]. Specifically, this R package predicts the probabilities of being white, black, Asian, Latino, and other races given a user's surname based on US census data with 0.215 overall error rate [15]. For example, the probabilities of being white, black, Asian, Latino, and other races for people with surname "Serwaa" are 0%, 99%, 0%, 0.004%, 0.004% consecutively, while for people with surname "Burbrink" are and 99%, 0%, 0.002%, 0%, 0.002% consecutively. We assigned black as users' race when the probability of being black was the highest among the probabilities. It should be noted that this process was the second step to validate that Twitter users having black identifiers in their bios were indeed black, not other races. Following this step, we predicted users' sex using 'gender' package [16]. This R package predicts whether users are male, female, or unidentified based on historical data such as US census and Social Security data [17]. For example, we classify "Tom", "Nick", and "David" as male; "Linda", "Yasmeen", and "Elaina" as female; "Kirito", "Zeoia", and "Noire" as unidentified.

Counting. In this step, we run SQL queries to count the number of all Twitter users observed in 2017 and 2018 in both yearly and daily basis. As explained earlier, this number functions as the denominator in calculating the black prevalence. Following this, we run other SQL queries to count the number of validated Twitter users on both an annual and daily basis. Validated users are those users whose accounts had black identifiers and were predicted as black in the previous step. This number functions as the numerator in calculating annual and daily black prevalence. Once we had the denominators and the numerators, we calculated the black prevalence at annual and daily scales. As mentioned earlier, these are the standardized measures used for further analyses.

3   Results

3.1   Descriptive Statistics

Black prevalence was 167 in 2017 and 203 in 2018, as can be seen in Fig. 1. These numbers revealed a 36 point increase in black prevalence in 2018 compared to 2017. In other words, an additional 36 Twitter users' bios contained black identifiers per 1 million users observed in 2018.

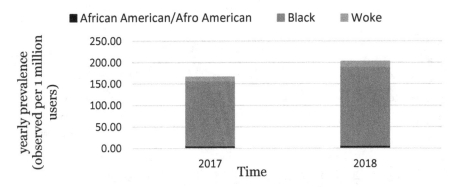

Fig. 1. Yearly prevalence of Twitter users with black identifiers

To look at the increase of black prevalence in 2018 in more detail, we calculated means of daily black prevalence and visualized them on a monthly basis. As can be seen in Fig. 2, there was a relatively steady trend of daily black prevalence throughout 2017 followed by a dramatic increase in January 2018. As of March 2018, however, the trend slightly declined and reached its lowest point in April 2018 for that year. The daily black prevalence continued to increase again in May 2018. It should be noted that the bottom of 2018 was still higher than the peak of 2017.

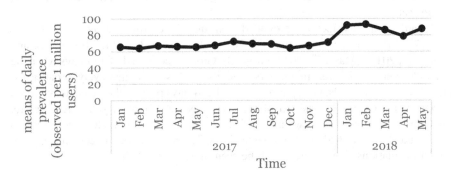

Fig. 2. Means of the daily prevalence of Twitter users with black identifiers

To reveal how the daily black prevalence fluctuated according to the users' sex, we calculated the means of daily black prevalence based on predicted sex and visualized the results in monthly basis. As can be seen in Fig. 3, the sex-based trends relatively followed the same patterns as the general trend (all predicted sex combined as shown in Fig. 3). However, they branched out dramatically as of January 2018 in which the number of unidentified users plummeted while the numbers of both male and female users increased and fluctuated at relatively the same rate.

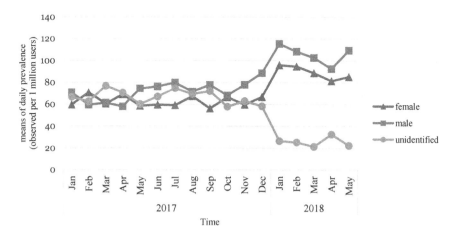

Fig. 3. Means of the daily prevalence of Twitter users with black identifiers based on sex

3.2 ANOVA

Even though the visualizations in Figs. 1, 2, and 3 suggest that there were differences in both yearly and daily black prevalence in 2017 and 2018 and between male and female, these visualizations do not confirm statistical significance. To that ends, we performed a two-way between-subject ANOVA by treating daily black prevalence as the number of participants, observed dates as the first factor, and predicted sex as the second factor.

Regarding the first factor, we divided them into three groups: January 1st, 2018 – May 24th, 2018 (Group 1), August 2nd, 2017 – December 31st, 2017 (Group 2), and January 1st, 2017 – May 24th, 2017 (Group 3). Group 1 consisted of 144 days when the Black Panther movie was in theaters, and its trailers were massively broadcasted through various channels. Group 2 consisted of 144 days prior to the first date of Group 1. Meanwhile, Group 3 consisted of the same days as Group 1, yet, a year before. Regarding the second factor, we included female (Group A) and male only (group B) and excluded unidentified sex from the analysis. The numbers of subjects, means, and standard deviations of each group can be seen in Table 1.

The ANOVA revealed that both observed dates, $F(2, 858) = 92.097, p < .001$, and sex, $F(1, 858) = 19, 239, p < .001$, were significant, while the interaction between the two factors was not, $F(2, 858) = 1.508, p = .222$, as can be seen in Table 2[3].

Table 1. Daily prevalence of Twitter users with black identifiers (per 1 million observed users)

		Female (a)			Male (b)	
Observed Date	n	Mean	SD	n	Mean	SD
Jan 1 – May 24, 2018 (1)	144	88.80	44.73	144	105.53	50.71
Aug 2 – Dec 31. 2017 (2)	144	47.79	39.27	144	64.63	45.05
Jan 1 – May 24, 2017 (3)	144	49.41	40.05	144	55.18	42.97

Table 2. The result of two-way ANOVA of the daily prevalence of Twitter users with black identifiers

Source	df	Sum of Square	Mean Square	F	p	Sig.
Observed date	2	355701	177851	92.097	<2e−16	***
Sex	1	37153	37153	19.239	1.3e−05	***
Observed date*sex	2	5826	2913	1.508	.222	
Residuals	858	1656902	1931			

3.3   Tukey's HSD

To reveal the differences concerning the two factors in more detail, we continued the analysis using Tukey's HSD. More attention should be paid to the differences between Group 1 and Group 2, and between Group 1 and Group 3. The former would illuminate if the increase of the black prevalence could be explained by the observe dates dividing before and after the Black Panther movie release, which might give a signal regarding the association of Black Panther movie and black racial identity. While the latter would give a signal if the increase had something to do with an annual trend or year over year comparison, and therefore was not associated with the Black Panther movie release.

As shown in Table 3, there were significant differences between Group 1 and Group 2, and between Group 2 and Group 3, for both male and female and cross-sex comparisons, at significant level $p < .01$. Regarding differences in sex, the results of the Tukey's HSD showed that there was no significant difference between male and female throughout 2017 but between male in group 2 and female in group 3. These findings explain why the interaction effect was not significant in the ANOVA result as previously shown in Table 2.

---

[3] We also performed two-way between-subject ANOVA with cutoff points on January 29th, 2018 – the premier of the Black Panther movie – and mixed ANOVA with observed dates treated as a repeated measure. These analyses yielded similar results. Both factors were significant at $p < .05$, while the interaction was not.

Table 3. The results of multiple comparisons – Tukey's HSD Dependent variable: daily prevalence

Group		Mean difference	Sig.	Lower bound	Upper bound
Jan 1-May 24, 2018 (1)	Aug 2-Dec 31, 2017 (2)				
Female (a)	Female (a)	41.09	0.00	26.22	55.80
	Male (b)	24.17	0.00	9.38	38.96
	Jan 1-May 24, 2017 (3)				
	Female (a)	39.38	0.00	24.60	54.17
	Male (b)	33.61	0.00	18.82	48.40
Jan 1-May 24, 2018 (1)	Aug 2-Dec 31, 2017 (2)				
Male (b)	Female (a)	57.74	0.00	42.95	72.53
	Male (b)	40.90	0.00	26.11	55.69
	Jan 1-May 24, 2017 (3)				
	Female (a)	56.12	0.00	41.32	70.91
	Male (b)	50.34	0.00	35.55	65.13
Aug 2-Dec 31, 2017 (2)	Jan 1-May 24, 2017 (3)				
Female (a)	Female (a)	−1.63	0.99	−13.17	16.42
	Male (b)	−7.40	0.71	−22.19	7.39
Aug 2-Dec 31, 2017 (2)	Jan 1-May 24, 2017 (3)				
Male (b)	Female (a)	15.21	0.04	0.42	30.01
	Male (b)	9.44	0.45	−5.35	24.24

4 Discussion

The significant results of both ANOVA and Tukey's HSD for Group 1 and Group 2 confirm the first hypothesis that the black prevalence on Twitter has increased significantly after the Black Panther movie release. This increase is not likely an annual trend, as Group 1 also differs significantly from Group 3. Those findings, we argue, highlight the association between the Black Panther movie release and black racial identity. Since we did not directly measure if the users have watched the movie or not nor ask them why they put black identifiers in their bios in the first place, one may argue that this increase might not be associated with the Black Panther movie at all let alone being affected by it. Rather, this increase might be due to a mere tendency that black Twitter users simply improve their bios over time or due to other significant events related to black community in the United States such as Martin Luther King Jr. Day, Black Lives Matter, or Black History Month.

However, if those alternative explanations were the case, we would then expect random patterns throughout 2017 and 2018 or slight spikes or at least some meaningful increases of black prevalence surrounding the periods of those alternative events in the previous year, which are in January, February, and July 2017. In fact, none of the visualizations and statistical analyses support those alternative arguments. In this respect, the discrepancy between the black prevalence in 2017 and 2018 is very dramatic and therefore is less likely due to a random chance. Moreover, the black prevalence throughout 2017 is relatively steady with no spike in the periods in which the alternative events occurs. Furthermore, the fact that Black Panther was the most tweeted movie in 2018 [18] may give further evidence supporting our argument that the increase of the black prevalence in 2018 is indeed associated with the Black Panther movie release.

Some possible scenarios may explain why this phenomenon has happened. First, the number of black Twitter users remain the same before and after the Black Panther movie release, and many of them then add black identifiers to their bio. Second, more black users open new Twitter accounts after the movie release and write black identifiers in their bios. Regardless of which scenario holds, both will end up with the significant increase in black prevalence. Thus, when our computer program randomly samples the Twitter accounts, this change is captured.

The dramatic increase of black prevalence, which occurred after the Black Panther movie release, might be due to a direct effect of the movie on black racial identity. Assuming that the users truly put black identifiers in their bios after they watch the movie, we may assert that the Black Panther movie strengthened racial identity among African Americans. This idea resonates with the previous findings of the study on similar topic. For instance, Musambira and Jackson [19] found that those who watched Tyler Perry's House of Payne regularly had a stronger black identity compared to those who watched it less. Sullivan and Platenburg [20] also came to the same conclusion when they examined the relationship between black media consumption and African American racial identity. The more African Americans consume black media, the stronger their racial identity is.

The effect of the Black Panther movie on black racial identity, assuming it holds, can be explained through the lens of the social identity theory. Tajfel and Turner [11] argue that individuals strive for positive social identity. Meanwhile, whether social identity is valued positive or negative depends on stereotypes associated with the groups, which most of the time are beyond an individual's control. When the social groups have positive stereotypes, individuals tend to stay and acknowledge their memberships. For instance, a hypothetical racial group named *green* is perceived as a social group achieving a higher degree of socioeconomic success than other racial groups. Delta, a hypothetical person, as a member of green then proudly acknowledge that he belongs to green. On the other hand, when the groups have negative stereotypes, individuals tend to leave or conceal their social identity. Using the same social group as the example, if green is perceived as an inferior group, then Delta would disassociate themselves with green and tend to acknowledge that he belongs to other social groups, which have better stereotypes.

Historically, the African American community has been subjected to strong negative stereotypes such as most black males are criminals and less educated [21] and most black females are loud, angry, demanding, and uncivilized [22]. These conditions may motivate African Americans to conceal their social identity in particular situations. In Twitter context, for example, they may hide their real name or avoid using real profile picture since those two can reveal their racial group. African Americans may also prefer to write things related to their professions or social roles such as mother or father, which are perceived having neutral or positive stereotypes, instead of black identifiers in their bios. However, as the Black Panther movie has succeeded in depicting black as a superior and technological advanced group, the stereotypes associated with the African American community have been changed from negative to positive. Indeed, this stereotype change may not entirely apply at the societal level yet, but, at least, at the individual level, it may hold true for many black people. Therefore, these improved stereotypes empower those black, who were previously insecure, shy, and less confident, to feel secure, proud, and more confident in revealing themselves as a member of black community on Twitter by putting black identifiers in their bios.

Furthermore, the statistical analyses also confirm the second hypothesis that the black male prevalence is significantly higher than black female prevalence after the Black Panther movie release. Even though our assertion, black males may be more inspired by the lead man figure in the movie than black females, may hold true, we also consider an alternative explanation, after carefully examining the visualizations. That is, this change seems reflect the demographic differences in Twitter and may not relate to ways in which the movie may affect black male and female differently. As can be seen in the Fig. 3, before the Black Panther movie release, the black male prevalence is already higher than black female prevalence. Thus, assuming the Black Panther movie release affecting both sexes, male prevalence still tend to be higher than female prevalence. Unfortunately, we have less evidence in supporting which one is the better explanation.

Finally, we shall reemphasize that this study does not claim to reveal a causal relationship between the Black Panther movie release and black racial identity. Instead, this study examines the association between the two. Further research is needed to test for a causal relationship and a mechanism of action.

4.1 Limitations

To our knowledge, this study is one of the earliest studies that empirically investigates the association of the Black Panther movie release and racial identity among African Americans. There are, at least, two points that make this study unique. First, unlike mainstream psychological research, this study uses a non-self-report instrument to measure racial identity. It may reduce biases such as social desirability and lack of attention. Second, concerning data gathering, this study takes advantage of publicly available massive data on Twitter. While traditional psychological research typically works on the data of hundreds of participants, this study works on the data of millions of participants gathered from the Twitter platform.

Apart from its strengths, several limitations should be of consideration. As mentioned earlier, this study did not ask Twitter users directly whether they had watched the Black Panther movie or not. It could be the case that the reasons why they had the black identifiers in their bios were not related with the Black Panther movie at all. Another limitation is regarding data processing. Because this study inferred demographics rather than directly measuring this data, the analysis process very much relied on machine learning employed by the R packages. Even though those packages have been validated in past research, we have no information yet regarding the type-1 and type-2 error rates for this current study. Indeed, perhaps these errors could be estimated or eliminated by performing human validation or employing more advanced algorithms. However, budget and time constraints make it less practical for doing so.

4.2   Direction for Future Research

Using the same datasets, we suggest future research to replicate this study and incorporate other races such as white and Asian. Doing so will answer questions such as whether the Black Panther movie is also associated with the prevalence of other races or exclusively associated with black only. We also suggest investigating the association between the Black Panther movie and black racial identity directly, for example, by doing a survey study resembling what Musambira and Jackson [19] did. Regarding the method, we highly suggest validating the use of the R packages in inferring the demographics of the Twitter users, for example, by employing human validation or examining the inter-reliability with other similar packages. We also suggest validating and standardizing the use of Twitter bios as a proxy to measure racial identity so that it will benefit future studies related to this topic, such as the Crazy Rich Asian movie with Asian identity.

4.3   Ethical Consideration

Doing study with Twitter data may raise some ethical concerns. As explained earlier, this study utilizes users' information that is visible to the public including those who do not have a Twitter account. This study also assumes that Twitter users are familiar with the nature of Twitter, which is more open compared to other social networking sites. Furthermore, this study does not violate any Twitter privacy policy nor does any harm to Twitter users.

Acknowledgements. We would like to thank the Institute for Advanced Computational Science (IACS) for material support and anonymous reviewers for their helpful comments and suggestions.

References

1. Disney. Black Panther (2018). https://movies.disney.com/black-panther. Accessed 18 Dec 2018
2. Box Office Mojo. 2018 domestic grosses (2018). https://www.boxofficemojo.com/yearly/chart/?yr=2018&p=.htm. Accessed 24 July 2019
3. France, L.R.: Golden Globe nominations kick off Hollywood's award season. CNN (2018). https://www.cnn.com/2018/12/06/entertainment/golden-globe-nominations/index.html. Accessed 19 Dec 2018
4. Wylie, J.: Black Panther wins 2019 Oscar for production design. OSCARS (2019). https://oscar.go.com/news/winners/black-panther-is-the-2019-oscar-winner-for-production-design. Accessed 23 July 2019
5. White, R.T.: I dream a world: black panther and the re-making of blackness. New Polit. Sci. **40**, 421–427 (2018)
6. Wallace, C.: Why 'Black Panther' is a defining moment for Black America. The New York Times (2018). https://www.nytimes.com/2018/02/12/magazine/why-black-panther-is-a-defining-moment-for-black-america.html. Accessed 19 Dec 2018

7. Turner, E.: Why 'Black Panther' means so much to the black community. Houston Chronicle (2018). https://www.houstonchronicle.com/local/gray-matters/article/black-panther-racial-and-ethnic-socialization-12741221.php. Accessed 19 Dec 2018

8. Kuhn, M., McPartland, T.S.: An empirical investigation of self-attitudes. Am. Sociol. Rev. **19**, 68–76 (1954)

9. Scottham, K.M., Sellers, R.M., Nguyên, H.X.: A measure of racial identity in African American adolescents: the development of the Multidimensional Inventory of Black Identity-Teen. Cult. Divers. Ethn. Minor. Psychol. **14**, 297–306 (2008)

10. Sellers, R.M., Smith, M.A., Shelton, J.N., Rowley, S.A.J., Chavous, T.M.: Multidimensional model of racial identity: a reconceptualization of African American racial identity. Pers. Soc. Psychol. Rev. **2**, 18–39 (1998)

11. Tajfel, H., Turner, J.: An integrative theory of intergroup conflict. In: Organizational Identity: A Reader, pp. 33–47 (1979)

12. Merriam-Webster. Stay woke, the new sense of 'woke' is gaining popularity (2017). https://www.merriam-webster.com/words-at-play/woke-meaning-origin. Accessed 19 Dec 2018

13. Kearney, M.W.: Collecting Twitter Data, p. 73 (2018)

14. Khanna, K., Imai, K., Jin, H.: Who are You? Bayesian Prediction of Racial Category Using Surname and Geolocation 14 (2017). https://doi.org/10.1093/pan/mpw001

15. Imai, K., Khanna, K.: Improving ecological inference by predicting individual ethnicity from voter registration records. Polit. Anal. **24**, 263–272 (2016)

16. Mullen, L., Blevins, C., Schmidt, B.: Predict gender from names using historical data, pp. 1–7 (2018)

17. Blevins, C., Mullen, L.: Jane, John … Leslie ? A historical method for algorithmic gender prediction. DHQ Digit. Humanit. Q. **9** (2015, online). http://www.digitalhumanities.org/dhq/vol/9/3/000223/000223.html

18. Pallotta, F.: 'Black Panther' is the most tweeted about movie ever. CNN Business (2018). https://money.cnn.com/2018/03/20/media/black-panther-twitter/index.html. Accessed 23 July 2019

19. Musambira, G.W., Jackson, N.E.: A preliminary analysis of Tyler Perry's 'House of Payne' and 'Meet the Browns': effect on the black identity, African American's frequency of exposure, perception of accuracy and affective evaluation. J. Creat. Commun. **13**, 212–231 (2018)

20. Sullivan, J.M., Platenburg, G.N.: From black-ish to blackness. J. Black Stud. **48**, 215–234 (2017)

21. Welch, K.: Black criminal stereotypes and racial profiling. J. Contemp. Crim. Justice **23**, 276–288 (2007)

22. Harris-Perry, M.V.: Sister Citizen: Shame, Stereotypes, and Black Women in America. Yale University Press, New Haven (2011)

Gender and Racial Diversity in Commercial Brands' Advertising Images on Social Media

Jisun An[✉][iD] and Haewoon Kwak[iD]

Qatar Computing Research Institute, Hamad Bin Khalifa University,
Doha, Qatar
{jisun.an,haewoon}@acm.org

Abstract. Gender and racial diversity in the mediated images from the media shape our perception of different demographic groups. In this work, we investigate gender and racial diversity of 85,957 advertising images shared by the 73 top international brands on Instagram and Facebook. We hope that our analyses give guidelines on how to build a fully automated watchdog for gender and racial diversity in online advertisements.

Keywords: Gender diversity · Racial diversity · Face detection · Advertisement

1 Introduction

"The *perception of the other* is a core aspect of the integration of ethnic minorities and immigrants [55]". Integration and cooperation in a multicultural society can be easy or challenging, depending on the perception of self and other groups. One of the notable channels that affect people's perception of the other is mass media [21,32]. After being repeatedly exposed, viewers' belief and attitudes are shaped by the mediated images from the media. Thus, the portrayal of different demographic groups in media, particularly advertisements, can play an essential role in shaping the formation of identities of those groups [14].

For the decades, scholars have studied the portrayals of demographic groups (mainly ethnic minorities compared to Whites) in advertisements in print and broadcast media [47,50]. Minority groups have been found to be continuously under- or misrepresented in the advertisements. For example, advertisements perpetuate conventional stereotyped images of races and gender, which are, for instance, African Americans depicted as aggressive and active, and women portrayed as young, thin, and smiling [16]. Despite the warnings from these studies, controversial advertisements, such as the one by Hornbach [3], are still being created. Thus, the continuous monitoring of advertisements and raising public awareness are essential.

In monitoring advertisements, analyzing the visual content is one of the main components because most advertisements include visual elements because of

© Springer Nature Switzerland AG 2019
I. Weber et al. (Eds.): SocInfo 2019, LNCS 11864, pp. 79–94, 2019.
https://doi.org/10.1007/978-3-030-34971-4_6

their effectiveness in marketing [38]. However, previous studies on examining advertisements largely depend on manual efforts for analyzing the visual content [8,46,47]. In the modern world, which is overloaded by digital content published on the web and social media, how to minimize such manual efforts and build an automated solution is the key to monitoring the tremendous volume of advertisements.

In this work, as a first step, we propose an automated way to examine gender and racial diversity in online advertisements in a large scale using modern image analysis techniques. Through a comprehensive review of previous literature, we define three metrics of the gender and racial diversity in advertisements that can be computed by automated tools: (1) how many times each gender and race appear, (2) how many times each gender and race appear in cross-sex interaction context, and (3) how many times each gender and race appear as smiling faces.

Using the three metrics, we demonstrate a large-scale analysis of the gender and racial diversity in the 85,957 advertising images of 73 international brands on Instagram and Facebook. We define advertising images of brands in a broad sense: as images posted on social media by their official accounts. Considering the definition of advertisement, which is "a picture, sign, etc. that is used to make a product or service known and persuade people to buy it", it is reasonable to consider the images posted on social media by brands' official accounts as their advertising images. As the marketing in social media has been differentiating from that in traditional media [24], our analysis of advertising images on social media adds new dimensions to the stream of previous research on U.S.-based empirical studies of advertisements in mass media [8,17,47]. In particular, the following research questions drawn from previous literature guide our analysis:

RQ1: How many times does each demographic group appear in advertising images? How different are they across the brands?
RQ2: Which pairs of demographic groups are preferred in advertising images for cross-sex interaction context?
RQ3: Is there a specific demographic group depicted more with smiling faces?

Our study provides a holistic view of the gender and racial diversity in today's advertising images by global brands on social media and is a great demonstration of the feasibility of our proposed metrics computed in an automated way.

2   Related Work

For decades there has been a long research stream on depictions of different demographic groups in marketing communications including advertisements [8,16,17,46,47]. Both cross-sectional and longitudinal U.S.-based studies have looked into the racial mix of models in TV commercials and print advertisements [12,39,52].

While some variations exist across the different data sources [8,41], a general consensus on depictions of ethnic minorities in advertisements, African American models in particular, has emerged: (1) increasing appearances, even compared to the incidence of their population relative to the entire U.S. population [50], (2) decreasing portrayals of blue-collar workers and increasing portrayals of professionals [60], and (3) taking more major roles [35]. Along with studies on African American models, representations of Asians and Hispanics in advertisements have also been investigated [12,35,40]. Compared to other demographic groups, Asian American models are frequently portrayed as a work-centric 'model minority' [53], while Hispanic models are still underrepresented compared to their populations [40]. Nonetheless, the images of 'White hegemonic masculinity and White feminine romantic fulfillment' are perpetuated in virtually all forms of television marketing [16].

Such racial stereotypes determine the roles of models and the types of products. For example, Black models are frequently depicted in sports/athletic contexts and thus are overrepresented in advertisements of sports/athletic products [36]. As Asian models are excessively depicted in work settings, they tend to appear in advertisements associated with affluence or work life and not to appear in advertisements of home-or social life-related products [53]. By contrast, White models are depicted more in home settings or cross-sex interactions because their stereotypes have both masculinity and feminine. As a result, they are overrepresented in the advertisements for upscale, beauty, and home-related products [26].

The impact of these stereotyped-or biased advertisements has been extensively discussed. Simply, those advertisements make people hold a biased belief by reinforcing negative stereotypes [15]. In communication studies, two theories have offered a theoretical foundation for a better explanation: social learning theory [9] and cultivation theory [21]. Both theories explain how our perception can be influenced by the depictions of different demographic groups in advertisements. Social learning theory posits that we can learn general behaviors and attitudes through observing others instead of through first-hand experience. Similarly, watching stereotyped depictions in advertisements are known to have a negative impact on people's perceptions [37,48]. On the other hand, cultivation theory suggests viewers' beliefs and attitudes are shaped by the mediated images to which they are repeatedly exposed. Particularly, our perception is likely to be cultivated when our social reality is close to the mediated images in advertisements [14]. For example, Asian viewers' perception is likely to be cultivated when they see Asian models in advertisements.

Subliminal effects of depictions in advertisements have also been studied [28]. They are typically tested by the Implicit Association Test [23], measuring response latencies to a given stimulus. For example, by comparing the response latencies to good/bad words associated with images of the faces of the same and different races, implicit in-group preferences are observed [44].

3   Data Collection

We begin by compiling a list of global brands and their sectors (e.g., apparel, beverage, and so on) by merging lists of global brands in Brand Finance's Global

500 2016 [4] and Interbrand's Best Global Brands 2016 [1]. We then refine the list of the brands by using the following criteria: First, as business-to-business (B2B) and business-to-consumer (B2C) brands exhibit significant differences in their social media usage [51], in this work, we focus only on B2C brands, which directly face users in their business. Second, to mitigate differences in cultures and attitudes toward diversity, we consider only the brands that originated from the U.S. We then filter out the brands that do not have an official Instagram or Facebook account. We note that these brands tend to have multiple Instagram or Facebook accounts targeting other regions (e.g., Starbucks Middle East) as they are international brands. In that case, we consider only the primary account. We then use Facebook Graph API and Instagram API to collect all the images uploaded till November 2017 based on the list of Instagram and Facebook accounts. After collecting the data, we eliminate the brands that do not have more than 50 images with faces. Finally, we have 73 international brands and their 85,957 advertising images posted on Instagram and Facebook.

To infer demographic attributes of models in advertisements automatically, we use Face++ [2], which is one of the widely used commercial tools for face detection. Face++ has been popularly used in computational social science research, showing reliable performance in inferring gender (Male or Female) and race (White, Asian, or Black) [6,7,43,59]. In a recent study [27], Face++ achieved more than 90% accuracy in gender and race detection and performed better than or as good as other commercial tools across diverse datasets. We note that we do not use the age inference of Face++ because the reliability of age inference has not been widely tested. Face++ also detects smiling levels (the degree of smile) of each face, which is used for answering RQ3. We do not consider images that Face++ returns an inference with low confidence scores (<0.7).

In the remaining part of this paper, we use the `typewriter` font to refer to a demographic group inferred by Face++. For example, we use `Asian` or `Black male`, to shorten the phrase 'inferred as Asian by Face++' or 'inferred as Black male by Face++' for brevity.

4   Frequencies of Appearances of Each Demographic Group

Along with a line of previous studies [16,17,36,53], we start with examining frequencies of appearances of each demographic group in advertising images on social media. Each brand might have different strategies to use models for the best promotion of their products and services. Accordingly, our 73 brands across different sectors might have a wide range of variations in the proportions of each demographic group.

Figure 1 shows the proportion of appearances of each demographic group that appeared in advertising images on Instagram and Facebook. While there are some differences between the platforms, we observe consistent trends. Notably, appearances of `White female` (Mean: 0.38 on Instagram, and 0.41 on Facebook)

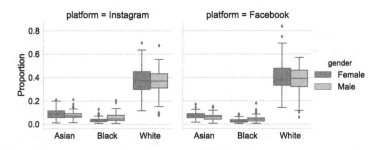

Fig. 1. Proportions of appearances of each demographic group in advertising images

and `White male` models (Mean: 0.36 on Instagram, and 0.38 on Facebook) out-number the other demographic groups on both Instagram and Facebook. These results are statistically significant as confirmed by Kruskal-Wallis 1-way ANOVA test with Dunn's post-hoc test ($H = 324.9$ for Instagram and 331.9 for Facebook and all the adjusted p from Dunn's test are lower than 2.34e−12). By contrast, `Black female` and `Black male` models show a considerably lower number of appearances. The percentage of appearances of `Black female` models is strikingly low, which is on average 2.9% and 3.6% of models on Instagram and Facebook, respectively. Considering the recent trends in which the percentage of Black female models is increasing in other media [46], they are quite underrepresented in advertising images on social media.

Compared with the actual population, the percentage of the appearances of each racial group in advertising images is enticing our attention. In the 2010 Census [5], Asian, Black, and White groups account for 5%, 13%, and 72% of the U.S. population, respectively. As the percentages in the census are computed with other racial groups (e.g., American Indian) as well, for a fair comparison, the percentage of each race should be normalized by considering the three races only, which are 5.6%, 14.4%, and 80% for Asian, Black, and White groups, respectively. In the advertising images on social media, we find that `Asian`, `Black`, and `White` models account for 16.8%, 8.9%, and 74.2% on Instagram and 13.3%, 7.4%, and 79.3% on Facebook, respectively.

We observe that the percentage of Whites in the actual population and those that appeared in social media advertisements are comparable. In contrast, `Black` models appear much less in social media advertisements considering their actual population. Surprisingly, Asians are overrepresented almost three times relative to their population in the U.S. Our results on social media show some commonality and contrasts from previous work on TV commercials (See [46] for detailed reviews since 1950s). One possible reason, of course, is the difference of target markets.

To show the variances in frequencies of appearances of each demographic group in advertising images across the brands, we propose two metrics: gender diversity and racial diversity. We define gender diversity of a brand b as a

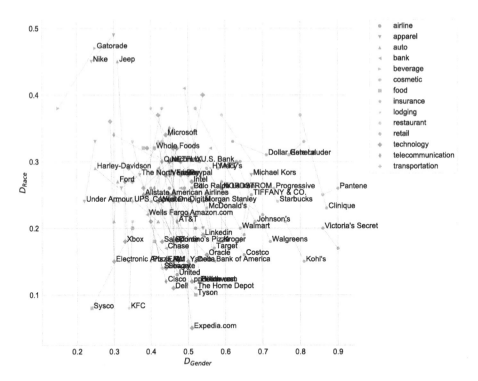

Fig. 2. Gender and racial diversity in advertising images of brand on Instagram and Facebook. Each brand is represented by two markers linked by a dotted line, which are a marker with a label (Instagram) and that without a label (Facebook).

ratio of appearances of female models in advertisements of the brand b as follows: $D_{gender}^b = \frac{N_{Female}^b}{N_{Female}^b + N_{Male}^b}$ where N_{gender}^b is the number of appearances of models of that gender group in the advertisements of the brand b. Similarly, we define racial diversity of a brand b as a ratio of appearances of non-white models in advertisements of the brand b as follows: $D_{race}^b = \frac{N_{Asian}^b + N_{Black}^b}{N_{Asian}^b + N_{Black}^b + N_{White}^b}$ where N_{race}^b is the number of appearances of models of that racial group in the advertisements of the brand b. While the entropy is often used to measure the diversity, we simply use non-white ratio because (1) it has been widely used for racial diversity studies [46], and (2) it is easy to interpret.

Figure 2 shows the gender and racial diversity of the 73 brands on their advertising images on social media. The diversity values are separately computed from the advertisements on Instagram and Facebook. Each brand is thus represented as two markers (one for Instagram and the other for Facebook) connected by a dotted line. To distinguish the two markers of one brand, we place a brand label at the marker for Instagram only.

We find some interesting trends in Fig. 2. First, there is a huge variation in both diversity measures among the brands. For example, $D_{race}^{Expedia.com@Instagram} = 0.05$, which means that more than 90% of models who appeared in their advertising images on Instagram are `White`, while $D_{race}^{Nike@Facebook} = 0.49$, which means that around 50% of models who appeared in their advertising images on Facebook are `Asian` or `Black`. Second, by comparing the distributions of D_{gender}^{b} and D_{race}^{b}, we can say that racial diversity should be more carefully considered. On average, D_{gender}^{b} is 0.471 on Facebook and 0.505 on Instagram, but D_{race}^{b} is 0.281 on Facebook and 0.219 on Instagram.

While the small sample size per sector does not allow us to conduct a statistical test for the sector differences, we observe that some brands show similar patterns on Instagram and Facebook regarding D_{gender}. The top three sectors are cosmetic, retail, and insurance, and the bottom three sectors are auto, beverage, and transportation on both platforms. Such strong patterns do not emerge in D_{race}, but beverage is the sector with the highest D_{race} and food falls in bottom three sectors on both platforms.

5 Diversity in Cross-Sex Interactions

When multiple models appear in an advertisement, it delivers cues that these models are interacting, thus providing a better integration of models in advertising [18,20]. In particular, advertising images in which models of different genders appear together, which are called cross-sex interactions, bring two specific situational contexts. One is a romantic context. Cross-sex interactions in advertisements fulfill romantic fantasies [16], making viewers fall into the emotional experience and pay less attention to the sales pitch behind it [25]. This means that models appearing in cross-sex interactions are likely to have some attractive qualities, such as beauty or masculinity, that can fulfill viewers' romantic fantasies. In this sense, Coltrane and Messineo [16] reveal the stereotyped White romantic fulfillment by reporting the prevalence of Whites, particularly females, in cross-sex interactions in TV commercials. The other is a family context. Cross-sex interactions also imply another common setting in advertisements, which is a family. The happy family scene is one of the well crafted moments or fantasies that resonate with viewers [54]. In other words, models depicted in this setting signify family relationships to viewers and deliver cues to intimate relationships [16].

Figure 3 shows the proportion of each demographic group appearing in cross-sex interaction, same-sex interaction (either men or women only), and by the self (a single person). From the figure, three interesting patterns emerge. First, long whiskers show that there is a considerable variation of depictions of each demographic group. For example, in the advertising images posted by Victoria's Secret on Facebook, only 3.8% of `Asian female` models ($N = 8$) are depicted in cross-sex interactions, while 65.9% of `Asian female` models (137) appear in the form of a single person (by the self). In contrast, in the advertising images of Citi on Facebook, 74.3% of `Asian female` models (26) are depicted in cross-sex interactions. This huge difference in cross-sex interactions across the brands, in addition to Fig. 2, warns that selective exposure (i.e., following on social media) to certain brands can make the diversity problem more complicated.

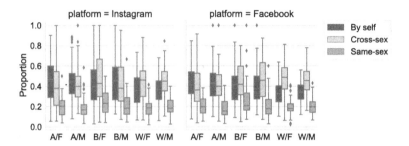

Fig. 3. Proportion of each demographic group in cross-sex interactions, same-sex interaction, or by the self. A/, B/, and W/ stand for `Asian`, `Black`, and `White`, and /F and /M stand for `Female` and `Male`, respectively.

Second, for any demographic group on both platforms, we can see a consistent trend that same-sex interaction is underrepresented compared to other forms of depictions. The statistically significant difference between the proportion of the same-sex interactions from that of cross-sex interactions and by-self are confirmed by Kruskal-Wallis 1-way ANOVA test with Dunn's post-hoc test (all the adjusted $p < 1.159e{-}06$ from all the comparisons). This indicates that same-sex interactions are less preferred in advertising. Rather, a single model or cross-sex interactions tend to more appear.

Third, from the above post-hoc test, we confirm that the difference between by the self and cross-sex interactions is significant for `White` `male` ($p = 3.15e{-}02$) on Instagram, `White` `female` ($p = 5.81e{-}05$) on Facebook, and `White` `male` ($p = 1.45e{-}05$) on Facebook. The difference in other demographic groups is not statistically significant. In other words, `White` models are more engaged in cross-sex interactions, while `Asian` and `Black` models are not. This aligns with the preference toward Whites in cross-sex interactions that have been repeatedly observed from TV commercials [16].

Then, how is the bias toward the Whites presented at the level of the pairs in cross-sex interactions? To answer this question, we compute the proportion of all possible 9 combinations (3 races (Female side) × 3 races (Male side) = 9 combinations) of demographic groups from the advertising images that include cross-sex interactions. When there are more than two models in an advertisement, we take all the possible combinations of races between different genders into account. For example, if one Asian Female (A/F), one Asian Male (A/M), and one Black Male (B/M) models appear in an advertising image, we find two cross-sex interactions, which are (A/F-A/M) and (A/F-B/M).

Figure 4(a) shows proportions of each pair of demographic groups in cross-sex interactions. To capture the variances between brands, we compute the proportions of each demographic group pair at the brand-level. From the figure, we observe that `White` `female` and `White` `male` models dominantly appear together. On average, 60.3% and 68.9% of cross-sex interactions in the advertising images are with `White` `female` and `White` `male` models on Instagram and Facebook, respectively. It is also noticeable that pairs with either `White`

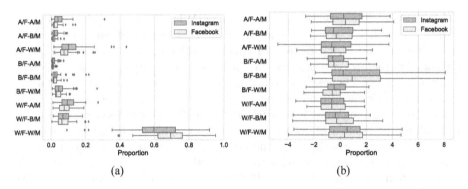

Fig. 4. (a) Proportions of each pair of different demographic groups in cross-sex interactions (b) Z-score of demographic group pairs in cross-sex interactions. Outliers are omitted for clarity

`female` or `White male` models are more frequent than those without any `White` model. However, this tendency does not mean that there is a systematic bias toward White models in pairing because, as we see in Fig. 1, `White` models simply outweigh other groups. Thus, `White` models naturally have a higher chance to be shown in any cross-sex interactions than other groups due to its high number, even though there is no actual preference toward `White female` or `White male` models as a partner in cross-sex interaction.

To compute the corrected preference toward a pair of demographic groups in cross-sex interactions, we compare the actual proportion of each pair with the proportions of the corresponding pair from a null model. To build the null model, we randomly shuffle the placement of models across the advertising images while preserving the number of models of each gender in every advertising image. As we only "shuffle" the placement of existing models without addition or deletion of models, the total number of models in each demographic group stays the same. After shuffling a significant number of times (e.g., until each model is moved 10 times from one image to the other), we can get a null model that randomly locates models of each demographic group but preserves the number of the models of each gender in every advertising image. This null model shows the case that models appear in cross-sex interaction by chance. To avoid the errors of outliers, we build 1,000 null models and compute the average and the standard deviation of proportions of each pair of demographic groups. Then, Z-score can be computed as follows: $Z_{p_i} = \frac{N_{p_i}^{original} - avg(N_{p_i}^{rand})}{std(N_{p_i}^{rand})}$ where p_i is a pair of certain demographic groups, $N_{p_i}^{original}$ is the number of pair p_i observed in the original data, and $N_{p_i}^{rand}$ is the number of pair p_i observed in a null model. The function of $avg(\cdot)$ is an average, and $std(\cdot)$ is a standard deviation. This Z-score shows how significant the observed frequency is compared to random.

Figure 4(b) shows Z-score of each pair of demographic groups engaged in cross-sex interactions on Instagram and Facebook. The most noticeable difference, compared to Fig. 4(a), is that the preference toward pairing of the same race in cross-sex interactions becomes apparent. While there are variances among brands, the median Z-scores of pairs of `Asian female` and `Asian male` models, `Black female` and `Black male`, and `White female` and `White male` models in cross-sex interactions are positive on both Instagram and Facebook. Although `White` models are frequently involved in cross-sex interactions as in Fig. 4(a), interestingly, interracial interactions with `White` models actually have the negative Z-score, meaning that those pairs are less preferred in cross-sex interactions once taking the number of models in each demographic group into account.

The preference toward pairs of the same race in cross-sex interactions implies that there is an implicit opposition to interracial relationships in cross-sex interaction context. According to the 2010 Census [5], in the U.S., only 7% of married couples are of different races, implying cross-race marriages are not common in society yet. Moreover, in a recent population-based survey experiment ($N = 2{,}035$) [42], 39% of respondents support the refusal of services to interracial couples. All these statistics prove that there is still a long way to go to the acceptance of interracial relationships, and advertising images reflect such reality to some extent.

6   Demographic Groups with More (Less) Smiles

Based on the premise that non-verbal communications in human interaction are as important as verbal communications [30], there have been numerous attempts to understand facial expressions in advertisements [10,45]. Since typical advertisements are made to capture attention, arouse interest, and lead to action [22], the most common facial expression of models is the *smile* among ten basic facial expressions [19], and its positive impact on consumer attitude has been reported [10]. While there are some nuanced differences in emotions expressed by the smiles between females and males [57], the smiling expression is quickly assessed with a high level of agreement and is more closely linked to happiness than other facial expressions to other emotions [34,58]. Particularly, as advertisements usually deliver the positive side of products or services, the fact that happy faces accelerate the cognitive processing of positive words [49] highlights the importance of smiling of the models in advertisements. Based on this line of research, we examine how differently each demographic group expresses smiles in advertising images.

Figure 5 shows the box plots of smiling levels (the degree of smile) of each demographic group. The smiling level ranges from 0 (no smile) to 100 (full smile) estimated by Face++. First, we find that `Female` models smile more than `Male` models where the mean smiling levels for `Female` and `Male` models are 55.6 ad.nd 42.8, respectively. The result is also statistically significant, confirmed by the independent t-test (Levene's test for equality of variance confirms that two sets have approximately equal variance ($W = 1.044$, $p = 0.309$), $t = 6.696$, $p < 0.001$). The effect size, measured by Cohen's d, is 1.047, showing that there is a large effect of gender on smiling levels. This finding is consistent with previous studies that women smile more than men in various media [31,33,45]. Of the

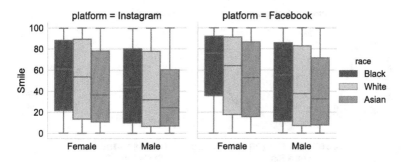

Fig. 5. Smiling level of each demographic group

same gender, differences between the races are also statistically significant. Any pair of different races of the same gender show significantly different levels of the smiles, confirmed by Kruskal-Wallis 1-way ANOVA test and the following Dunn's post-hoc test; all the p-values for the comparison of the different races are less than 3.30e−03. Additionally, long boxes and whiskers reaching zero and one indicate that there exists a huge variance of the smiling levels even within one demographic group.

Figure 6 shows the distribution of the smiling levels of each race group of females (top) and males (bottom), respectively. Here we quantize the smiling levels into 20 bins. From all figures, U-shaped (balanced and unbalanced) curves consistently emerge; every demographic group has a larger proportion of non-smile faces (leftmost bin) or full-smile faces (rightmost bin) than faces with other smiling levels. Also, Male models are more often depicted with non-smile than full-smile, while Female models are more often depicted with full-smile than non-smile except Asian female models. Together with Fig. 5, these results resonate with previous work [57] that social constraints imposed on females who live in a male-biased society make themselves to rely on "behaviors designed to advertise their trustworthiness through higher levels of submissive displays", and smiling works in that way, as a cue for the trustworthiness of women [56].

7   Discussions and Conclusions

In this work, we proposed an automated way to examine gender and racial diversity in online advertisements using modern image analysis techniques. We demonstrated its feasibility through a large-scale analysis of 85,957 advertising images of 73 international brands on Instagram and Facebook.

The quantitative analysis has shown several interesting findings. First, we observed huge variations of gender and racial diversity in advertising images across the brands, as those images are made to fit their models and representations in social norms, cultural values, target market, and social media audiences [15]. As brands have their own target audiences, it is reasonable to have even very skewed model representations (e.g., Victoria's Secret uses more than 90% Female models). Second, nevertheless, we found consistent trends that

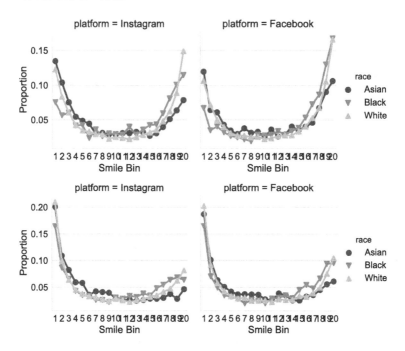

Fig. 6. Proportions of each race in different smiling levels (Top: `Female`, Bottom: `Male`)

`White` models outnumber other races. Also, we observed `Asian` models are over-represented which could be due to brands' efforts to appeal to a huge Asian market. By contrast, `Black` models are quite underrepresented. In contrast to a recent study of increasing appearances of Black models in advertisements in broadcast and print media [46], their presence on advertising images in social media still stays low. Third, there are some differences in gender and racial diversity between Instagram and Facebook. The observed differences, higher percentages of racial diversity on Facebook and higher gender diversity on Instagram, are well aligned with their userbase [7]. Fourth, `White` models are more engaged in cross-sex interactions, as previous literature reported [16]. In addition, by comparing the actual data with random null models, we revealed the preference toward the same race pairs in cross-sex interactions. In other words, inter-racial cross-sex interactions are underrepresented. Finally, we captured gender bias that `Female` models smile more than `Male` models, which is consistent with previous studies in various media [31,33,45].

Our work is not without limitations. First, the use of Face detection for inferring gender and race may have inherent biases [13]. Second, we consider global top brands and do not take cultural differences into account. Since there could exist huge variances in gender and racial diversity in advertising images across regions and cultures, follow-up studies with ore data are required for generalization. Third, we were unable to analyze the nuanced portrayals of models. For example, an advertisement with female chefs and male engineers might have a high gender diversity but reinforce gendered stereotypes. Recently, such 'stereotyped gender roles' have been actively studied [11,29]. For future work, we aim to develop new computational methods that can capture more sophisticated representations of models in advertisements.

Notwithstanding the limitation, this work contributes to the stream of research on gender and racial diversity in advertisements by introducing the fully automated computational tools on advertisement studies and conducting a large-scale analysis. The entire process, which is collecting advertising images, labeling faces, and computing the diversity scores, is automated and will become more accurate as the image recognition technology improves. It is thus possible to monitor the diversity efforts of brands with extremely low cost and near real-time. This approach is a substantial advantage compared to the required time and resource in previous research, such as collecting TV commercials or magazine advertisements, labeling faces by educated workers, and so on. While there is room for improvement particularly in capturing a nuanced representation of models, our effort is the first step to build an automated pipeline for tracking gender and racial diversity in the advertisements and raising public awareness toward the right depiction of an ethnic minority in the media.

References

1. Best Global Brands 2016. https://www.interbrand.com/best-brands/best-global-brands/2016/. Accessed 16 Apr 2019
2. Face++. https://www.faceplusplus.com. Accessed 16 Apr 2019
3. German DIY chain's 'racist' advert provokes anger in South Korea. https://www.theguardian.com/world/2019/mar/28/german-diy-chain-hornbach-racist-advert-provokes-anger-south-korea. Accessed 16 Apr 2019
4. Global 500 2016—rankings—brandirectory. https://brandirectory.com/rankings/global-500-2016. Accessed 16 Apr 2019
5. Households and families: 2010. https://www.census.gov/prod/cen2010/briefs/c2010br-14.pdf. Accessed 16 Apr 2019
6. An, J., Weber, I.: #greysanatomy vs. #yankees: Demographics and hashtag use on Twitter. In: ICWSM (2016). https://www.aaai.org/ocs/index.php/ICWSM/ICWSM16/paper/view/13021
7. An, J., Weber, I.: Diversity in online advertising: a case study of 69 brands on social media. In: Staab, S., Koltsova, O., Ignatov, D.I. (eds.) SocInfo 2018. LNCS, vol. 11185, pp. 38–53. Springer, Cham (2018). https://doi.org/10.1007/978-3-030-01129-1_3
8. Bailey, A.A.: A year in the life of the African-American male in advertising: a content analysis. J. Advert. **35**(1), 83–104 (2006)
9. Bandura, A.: Social-learning theory of identificatory processes. Handb. Social. Theory Res. **213**, 262 (1969)
10. Berg, H., Söderlund, M., Lindström, A.: Spreading joy: examining the effects of smiling models on consumer joy and attitudes. J. Consum. Mark. **32**(6), 459–469 (2015)

11. Bolukbasi, T., Chang, K.W., Zou, J.Y., Saligrama, V., Kalai, A.T.: Man is to computer programmer as woman is to homemaker? debiasing word embeddings. In: Advances in Neural Information Processing Systems, pp. 4349–4357 (2016)
12. Bowen, L., Schmid, J.: Minority presence and portrayal in mainstream magazine advertising: an update. Journal. Mass Commun. Q. **74**(1), 134–146 (1997)
13. Buolamwini, J., Gebru, T.: Gender shades: intersectional accuracy disparities in commercial gender classification. In: Conference on Fairness, Accountability and Transparency, pp. 77–91 (2018)
14. Choudhury, P.K., Schmid, L.S.: Black models in advertising to blacks. J. Advert. Res. **14**(3), 19–22 (1974)
15. Cohen-Eliya, M., Hammer, Y.: Advertisements, stereotypes, and freedom of expression. J. Soc. Philos. **35**(2), 165–187 (2004)
16. Coltrane, S., Messineo, M.: The perpetuation of subtle prejudice: race and gender imagery in 1990s television advertising. Sex Roles **42**(5), 363–389 (2000)
17. Cox, K.K.: Changes in stereotyping of negroes and whites in magazine advertisements. Public Opin. Q. **33**(4), 603–606 (1969)
18. Dominick, J.R., Greenberg, B.S.: Three seasons of blacks on television. J. Advert. Res. **26**, 169–173 (1970)
19. Ekman, P., Friesen, W.V.: Measuring facial movement. Environ. Psychol. Nonverbal Behav. **1**(1), 56–75 (1976)
20. Elliott, M.T.: Differences in the portrayal of blacks: a content analysis of general media versus culturally-targeted commercials. J. Curr. Issues Res. Advert. **17**(1), 75–86 (1995)
21. Gerbner, G., Gross, L., Morgan, M., Signorielli, N., Shanahan, J.: Growing up with television: cultivation processes. Media Eff. Adv. Theory Res. **2**, 43–67 (2002)
22. Goddard, A.: The Language of Advertising: Written Texts. Psychology Press, Abingdon (2002)
23. Greenwald, A.G., McGhee, D.E., Schwartz, J.L.: Measuring individual differences in implicit cognition: the implicit association test. J. Pers. Soc. Psychol. **74**(6), 1464 (1998)
24. Hanna, R., Rohm, A., Crittenden, V.L.: We're all connected: the power of the social media ecosystem. Bus. Horiz. **54**(3), 265–273 (2011)
25. Illouz, E.: Consuming the Romantic Utopia: Love and the Cultural Contradictions of Capitalism. University of California Press, Berkeley (1997)
26. Jacobs Henderson, J., Baldasty, G.J.: Race, advertising, and prime-time television. Howard J. Commun. **14**(2), 97–112 (2003)
27. Jung, S., An, J., Kwak, H., Salminen, J., Jansen, B.: Assessing the accuracy of four popular face recognition tools for inferring gender, age, and race. In: ICWSM (2018)
28. Katz, I., Hass, R.G.: Racial ambivalence and American value conflict: correlational and priming studies of dual cognitive structures. J. Pers. Soc. Psychol. **55**(6), 893 (1988)
29. Kay, M., Matuszek, C., Munson, S.A.: Unequal representation and gender stereotypes in image search results for occupations. In: Proceedings of the 33rd Annual ACM Conference on Human Factors in Computing Systems, pp. 3819–3828. ACM (2015)
30. Knapp, M.L., Hall, J.A., Horgan, T.G.: Nonverbal Communication in Human Interaction. Cengage Learning, Boston (2013)
31. Kwak, H., An, J.: Revealing the hidden patterns of news photos: analysis of millions of news photos using GDELT and deep learning-based vision APIS. In: ICWSM Workshop on News and Public Opinion (NECO) (2016)

32. Kwak, H., An, J., Salminen, J., Jung, S.G., Jansen, B.J.: What we read, what we search: media attention and public attention among 193 countries. In: Proceedings of the 2018 World Wide Web Conference on World Wide Web, pp. 893–902. International World Wide Web Conferences Steering Committee (2018)

33. LaFrance, M., Hecht, M.A., Paluck, E.L.: The contingent smile: a meta-analysis of sex differences in smiling. Psychol. Bull. **129**(2), 305 (2003)

34. Lau, S.: The effect of smiling on person perception. J. Soc. Psychol. **117**(1), 63–67 (1982)

35. Lee, K.Y., Joo, S.H.: The portrayal of Asian Americans in mainstream magazine ads: an update. Journal. Mass Commun. Q. **82**(3), 654–671 (2005)

36. Mastro, D.E., Stern, S.R.: Representations of race in television commercials: a content analysis of prime-time advertising. J. Broadcast. Electron. Media **47**(4), 638–647 (2003)

37. McCullick, B., Belcher, D., Hardin, B., Hardin, M.: Butches, bullies and buffoons: Images of physical education teachers in the movies. Sport Educ. Soc. **8**(1), 3–16 (2003)

38. McQuarrie, E.F.: Differentiating the Pictorial Element in Advertising. Visual Marketing: From Attention to Action, pp. 91–112. Erlbaum, New York (2008)

39. Millard, J.E., Grant, P.R.: The stereotypes of black and white women in fashion magazine photographs: the pose of the model and the impression she creates. Sex Roles **54**(9–10), 659–673 (2006)

40. Paek, H.J., Shah, H.: Racial ideology, model minorities, and the" not-so-silent partner:" stereotyping of Asian Americans in US magazine advertising. Howard J. Commun. **14**(4), 225–243 (2003)

41. Plous, S., Neptune, D.: Racial and gender biases in magazine advertising: a content-analytic study. Psychol. Women Q. **21**(4), 627–644 (1997)

42. Powell, B., Schnabel, L., Apgar, L.: Denial of service to same-sex and interracial couples: evidence from a national survey experiment. Sci. Adv. **3**(12), eaao5834 (2017)

43. Reis, J.C., Kwak, H., An, J., Messias, J., Benevenuto, F.: Demographics of news sharing in the US twittersphere. In: Proceedings of the 28th ACM Conference on Hypertext and Social Media, HT 2017, pp. 195–204. ACM (2017). https://doi.org/10.1145/3078714.3078734

44. Richeson, J.A., Shelton, J.N.: Brief report: thin slices of racial bias. J. Nonverbal Behav. **29**(1), 75–86 (2005)

45. Rodgers, S., Kenix, L.J., Thorson, E.: Stereotypical portrayals of emotionality in news photos. Mass Commun. Soc. **10**(1), 119–138 (2007)

46. Shabbir, H.A., Hyman, M.R., Reast, J., Palihawadana, D.: Deconstructing subtle racist imagery in television ads. J. Bus. Ethics **123**(3), 421–436 (2014)

47. Shuey, A.M., King, N., Griffith, B.: Stereotyping of negroes and whites: an analysis of magazine pictures. Public Opin. Q. **17**(2), 281–287 (1953)

48. Skill, T., Wallace, S.: Family interactions on primetime television: a descriptive analysis of assertive power interactions. J. Broadcast. Electron. Media **34**(3), 243–262 (1990)

49. Stenberg, G., Wiking, S., Dahl, M.: Judging words at face value: interference in a word processing task reveals automatic processing of affective facial expressions. Cogn. Emot. **12**(6), 755–782 (1998)

50. Stevenson, T.H.: A six-decade study of the portrayal of African Americans in business print media: trailing, mirroring, or shaping social change? J. Curr. Issues Res. Advert. **29**(1), 1–14 (2007)

51. Swani, K., Brown, B.P., Milne, G.R.: Should tweets differ for B2B and B2C? an analysis of Fortune 500 companies' Twitter communications. Ind. Mark. Manag. **43**(5), 873–881 (2014)
52. Taylor, C.R., Lee, J.Y.: Not in vogue: portrayals of Asian Americans in magazine advertising. J. Public Policy Mark. **13**(2), 239–245 (1994)
53. Taylor, C.R., Stern, B.B.: Asian-Americans: television advertising and the "model minority" stereotype. J. Advertis. **26**(2), 47–61 (1997)
54. Taylor, E.: Prime-Time Families: Television Culture in Post-War America. University of California Press, Berkeley (1989)
55. Trebbe, J., Schoenhagen, P.: Ethnic minorities in the mass media: how migrants perceive their representation in swiss public television. J. Int. Migr. Integr. **12**(4), 411–428 (2011)
56. Vazire, S., Naumann, L.P., Rentfrow, P.J., Gosling, S.D.: Smiling reflects different emotions in men and women. Behav. Brain Sci. **32**(5), 403–405 (2009)
57. Vigil, J.M.: A socio-relational framework of sex differences in the expression of emotion. Behav. Brain Sci. **32**(5), 375–390 (2009)
58. Wallbott, H.G.: Recognition of emotion from facial expression via imitation? Some indirect evidence for an old theory. Br. J. Soc. Psychol. **30**(3), 207–219 (1991)
59. Zagheni, E., Garimella, V.R.K., Weber, I., et al.: Inferring international and internal migration patterns from Twitter data. In: Proceedings of WWW Companion (2014)
60. Zinkhan, G.M., Quails, W.J., Biswas, A.: The use of blacks in magazine and television advertising: 1946 to 1986. Journal. Q. **67**(3), 547–553 (1990)

our extracted textual features. In Sect. 5, we present details of the correlation analysis between textual features and deprivation indices for properties in various locations of Dublin, and present a discussion on the implications of the findings. In Sect. 6, we conclude the paper.

2   Related Work

We group related work into three areas whereby the first includes an overview of works on real estate appraisal. Secondly, we present a brief overview of works that analyze correlations between house prices and various external factors. Finally, we present works that take into account textual features of online housing listings for various purposes.

Traditional research on real estate appraisal is based on financial real estate theory [17] and financial time series analysis [20], whereby the former builds an index of real estate values while the latter investigates the trends, periodicity and volatility of real estate prices. Another class of methods known as hedonic methods [27] approach the problem from an econometric angle, while operating on the assumption that the price of a property depends on its characteristics and location. With the recent advances in computational methods there has been an increasing interest in applying machine learning models [16,18] for real estate appraisal, and furthermore using diverse data sources such as online reviews, geospatial data from mobile devices, images etc. [6,8,25,29]. The work reported in this paper differs somewhat from real estate appraisal in that we analyse textual descriptions associated with online housing advertisements in an attempt to identify certain patterns that can be used as complementary evidence for real-estate appraisal.

Within the area of urban economics, researchers have performed an analysis of external influences that play a role in changing house prices. Of these, *walkability* [5] is a dominant factor followed by *culture* [13], *perception* [2] and *design* [25]. Essentially, these external factors affect urban development which in turn leads to high house prices. The analysis in this paper does consider the influence of external factors; however, the main difference is that we analyse how these factors influence the way in which a property description is written instead of the house price.

To the best of our knowledge, the research community has not traditionally devoted much attention to the textual descriptions associated with real estate advertisements. Some recent work in this regard includes Shahbazi et al. [26], in which a semantic text analysis of property listings on Multiple Listing Service (MLS)[3] is performed; more specifically, their work utilises an unsupervised method for annotation of domain-specific real estate concepts using word2vec after which a goodness score is assigned to the property listing. In another work, Nowak and Smith [22] incorporate text data (in the form of word tokens) from

---

[3] MLS is the singularly most important database in United States where real estate agents and brokers list real estate properties for sale.

MLS listings into a hedonic pricing model, leading to a reduction of pricing prediction error of more than 25%. The textual analysis in this paper is mostly centred around the influence location affluence measures have on the various aspects of the descriptions. This to the best of our knowledge is the first such work with significant implications for the design of online property portals as we detail in Sect. 5.

3 Motivation for the Textual Analysis of Online Housing Advertisements

The underlying intuition behind the textual analysis of online housing advertisements is the common consensus that there are potential problems with these advertisements posted by realtors or owners; for example, vague advertisements, the inclusion of misleading photos, and/or the omission of important details. We conducted an online survey to analyze the problems faced by users of online real estate portals and distributed the survey via university mailing lists and social media services; in particular, users who have previously searched for a property to buy/rent in Dublin were targeted. Our main motivation was to observe whether or not users feel that online housing advertisements contain some inaccuracies and/or were misleading in some manner.

We received 314 responses during the period March to May 2016. 62% of the respondents reported using online real estate portals several times in the past[4], and the remaining 38% reported using these online real estate portals at least once. The most significant outcome of this survey was that 41% of respondents (129 out of 314) reported that they considered textual descriptions associated with online housing advertisements as important whereas 78% of respondents (245 out of 314) reported that they considered both textual descriptions and photos associated with online housing advertisements as important. Another important outcome of the survey was that 47% of respondents (148 out of 314) reported that textual descriptions associated with online housing advertisements contain some inaccuracies. We also asked the respondents to provide detailed comments on these.

Of these the highest reported inaccuracy was with regards to omission of details on the condition of a property with regards to need for repair followed by too little details on the property's age, layout and condition. Some respondents commented that the advertisements for a large part contained a detailed focus on location aspects of properties as opposed to aspects related to layout and conditions. The example property advertisement shown in Fig. 1 shows a typical scenario whereby most of the description emphasized location aspects rather than property aspects.

The results of this brief survey prompted us to investigate the relationship between textual features in advertisements and location affluence measures as described in the following sections.

---

[4] Note that a majority of these used online real estate portals multiple times on account of moving house.

Property Description

No.3 is a superb two bedroom first floor apartment ideally
situated within walking distance of Dundrum Town Centre, a
6-7 minute walk to Dundrum LUAS and just a 20 minute walk
to UCD. Presented in walk-in condition having been recently
refurbished and measuring approx. 74m2 (796ft2), this dual
aspect property located in a private, quiet setting, comes with a
host of superior features including spacious living area,
separate utility room double-glazed windows and ample
parking. This property would represent an ideal first time buy
or a lucrative investment due to the premium rents being
achieved in the area.

Accommodation briefly comprises; hallway, living/dining
room, kitchen with utility, two double bedrooms and bathroom.
There is additional dedicated storage located in the common area
hallway.

All amenitites are within easy reach with Dundrum town centre
being within a short 10 minute walk. There one will find a myriad of
different speciality shops, restuarants, coffee shops as well as
the cinema and other leisure pursuits. Public transport facilities are
well catered for with the LUAS being within walking distance and
there is also as regular bus service on your doorstep. The M50 is
within a very short drive and provides easy access to most major route-
ways.

Fig. 1. An example property advertisement

4   Dataset and Available Property Features

The study reported in this paper is based on two property advertisements corpora compiled from a popular Irish real estate information access portal. We
restrict our crawl to Dublin-based properties for the purpose of analysing the
diverse range of heterogeneous locations in Dublin city. The first crawl covers
the period from September, 2016 to January, 2017 while the second crawl covers
the period from December, 2018 to March, 2019. The first crawl includes a total
of 3,682 properties in Dublin while the second crawl includes a total of 1,533
properties in Dublin. Table 1 summarizes the various features of properties that
can be extracted from our dataset. The features based on housing attributes
include the type of the property (house, apartment, studio etc.), the number of
bedrooms and bathrooms, and whether or not a garden, parking or heating is
included in the property. The features based on urban infrastructure relate to
public transport linkages near a property; in Dublin, the three essential modes
of public transport are bus, Luas[5] and DART[6]; it is noteworthy that properties
located close to the Luas and DART have a marginally higher value than others [14]. Finally, the textual features are those that we mine from the textual
descriptions in advertisements as explained in the following section. For a sample
textual description see Fig. 1. One could argue that due to time difference in the
crawl from which two different corpora were obtained there may be significant
differences in property market (specifically, house prices); however, the factors
that we analyse i.e. location affluence indicators explained in the following do

---

[5] https://en.wikipedia.org/wiki/Luas.
[6] https://en.wikipedia.org/wiki/Dublin_Area_Rapid_Transit.

not change over the period covered in our crawl and hence, our analysis holds for the two corpora.

For location affluence indicators, we utilise the recently developed Pobal HP Deprivation Index for Ireland [10]. This index provides a method of measuring the relative affluence or disadvantage of a particular geographical area using data compiled from various censuses. We use the latest version of this index from 2016 and this particular index is novel in that it is based on three dimensions of affluence/disadvantage: Demographic Profile, Social Class Composition and Labour Market Situation. Specifically, the Pobal data gives an index for deprivation which has been classified as shown in Table 2 based on a relative index score[7]. From this point onwards in the paper, we use the term deprivation index score to refer to the relative index score where a high score indicates affluence. It is these scores that are used to characterise our two advertisements' corpora based on location distributions (by affluence) as shown in Table 3.

Table 1. Features extracted for each property.

Feature type	Feature
Housing attributes	Property type
	No. of bedrooms
	No. of bathrooms
	Parking
	Garden
	Heating
	Floor area
Urban infrastructure	Bus routes
	Tram (Luas)
	Train (DART)
Textual features	Named entities
	Topical consistency
	Location contribution

4.1 Extracted Textual Features

As shown in Table 1, we extract three types of textual features for the purpose of our analysis. Of these named entities are well-defined in the NLP community whereas *topical consistency* and *location contribution* are devised for the purpose of the analysis in this paper. Each of these feature types is described in the subsections below.

---

[7] Note that relative index score is included as part of the Pobal index.

Table 2. Details of locations based on relative score index from POBAL dataset.

Relative Index Score	Label
over 30	Extremely affluent
20 to 30	Very affluent
10 to 20	Affluent
0 to 10	Marginally above average
0 to −10	Marginally below average
−10 to −20	Disadvantaged
−20 to −30	Very disadvantaged
below −30	Extremely disadvantaged

Table 3. Location distributions for crawled dataset(s)

Dataset	Affluent	Marginally above average	Marginally below average	Disadvantaged
Sept. 2016–Jan. 2017	542	421	1473	1246
Dec. 2018–Mar. 2019	245	387	586	315

Named Entities. Named entities are extracted per location from within the textual descriptions in advertisements of each property in a given location. Named entity recognition (NER) is a sub-task within information extraction whereby named entity mentions in unstructured text are identified; the extracted entities are person names, organizations, locations, medical codes, time expressions, quantities, monetary values, percentages. For the specific case of online housing advertisements, the extracted entities mostly fall into two categories, i.e. locations and organizations. For each of these, we compute a feature called *locationNorm* and *organizationNorm* which is a measure of the normalized mentions of locations and organizations, respectively, in a given property location. For each property, location and organization mentions are normalized by the total number of words in the property description under consideration. Then, for a certain location, the values of *locationNorm* and *organizationNorm* for properties in that location are averaged so that its value remains less than 1.0.

Topical Consistency. *Topical consistency* is a measure extracted per location from within each property in a given location. We do this in two steps whereby we first apply topic modelling over the property descriptions to determine their topical associations, and, in the second step we compute the mean pairwise Jaccard similarity over the top-3 topics extracted for each property in a given location. For the purpose of analysis of locations in this paper, the number of topics is set to 10 as that was empirically found to be representative of different themes in the property advertisements. Note that the value of *topical consistency* varies between zero and one, where a value close to zero implies that the *topical con-*

sistency is negligible and a value of one implies maximum *topical consistency*. In essence it measures the proportion of various topics (see examples are shown in Table 6) within textual descriptions where topics are different threads of information, and the model itself distributes words per topics using a probabilistic graphical model.

Location Contribution. *Location contribution* is also a measure extracted per location from within each property in a given location. This involves the text classification of sentences that make up the textual description of a property with each sentence belonging to one of three classes: *describing the property, describing the location* or *none*. A portion of sentences (1050 sentences in total with 413 sentences describing property, 573 sentences describing location, and 54 sentences belonging to none category) in property descriptions were first manually tagged via the crowdsourcing platform Figure-Eight[8] in order to obtain ground truth labels for the dataset. Our text classification framework utilises unigram and bigram tokens in a support vector machine model to classify the sentences as either describing the property, location or none. The classification results on a held-out dataset (containing all sentences in a randomly selected 20% of properties from the training data of the two corpora) are shown in Table 4. The high accuracy shows that the classification model performs sufficiently well, and it can be safely assumed that the final labels for non-tagged part of the corpora will be correct. Finally, based on the label for each sentence in a property description, a cumulative *location contribution* score is computed which is then aggregated over the properties in each location; this score provides the percentage of sentences in property descriptions, per location, that pertain to location-specific characteristics. There is a notable difference between *locationNorm* and *location contribution* in that the former operates only on named entities thereby being more limited whereas the latter is able to operate on common nouns and noun phrases thereby picking more granular details on location aspects within text.

Table 4. Accuracy on hold-out dataset for sentence classification.

Dataset	Accuracy
Sept. 2016–Jan. 2017	84.7%
Dec. 2018–Mar. 2019	86.8%

5   Analysed Correlations and Results

A correlation analysis was performed to investigate the relationship between indicators of a location's affluence and the extracted textual factors explained

---

[8] https://www.figure-eight.com/.

in Sect. 4. As mentioned previously, deprivation indices based on census data developed by Pobal HP have been used for our analysis.

We report Spearman correlation over all properties (see Table 5) between the 2016 HP Relative Index Score or more commonly Deprivation Index score and *"locationNorm"*, *"organizationNorm"*, *"topical consistency"*, and *"location contribution"*. Note that all reported correlations are statistically significant at a level of $p < 0.01$.

Investigating the table, we find no significant correlation between *"location-Norm"* and deprivation indices for an area. However, we find a strong, positive correlation between *"organizationNorm"* and deprivation indices for an area implying that online housing advertisements for locations with high affluence have high mentions of organizations within the advertisement text. Typically organisations within an advertisement include names of shopping centres, supermarkets, reputed schools/colleges and other potentially significant landmarks. Hence, advertisements for affluent locations place a high emphasis on organization entities so as to highlight specific aspects that could potentially lead to "higher prices."

Secondly, *"topical consistency"* and deprivation indices are moderately, negatively correlated. This is very interesting and shows that a high location affluence leads to topical inconsistencies in the textual descriptions. On a closer analysis we find that certain properties in affluent locations have a balance of different topics with the advertisement itself being partially about the property and partially about the location; however, some properties (especially old ones in need of repair) cover more topics that discuss location with a tendency to hide the aspects that can help lower the property's price.

Finally, there is a strong, positive correlation between *"location contribution"* and deprivation indices implying that property advertisements for locations with higher affluence have a high proportion of sentences that describe the location. Overall, this is not a surprising conclusion and is in line with [23].

In the following subsections we present a detailed analysis of various textual features in areas with similar affluence in an attempt to explain how our analysis can have a variety of implications within the housing market of Dublin. We first present statistics on two of our measures *"topical consistency"* and *"location contribution"* within areas of similar levels of affluence followed by an explanation of some ways in which our findings can help towards meaningful interpretation of online property advertisements.

Table 5. Correlations between textual features and deprivation indices

	2016 HP Relative Index Score
locationNorm	0.12
organizationNorm	0.63
topical consistency	−0.39
location contribution	0.74

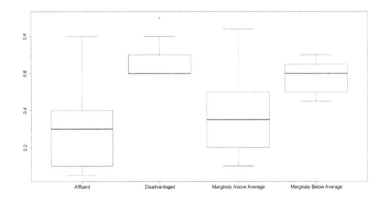

Fig. 2. Boxplot showing variations in "topical consistency"

5.1 Analysis of Areas with Similar Affluence

Figure 2 shows the box plots for *"topical consistency"* in different areas with the same levels of affluence whereas Fig. 3 shows the box plots for *"location contribution"*. As can be seen there is more variability for both the measures in affluent areas (see areas with label "Affluent" and "Marginally Above Average"). As is clear from examples of topics in Table 6, the high variability in *'"topical consistency"* together with a similar high variability in *"location contribution"* for affluent areas shows evidence for an unbalanced proportion of stress on location aspects within some advertisements particularly where certain properties are not in perfect conditions. To further illustrate we present example topics in Table 6; as can be seen the topics themselves are representative of location aspects, property aspects or mixed aspects and the fact that *"topical consistency"* shows wide variability in areas of high affluence together with low values depicts that users need to be cautious in dealing with properties in such locations. On the other hand, less affluent locations do not show such high variability for the measures *"topical consistency"* and *"location contribution"*; moreover, the values for these measures themselves in less affluent areas depicts an overall focus on aspects of the property. We report statistics on a more granular level for some of the affluent areas namely Rathmines, Blackrock, Dundrum and Pembroke and the less affluent areas namely Firhouse, Lucan, Drumcondra and Blanchardstown; as seen the mean for *"location contribution"* within the affluent areas is higher as compared to less affluent areas and with the exception of Pembroke the standard deviation varies quite a bit. This further confirms the findings on exercising caution in affluent areas in terms of the condition of a property, and the emphasis on location. Hence, the values of our novel textual features particularly *"topical consistency"* and *"location contribution"* aid the user in meaningful interpretation of online advertisements.

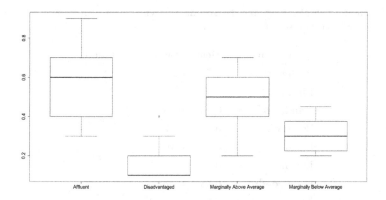

Fig. 3. Boxplot showing variations in "location contribution"

Table 6. Example topics

Words describing topic	Topic related to
center, space, garden, rear, parking	property
luxurious, room, located, hallway, light	property
m50, amenities, schools, shopping, access	location
rooms, bright, access, shopping, schools	mixed
centre, garden, immaculate, leisure, colleges	mixed
window, fireplace, hallway, rooms, open	property
suburban, access, transport, , cafes	location

5.2   Discussion

The work reported in this analysis fundamentally informs research within the theme of "Data Science for Good", and below we present few ways in which our analysis can aid property price management.

Implications: On its own the outcome of location aspects being highly emphasized in online housing advertisements for affluent locations is not surprising; and in urban sectors this is something potential buyers or tenants would have in mind. However, when combined with other factors such as *topical consistencies* being mixed with some advertisement having both property aspects and location aspects while some having more of location aspects reveals interesting insights. It also becomes obvious that realtors/owners in affluent locations in an attempt to sell an affluent location's amenities sometimes hide the aspects of the property that should be made known to potential buyers or tenants. In such a scenario our textual features could aid in first steps towards price control in the housing market which has been an area in which current Irish government is heavily struggling. This can for example be done via automated price prediction models built on top of our textual features, and detecting realtors/landlords/owners who market the property at a price much higher than predicted price. Moreover,

Table 7. Some examples showing the standard deviation of well-known affluent and less affluent areas of Dublin

Location name	Mean	Standard deviation
Rathmines	0.55	0.31
Blackrock	0.73	0.42
Dundrum	0.65	0.38
Pembroke	0.78	0.12
Firhouse	0.41	0.16
Lucan	0.48	0.23
Drumcondra	0.38	0.15
Blanchardstown	0.32	0.08

we argue for more crowd-sourced controls over online property portals such as the ones on the Multiple Listings Service database in United States whereby users can leave comments, and these comments could potentially include property aspects that realtors/owners may not have pointed out. This can eventually help give back control to the buyer or tenant adding more transparency thereby leading to lesser exploitation by realtors/owners/landlords (Table. 7).

6　Conclusion

In this paper, we have presented a textual analysis of online housing advertisements for Dublin, and have attempted to present details of how locations with high affluence have a majority of online housing advertisements in which realtors and landlords overemphasize location aspects. This became evident by means of correlating deprivation indices with various textual features namely named entities (organizations were strongly, positively correlated), *topical consistency* which was moderately, negatively correlated, and *location contribution* which was strongly, positively correlated. The work in this paper can serve as a first step in utilising more advanced textual features in real-estate appraisal, and this is the aim of our future work. Finally, such an analysis can aid incorporation of a price estimator within online property portals such as the ones in Zillow.com.

Acknowledgments. This work is supported by Science Foundation Ireland through the Insight Centre for Data Analytics under SFI/12/RC/2289_P2.

References

1. Brown, V.J.: Give me shelter: the global housing crisis. Environ. Health Perspect. **111**(2), A92 (2003)

2. Buonanno, P., Montolio, D., Raya-Vílchez, J.M.: Housing prices and crime perception. Empir. Econ. **45**(1), 305–321 (2013)
3. Byrne, M., et al.: The financialization of housing and the growth of the private rental sector in Ireland, the UK and Spain. Technical report (2019)
4. Carstairs, V.: Deprivation indices: their interpretation and use in relation to health. J. Epidemiol. Community Health **49**(Suppl 2), S3–S8 (1995)
5. Cortright, J.: Walking the walk: How walkability raises home values in US cities (2009)
6. De Nadai, M., Lepri, B.: The economic value of neighborhoods: predicting real estate prices from the urban environment. In: 2018 IEEE 5th International Conference on Data Science and Advanced Analytics (DSAA), pp. 323–330. IEEE (2018)
7. Elliot, P., Cuzick, J.: Geographical and Environmental Epidemiology: Methods for Small Area Studies. World Health Organization, Geneva (1992). (Number 614.42 G3)
8. Fu, Y., et al.: Sparse real estate ranking with online user reviews and offline moving behaviors. In: 2014 IEEE International Conference on Data Mining, pp. 120–129. IEEE (2014)
9. Gelman, I.A., Wu, N.: Combining structured and unstructured information sources for a study of data quality: a case study of Zillow.com. In: 2011 44th Hawaii International Conference on System Sciences (HICSS), pp. 1–12. IEEE (2011)
10. Haase, T., Pratschke, J.: The 2016 Pobal HP Deprivation Index (SA) (2016)
11. Haase, T., Pratschke, J., Gleeson, J.: The 2011 All-Island HP Deprivation Index. Pobal, Dublin (2014)
12. Hearne, R.: A home or a wealth generator. Inequality, financialisation and the Irish housing crisis. TASC, Dublin (2017)
13. Hristova, D., Aiello, L.M., Quercia, D.: The new urban success: how culture pays. Front. Phys. **6**, 27 (2018)
14. Keenan, M.: Revealed: how much living close to Luas and Dart adds to your house price (2018). https://www.independent.ie/irish-news/revealed-how-much-living-close-to-luas-and-dart-adds-to-your-house-price-36933179.html
15. Kiel, K.A., Zabel, J.E.: Location, location, location: The 3L approach to house price determination. J. Hous. Econ. **17**(2), 175–190 (2008)
16. Kontrimas, V., Verikas, A.: The mass appraisal of the real estate by computational intelligence. Appl. Soft Comput. **11**(1), 443–448 (2011)
17. Krainer, J., Wei, C., et al.: House prices and fundamental value. FRBSF Econ. Lett. (2004)
18. Lam, E.: Modern regression models and neural networks for residential property valuation. Royal Institute of Chartered Surveyors (1996)
19. Li, X.-B., Motiwalla, L.: For sale by owner online: who gets the saved commission? Commun. ACM **52**(2), 110–114 (2009)
20. Nagaraja, C.H., Brown, L.D., Zhao, L.H., et al.: An autoregressive approach to house price modeling. Ann. Appl. Stat. **5**(1), 124–149 (2011)
21. Nowak, A., Smith, P.: Textual analysis in real estate. J. Appl. Econ. (2016)
22. Nowak, A., Smith, P.: Textual analysis in real estate. J. Appl. Econ. **32**(4), 896–918 (2017)
23. O'Brien, C.: Dublin's north/south divide apparent in property prices (2018). https://www.irishtimes.com/business/construction/dublin-s-north-south-divide-apparent-in-property-prices-1.3660146. (Irish Times)

24. Orford, S.: Valuing location in an urban housing market. In: The Proceedings of the 3rd International Conference on GeoComputation, United Kingdom, University of Bristol, Bristol, BS8 1SS, UK, pp. 56–58 (1988)
25. Poursaeed, O., Matera, T., Belongie, S.: Vision-based real estate price estimation. Mach. Vis. Appl. **29**(4), 667–676 (2018)
26. Shahbazi, M., Barr, J.R., Hristidis, V., Srinivasan, N.N.: Estimation of the investability of real estate properties through text analysis. In: 2016 IEEE Tenth International Conference on Semantic Computing (ICSC), pp. 301–306. IEEE (2016)
27. Taylor, L.O.: The hedonic method. In: Champ, P.A., Boyle, K.J., Brown, T.C. (eds.) A Primer on Nonmarket Valuation, pp. 331–393. Springer, Dordrecht (2003). https://doi.org/10.1007/978-94-007-0826-6_10
28. Wong, C.: Indicators for Urban and Regional Planning: The Interplay of Policy and Methods. Routledge, Abingdon (2006)
29. You, Q., Pang, R., Cao, L., Luo, J.: Image-based appraisal of real estate properties. IEEE Trans. Multimedia **19**(12), 2751–2759 (2017)

Into the Dark: A Case Study of Banned Darknet Drug Forums

Selina Y. Cho(✉) and Joss Wright(✉)

University of Oxford, Oxford, UK
selina.cho@cs.ox.ac.uk, joss.wright@oii.ox.ac.uk

Abstract. In March 2018, to the surprise of many users, the largest Reddit forums related to darknet markets (DNM) were banned overnight. For users, whose trading activity relied heavily on these forums, the ban was a threat to the community as a whole. In this study we use a complete set of posts from the newly founded forums in the darknet-based "Dread" platform to examine key discussion topics and the sentiment of the community towards the ban. We look at the level of user engagement in the new forums, and the number of users who retain their old usernames. Applying topic modelling to posts on the new forum, we show that there are many overlapping themes across both the banned and new forums, and that discussions on drugs are the most prominent, followed by vendors, shipping reviews, and payment methods. We observe that the new community demonstrates negative sentiment toward the unexpected ban and the loss of accumulated information, but also holds a favourable view of Dread in the hopes that it will offer greater features and security for the users. Users across both platforms express attachment and affinity to the general DNM community, and demonstrate relation to it beyond the commercial purpose.

Keywords: Community · Darknet · Topic modelling · Sentiment analysis · Speech ban · Social support

1 Introduction

Reddit is one of the largest and most popular platforms on the web, and users of darknet markets (DNM) had long used Reddit as a platform to share information. Despite the risks of revealing sensitive discussions in public, Reddit's forums thrived among DNM users as large repositories of information were regularly updated and curated by its active userbase [29]. After years of collective contribution, the forums had become a key reference point for DNM users, with guidance on safely purchasing products, anonymous communications, and vendor and scam alerts. Each forum, or "subreddit", had a dedicated topic of discussion, and the forum subscribers were typically anonymous. The ease with which users could access and contribute information in Reddit's forums helped create a sense of community and a public discourse that welcomed experts, newcomers, and enthusiasts of DNMs from around the world [10,21].

© Springer Nature Switzerland AG 2019
I. Weber et al. (Eds.): SocInfo 2019, LNCS 11864, pp. 109–127, 2019.
https://doi.org/10.1007/978-3-030-34971-4_8

On the 21st of March 2019, however, many of the largest DNM subreddits came to a halt when Reddit updated their policy [24] to forbid discussions facilitating transactions of illicit goods. Over 40 subreddits pertaining to DNMs were banned overnight, and a large portion of the public data previously displayed in subreddits became irretrievable to users. The incident stirred much criticism within the community, and the users on neighbouring subreddits advertised alternative platforms to which users could migrate. In particular, a new platform named Dread rose to prominence after positive reviews were spread across existing forums and websites beyond Reddit.

1.1 Research Questions

This study aims to highlight the social phenomenon ensuing from a speech ban in a community that is associated with the use of illicit goods and anonymous communications. Examining posts from both banned Reddit and new Dread forums, we highlight the core themes of discussion, and assess the extent to which the unexpected disruption has sparked change in the overall dialogue, as analysed through topic modelling and user sentiment. We examine the following questions:

RQ1 What are users discussing in the new platform? Are key topics preserved in the move to Dread?

RQ2 How do users perceive the ban and, by extension, Reddit?

RQ3 How has user engagement changed in the new platform?

2 Related Work

2.1 Community Response and Support

Social media platforms with user-generated contents enable users to have a wide scale public discourse and bring about a collective motion [10]. Reddit is known to have a community base that is particularly active and vocal in achieving its goals [22], making it an appropriate platform in which to observe community responses to structural changes. For instance, a group of influential moderators on Reddit once went on a mass protest by preventing millions of users from accessing the platform in order to demand a better treatment of the employees by the company [1].

During a period of community unrest after a ban on hate-speech, supporters of hate-speech on Reddit migrated to new platforms such as Voat, carrying with them their grievances and public perceptions of hate speech [23]. A large number of accounts discontinued using Reddit, with those that stayed drastically decreasing their usage of hate speech [8]. The lack of suitable alternative subreddits and the discomfort from hiding from Reddit's administration were given as the leading reasons to migrate to other platforms. In a social networking app Instagram, on the other hand, banning tags [7] have been shown to influence the community to evade the ban efforts by adopting non-standard lexical variants, which were actually found to contain more toxic contents than the previous ones.

Platforms with anonymity features have shown to enable more intimate and open conversations when seeking advice and discussion [4], where the ephemeral nature of the posts have been suggested to encourage participation. Information seeking and sharing practices were seen in mental health communities of Reddit where the users were able to openly discuss socially stigmatised issues in anonymity [9]. Its study by Choudhury and De found that feedback to queries posted on subreddits were of noticeably high quality, even when these contributors were not compensated for their effort, and reflected how such self-disclosing attitudes attracted greater social support within the community. This dimension of social support contrasted with other social media platforms, such as Twitter or Facebook, in which users would be more conscious of being watched and identifiable. Reddit's design and support for niche communities, and the scale of its existing userbase play a key role in retaining the remaining users, and potentially in promoting a homophilic and polarised culture in the Internet [21].

To the knowledge of the authors, the study of communities on social media platforms so far focuses only on those on the publicly indexed web pages, and there is a limited understanding of the equivalent social community that co-exist across the darknet.

2.2 Disruption in Darknet Markets

Based on the concept of collective consciousness by Durkheim [12,13], Ladegaard [18] argues that law enforcement crackdowns in DNMs and their forums had fostered community spirit and solidarity, enabling users to survive and migrate to new platforms as a collective unit. More recent work [6] suggests that the effects of law enforcement disruptions on markets tend only to last briefly, and that the number of vendors can continue to increase despite disruptions. Trust play a significant role in vendor selection among the users over other factors such as product differentiation or affordability [14]. Trade levels in DNMs have actually been found to increase even during law enforcement interventions, as the users place loyalty above law and resist excessive policing measures [19].

Hardy and Norgaard [16] demonstrate that feedback mechanisms and reputation create an informal institutional framework, providing users enough confidence and momentum for markets to exist without government regulation. Armona [3] finds that consumer demand is approximately equally influenced by communication on both formal and informal networks such as product reviews in darknet market forums and public discussion forums as Reddit. However, due to the confidentiality concerns of Reddit as a public platform, reviews on markets have shown to be far more sought after than those on subreddits.

3   Methods

3.1   Terminologies

We refer to both subreddits and subdreads simply as forums. Each forum has a creator and at least one moderator; responsible for the establishment and maintenance of the forum.

DNM refers to a commercial website accessible via an anonymous overlay network such as Tor or I2P in which buyers and sellers present and accept offers. Payments are typically facilitated through cryptocurrencies. Forums contain a blend of questions, reviews, and discussions on drugs, vendors, arrests, and markets. In this study, the market forums with some of the highest number of users included Dream Market, Wallstreet Market, and Rapture Market. General discussions were posted on "DNM" and "Darknet Markets" forums. A notable one was DNMSuperlist, which had an updated list of all latest operating markets, as well as a "Wall of Shame" that listed markets that had ceased to exist.

3.2   Datasets

We use publicly available data on Reddit and scraped data from Dread to construct a dataset of all posts in relevant banned forums. Our Reddit data runs from November 2017 up until the ban on the 21st March 2018. Dread data runs since its inception in February 2018 until Aug 2018. The features in the dataset include forum names, posting dates, usernames, thread titles, and contents. We analyse a total of 35,589 Reddit postings and 8,270 Dread postings, representative of the top 10 DNM-related forums by volume, shown in Table 1. Figure 1 in Appendix A.1 shows the total number of postings over the months overlapping the ban.

All work was carried out with institutional approval[1], and with consideration for the rights and protection of users and their respective services.

To analyse banned Reddit forums, we made use of an archived set of posts on Google BigQuery[2], as the forums themselves are no longer usable directly or by their communities. Through manual search, we identified not only forums that were banned in March 2018, but also those banned in preceding weeks. This resulted in a total of 42,418 posts, from which we excluded non-English forums and selected the top 10 DNM-related forums by posting volume between 1st November 2017 and 31 March 2018. After applying duplicate checks, this resulted in 35,589 posts.

For Dread, we used the Python scraping framework *scrapy* to access the main onion link (*dreadditevelidot.onion*) and scrape all post contents. Upon first accessing the website we were redirected to a CAPTCHA automation challenge image. We applied image transformation and the Tesseract optical character recognition engine to convert CAPTCHA images into characters and overcome

---

[1] Reference Number from Oxford Internet Institute's Departmental Research Ethics Committee (DREC): SSH OII C1A 18 070.

[2] https://bigquery.cloud.google.com/dataset/fh-bigquery:reddit_posts.

the original format. This scraping resulted in a total of 12,612 posts. After excluding non-English forums and selecting the top 10 DNM-related forums by volume, the dataset comprised a total of 8,270 posts.

Table 1. Overview of the top 10 forums in Reddit and Dread

Reddit	# of posting	Dread	# of posting
DarkNetMarkets	9275	DarkNetMarkets	2,356
fakeid	6782	WallStreetMarket	1,146
DNMUK	5041	Xanax	791
RCSources	4132	DNMUK	734
DankNation	3417	DankNation	713
Xanaxcartel	3284	DarkNetAustralia	658
darknetmarketsOZ	1174	Dread	554
afinil	1119	fraud	476
EU_RCSources	773	rcsources	449
Darknet_Markets	592	DNMAds	393
Total:	35,589	Total:	8,270

3.3   Analysis Tools

Topic modelling and sentiment analysis were used to identify the overlapping trends in discourse and the users' tones on the subject matter to reflect their views and concerns in response to Reddit's ban.

RQ1: Topic Modelling. Latent Dirichlet Allocation (LDA) [5] is a generative model widely used for unsupervised topic modelling. Using large collections of discrete data, LDA can develop probabilistic topics, or groups of words, where each word is given a probability of belonging to the topics. The words with the highest probabilities in each topic can be used to interpret its underlying theme.

We used LDA to capture major discussion topics in both Reddit and Dread. Using Gensim[3] and MALLET[4], we ran two LDA models based on the posts from the top 10 forums. We created a corpus containing a list of all the string elements extracted from post contents. All the titles and post contents were transformed as standard for topic modelling: lower cased, punctuation removed, linebreaks removed, whitespace collapsed, lemmatised (via *spacy*), duplicate checked, and standard stopwords removed using NLTK. We removed words that had fewer than 3 characters and more than 15 characters [2]. Title and contents were then concatenated to be analysed together, and filtered only for nouns and adjectives to avoid degradation of preprocessed words and content.

---

[3] https://radimrehurek.com/gensim/.
[4] http://mallet.cs.umass.edu/.

From Reddit, we obtained 34,390 terms in the total corpus; from Dread we obtained 34,077 corpus terms. We generated an LDA model for 2000 iterations on the whole corpus, and set both the α and β values to the default value of 1.0 divided by the number of topics. We found that using fewer than seven topics caused a general overlap in the keywords assigned to each topic, and that more than seven topics resulted in redundancy and overfitting of topic assignments. The perplexity assessment of the analysis is shown in Fig. 3 in Appendix A.3. Given the results of these trials and manual inspection for suitability, a model based on seven topics was selected as most coherent for Reddit and six for Dread.

RQ2: Sentiment Analysis. We used TextBlob [20] to analyse the quality of sentiments spanning across posts that mention "Reddit". TextBlob is a well-established tool to perform common natural language processing tasks such as part-of-speech tagging, sentiment analysis, and text translation using its public API. The tool has been used in Twitter on patients for hospital quality survey [17] and dispersion of Brexit sentiments spread by bots [15], newspaper readers' comments [27], and sarcasm detection through text and image [25].

TextBlob scores posts for *polarity* and *subjectivity*, determining whether a post is positive, negative, or neutral for a given topic, and how subjective each statement is likely to be. Polarity is given within the range $[-1.0 \text{ to } 1.0]$ in which -1.0 represents a highly negative sentiment and $+1.0$ indicates a highly positive sentiment; subjectivity is given between the range $[0.0 \text{ to } 1.0]$ where 0.0 is highly objective and 1.0 is highly subjective. Figure 4 in Appendix A.4 shows the probability distribution of polarity rates seen in Reddit and Dread.

RQ3: Community. To assess the effects of the ban on user activity, we first looked up the complete list of DNM-related subreddits banned in March 2018, and manually identified the most likely equivalent forums in Dread. In some cases, multiple Reddit forums corresponded to a same Dread forum, and so we accumulated the alternatives to reflect the average number of user engagement across different forums. Then we calculated the percentage of unique usernames present in a forum from the total subscription number of the respective forum, to gain the proportion of users actively engaging in a discussion. We also compiled a list of unique username from Reddit, and compared each to usernames across Dread forums to find overlapping pairs, to find signs of username preservation.

4   Results

4.1   RQ1: Topic Analysis

Tables 2 and 3 shows the list of the most frequently appearing keywords in the topic models, in descending order of probability. The key themes are manually assessed by the authors in Table 4 based on the topic keywords. In general it appears that forums are dedicated to a small range of topics, particularly around the experience of using a drug and interacting with vendors. Some of the present keywords most applicable to the drug products are *experience, chemical, sample, legit,* and *quality,* and to the vendors are *communication, experience, good, guy,* and *review.*

Table 2. Top ten most frequent corpus terminologies for seven topics from Reddit

1	2	3	4	5	6	7
btc	good	modafinil	vendor	order	bud	amp
source	vendor	drug	review	day	sample	value
fee	dream	bitcoin	gram	anyone	cgmc	cost
coin	time	use	shatter	pack	cart	price
payment	market	year	product	week	test	product
monero	day	wallet	kush	description	legit	shipping
free	anyone	new	pill	time	usa	good
link	experience	way	dose	post	result	high
christmas	guy	people	chemical	package	forum	quality
new	bar	site	mdma	email	product	communication

Table 3. Top ten most frequent corpus terms for six topics from Dread

1	2	3	4	5	6
hash	vendor	signature	vendor	cocaine	card
good	good	pgp	anyone	good	bank
quality	price	key	market	product	account
high	order	public	order	quality	panama
distillate	product	end	time	pure	monero
paypal	review	block	new	market	guide
available	shipping	sha	people	gram	cash
something	dream	shop	good	flake	bitcoin
wax	day	gram	post	top	credit
pack	quality	hash	day	high	btc

From Reddit's seventh topic and Dread's second topic, we see that some of the common user interests when purchasing a product are its *value, price, quality* and *shipping* method. Drugs that appeared most frequently are cocaine, cannabis, Modafinil, and MDMA. Words such as *pure, legit,* and *top* show that drugs with the highest quality and purity are of interest. For instance, *flake* in Dread's fifth topic refers to a more premium type of cocaine with above 40% purity[5]; *shatter* in Reddit's fourth topic refers to a concentrate that contains 80–

---

[5] London, This Is What's Actually in Your Cocaine (2015 (accessed March 30, 2019)), https://www.vice.com/en_uk/article/nnq8k8/london-theres-no-cocaine-in-your-cocaine-940.

Table 4. Interpretation of Topics

T	Themes (Reddit)	T	Themes (Dread)
1	Payment methods	1	Drug review and payment method
2	Vendor review and enquiry	2	Vendor and drug review
3	Payment methods for drugs	3	Secure communication methods
4	Vendor and drug review	4	Vendor enquiry
5	Product delivery review	5	Cocaine review or advertisement
6	Drug sampling	6	Payment methods used in markets
7	Product review		

90% cannabinoid content. In the payment topic, Bitcoin and Monero are clearly dominant across the platforms.

From several matching keywords across the topics, we see that the majority of the discussion themes that existed in Reddit prior to the ban have continued to dominate in Dread. In Dread, however, there is an additional topic of secure communication tools, including PGP (Pretty Good Privacy) and SHA (Secure Hash Algorithm). On manual inspection, several posts on the forums are signed with users' PGP-keys, and contain strings as "BEGIN PGP SIGNED MESSAGE" and "END PGP SIGNATURE", which likely contributed to formation of this topic. PGP is an encryption program used for signing, encrypting, and decrypting text-based data to increase the security of communications and verify the associated identity. As these weren't as prominent in Reddit's corpus terminologies, it can be inferred that Dread has more users who are likely to PGP-sign a post and care more about familiar identities, given Dread's relatively new environment.

4.2   RQ2: User Sentiments - Are Users Happy?

Contrary to the assumption that the crowd is unhappy and critical of a speech ban, sentiment analysis showed that more users offered positive remarks than negative when mentioning the term *Reddit*. 21.9% of the posts on Reddit indicated a positive sentiment, 19.7% a negative sentiment, and 58.4% a neutral sentiment. On the other hand on Dread, 30% of posts indicated a positive sentiment, 17.7% a negative sentiment, and 52.3% a neutral sentiment. The higher percentage of positive sentiment in Dread may be due to the excited praising of the still-new platform. Manual inspection of the posts marked as positive sentiment showed that the majority of them actually demonstrated mixed sentiments; a post would begin by criticising Reddit's decision to ban, and end by praising the design of Dread and the increased sense of security or freedom from Reddit's policies. Posts with positive sentiment are seen in Table 5 below with polarity (P), subjectivity (S), and the text body. Some original quotes in the following have been reduced for space, and names of users have been pseudonymised for ethical reasons. Users whose usernames appeared in both Reddit and Dread

Table 5. Positive sentiments in Dread based on polarity (P) and subjectivity (S). Original texts are displayed for legibility.

P	S	Text
0.83	0.6	Dread has the best UI better than reddit!
0.6	0.25	Thanks to the staff of Dread for allowing Newb to create this sub as a refuge from the persecution of Reddit. [Moderator A] is one of the best Mods I've encountered. Viva la Revolution Chemico!
0.51	0.58	It's cool to see the community growing. In some ways Dread is already better than Reddit. Keep up the good work [User A]!
0.28	0.73	[User A] is a gentle soul... He doesn't deserve any harm. He's just trying to keep people safe. It's like people hiding jews in WW2. FUCK REDDIT!!!
0.37	0.54	[...] the fact that reddit, an easy access cleannet site, was used to store lots of information related to darknet markets was not the greatest idea - why had no one thought for making a website like that before? [...] I see it as a good thing. Now kids wont be able to just go on reddit and learn how to buy and sell drugs literally in a day. I feel this is an opportunity as now its not as easy as a google search to find lots of information [...] (Cont. in Appendix A.5)

posts, in particular, expressed positive views on the new platform and its features. The view was often backed by the genuine concern and affinity the users held toward the existing community. One user had expressed that despite the reduced size of the community, the new platform enabled users to feel more intimate, and even encouraged them to act more decently than they had previously in Reddit (P: 0.21, S: 0.53): "[...] What I have noticed in the last few weeks is a great thing, this community is not arguing, we are not picking fights, we are helping each other out, offering opinions, being honest [...] our community knows the rules, abides them and calls out ones that don't. [...] ALTHOUGH much smaller this community is much closer than it ever has been [...]." Another user conveyed the affection he or she holds for a specific forum community, DankNation, and even offered help to other users (P: -0.003, S: 0.57): "[...] Sad day for DNMs as a whole, its unfortunate that the mass of other subs couldn't contain their subs which IMO ultimately led to the shut down of EVERYTHING. [...] Love all you DankNation users, hopefully we can make this something worth using, and hope for your continued support. [...]." The extension of the quotes can be found in Table 7 in Appendix A.5.

The negative expressions frequently refers to the sudden loss of previous content on drugs and vendor reviews on Reddit that will now make it harder for the users to safely navigate their way around in DNMs against fraud and scams. However, the authors found no negative sentiments geared toward Dread itself, upon inspection of the posts indicated as negative; if any, the sentiments expressed contempt toward the existing features of the platforms such as moderators, vendors, and administrators in both Reddit and Dread. Posts with negative sentiments are seen in Table 6 below. It is worth mentioning that negative remarks expressed through profanity are often not recognised by the processing tool, and as such are skipped or labelled as 0, increasing the number of contents with neutral rating. Manual investigation of neutral categories showed that most users were sending out warnings about activities on the web with regards to Reddit's ban, while praising how the developer(s) of Dread had the alternative environment ready in time for them to migrate. The posts with mixed sentiments can be seen in Table 8 in Appendix A.5.

Table 6. Negative sentiments found in Dread.

P	S	Text
-0.37	0.65	Anyone make it over here? Reddit is fucked, hope everyone makes it either over here or somewhere else
-0.6	0.7	reddit fucked us during the draw, but here are the results for lotto [...]
-0.23	0.59	[mods] censor any mention of my name, and yet actively promote scam vendors like [Vendor A] and [Vendor B]. Vendors who DOX customers, and selective scam by sending out empty packages. You cannot mention mine name, without automod deleting it immediately. Very blatant censorship from blatantly corrupt mod team. The cancer of reddit is officially spreading. Dread is dead

4.3   RQ3: Community Engagement

13 of the 20 Dread forums that we obtained information on showed an increase in per user engagement in the forums. On country-specific forums in particular, the posting activity rate had increased by a noticeable amount; an increase from 45.11% to 53.75% and from 20.37% to 44.6% in DarkNetMarketsNO and DNMUK, respectively. The overall subscription number of such forums is much lower than other major market forums but the users in it were more engaged in terms of contributing new posts. Table 9 in Appendix A.6 lists the total proportions (%) of user engagement in forums from the number of subscribers (S) per forum and the number of unique usernames (N) present in the corresponding forum.

On the other hand, four market-focused forums in Dread - including Tochka-FreeMarket, WallStreetMarket, LibertasMarket, and DarkNetMarkets - had particularly low numbers of contribution despite their high number of subscribers. It is possible that these forums were among the first to be created in Dread, and thus new Dread visitors subscribed as default options with no particular inclination to these actual markets. One can deduce that the ones that take the extra measure to find the country or drug-specific forums and that are knowledgeable enough to carry out discussions in these respective forums are the ones who actually have hands-on experience engaging in DNMs.

Across 14,523 unique usernames in Reddit and 5,136 in Dread, including those of identified moderators, there were 236 matching usernames appearing in the six months prior to and after the ban. In Dread, only 88 users out of the 236 matching usernames had mentioned the term "Reddit" in their posts. It may be that preservation of reputation between forums is not the major concern except for a particularly well known few, and securing one's anonymity is deemed more important for the users.

5 Discussion

5.1 Implications

Solidarity in Times of Uncertainty. Even with the sudden ban of several top forums and the nuisance of relocating to a new platform, there is a sense of increased comfort and reassurance among users in the new platform, as seen across wide majority of the sentiment analysis outputs; this may be relevant to both increasing chances of survival of the DNM community and the idea of having a discourse more free from prior policies.

Despite the fact that the size of the community is much smaller in Dread, there is an underlying assumption that users who are willing to put in the effort to migrate to the new platform are the kind of users that, in mass numbers, will help ensure the community survives through such unexpected changes. Dread's new environment may thus promote more intimacy and tacit trust amongst users who had been initially unhappy about Reddit's change of policy – a phenomenon similar to those seen in mental health subreddits and 4chan boards [4,9]. This is also aligned with the previous finding by Ladegaard [18] on how some DNM communities embrace a sense of non-commercial and altruistic culture, elevating the relationship beyond that of efficient trading of products, which had brought them together in the first place.

The analysed posts on forums show that users are willing to reach out and provide assistance to users who are not as experienced or knowledgeable in navigating around DNM markets at times of uncertainty and absence of information. We also see that core members of the community, such as the frequently mentioned *User A*, play a crucial role in preserving trust in a platform.

Key User Interests. The frequent terms illuminate general user concerns and trends that surfaced before and after the Reddit ban. The frequent appearance of *vendor, good,* and *quality* over the topics show that verification of vendor quality is one of the top interests of the users, alongside drug quality, shipping experiences, and payment mediums. Monero and bitcoin dominated discussion of the cryptocurrency topics revealing its prevalence in DNMs. These findings validate the use of LDA topics as proxies for understanding the common interests of the community.

Country-Specific Communities. One unexpected finding was that the country-specific forums in Dread demonstrated greater community contribution than other forums with a more general audience. There are several potential reasons for this. The physical proximity of drug sellers and buyers can make transactional process much easier for both parties [11], including a lower likelihood of package inspection. There may also be a higher degree of trust and bond for communities that are bound by their geographical region, which can concern language dialect, culture, and trends. Thus, the users may deem the country-specific communities more reliable at a time when information is scarce and users are acclimatising to the new setting. Consumers may also be conscious of differing laws in the prospective countries with regards to using a product.

5.2   Limitations

At the time of data collection, Dread was still an emerging community, and it is thus hard to predict whether the discussion themes and the user engagement rate will remain stable. Alternative websites, such as Voat or The Hub, were considered alongside Dread to alleviate this concern, but the number of posts in DNM-related forums in those websites were so low that it would not have contributed significantly to the existing data on Dread.

Topic modelling requires a number of topics to be specified manually, and thus such models necessarily involve an element of subjectivity. Excluding stopwords and lemmatisations have been argued to produce better topic model [26], but in our case stopwords appeared to result in more coherent and interpretable models.

For sentiment analysis, we suspect that a large portion of the neutral sentiment may have been influenced by the inability of TextBlob to handle negations, sarcasm, and expletives. This is a known limitation of general-purpose sentiment analysis tools, which can be partially alleviated by compiling lists of frequently occurring words and manually assigning them as positive or negative.

5.3   Future Work

Further observation of user activity on clearnet social media could help uncover any linkage of the darknet community with online criminal markets, beyond the scope of the illicit products. One could look into publicly accessible cybercriminal communities [28] to find how a ban in cybercriminal markets affects the communities' information sharing behaviour.

Encrypted chat applications as Telegram, Whatsapp, and Discord enable users to transition their talk from public forums to a still public, but seemingly more intimate chat groups. These applications come at a time when majority of the users are losing trust in large centralised structures due to the continuous disruption of the law enforcement and the fear of being scammed by vendors. The type of discourse that transpire in such mediums can reinforce a broader understanding of how the community's norms and values develop as a whole.

A   Appendices

A.1   Timeline of the number of postings

Forums were banned intermittently prior to March as seen by a gradual drop since December in Fig. 1. May's sudden drop is when the platform had a brief downtime. Reddit provided a much richer variety of DNM-related forums specialising in specific drugs and countries, and such details had not yet transferred over to Dread, including popular market forums as Agora, TradeRoute, and The-MajesticGarden. Reddit potentially had more passer-bys who subscribed to the forums out of fleeting curiosity, without intending to access the DNM themselves.

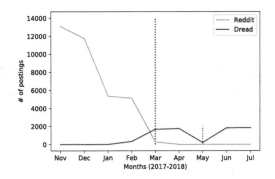

Fig. 1. Number of postings over the months (2017–2018) overlapping the ban

A.2   Document Word Counts

See Fig. 2.

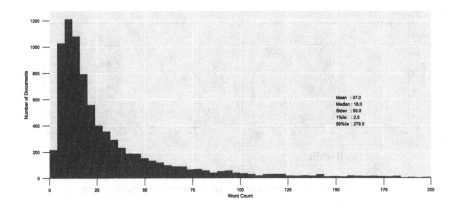

Fig. 2. Distribution of the word counts in documents to which the LDA was applied

A.3   Perplexity

In Fig. 3b, we obtained a string of negative bound values ranging between −8.115 and −8.150. Even though a lower perplexity is desired, the value likely denotes deterioration of the sample data from infinitesimal probabilities being converted to the log scale by Gensim. As a result, we found the number of topics for Dread by inspection rather than relying on the perplexity per se.

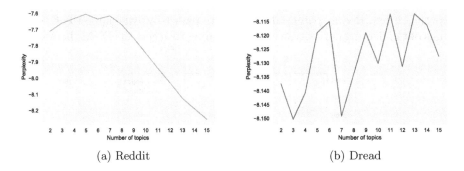

(a) Reddit   (b) Dread

Fig. 3. Perplexity results when run up to 15 topics

A.4   Histogram of Polarity

See Fig. 4 for the histogram of the polarity seen in Reddit and Dread. The common threshold of −0.1 < x < 0.1 for neutral gave an abnormally high level of positive sentiments, which weren't always the case upon inspection of the original posts by the authors, with 391 positive, 61 negative, and 299 neutral categories. To suit the histogram fit better, we adjusted the threshold upwards to −0.001 < x < 1.999 for the neutral category.

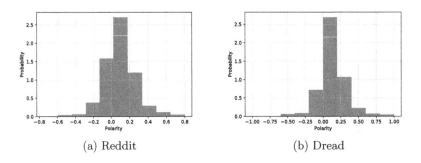

(a) Reddit   (b) Dread

Fig. 4. Histogram showing the probability of polarity rate

A.5   Extended Posts from Sentiment Analysis

Table 7 shows posts with positive or negative sentiments, from Sect. 4.2. Table 8 shows posts with mixed sentiments.

Table 7. Extended posts with positive or negative sentiments from Sect. 4.2.

P	S	Text
0.21	0.53	As you all know I have put a lot of hard work into this community, a lot of time, and put up with a lot of bs. I love this fucking place and its like a second home for me, long before being modded I was on everyday keeping up with banter, ads etc. Reddit became really shitty, users became really shity and even vendors became really shitty... What I have noticed in the last few weeks is a great thing, this community is not arguing, we are not picking fights, we are helping each other out, offering opinons, being honest [...] our community knows the rules, abides them and calls out ones that don't. I really feel like ALTHOUGH much smaller this community is much closer than it ever has been. I want to thank ALL of the vendors that took time to verify with me, I want to take time for the ads you are putting up, I want to thank our wonderful users for spreading reviews and getting names out there, we can only help each other [...]
0.37	0.54	being honest, the recent media attention that DNM's have been receiving in the last two/three years and the fact that reddit, an easy access cleannet site, was used to store lots of information related to darknet markets was not the greatest idea - why had no one thought for making a website like that before? but ye now that nearly every single sub-reddit is banned now, I see it as a good thing. Now kids wont be able to just go on reddit and learn how to buy and sell drugs literally in a day. I feel this is an opportunity as now its not as easy as a google search to find lots of information - but this will make it harder to verify vendors authenticity as there would be no reviews. (obvs can verify with PGP) [...] It honestly saddens me to see all these scammers and shitty vendors get away with so much nowadays
−0.03	0.65	So anyone who has made it this far is aware of the situation, so no need for me to repeat... Sad day for DNMs as a whole, its unfortunate that the mass of other subs couldn't contain their subs which IMO ultimately led to the shut down of EVERYTHING Our sub had no problems recently as we have been extremely on top of shit, but this is not tied to us, it was a reddit crack down. [...]

Table 8. Posts with mixed sentiment rating.

P	S	Text
0.19	0.68	[...] who trusts this onion? who's on it? how many users did r/darknetmarkets have before we were supposedly sent here? are these really the mods from that subreddit? was this place the backup plan all along? we all saw it coming i just never heard anything about where to go if shit hit the fan. seems great. convenient. well thought out. just dont trust it atm to be honest. vendor ad thread is an alright idea. i do know its a temporary solution so, its obviously not ideal. if vendors start coming here (even though its looking pretty sparse right now) we need some sort of database feature, specifying what market vendors on, products vendor has, vendors shipping location, etc. [...]
0.018	0.28	So I read a bunch of places all of the redditors from the DNM's that got closed down were moving en masse to Dread. But that hasn't seemed to happen in my estimation. So where is everyone now? DNMA's? The hub? Or am I mistaken, is Dread the place to be?
0.17	0.57	Since most of us here are seeking asylum after the great Reddit ban of March 21st 2018 there no searching history to be able to look up inside jokes, infamous people events, etc. the newbies are very much OOTL. [...]
0.17	0.60	Hey! We are still alive and kicking despite the man coming down on us all. I am surprised it took THIS long for them to rid reddit of our glorious freedom fighting communities. Darn it. [...]
0.16	0.58	Hey everyone, took a loooong break since everything was banned from reddit. Now I'm fucking back, under a different name, and I'm so excited to spend all my free time on here again [...]
0.15	0.52	Any chance we can get this list of ok markets and lists of ones to avoid and they whys? I'm not sure if this information was backed up before The Great Reddit ban of 2018. Or if it's got to be created all new and from memory but so far I've seen a couple of marketplaces that I know where listed as being no good and would hate to lose our new sanctuary place so soon with LE getting all our new stuff
0.12	0.43	I like dread quite a lot since reddit banned all sourcing related subreddits. but considering that the site gets ddosed and might not want to much publicity i would understand if it might be better to keep it low key. what do you think. should I share this as much as I can or just with well trusted people? Interested in hearing your opinions on the subject
0	0	So as we've all noticed it seems that reddit has turned into a Hitler style iron fist rule
0	0	Everyone delete our reddit accounts?

A.6   Proportion of the User Engagement

See Table 9 to see the proportion of user engagement. As mentioned in the methodology, multiple Reddit forums corresponded to a same Dread forum, and so we accumulated the alternative forums to reflect the average number of user engagement across different forums that had appeared in the forum's posts.

Table 9. The proportion (%) of user engagement by subscription rate, based on the list of main banned subreddits and its equivalent forums present in Dread, alongside the number of subscribers (S) per forum and the number of unique usernames (N).

Reddit	S	N	%	%	N	S	Dread
TochkaFreeMarket	89	44	49.44	0.36	44	12,215	TochkaFreeMarket
ZionMarket,	124	49	40.40	17.50	7	40	zionmarket
Zion_Market	252	104					
RaptureMarket	291	114	39.18	24.21	91	376	RaptureMarket
WallStreetMarket	370	81	21.90	5.34	693	12,982	WallStreetMarket
DreamMarketDarknet,	950	309	21.58	28.25	259	917	DreamMarket
dnDreamMarket,	281	23					
DreamMarketplace	508	122					
LibertasMarket	363	75	20.67	0.42	51	12,097	LibertasMarket
DarkNetMarkets,	178,360	4,859	11.17	10.88	1480	13,603	DarkNetMarkets
DarkNetMarketsLinks,	476	200					
DarkWebMarkets,	5,941	15					
Darknet_Markets,	9,080	538					
TorMarketplaces	959	47					
fakeid	35,000	3,511	**10.03**	**20.93**	95	454	FakeID
DankNation	18,562	1,585	**8.54**	**29.94**	355	1,186	DankNation
murderhomelesspeople	772	24	**3.11**	**11.32**	50	442	murderhomelesspeople
Xanaxcartel	4,736	1,076	**22.72**	**46.33**	340	734	Xanax
RCSources	25,655	2,087	**8.13**	**33.26**	293	881	rcsources
EU_RCSources	2,710	431	**15.90**	**3.90**	3	77	EUrcsources
DarkNetMarketsNoobs	54,780	1523	**2.79**	**14.90**	98	658	DarknetMarketsNoobs
DarkNetMarketsNO	1,113	502	**45.11**	**53.75**	158	294	DarkNetMarketsNO
DarkMarketsBrasil	1,065	265	**24.89**	**49.68**	77	155	DarkMarketsBrasil
DNMUK	8,940	1,821	**20.37**	**44.6**	462	1,036	DNMUK
DNMIndia	566	64	**11.31**	**31.15**	19	61	DarknetMarketsIndia
DarkNetMarketsNZ	677	120	**17.73**	**30.71**	35	114	DarknetMarketsNZ
darknetmarketsOZ	4,170	659	**15.81**	**22.5**	9	40	DarknetmarketsOZ

References

1. Reddit in uproar after staff sacking. BBC News, July 2015. https://www.bbc.com/news/technology-33379571
2. Aoyama, H., Constable, J.: Word length frequency and distribution in English: part I. Prose. Lit. Linguist. Comput. **14**(3), 339–358 (1999). https://doi.org/10.1093/llc/14.3.339
3. Armona, L.: Measuring the demand effects of formal and informal communication: evidence from online markets for illicit drugs. ArXiv e-prints, February 2018. https://arxiv.org/abs/1802.08778v1

4. Bernstein, M.S., Monroy-Hernández, A., Harry, D., André, P., Panovich, K., Vargas, G.G.: 4chan and/b: an analysis of anonymity and ephemerality in a large online community. In: Proceedings of the Fifth International AAAI Conference on Weblogs and Social Media (ICWSM) (2011)

5. Blei, D.M., Ng, A.Y., Jordan, M.I.: Latent dirichlet allocation. J. Mach. Learn. Res. **3**, 993–1022 (2003). http://www.jmlr.org/papers/v3/blei03a.html

6. Buskirk, J.V., et al.: The recovery of online drug markets following law enforcement and other disruptions. Drug Alcohol Depend. **173**, 159–162 (2017). https://doi.org/10.1016/j.drugalcdep.2017.01.004, http://www.sciencedirect.com/science/article/pii/S0376871617300741

7. Chancellor, S., Pater, J.A., Clear, T., Gilbert, E., De Choudhury, M.: #thyghgapp: Instagram content moderation and lexical variation in pro-eating disorder communities. In: Proceedings of the 19th ACM Conference on Computer-Supported Cooperative Work & Social Computing, CSCW 2016, pp. 1201–1213. ACM, New York (2016). https://doi.org/10.1145/2818048.2819963

8. Chandrasekharan, E., Pavalanathan, U., Srinivasan, A., Glynn, A., Eisenstein, J., Gilbert, E.: You can't stay here: the efficacy of reddit's 2015 ban examined through hate speech. Proc. ACM Hum.-Comput. Interact. **1**(CSCW), 31:1–31:22 (2017). https://doi.org/10.1145/3134666

9. Choudhury, M.D., De, S.: Mental health discourse on reddit: self-disclosure, social support, and anonymity. In: Proceedings of the Eighth International AAAI Conference on Weblogs and Social Media (ICWSM) (2014). https://www.aaai.org/ocs/index.php/ICWSM/ICWSM14/paper/view/8075

10. Dijck, J.V.: The Culture of Connectivity: A Critical History of Social Media. Oxford University Press, Oxford (2013)

11. Dittus, M., Wright, J., Graham, M.: Platform criminalism: the "last-mile" geography of the darknet market supply chain. In: Proceedings of the 2018 World Wide Web Conference, WWW 2018, pp. 277–286. International World Wide Web Conferences Steering Committee (2018). https://doi.org/10.1145/3178876.3186094

12. Durkheim, E.: The Division of Labor in Society. Translated by G. Simpson. Free Press, Collier Macmillan, New York (1964)

13. Durkheim, E.: The Rules of Sociological Method: And Selected Texts on Sociology and Its Method. Free Press (2014). Free press trade paperback edition

14. Duxbury, S.W., Haynie, D.L.: Building them up, breaking them down: topology, vendor selection patterns, and a digital drug market's robustness to disruption. Soc. Netw. **52**, 238–250 (2018)

15. Gorodnichenko, Y., Pham, T., Talavera, O.: Social media, sentiment and public opinions: evidence from #Brexit and #USElection. Working Paper 24631, National Bureau of Economic Research, May 2018. https://doi.org/10.3386/w24631, http://www.nber.org/papers/w24631

16. Hardy, R.A., Norgaard, J.R.: Reputation in the internet black market: an empirical and theoretical analysis of the deep web. J. Inst. Econ. **12**(3), 515–539 (2016). https://doi.org/10.1017/S1744137415000454

17. Hawkins, J.B., et al.: Measuring patient-perceived quality of care in us hospitals using twitter. BMJ Qual. Saf. **25**(6), 404–413 (2016). https://doi.org/10.1136/bmjqs-2015-004309. https://qualitysafety.bmj.com/content/25/6/404

18. Ladegaard, I.: "I pray that we will find a way to carry on this dream": how a law enforcement crackdown united an online community. Crit. Sociol. (2017). https://doi.org/10.1177/0896920517735670

19. Ladegaard, I.: We know where you are, what you are doing and we will catch you: testing deterrence theory in digital drug markets. Br. J. Criminol. **58**(2), 414–433 (2018). https://doi.org/10.1093/bjc/azx021

20. Loria, S.: Textblob documentation page (2018). https://textblob.readthedocs.org/en/dev/index.html. Accessed 11 July 2019

21. Massanari, A.: #Gamergate and the fappening: how reddit's algorithm, governance, and culture support toxic technocultures. New Media Soc. **19**(3), 329–346 (2017). https://doi.org/10.1177/1461444815608807

22. Matias, J.N.: Going dark: social factors in collective action against platform operators in the reddit blackout. In: Proceedings of the 2016 CHI Conference on Human Factors in Computing Systems, CHI 2016, pp. 1138–1151. ACM, New York (2016). https://doi.org/10.1145/2858036.2858391

23. Newell, E., et al.: User migration in online social networks: a case study on reddit during a period of community unrest. In: Proceedings of the Tenth International Conference on Web and Social Media (ICWSM), Cologne, Germany, pp. 279–288, May 2016

24. Reddit-Policy: New addition to site-wide rules regarding the use of Reddit to conduct transactions (2018). https://www.reddit.com/r/announcements/comments/863xcj/new_addition_to_sitewide_rules_regarding_the_use/. Accessed 10 Aug 2018

25. Schifanella, R., de Juan, P., Tetreault, J., Cao, L.: Detecting sarcasm in multimodal social platforms. In: Proceedings of the 24th ACM International Conference on Multimedia, MM 2016, pp. 1136–1145. ACM, New York (2016). https://doi.org/10.1145/2964284.2964321

26. Schofield, A., Magnusson, M., Mimno, D.: Pulling out the stops: Rethinking stopword removal for topic models. In: Proceedings of the 15th Conference of the European Chapter of the Association for Computational Linguistics: Volume 2, Short Papers, Valencia, Spain, pp. 432–436. Association for Computational Linguistics, April 2017. https://www.aclweb.org/anthology/E17-2069

27. Schuth, A., Marx, M., de Rijke, M.: Extracting the discussion structure in comments on news-articles. In: Proceedings of the 9th Annual ACM International Workshop on Web Information and Data Management, WIDM 2007, pp. 97–104. ACM, New York (2007). https://doi.org/10.1145/1316902.1316919

28. Talos, C.: Hiding in Plain Sight (2019). https://blog.talosintelligence.com/2019/04/hiding-in-plain-sight.html. Accessed 06 Apr 2019

29. Weninger, T., Zhu, X.A., Han, J.: An exploration of discussion threads in social news sites: a case study of the reddit community. In: Proceedings of the 2013 IEEE/ACM International Conference on Advances in Social Networks Analysis and Mining, ASONAM 2013, pp. 579–583. ACM, New York (2013). https://doi.org/10.1145/2492517.2492646

A Longitudinal Study on Twitter-Based Forecasting of Five Dutch National Elections

Eric Sanders[1(✉)] and Antal van den Bosch[1,2]

[1] CLS/CLST, Radboud University, Nijmegen, The Netherlands
e.sanders@let.ru.nl
[2] KNAW Meertens Institute, Amsterdam, The Netherlands
antal.van.den.bosch@meertens.knaw.nl

Abstract. We report on an eight-year longitudinal study of predicting the outcome of elections based on party mentions in tweets. Five Dutch national elections for the parliament and senate between 2011 and 2019 were examined. Configurations with four parameters were tested. For three elections, reasonably accurate predictions can be obtained that are under twice the error of the classic polls, but only after post-hoc optimization. When the same optimal parameter configuration is used for all elections, the results worsen.

Keywords: Twitter · Election forecasting · Longitudinal study

1 Introduction

A range of studies have reported attempts to predict the outcome of elections based on counts in tweets [7]. Some claim success [3,10,20,21], others report failure [1,8] or are undecided [14,18]. All studies have one element in common: they study only one election, except for a few studies that report on predicting two or three elections in different countries at the same time [4,12,19]. As Gayo-Avello points out, "predicting" the outcome of an election after the election is not a convincing proof that it works: "you cannot (consistently) predict elections from Twitter!" [6]; the model can be tweaked afterwards to match the prediction with the results. As Jungherr et al. showed in [11] that the prediction of the German elections by Tumisjan et al. in [20] was too optimistic because of unrealistic choices in their experiment design.

The study presented in this paper seeks to critically evaluate the claim that only through post-hoc and unrealistic optimization, tweet counts may be used to predict election outcomes. We do so by examining a series of similar elections from the same country. We investigated five elections for the Dutch parliament and senate that took place between 2011 and 2019. First we investigated if we could approximate the outcome of elections based on tweet counts for five different elections, following a standard approach. Second, we optimized a set of

© Springer Nature Switzerland AG 2019
I. Weber et al. (Eds.): SocInfo 2019, LNCS 11864, pp. 128–142, 2019.
https://doi.org/10.1007/978-3-030-34971-4_9

parameters on the five elections to see whether an optimal configuration could be found that would score high on all five elections or whether for each election a different optimal setup would be needed. As an additional evaluation to comparing the Twitter-based predictions to the election results, we also compare them to predicted results obtained with classical polling methods.

When we tried to predict the Dutch parliamentary elections of 2012 based on party mentions in tweets we reported moderate success in [14]. However, we were already aware of criticism on Twitter-based forecasting of election outcomes. Gayo-Avello raises several points of attention in various papers [5,7]. Although we can not address all his points in this study, we focused on the point concerning post-hoc optimization of a winning model. We did not take into the potential effect of sentiment analysis and demographic statistics in this study. For sentiment analysis, usually simple methods are used that are reported to hardly improve prediction [9]. In other work, we described our method to use demographic statistics in predicting election results from tweets [15]. We restricted ourselves to gender and age, as other demographic features are virtually impossible to get from both elections and tweets. Again, we showed that taking demographic statistics into account does not really help forecasting the elections. In sum, in this paper we focus on simple count-based prediction; the parameters we optimize all regulate an direct aspect of what precisely to count.

This paper is organized as follows. In Sect. 2 we explain the Dutch electoral system and show the elections and their outcomes that are used in this study. In Sect. 3 the set-up of our experiments is explained, and the results of the experiments are shown in Sect. 4. In Sect. 5 we reflect on the outcome of this study, and we conclude in Sect. 6.

2   Dutch Elections

In the Netherlands, four types of elections take place: (1) national parliament, (2) provinces/senate, (3) municipality, and (4) European parliament. European elections are held every five years, while the other elections are in principle held every four years. The elections we study in this paper are the national parliamentary and province/senate elections. Politically speaking they are related as they determine the seat distributions in the two chambers of the Dutch parliament. In the national parliamentary elections the members of the *Tweede Kamer* (TK), consisting of 150 seats, are directly elected by Dutch citizens older than 18 years of age (voting in the Netherlands is voluntary). Several parties participate in the elections and after the elections a coalition of parties forms a government; typically this coalition has more than half of the seats. In the province/senate elections the *Provinciale Staten* (PS) are elected. These are the local parliaments of the 12 provinces in the Netherlands. In a second phase of the same elections, three months later, the *Eerste Kamer* (EK), the national senate consisting of 75 seats, is elected by the members of the PS. Because all laws have to pass both the TK and the EK, both elections are of national importance; also, the government coalition is handicapped if they do not have the majority in both chambers. In the remainder of this paper we will refer to these two elections as TK and EK. The elections of the European parliament and the municipalities are quite different in nature. Many other political parties, e.g. local parties, participate in these elections.

The elections studied in the experiments in this paper are the EK of 2011, 2015 and 2019, and the TK of 2012 and 2017. Table 1 lists all parties that gained seats in these elections, along with the percentage of votes they received. The table also lists the turnout, which is generally higher for TK.

Table 1. Results of five Dutch elections with percentages and number of seats for all parties that got a seat in the real elections or in the Twitter predictions

	2011 EK		2012 TK		2015 EK		2017 TK		2019 EK	
Turnout	56.0%	7.0 M	76.6%	9.4 M	47.8%	6.1 M	81.6%	10.6 M	56.0%	7.0M
	%votes	#seats	%	#	%	#	%	#	%	#
VVD	19.6	16	26.6	41	15.9	13	21.3	33	14.1	12
PVDA	17.3	14	24.8	38	10.1	8	5.7	9	9.9	7
CDA	14.1	11	8.5	13	14.7	12	12.4	19	13.5	9
PVV	12.4	10	10.1	15	11.7	9	13.1	20	7.5	5
SP	10.2	8	9.7	15	11.7	9	9.1	14	6.5	4
D66	8.4	5	8.0	12	12.5	10	12.2	19	7.1	6
GroenLinks	6.3	5	2.3	4	5.4	4	9.1	14	10.5	9
ChristenUnie	3.3	2	3.1	5	4.0	3	3.4	5	5.5	4
50Plus	2.3	1	1.9	2	3.4	2	3.1	4	2.8	2
SGP	2.2	1	2.0	3	2.8	2	2.1	3	2.6	1
PVDD	1.9	1	1.9	2	3.5	2	3.2	5	3.8	3
DENK							2.1	3		
FVD							1.8	2	15.8	13
PPNL							0.3	0		
VNL							0.4	0		
Artikel1							0.3	0		
GeenPeil							0.1	0		
Other	2.1	1	1.0	0	4.4	1	0.5	0	0.4	0
Total	100	75	100	150	100	75	100	150	100	75

The parties VVD (conservative liberals), PVDA (social democrats), CDA (christian democrats), PVV (anti muslims), SP (socialists), D66 (social liberals), GroenLinks (greens), ChristenUnie (socially conservative christians), 50PLUS (pensioners), SGP (reformed christians), PVDD (animal rights) gained a seat in all elections. The parties DENK (muslims) and FVD (national conservative) are new parties that participated successfully in 2015 for the first time. PPNL, VNL, Artikel1 and GeenPeil did not gain a seat in the 2015 election, but got a virtual seat in the Twitter polls and are therefore included. The 'other' party in the table that has a seat in the EK is an independent party that is elected by provincial senators that do not belong to one of the national parties. It is ignored in the experiments.

After the second world war until 1998 the political landscape in the Netherlands was pretty stable. VVD, PVDA and CDA (or the parties of which CDA is a merger party) always amassed at least two thirds of the votes, and two of them always had a majority and formed the government coalition together. In a few cases one or two other parties joined the coalition, although they were not necessary for a majority. From 2002 onwards the situation has shifted. New, so called "populist" parties, gained a fair amount of seats and the three traditional big parties fell to new lows. In 2017, VVD, PVDA and CDA received only 40% of the votes together. Voters change from one party to another much more easily than before, resulting in big shifts in power ratios. E.g. the PVDA went from 38 seats at TK 2012 to 9 seats at TK 2017. In the last election the populist party Forum voor Democratie (FVD) became the largest of the country where it did not exist yet three years earlier.

3   Experiments

3.1   Count Parties in Tweets

The tweets used in the experiments are from TwiNL [17], a large collection of automatically harvested Dutch tweets. It covers an estimated 40% of all Dutch tweets posted since December 2010. In our experiments we collected all tweets containing the name of a Dutch political party from 25 days before election day until the final day before the elections. We only searched for parties that were either significantly in the news or that were included in the polls. Parties were searched via regular expression of the common names of the parties. These are mostly abbreviations and sometimes full names. Most party names are so long that the full name is never used, certainly in tweets. The search was case-insensitive. In a few cases variants with an error in the name (e.g. 'voor' (for) instead of 'van' (of) and vice versa) were used. For abbreviations, variants with and without dots between the letters were matched. For example, 'pvda', 'P.v.d.A', and even 'p.VDa' all match for 'Partij van de Arbeid'. After some initial investigation of the names that were used in the tweets to refer to the political parties, we used the regular expressions in Table 2.

Some of the party names have other meanings. The abbreviations GL and CU can mean 'good luck' and 'see you', but these are not often used in that sense and regarded as little noise in the data. A considerably larger problem is the ambiguity of 'Denk'. Besides the name of the political party is it a conjugation of the verb 'denken' (to think). To circumvent this problem we built an automatic classifier (SVM), trained on manually annotated data, with an accuracy of over 90%. The errors of the classifier are in both ways (verb classified as party and vice versa). We estimate the count for 'denk' as political party at least 95% accurate.

The procedure for counting party names is as follows. All the tweets from 25 days before election day until the final day before election day in the TwiNL corpus are searched for occurrences of the names of all political parties. The corpus is in json format with metadata. If there is a match, the (text of the) tweet

Table 2. Regular expressions used to detect parties in tweets

Party (short and full name)	Regular expressions
VVD Volkspartij voor Vrijheid en Democratie	"v\.?v\.?d\.?"
PVDA Partij van de Arbeid	"p\.?v\.?d\.?a\.?", "partij\s+v(oor\s+—an\s+—\.)?d(e—\.)?\s+arbeid"
CDA Christen Democratisch Appel	"c\.?d\.?a\.?"
PVV Partij Voor de Vrijheid	"p\.?v\.?v\.?", "partij\s+v(oor\s+—an\s+—\.)?d(e—\.)?\s+vrijheid"
SP Socialistische Partij	"s\.?p\.?"
D66 Democraten 1966	"d\'?66"
GroenLinks	"g\.?l\.?", "groen.?links"
ChristenUnie	"c\.?u\.?", "christen.?unie"
50Plus	"50[^\d]?\s(\+—plus)*"
SGP Staatkundige Gereformeerde Partij	"s\.?g\.?p\.?"
PVDD Partij Voor De Dieren	"p\.?v\.?d\.?d\.?", "partij\s+v(oor\s+—an\s+—\.)?d(e—\.)?\s+dieren"
DENK	"denk"
FVD Forum Voor Democratie	"f\.?v\.?d\.?", "forum\s*v(oor)?\s*democratie"
PPNL PiratenPartij NederLand	"p\.?p\.?n\.?l\.?", "piraten\s*partij"
VNL Voor NederLand	"v\.?n\.?l\.?", "voor\s*nederland"
Art1kel Artikel1	"art1kel", "artikel\s*1"
GeenPeil	"geen\s*peil"

is saved together with tweet id, the name or names of the political party/parties, whether the tweet is a retweet or a reply, whether it contains a url and the date and time of the tweet. In a second phase, the denk-classifier will classify the tweets containing 'denk'. If the classifier classifies 'denk' as a verb it will be removed from the list of parties in that tweet. Equation 1 shows how the percentages of tweets per party are computed.

$$Perc(p) = \frac{\sum_{d=1}^{M} TM(d)(p)}{\sum_{i=1}^{N} \sum_{d=1}^{M} TM(d)(i)} \tag{1}$$

Where $Perc(p)$ is the percentage of mentions of party p, $TM(d)(i)$ is the number of times party i is mentioned in the tweets on day d, M is the total number of days, N is the total number of parties

When computing percentages of party mentions or election outcome, we only take parties into account that get a virtual seat in the tweet counts and/or an actual seat in the elections. All other mentions and votes are ignored.

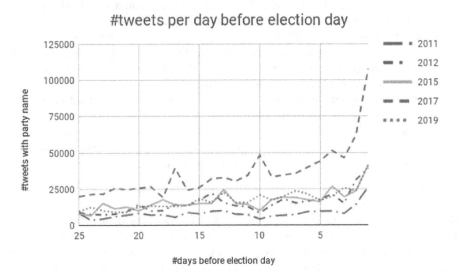

Fig. 1. Number of tweets per day before election day for the five elections

See Fig. 1 for the number of tweets with at least one political party mentioned for the 25 days before the day of the elections for the five elections. For all elections, the number of tweets increases slowly towards the day of the elections and is rarely below 5,000 tweets. The elections of 2011 generated the least number of tweets. Twitter was not as big then as it would become later and these were the elections for the provinces/senate, which are not as popular as those of the national parliament. The elections that were most tweeted about were those of 2017, when Twitter was huge and the elections were for the national parliament and had the highest turnout of the five (see Table 1). The number of tweets with a party name in it exceeded the 100,000 the day before the elections in 2017.

3.2   Parameters

Four parameters determine the set-up of a single experiment:

– The number of days before the election day that are taken into the counts. One would expect the closer to the actual election day, the more precise count will be. On the other hand, a higher volume might also lead to a more

precise count. Also, sudden peaks in counts of one party (for whatever reason), will be less influential with more days in the counts. We experimented with $[1, 2, 3, 4, 5, 6, 7, 8, 9, 10, 15, 20, 25]$ days of tweets before the election day.
– Whether retweets and replies are taken into the counts or not.
  Retweets and replies are a different kind of tweets than original tweets. They support an original tweet and in that sense do they mostly reflect the meaning of the retweeter. There is much randomness in retweeting, however. Leaving out retweets and replies might yield a more accurate count of actual support.
– Whether tweets with URL are taken into the counts or not.
  Tweets with an URL are often a post from the page of another website. In our experiments these are often news websites. These tell less about a person's opinion or support than an original tweet. Therefore we test whether counts are more accurate when we leave them out.
– Whether tweets with more than one party mentions are taken into account, or only tweets with one party mentioned.
  One can only vote for one party. Thus it makes sense to only count tweets in which one party is mentioned. On the other hand, one can support several parties and not have decided which party one will vote for.

There are also a few parameters that we do not take into account. We do not look at sentiment and speaker demography. Sentiment analysis and speaker demography is used in predicting election outcomes based on tweets [15] by taking only positive tweets in account. This produces moderately positive results. It goes beyond the scope of this paper though, in which we want to investigate whether with simple methods a correlation can be found between party mentions in tweets and election results. Sentiment and demography are far from simple to determine, and since the improvements on results are only minor at best, we decided to leave them out of our experiments.

4   Results

The results of comparing counts in tweets and election results are often given in Mean Absolute Error (MAE). This is the average over all parties of the absolute difference between the percentage of the counts in the tweets and the results in the elections. We argue that this is not a good measure, because the number becomes smaller (thus more optimistic) when there are a lot of small parties of which the difference between the counts and the actual results is small, because of the high denominator. Therefore we do not average the parties and show results of the total Absolute Error (AE). That is the total sum over all parties of the positive difference between the election result of a party and the predicted result. In our case we give the AE in percentage points instead of number of seats, because the number of seats varies between TK and EK. See Eq. 2 for the computation of the Absolute Error.

$$AE = \sum_{i=1}^{N} |Perc_{el}(i) - Perc_{tm}(i)| \tag{2}$$

Where AE is the Absolute Error, $Perc_{el}(i)$, the percentage of the votes for party i in the elections, $Perc_{tm}(i)$ the percentage of mentions of party i in the tweets and N is the total number of parties.

One of the criticisms from Jungherr et al. on the work by Tumisjans et al. was that they had not included the Pirate Party in their prediction. The Pirate Party had a high social media presence, also on Twitter, but did not get seats in the German parliament. That could not be known beforehand. By not including them in the counts, they were getting unrealistic results, claimed Jungherr [11]. In our experiments we included all parties that got a seat according to the tweet counts, whether or not they earned a seat in the elections. This way all significant errors are included in our error measurement and only errors smaller than one seat in the prediction or in the elections are missed.

We computed the lowest absolute errors by computing the AE of each possible configuration by doing a grid search over all parameters. We determined the lowest possible AE and best configuration for each election separately and also the overall best configuration and lowest AE. This is the one configuration that scores the lowest AE on average over all elections. Finally, we also computed the AE of the prediction by the same leading polling organisation for each election.[1]

Table 3 lists the AEs for each year of the prediction of the best configuration per election, overall and of the polls. The scores with all parties included can be found in Tables 6, 7 and 8 in the Appendix. The best configurations leading to these AEs can be found in Table 4.

Table 3. Absolute error for the five elections of the best configuration per year, the best overall configuration and of the polls

	2011 EK	2012 TK	2015 EK	2017 TK	2019 EK
AE (%) best configuration per year	23.8	18.0	20.7	32.8	40.2
AE (%) best configuration overall	29.4	23.8	28.2	41.5	45.4
AE (%) polls	16.8	11.9	12.5	17.7	14.9

As can be seen in Table 3, the AE for the parliamentary elections of 2012 was the lowest of the five with a score of 18.0. This was the first election we investigated, and reported about in [14]. The best scoring Twitter-based AE of 2015 and 2011 are only 2.7 and 5.8 higher than that of 2012 (first line of Table 3), but the AE of the two most recent election are 14.8 and 22.2 higher, and can be considered outright unreliable. Note that the optimal parameter configurations (Table 4) are quite different for the five elections. Notably, the number of days taken into account before the election day differs substantially for each model. The only feature that is constant is exclusion of retweets. The AE of the overall

---

[1] https://home.noties.nl/peil/.

Table 4. Configuration that gives the lowest AE for each year and over all years

	#days	#parties	Urls	Retweets replies
2011	5	All	Exclude	Exclude
2012	4	All	Include	Exclude
2015	1	One	Exclude	Exclude
2017	20	All	Exclude	Exclude
2019	25	All	Include	Exclude
Overall	7	All	Include	Exclude

best scoring configuration is 6.6% higher on average compared to the score of the optimal setting per year. The polls outperform the Twitter-based forecast in all circumstances.

We also inspected the best scoring parameters, averaged over all other parameters, per year. See Fig. 2 for the average AE per number of days included in the counts for each year.

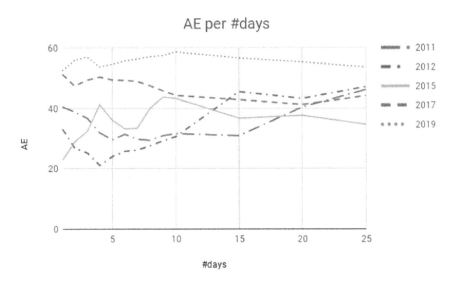

Fig. 2. Absolute Error per number of days averaged over all other parameters for the five elections

Three trends can be seen in the figure. For 2011 and 2012, the AE first reduces to a minimum at 5 or 6 days and then goes up again. 2015 shows an opposite trend, first up and then down, but starts with the minimum at only one day included in the counts. The AE of the elections of 2017 and 2019 are quite stable with a minimum AE at 20 and 1 days included respectively.

Table 5 shows for each parameter the AE averaged over all other parameters. The first two rows with results indicate that including tweets with multiple parties mentioned always score better and also by a fairly large margin. The difference between including or excluding urls and retweets/replies is much smaller and not consistent over the years. Only in 2019 it really matters whether or not urls and retweets/replies are included.

Table 5. Absolute Error per parameter averaged over all other parameters for the five elections

	2011	2012	2015	2017	2019
Multiparty	**31.0**	**28.4**	**35.3**	**42.1**	**53.4**
Monoparty	37.9	34.0	36.0	52.0	58.0
Exclude urls	**34.2**	31.6	38.2	**46.6**	57.9
Include urls	34.7	**30.8**	**33.2**	47.5	**53.5**
Exclude retweets	**33.6**	32.4	**34.7**	**45.3**	**47.8**
Include retweets	35.3	**30.0**	36.6	48.8	63.6

5 Discussion

Our golden standard in these experiments is the outcome of the elections. An AE of 0 would mean a perfect prediction. This is unrealistic and therefore, we also compare our results with one of the traditional pollers. These have a longstanding reputation in predicting the outcome of elections and are in general reliable indications of voter preference. If we could approach or even beat these, we can claim to be successful.

Table 3 shows the absolute errors of the polls compared to the Twitter-based AEs. As mentioned earlier, the polling results are taken from the oldest and most famous poller in the Netherlands, Maurice de Hond [2]. There are other polling organizations, however the difference is small in general and the polls by De Hond are as good as the others. The polls are from the day before election day, except for 2015. That year the most recent poll before the elections is from three days before election day. Note that the polls are originally in number of seats, which gives a slight inaccuracy when converted to percentages.

If we compare the AE of the polls with the AE of optimal configuration of the party counts in tweets one could claim moderate success for the first three years. The AE of the Twitter prediction is about 7% worse than the polls in 2011, 2012 and 2015. The problem is though that these best possible configurations were decided afterwards. If we compare the results with the same configuration for all years the difference is doubled in the best case, which is also decided afterwards. In that case, the AE of Twitter prediction is at least twice that of the polls. For 2017 and 2019 the difference is 15% and 25% respectively and already twice as big for the best possible configuration.

These figures show that it is possible to claim moderate success in predicting the outcome from elections based on tweets, but only in single cases and when configuring the model afterwards, since there is no way in knowing what the ideal configuration would look like beforehand. When using a constant configuration, the results are too poor to call them successful.

The underlying question remains, what do the party counts in tweets represent? Why do they seem to reflect election outcome to a certain extent in some cases and are far from it in other cases, where a 'case' can be both an individual party or an entire election? The answer probably lies in the direction of the arguments put forward by Murthy [13], who claims that tweets are mostly more reactive than predictive, e.g. to news and current affairs. People react on Twitter on what they see on television, read in the newspapers and elsewhere on the internet. This may have a fairly high correlation with the popularity of political parties and hence the election outcome. This is not so strange since popular parties are often talked about. However, parties may be talked about when they are not popular (anymore). E.g. in the parliamentary elections of 2015, the PVDA was the third party in Twitter mentions, because it was one of the two parties in the government coalition. Their voters, however, were disappointed by their policy, and in the elections they came out as seventh party with half the percentage of votes compared to mentions on Twitter (see Table 6).

Another factor in the difference between party mentions on Twitter and election outcome is difference in effort that parties or their followers invest in social media presence. Parties such as the Pirate Party (PPNL) and GroenLinks are known to be very active on Twitter, which results in overly positive Twitter predictions. On the other hand, the party 50Plus represents the elderly who are known to be less active on Twitter [16] and are consistently scoring too low in the Twitter prediction.

The Dutch electoral system is quite different from other elections that have been predicted with Twitter. Especially the number of parties that participate is large compared to most elections. Often, only the winner of two candidates has to be selected. That makes that our experiments and conclusions do not automatically generalise to all other elections, although we think we have a strong point in claiming that success in predicting one election does not necessarily means success in predicting other elections.

6   Conclusion

In this paper we described an eight-year longitudinal study of the prediction of election results based on how often political parties are mentioned in tweets in the period before the elections. We examined five similar Dutch elections from the period 2011–2019. Our prediction models were constrained by four parameters: (1) the number of days from which tweets are included, (2) inclusion or exclusion of retweets and replies, (3) inclusion or exclusion of urls, (4) inclusion or exclusion of tweets with more then one party mentioned. The results, measured in total absolute error, show that for three individual elections moderate results can be obtained, but only after tweaking the model post-hoc in the optimal configuration. When the same (optimal) model for all elections is used, the results drop considerably. From the parameters we used, the number of days and the number of parties included make a difference, while inclusion or exclusion of urls and retweets/replies appears not to do so in general.

From these results we conclude that predicting election outcome by counting tweets is not straightforward, especially not consistently over various elections. Our method was relatively simple and we ignored parameters that might have improved the results, such as sentiment analysis and demographical statistics, but we expect our conclusion would hold if we would have included them, based on previous experiments with these.

A suggested path for future research is to find out what the party mentions in tweets correlate with more precisely. We plan to look into the hypothesis that there is a strong correlation between the tweet counts and the publication patterns of news media such as television, newspapers and online news websites.

Appendix

A   Absolute Errors for all parties

Table 6. Results per party and Absolute Error for all elections of the configuration that scores best for that particular election (see Table 4)

	2011 EK		2012 TK		2015 EK		2017 TK		2019 EK	
	%election	%twitter	%el	%tw	%el	%tw	%el	%tw	%el	%tw
VVD	20.0	16.7	26.7	21.2	16.7	16.6	21.6	15.2	14.1	16.1
PVDA	17.7	13.1	25.0	23.7	10.6	13.0	5.8	11.7	9.9	7.3
CDA	14.4	14.2	8.6	9.2	15.4	11.5	12.6	9.0	13.5	7.8
PVV	12.7	21.4	10.2	9.9	12.3	14.3	13.3	15.1	7.5	9.7
SP	10.4	7.7	9.7	10.7	12.2	9.0	9.2	5.7	6.5	5.7
D66	8.5	8.7	8.1	7.0	13.0	14.4	12.4	9.8	7.1	14.3
GroenLinks	6.4	7.5	2.4	7.5	5.6	5.7	9.3	9.6	10.5	15.4
ChristenUnie	3.4	3.9	3.2	3.1	4.2	2.9	2.5	2.5	5.5	5.2
50Plus	2.4	1.8	1.9	1.9	3.5	1.6	3.2	3.1	2.8	1.5
SGP	2.2	1.7	2.1	2.2	2.9	5.7	2.1	2.0	2.6	1.7
PVDD	1.9	3.4	1.9	2.7	3.6	5.3	3.2	5.5	3.8	2.0
DENK							2.1	3.1	0.4	4.2
FVD							1.8	1.7	15.8	9.2
PPNL			0.3	1.7			0.3	1.7		
VNL							0.4	2.2		
Artikel1							0.3	0.8		
GeenPeil							0.1	1.2		
AE		23.8		18.0		20.7		32.8		40.2

Table 7. Results per party and Absolute Error for all elections of the configuration that scores best overall

	2011 EK		2012 TK		2015 EK		2017 TK		2019 EK	
	%election	%twitter	%el	%tw	%el	%tw	%el	%tw	%el	%tw
VVD	20.0	16.0	26.7	20.9	16.7	25.9	21.6	15.5	14.1	20.1
PVDA	17.7	12.1	25.0	19.6	10.6	13.9	5.8	10.7	9.9	6.0
CDA	14.4	16.4	8.6	9.2	15.4	10.3	12.6	7.4	13.5	6.6
PVV	12.7	21.7	10.2	10.6	12.3	10.9	13.3	17.0	7.5	10.1
SP	10.4	7.5	9.7	12.2	12.2	8.2	9.2	4.9	6.5	3.1
D66	8.5	7.9	8.1	8.4	13.0	14.3	12.4	9.8	7.1	12.9
GroenLinks	6.4	8.4	2.4	7.6	5.6	5.7	9.3	12.6	10.5	14.9
ChristenUnie	3.4	3.3	3.2	3.8	4.2	3.7	2.5	2.8	5.5	3.8
50Plus	2.4	1.5	1.9	1.2	3.5	1.3	3.2	1.5	2.8	1.4
SGP	2.2	1.4	2.1	2.3	2.9	2.1	2.1	1.4	2.6	1.6
PVDD	1.9	3.6	1.9	2.8	3.6	3.9	3.2	3.1	3.8	1.7
DENK							2.1	3.8	0.4	4.5
FVD							1.8	3.4	15.8	13.4
PPNL			0.3	1.5			0.3	2.5		
VNL							0.4	1.6		
Artikel1							0.3	0.7		
GeenPeil							0.1	1.4		
AE		29.4		23.8		28.2		41.5		45.4

Table 8. Results per party and Absolute Error for all elections of the polls

	2011 EK		2012 TK		2015 EK		2017 TK		2019 EK	
	%election	%poll	%el	%po	%el	%po	%el	%po	%el	%po
VVD	20.0	21.3	26.8	24.0	16.7	15.3	21.8	18.0	14.1	15.1
PVDA	17.7	14.7	25.1	24.0	10.6	9.3	5.9	6.0	9.9	8.2
CDA	14.4	12.0	8.6	8.0	15.4	14.7	12.7	14.7	13.5	10.1
PVV	12.7	16.0	10.2	12.0	12.3	16.0	13.4	16.0	7.5	9.6
SP	10.4	12.0	9.8	13.3	12.2	13.3	9.3	8.7	6.5	6.9
D66	8.5	6.7	8.1	7.3	13.0	14.0	12.5	10.0	7.1	8.2
GroenLinks	6.4	5.3	2.4	2.7	5.6	6.0	9.4	12.0	10.5	10.7
ChristenUnie	3.4	4.0	3.2	3.3	4.2	4.0	2.5	3.3	5.5	4.1
50Plus	2.4	2.7	1.9	1.3	3.5	2.0	3.2	2.7	2.8	2.7
SGP	2.2	2.7	2.1	2.0	2.9	2.7	2.1	2.0	2.6	2.7
PVDD	1.9	2.7	2.0	2.0	3.6	2.7	3.3	2.7	3.8	2.7
DENK							2.1	2.0	0.4	2.7
FVD							1.8	2.0	15.8	15.1
AE		16.8		11.9		12.5		17.7		14.9

References

1. Anuta, D., Churchin, J., Luo, J.: Election bias: comparing polls and twitter in the 2016 us election. arXiv preprint arXiv:1701.06232 (2017)
2. De Hond, M.: Dutch Election Polls (2011–2019). https://home.noties.nl/peil/wekelijkse-stemming/
3. Dwi Prasetyo, N., Hauff, C.: Twitter-based election prediction in the developing world. In: Proceedings of the 26th ACM Conference on Hypertext & Social Media, pp. 149–158. ACM (2015)
4. Gaurav, M., Srivastava, A., Kumar, A., Miller, S.: Leveraging candidate popularity on Twitter to predict election outcome. In: Proceedings of the 7th Workshop on Social Network Mining and Analysis, p. 7. ACM (2013)
5. Gayo-Avello, D.: I wanted to predict elections with Twitter and all I got was this Lousy Paper"-a balanced survey on election prediction using Twitter data. arXiv preprint arXiv:1204.6441 (2012)
6. Gayo-Avello, D.: No, you cannot predict elections with Twitter. IEEE Internet Comput. **16**(6), 91–94 (2012)
7. Gayo-Avello, D.: A meta-analysis of state-of-the-art electoral prediction from Twitter data. Soc. Sci. Comput. Rev. **31**, 649–679 (2013)
8. Gayo-Avello, D., Metaxas, P.T., Mustafaraj, E.: Limits of electoral predictions using twitter. In: Fifth International AAAI Conference on Weblogs and Social Media (2011)
9. Huberty, M.: Can we vote with our tweet? On the perennial difficulty of election forecasting with social media. Int. J. Forecast. **31**(3), 992–1007 (2015)
10. Ibrahim, M., Abdillah, O., Wicaksono, A.F., Adriani, M.: Buzzer detection and sentiment analysis for predicting presidential election results in a Twitter nation. In: 2015 IEEE International Conference on Data Mining Workshop (ICDMW), pp. 1348–1353. IEEE (2015)
11. Jungherr, A., Jürgens, P., Schoen, H.: Why the pirate party won the German election of 2009 or the trouble with predictions: a response to Tumasjan, A., Sprenger, T.O, Sander, P.G., Welpe, I.M. "predicting elections with Twitter: what 140 characters reveal about political sentiment. Soc. Sci. Comput. Rev. **30**(2), 229–234 (2012)
12. Kagan, V., Stevens, A., Subrahmanian, V.: Using Twitter sentiment to forecast the 2013 Pakistani election and the 2014 Indian election. IEEE Intell. Syst. **30**(1), 2–5 (2015)
13. Murthy, D.: Twitter and elections: are tweets, predictive, reactive, or a form of buzz? Inf. Commun. Soc. **18**(7), 816–831 (2015)
14. Sanders, E., Van den Bosch, A.: Relating political party mentions on twitter with polls and election results. In: Proceedings of DIR-2013, pp. 68–71 (2013). http://ceur-ws.org/Vol-986/paper_9.pdf
15. Sanders, E., de Gier, M., van den Bosch, A.: Using demographics in predicting election results with Twitter. In: Spiro, E., Ahn, Y.-Y. (eds.) SocInfo 2016. LNCS, vol. 10047, pp. 259–268. Springer, Cham (2016). https://doi.org/10.1007/978-3-319-47874-6_18
16. Sloan, L., Morgan, J., Burnap, P., Williams, M.: Who tweets? Deriving the demographic characteristics of age, occupation and social class from Twitter user metadata. PLoS ONE **10**(3), e0115545 (2015)
17. Tjong Kim Sang, E., Van den Bosch, A.: Dealing with big data: the case of Twitter. Comput. Linguist. Neth. J. **3**, 121–134 (2013)

18. Tjong Kim Sang, E., Bos, J.: Predicting the 2011 Dutch senate election results with Twitter. In: Proceedings of the Workshop on Semantic Analysis in Social Media, pp. 53–60. Association for Computational Linguistics (2012)
19. Tsakalidis, A., Papadopoulos, S., Cristea, A.I., Kompatsiaris, Y.: Predicting elections for multiple countries using Twitter and polls. IEEE Intell. Syst. **30**(2), 10–17 (2015)
20. Tumasjan, A., Sprenger, T.O., Sandner, P.G., Welpe, I.M.: Predicting elections with Twitter: what 140 characters reveal about political sentiment. ICWSM **10**, 178–185 (2010)
21. Wang, L., Gan, J.Q.: Prediction of the 2017 French election based on twitter data analysis using term weighting. In: 2018 10th Computer Science and Electronic Engineering (CEEC), pp. 231–235. IEEE (2018)

Measuring Personal Values in Cross-Cultural User-Generated Content

Yiting Shen$^{(\boxtimes)}$, Steven R. Wilson, and Rada Mihalcea

University of Michigan, Ann Arbor, MI, USA
{yiting,steverw,mihalcea}@umich.edu

Abstract. There are several standard methods used to measure personal values, including the Schwartz Values Survey and the World Values Survey. While these tools are based on well-established questionnaires, they are expensive to administer at a large scale and rely on respondents to self-report their values rather than observing what people actually choose to write about. We employ a lexicon-based method that can computationally measure personal values on a large scale. Our approach is not limited to word-counting as we explore and evaluate several alternative approaches to quantifying the usage of value-related themes in a given document. We apply our methodology to a large blog dataset comprised of text written by users from different countries around the world in order to quantify cultural differences in the expression of person values on blogs. Additionally, we analyze the relationship between the value themes expressed in blog posts and the values measured for some of the same countries using the World Values Survey.

Keywords: Content analysis · Personal values · User-generated content

1 Introduction

In psychological research, *values* are typically characterized as networks of ideas that a person views to be desirable and important [20]. Psychologists, historians, and other social scientists have long argued that people's basic values influence their behaviors [1,19]; it is generally believed that the values which people hold tend to be reliable indicators of how they will actually think and act in value-relevant situations [18]. Human values are thought to generalize across broad swaths of time and culture [21], and in fact, recent work suggests that the study of values plays a central role in cross-cultural analyses [11]. Further, values and are deeply embedded in the language that people use on a day-to-day basis [4], and we therefore expect that a strong relationship exists between the values of a cultural group and the type of content that is written about by people from that group.

Y. Shen and S. R. Wilson—Equal contributions

The original version of this chapter was revised: a citation was missing. The correction to this chapter is available at https://doi.org/10.1007/978-3-030-34971-4_23

ⓒ Springer Nature Switzerland AG 2019
I. Weber et al. (Eds.): SocInfo 2019, LNCS 11864, pp. 143–156, 2019.
https://doi.org/10.1007/978-3-030-34971-4_10

While values are commonly measured using tools such as the Schwartz Values Survey and the World Values Survey [9] – well established questionnaires that ask respondents to rate value items on a Likert-type scale [21] – it has recently been shown that topic modeling based approaches are another useful way to measure specific values, and can be applied to open-ended writing samples [3]. Even more recently, a lexicon for personal values has been introduced [24], which defines and organizes a set of dimensions related to personal values. This lexicon can be used to quantify the degree to which a text is *about* different value concepts.

Computational methods like these can be used at scale, potentially reaching larger populations. Further, these *observational* approaches do not rely on self-report data, but rather on naturally occurring data produced by authors of texts. However, it is important to measure value content in text that is personal in nature so that we can have more confidence that when value-related terms are used, they are used in connection with the author's own thoughts and beliefs. One possible source of such data is social media such as blogs, where people commonly write things about themselves in ways that might reflect their values. For example, one user in the dataset that we will explore who had a high lexicon score for the value of "Family" writes, "Happy Mother's Day to my dear mom in law, our two daughters, my sister, sister in laws, nieces, aunts, cousins, and many other beautiful women in my life", while another user with a high score for "Hard Work" writes that "Self-discipline can make the difference between an averagely talented person doing something amazing with their lives and a naturally talented person realizing very little of their potential". Based on examples like these, we expect that computational linguistic approaches, like those mentioned above, should be able to capture values in user-generated content. Further, we can use attributes associated with users' profiles to infer aspects of their culture, adding another dimension to this text-based value analysis.

Our goal in this paper is to explore cultural differences in the usage of value-laden language in personal, online user-generated content. While there are many different ways to define culture [5], we use country of residence as one way in which to divide users culturally, based on the notion of National Culture [8], and while there are many types of user-generated content, we focus on blogs because they are an ideal platform for users to write, at length, about the things that are important to them. We use the lexicon for personal values to quantify the degree to which personal blogs reflect various dimensions of value-related content. We experiment with various extensions to the typical "word counting" based approaches for quantifying concept usage in a text with lexicons, and find that more sophisticated semantic matching allows us to better discover documents that are related to the value dimensions from the lexicon. Further, we explore the degree to which conclusions that might be drawn from this type of analysis corresponds to traditional survey-based findings from the world values survey, which also divides respondents across countries.

2   Methodology

As we seek to measure values-related content in text, we turn to the hierarchical values lexicon [24] that was created for this very purpose. This resource contains a hierarchy of concepts that are related to personal values and provides the ability to define categories based on subtrees of this hierarchy. We use the authors' recommended set of 50 value concepts,[1] which includes sets of words related to values such as "Family", "Religion", and "Justice". By examining how frequently words related to these values appear in texts, we aim to get a sense of the types of values that are being discussed.

While we use a pre-constructed lexicon in this study, we first consider how exactly we should use the lexicon to quantify the usage of themes within a given document. In this section, we describe the typical approach used, list some common issues with this approach, and propose and evaluate several solutions to these problems, finally reaching a conclusion about the methodology that we will employ for our cross-cultural analysis.

2.1   Quantifying Concept Usage with Lexical Resources

Typically, a dictionary-based lexical resource, $\mathcal{L}$, contains a list of m concepts $\mathcal{L} = \{\mathcal{C}_0, \mathcal{C}_1, \ldots, \mathcal{C}_m\}$, and each concept contains a list of n patterns that match words which are associated with that concept, i.e., $\mathcal{C}_i = \{p_0, p_1, \ldots, p_n\}$. Often, these patterns are specific strings that must be matched exactly, but they might also include wildcard characters (which we denote using the "*" character) that can match any sequence of characters within a single token, e.g., "happi*" which could match the tokens "happiness", "happily", "happier", and others. The purpose of such a lexicon is to assign m scores to a document, $\mathcal{D}$, one for each of the concepts in $\mathcal{L}$, in a way that accurately captures the degree to which $\mathcal{D}$ is *about* each of the concepts. $\mathcal{D}$ itself is composed of a sequence of k tokens, which, assuming a bag-of-words model, are represented as a multiset $\mathcal{D} = \{w_0, w_1, \ldots, w_k\}$. The most common approach to compute a score, $s_{WF}(\mathcal{D}, \mathcal{C}_i)$, for $\mathcal{D}$ for any concept $\mathcal{C}_i \in \mathcal{L}$ is what we will refer to as the Word Frequency approach:

$$s_{WF}(\mathcal{D}, \mathcal{C}_i) = \frac{|\{w_j \in \mathcal{D} : m(w_j, \mathcal{C}_i) = 1\}|}{|\mathcal{D}|}$$

where $m(w_j, \mathcal{C}_i)$ returns 1 if at least one pattern in $\mathcal{C}_i$ matches w_j, and 0 otherwise.

Indeed, such count- or frequency-based lexicon scoring has been successfully applied to various domains, such as the measurement of depression-related content [17], the measurement of morals [7], sentiment analysis [23], and various other psychologically relevant word classes [15]. However, there are several potential problems with the Word Frequency approach. The set of words related to a concept are typically well thought-out and do a good job of capturing the

---

[1] The words for each category are available from the resource available in the "Values Lexicon" section at http://nlp.eecs.umich.edu/downloads.html.

"essence" of the concept, but there may be other ways to express this concept that were not included in the lexicon for any number of reasons. Content words are, by nature, open class, and thus new words may come into existence or shift in meaning over time, yet we would still like to be able to quantify their relationship to lexicon themes. On the other hand, there may be words that are *somewhat* related to a concept in a lexicon, and it might be advantageous to be able to capture this. While the pattern-based nature of the paradigm that we have presented does allow for some morphological variation in the terms in a text, we may also want to match words that are semantically similar to those in a concept even if they are morphologically different. Further, simply using a wildcard may lead to some erroneous matches. Continuing our example from above, we would also match the pattern "happi*" with "happing", which, although not a commonly used word in most text corpora, is not related to the intended concept of positive emotion and could lead to false positives. This type of problem is extremely noticeable in short texts, such as a tweets, where the categories assigned to each word contribute to a substantial proportion of the total score for that text. Yet another issue with the pattern matching approach is polysemy. Should the word "father" be more related to the value of "family" or "religion"? This is highly dependent on the context in which this word appears. In this section, we describe and evaluate two alternative approaches that can be used to help ameliorate some of the aforementioned issues with the Word Frequency approach.

Distributed Dictionary Representation

The Distributed Dictionary Representation (DDR) method was introduced to both increase the coverage of lexicon categories, but also to perform matching between categories and documents at a deeper, semantic level than can be achieved using the Word Frequency approach. With DDR, the representation of the words in a given category is computed by averaging their word embedding vectors, and this averaged representation is used to represent the concept of this category. That is, given a set of d-dimensional word embeddings $\mathcal{E}_i^{\mathcal{C}} = \{e_0, e_1, \ldots, e_n\}$, one per each pattern in $\mathcal{C}_i$, we compute a single vector representation of $\mathcal{C}_i$ as the mean of all embeddings in $\mathcal{E}_i^{\mathcal{C}}$, and we refer to this averaged vector as $\bar{\mathcal{E}}_i^{\mathcal{C}}$. Similarly, the representation of the given document, $\mathcal{D}$, is computed by averaging the bag of word embedding vectors $\mathcal{E}^{\mathcal{D}} = \{e_0, e_1, \ldots, e_k\}$, one for each word in the text, to get the averaged embedding $\bar{\mathcal{E}}^{\mathcal{D}}$. Importantly, the word embeddings used come from the same vector space, and so each word maps to the same d-dimensional embedding regardless of whether it appears in the $\mathcal{L}$ or $\mathcal{D}$.

Given these averaged embeddings, DDR assigns scores to documents using cosine similarity:

$$s_{DDR}(\mathcal{D}, \mathcal{C}_i) = \frac{\bar{\mathcal{E}}_i^{\mathcal{C}} \cdot \bar{\mathcal{E}}^{\mathcal{D}}}{||\bar{\mathcal{E}}_i^{\mathcal{C}}|| ||\bar{\mathcal{E}}^{\mathcal{D}}||}$$

Using word embeddings instead of word-counting, DDR is able to capture the concept of a category or a piece of text at a semantic level, which is consistent with the original motivation of many lexicons which were designed to identify the presence of a semantic concept in a document. In this study, we obtain all word embeddings using the FastText[2] model [2], which also has the advantage of using subword information to obtain embeddings for words that were not seen during training.

Unsupervised Context-Based Relatedness Classification
We propose an additional technique that can be applied to an existing lexicon in order to tackle one glaring problem that is not addressed by DDR; namely, that every instance of a word will be counted toward a given category, regardless of whether or not the word present in the document has the same sense as the word in the lexicon. In this approach, which we call Unsupervised Context-Based Relatedness Classification (UCRC), we only count occurrences of tokens have the correct sense, which is inferred from the context. Similar to the Word Frequency approach, UCRC gives scores to documents as:

$$s_{UCRC}(\mathcal{D}, \mathcal{C}_i, \delta) = \frac{|\{w_j \in \mathcal{D} : m'(w_j, \mathcal{D}, \mathcal{C}_i, \delta) = 1|}{|\mathcal{D}|}$$

where the new function $m'(w_j, \mathcal{D}, \mathcal{C}_i, \delta)$ returns 1 if any pattern in, $\mathcal{C}_i$ matches w_j and the sense of w_j is the same as the sense of the matching pattern based on a context window of size δ. This means that we must determine both the sense of w_j based on the $\frac{\delta}{2}$ previous and $\frac{\delta}{2}$ next words in $\mathcal{D}$, as well as the sense of the pattern p that matched w_j based on the intended meaning of the lexicon, which we allow to be defined manually. Rather than looking for an exact sense-level match, we simplify this by group senses into two categories: lexicon-related and non-lexicon-related. In this case, we can say that we only need to determine if w_j in $\mathcal{D}$ is lexicon-related or not.

To achieve this, we first get a set of possible contexts of the pattern from the WordNet database [14]. We can get the possible contexts of a pattern by getting the usage examples of each synset that contains words which are matched by the pattern. We term the set of possible contexts of the pattern the *context set* for p.

Next, we determine, in the *context set*, what kind of context indicates that the pattern is relevant to the lexicon, and what kind of context indicates that the pattern is not. To complete this step, we need to know whether each synset is related to $\mathcal{L}$ or not. We begin by manually annotating synsets for a subset of patterns (i.e., patterns that match a word in the synsets) that belong to some concept in $\mathcal{L}$. We randomly select 50 patterns, examine all relevant synsets, and label whether or not each synset is related to the notion of personal values. Then, under the assumption that the set of value-relevant synsets are related to one another, we automatically expand the set of lexicon-related synsets to include all synsets with a WordNet path distance that is less than some hyperparamter

---

[2] While other contextual word embeddings like ELMo [16] do a good job of capturing the meanings of words in specific contexts, lexicons such as the values lexicon that we use is this study do not provide contexts along with the category-specific words, and so further research would be required to determine how to best create, e.g., value-specific dictionary embeddings with ELMo to use within the DDR framework.

N, following hypernym and hyponym links when searching across paths. To tune N, we label an additional set of 30 patterns' synsets and measure the F1-score on this test set when labeling all synsets with a path distance $<N$ to be lexicon-related, varying N from 1 to 25. We find the maximum F1-score of 0.747 when $N = 10$. Note that the default approach is to label *every* occurrence of a match as lexicon-related, leading to a high rate of false positives. Indeed, we find that in our sample, when we set $N = 10$, we *only* reduce false positives without introducing additional false negatives.

In the final step of our process, we find a single context from the *context set* of p that is most similar to the context of w_j in $\mathcal{D}$, where context is determined from a sequence of length δ surrounding the word or pattern. The similarity is computed using the cosine similarity between the average FastText embeddings for the two contexts, similar to the scoring function that was used in the DDR method. Finally, we consider the synset that appears in the most similar pattern context, and check to see if that synset was classified as lexicon-related in the previous step. If it is, then we say that the occurrence of w_j in $\mathcal{D}$ is also lexicon-related, and therefore we can count the match toward the score for the category in the lexicon.

2.2   Evaluation of Lexicon Quantification Approaches

Given our two proposed methods for improving the quantification of documents by lexicons, we design a series of evaluations that can be used to determine the viability of these approaches.

Category-Text Matching

First, we aim to determine how well the DDR quantification approach is able to accurately assign scores to documents based on the concepts defined in the lexicon. To do this, we obtain scores for each category in the lexicon across a text corpus in order to find the documents that have high, average, and low scores for each category. To test a category, we select two documents: one that has a high score for that category and another than doesn't. These two documents are presented to a set of judges on Amazon Mechanical Turk[3] who are given the category label and asked to decide which document best expresses the concept described by the label. If the judges can select the correct document significantly more than half of the time, we know that the lexicon is able to identify text that expresses the category being evaluated. There are two settings for this Category-Text Matching: *high-low* and *high-median*. In *high-low*, one of the top q scoring documents is paired with one of the bottom scoring q documents for the category, while high-median pairs this same high-scoring document with one of the q documents surrounding the median scoring document. The latter is a much more difficult version of the task since the judge must determine which of two texts that are related to a concept *most* expresses this concept.

The score for either version of the task is reported as the percentage of judges who correctly selected the high-scoring text. In each HIT, a crowd worker

---

[3] https://www.mturk.com.

Table 1. Accuracy of DDR and Word Frequency (WF) in the High-Median and High-Low settings.

	High-Median		High-Low	
	DDR	WC	DDR	WC
Baseline	*50%*	*50%*	*50%*	*50%*
Average	**81.06%**	67%	**97.92%**	72%

is shown seven pairs of texts, one of which is a randomly inserted checkpoint question based on a Wikipedia article title and contents: the title of the article is shown, and the first paragraph of the article is shown as one choice while the first paragraph of a *different* article is shown as an alternative. HIT are rejected when workers are unable to identify the correct article. For our set of documents, we collect posts from Reddit[4] that we expect to contain some value-related content based on their subreddit categorization, such as "/r/family" and "/r/christian". We assign lexicon scores to each post using either s_{DDR} or s_{WF}, and the results are presented in Table 1. We can see that the DDR method does a much better job selecting documents that are actually perceived to be related to the lexicon categories.

Word-Sense Disambiguation
To evaluate the UCRC method as a means of unsupervised word sense grouping, we run first it on the SemCor corpus [12]. The Semcor is a lexical resource where words are annotated in terms of their WordNet synsets. With UCRC we know, for any synset related to a pattern in the lexicon, whether that synset is lexicon-related or not. Therefore, we can simply check whether each lexicon pattern that matches a labeled instance in the SemCor is relevant to the lexicon or not, essentially creating a binary prediction task (in contrast to the sense-level classification that is typically performed on the SemCor dataset). Among 352 text files in the SemCor, there are 1419 in-text lexicon pattern matches, of which 1304 are relevant to the value lexicon, and 115 are not. If the Word Frequency approach is used and every instance is labeled lexicon-related, the F1-score is 0.92. On the other hand, if UCRC is used, the F1-score is 0.97. Among these 115 conceptually unrelated words, the UCRC method is able to detect 74 of them, increasing the specificity from 0% to 64.35%. Overall, UCRC indeed has a higher F1-score and a greatly improved specificity.

Document Ranking
Before considering asking human crowd-workers to do the Category Text Matching for the same set of Reddit posts used before to evaluate the DDR method, we wanted to determine how different the ranking generated by UCRC is from the ranking generated by the standard Word Frequency approach. If there is not much of a difference, then the pairs selected for the Category Text Matching will likely not change and so UCRC would not impact the Category Text Matching score. We hypothesize that the difference in rankings might be small because

---

[4] https://www.reddit.com.

the number of true negatives (with respect to lexicon-relatedness) is actually quite low in practice. To quantitatively show how those two rankings in order of relevance differ, we run Kendall's τ Rank Correlation Coefficients [10] to compare the ranking using s_{UCRC} and the ranking using the Word Frequency based score, s_{WF}, for each category. The closer the coefficient is to 1, the less different the two rankings are from each other (See Table 2 for specific results). We can see that all the coefficients are more than 0.83, and most of them are very close or equal to 1. Based on these results, we do not run the Category-Text Matching evaluation on UCRC, understanding that the results will likely not change. The effect of UCRC is maximized when it is run on the text where many false positives exists, but we do not find this to be the case in the corpora that we explore, and so we do not use UCRC in the following experiments. However, we do recommend the use of UCRC to those using lexicons containing many ambiguous terms or when applying lexicons to corpora containing these kinds of words.

Table 2. Kendall's τ rank correlation coefficients for each category

Category	τ	Category	τ	Category	τ
forgiving	1.0	accepting-others	0.99	emotion	1.0
society	0.96	helping-others	0.94	feeling-good	0.85
significant-other	1.0	achievement	0.98	honesty	0.95
family	1.0	life	0.97	animals	0.98
friends	1.0	purpose	0.99	self-confidence	1.0
career	1.0	perseverance	1.0	dedication	1.0
relationships	1.0	religion	1.0	social	0.96
nature	1.0	learning	0.99	advice	1.0
optimism	0.94	wealth	0.98	gratitude	0.97
siblings	1.0	truth	0.91	order	0.84
health	1.0	respect	0.97	thinking	0.99
creativity	1.0	work-ethic	0.96	marriage	1.0
cognition	0.99	parents	1.0	future	0.99
security	0.97	spirituality	0.92	justice	0.96
hard-work	0.97	autonomy	1.0	art	1.0
responsible	0.98	inner-peace	0.97	children	0.96
helping-others2	0.83	moral	1.0		

3   Data

As a source of a large amount of user-generated content from authors around the world, we collected a corpus of blog posts from the popular platform, Blogger.[5]

---

[5] https://www.blogger.com.

Since the values lexicon that we are using in this study was developed in the English language, we only consider text written by users from countries that have a large number of English speakers[6] which also have a significant presence on the Blogger platform[7]. As a result, we collect all posts written by a sample of authors from these countries: United States, India, Philippines, Nigeria, United Kingdom, Canada, Australia, Pakistan, South Africa, New Zealand, Tanzania, Ireland, and Singapore. For each country, we collect a list of blogs written by users from that country[8], and subsequently collect posts from those blogs. We preprocess each blog post them by removing all HTML tags[9], and since we seek text that is personal in nature, we remove any blog posts that do not contain the word "I". Next we perform language identification,[10] and we ignore any documents that are not mostly written in English, since that is the language in which the values lexicon is built. For each document, we compute value scores for the 50 value categories described above using the DDR method with FastText embeddings,[11] and then we average the scores across all documents written by each user, since we wish to avoid unfairly weighting the scores for a country in favor of a few high-producing authors. We only consider authors for which we could retrieve at least 5 posts and when a single user has written more than 100 posts, we randomly sample 100 posts to use as a representation for that user. Finally, we average the scores for all users from a given country in order to get overall scores for each of the 50 values for each of the thirteen countries.

4   Results and Analysis

Table 3 depicts the average value category scores for each of the thirteen countries. In order to emphasize differences across the value categories, the scores for each row were divided by the average score for that row. From this heatmap, we can see that values like "marriage" and "responsibility" were talked about to a higher degree in Nigeria, while values like "life" and "gratitude" were talked about more often in blogs written by users from the Philippines and Singapore. Interestingly, certain countries, like Nigeria, had highever average usage rates of words from all value categories, while others, like India and Pakistan, had lower average usage scores overall. This is not completely surprising due to the inter-correlations between many some of the value theme scores, but it also showcases the following phenomenon: writers of blogs in some countries write in general about things related to a wide range of values, while blogs in other countries more often focus on topics that are not value-related.

---

[6] Based on estimations provided at https://en.wikipedia.org/wiki/List_of_countries_by_English-speaking_population.

[7] At least 1,000 users claim to be from that country.

[8] We collected these using code from https://github.com/costaspappus/Blogs-Scraper.

[9] We use https://www.crummy.com/software/BeautifulSoup/ to clean the HTML.

[10] Using https://github.com/saffsd/langid.py.

[11] As the overall results are not expected to change by a noticeable degree based on our evaluation, we opt not to use the UCRC method in the present analysis.

Table 3. Heat map showing normalized average lexicon scores for blog data from thirteen countries.

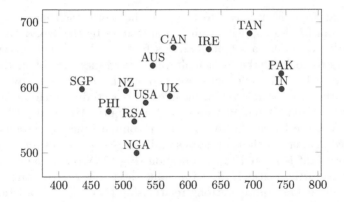

Fig. 1. T-SNE projection of countries' blogger content based on averaged value lexicon scores.

Interestingly, as we analyze the various cultural differences in the usage of value-related words, we notice several groups of countries that used words from the value categories to similar degrees, possibly indicating cultural similarities between these countries. In order to explore and emphasize the similarities between countries usage of value themes, we performed a projection of the countries into a 2-dimensional space using T-SNE [13] (Fig. 1). Here, we see some regional groupings, such as India and Pakistan, but also some countries that are not close as close to their neighbors in this "values space": USA is much close to the UK than it is to Canada, which is closer to countries like Australia and Ireland.

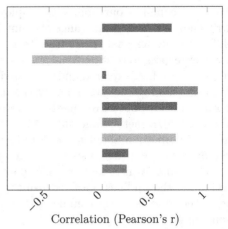

Fig. 2. Country-level correlation between aggregated WVS question responses and value lexicon scores.

As a final analysis, we seek to compare the scores for some of the value categories from the lexicon with values as measured by the World Values Survey (WVS)[12]. We select a set of questions from the WVS that measure similar concepts to some of the 50 default value categories present in the values lexicon. For each of the questions, we average the results for any countries included in the WVS that are also included in our study, which includes Australia, New Zealand, India, Pakistan, Nigeria, South Africa, the Philippines, Singapore, and the United States. Then, we compute the correlation between the averaged answers to these questions and the average scores for a value lexicon category that is related to the question (Fig. 2). While some of the WVS questions have little relationship to the value categories that we might expect, others actually exhibit quite a strong relationship that is even statistically significant with a small sample of measurements. For example, the average score for the "Religion" lexicon category is strongly correlated with people's answers to the question about their membership in a church or other religious organization. Two interesting cases are those of "Security" and "Trust": people from countries with high average lexicon scores for these categories actually reported feeling less secure in their neighborhoods and had less overall trust in other people. These inverse relationships may point to the level of activation of these values as a consequence of the residents' environments. Certain values may be activated in relevant situations [22], and we may be observing cases where people actually talk more about values that they feel are threatened, thus making them more relevant that they are in places where things like security and trustworthiness might be taken for granted.

5   Conclusions

We have explored our ability to employ these lexicons on a set of blog data written by authors from a range of countries in order to investigate cross-cultural differences in personal values from text. We used a lexicon that was designed to measure expressions of personal values in text data, but rather than just using it "as is", we first explored and evaluated several techniques that can be used to improve the way that we quantify the usage of lexicon themes. We found that both the DDR and UCRC methods have their merits, but for our analyses, we chose the DDR method and applied it to blogs from thirteen countries in order to gather information about the expressions of values in these countries. We used the average value theme scores to group these countries in a low-dimensional space to show which countries share similar value theme usage rates, and we compared the findings obtained using this text-based method with the results from the most recently completed round of the World Values Survey, finding some interesting correlations.

---

[12] We use data from round 6 of the WVS, available at http://www.worldvaluessurvey.org/.

Acknowledgments. This material is based in part upon work supported by the Michigan Institute for Data Science, by the National Science Foundation (grant #1815291), and by the John Templeton Foundation (grant #61156). Any opinions, findings, and conclusions or recommendations expressed in this material are those of the author and do not necessarily reflect the views of the Michigan Institute for Data Science, the National Science Foundation, or the John Templeton Foundation.

References

1. Ball-Rokeach, S., Rokeach, M., Grube, J.W.: The Great American Values Test: Influencing Behavior and Belief Through Television. Free Press, New York (1984)
2. Bojanowski, P., Grave, E., Joulin, A., Mikolov, T.: Enriching word vectors with subword information. arXiv preprint arXiv:1607.04606 (2016)
3. Boyd, R.L., Wilson, S.R., Pennebaker, J.W., Kosinski, M., Stillwell, D.J., Mihalcea, R.: Values in words: using language to evaluate and understand personal values. In: Ninth International AAAI Conference on Web and Social Media (2015)
4. Chung, C.K., Pennebaker, J.W.: Finding values in words: using natural language to detect regional variations in personal concerns. In: Geographical psychology: Exploring the interaction of environment and behavior, pp. 195–216 (2014). https://doi.org/10.1037/14272-011
5. Faulkner, S.L., Baldwin, J.R., Lindsley, S.L., Hecht, M.L.: Layers of meaning: an analysis of definitions of culture. In: Redefining Culture: Perspectives Across the Disciplines, pp. 27–51 (2006)
6. Garten, J., Hoover, J., Johnson, K.M., Boghrati, R., Iskiwitch, C., Dehghani, M.: Dictionaries and distributions: Combining expert knowledge and large scale textual data content analysis. Behav. Res. Methods **50**(1), 344–361 (2018)
7. Graham, J., Haidt, J., Nosek, B.A.: Liberals and conservatives rely on different sets of moral foundations. J. Pers. Soc. Psychol. **96**(5), 1029 (2009)
8. Hofstede, G.: Dimensionalizing cultures: the hofstede model in context. Online Readings Psychol. Cult. **2**(1), 8 (2011)
9. Inglehart, R., et al.: World values survey: round six-country-pooled datafile 2010–2014. JD Systems Institute, Madrid (2014)
10. Kendall, M.G.: The treatment of ties in ranking problems. Biometrika **33**(3), 239–251 (1945)
11. Knafo, A., Roccas, S., Sagiv, L.: The value of values in cross-cultural research: a special issue in honor of shalom schwartz (2011)
12. Landes, S., Leacock, C., Tengi, R.I.: Building semantic concordances. WordNet Electron. Lexical Database **199**(216), 199–216 (1998)
13. Maaten, L.V.D., Hinton, G.: Visualizing data using t-SNE. J. Mach. Learn. Res. **9**, 2579–2605 (2008)
14. Miller, G.: WordNet: An Electronic Lexical Database. MIT press, Cambridge (1998)
15. Pennebaker, J.W., Boyd, R.L., Jordan, K., Blackburn, K.: The development and psychometric properties of liwc2015. Technical report (2015)
16. Peters, M.E., et al.: Deep contextualized word representations. arXiv preprint arXiv:1802.05365 (2018)
17. Ramirez-Esparza, N., Chung, C.K., Kacewicz, E., Pennebaker, J.W.: The psychology of word use in depression forums in English and in Spanish: testing two text analytic approaches. In: In the International AAAI Conference on Web and Social Media (2008)

18. Rohan, M.J.: A rose by any name? the values construct. Pers. Soc. Psychol. Rev. **4**(3), 255–277 (2000). https://doi.org/10.1207/S15327957PSPR0403_4
19. Rokeach, M.: Beliefs, Attitudes, and Values, vol. 34. Jossey-Bass, San Francisco (1968)
20. Rokeach, M.: The Nature of Human Values, vol. 438. Free press, New York (1973)
21. Schwartz, S.H.: Universals in the content and structure of values: theoretical advances and empirical tests in 20 countries. Adv. Exp. Soc. Psychol. **25**, 1–65 (1992). https://doi.org/10.1016/S0065-2601(08)60281-6
22. Schwartz, S.H.: An overview of the Schwartz theory of basic values. Online Readings Psychol. Cult. **2**(1), 11 (2012)
23. Taboada, M., Brooke, J., Tofiloski, M., Voll, K., Stede, M.: Lexicon-based methods for sentiment analysis. Comput. Linguist. **37**(2), 267–307 (2011)
24. Wilson, S.R., Shen, Y., Mihalcea, R.: Building and validating hierarchical lexicons with a case study on personal values. In: Staab, S., Koltsova, O., Ignatov, D.I. (eds.) SocInfo 2018. LNCS, vol. 11185, pp. 455–470. Springer, Cham (2018). https://doi.org/10.1007/978-3-030-01129-1_28

Perceptions of Social Roles
Across Cultures

MeiXing Dong[✉], David Jurgens, Carmen Banea, and Rada Mihalcea

University of Michigan, Ann Arbor, MI, USA
{meixingd,jurgens,carmennb,mihalcea}@umich.edu

Abstract. In this paper we introduce a data set of social roles and their aspects (descriptors or actions) as emerging from surveys conducted across a sample of over 400 respondents from two different cultures: US and India. The responses show that there are indeed differences of role perceptions across the cultures, with actions showcasing less variability, and descriptors exhibiting stronger differences. In addition, we notice strong shifts in sentiment and emotions across the cultures. We further present a pilot study in predicting social roles based on attributes by leveraging dependency-based corpus statistics and embedding models. Our evaluations show that models trained on the same culture as the test set are better predictors of social role ranking.

Keywords: Social role perceptions · Cultural differences · Word associations · Cultural biases · Natural language processing · Word representations

1 Introduction

Beliefs we hold about the world often manifest themselves in the way we use language. Understanding what people say or write can help us gain insight into their worldview, beliefs, and the way they are primed to interact with the surrounding world. Such analyses of language can also lead to new insights into cultural differences. Groups of people sharing certain characteristics – e.g., nationality, region, state, gender, or religion – would often have a shared understanding of the world, which in turn is reflected in their use of language.

While the connections between language and culture have traditionally been the purview of cultural psychology [42], more recent work in computational linguistics has also started to address these connections, resulting in models that can uncover the different use of words across cultures [22,24], the various distribution of topics in different cultures [34], or the word associations that people with different demographics tend to make [21,25].

The hypothesis driving our work is that we can use language to identify and understand the implicit perceptions and expectations that people hold with regards to social roles in our society. For instance, the frequent use of the descriptor *kind* or the action *help* in connection to the role *friend* can be an indication

© Springer Nature Switzerland AG 2019
I. Weber et al. (Eds.): SocInfo 2019, LNCS 11864, pp. 157–172, 2019.
https://doi.org/10.1007/978-3-030-34971-4_11

that friends are usually regarded as people who are kind and provide help. Moreover, we also hypothesize that there may be cultural differences in these social role perceptions, and that different groups of people may correspondingly use different descriptors or actions when they refer to the same social role.

This paper makes four main contributions. First, we examine what constitutes a social role, and we propose the use of descriptors (adjectives) and actions (verbs) as a way to understand the implicit perception of social roles as reflected in language. Second, we introduce a new data set, consisting of 49 frequent social roles (e.g., *mother, friend, lawyer*) and the associated descriptors and actions, as contributed by over 400 human judges from two different cultures (United States and India). Third, we perform several analyses to uncover cross-cultural variations in social role perception, and we identify roles with high, medium, and low variations. Finally, we propose two computational models that can predict the most likely social role based on a descriptor or an action. One model is based on statistics collected over a large syntactically annotated collection of texts authored by people from two cultures, while the second one relies on neural models that are aware of the syntactic relations between words.

Our main findings show that there are indeed differences in the perceptions associated with the roles between the two cultures, and that the degree of cultural similarity varies across the roles. The computational models show that it is possible to predict roles from the attributes that people associate with them. Furthermore, our models exhibit higher performance when the train and test set cultures match, indicating that our models encode cultural differences.

2   Related Work

The concept of "roles" is frequently considered by those in the social sciences as a way to analyze social structures and behaviors [2,7,18,26,38]. Roles can be characterized by the norms and expectations that society places on people of particular social or functional positions [26]. Such norms greatly influence how people act and interact with others [12], especially when one is acting as a member of a role [43]. The perceptions of others are important; depending on whether one acts according to role expectations, there exist rewards or punishments doled out by society [18]. By asking members of a group about the behaviors that a role is likely to participate in, one can analyze the differences in perceptions of roles between cultural groups, such as Hispanics versus the general US population [44].

We take inspiration from previous work that models latent character types, or personas (such as the "love interest" or "best friend") and their typical characteristics in films [4]. To extract character aspects, the authors look at a subset of the syntactic dependencies that involve the personas. We extract aspects in a similar way and focus on predicting a role based on its expected characteristics, in contrast to Bamman et al. that focus on partitioning types of roles. Additionally, films tend to create stereotypical personas with strong associations to their characteristics. Social roles, however, are constructed from societal expectations in aggregate and can be much more nuanced.

Another related line of research has considered the prediction of words that are most likely to be associated with a stimulus word [21]. Our task differs in that we go beyond free-form associations and instead hone in on specific aspect types, namely actions and descriptors as they relate to a given social role.

To use natural language, we must build word representations. A straightforward approach is to treat words as discrete symbols, leading to many bag-of-words methods for representing text [41,46]. While useful for many tasks, this representation does not encode relations between words or semantics. Many recent word representation methods model words as continuous, dense vectors derived from neural networks [5,30] or word co-occurrence information [35], also known as word embeddings. These have been shown to perform well across numerous tasks [39]. Additionally, [1,3,10,20,21] have sought to encode additional sources of information to be captured in word embedding vectors.

One of our models is derived from dependency-based embedding models [28], where dependency links are used to form the contexts in a skip-gram model. The resulting embeddings encode functional similarity rather than topical similarity. For instance, *rapping*, *busking*, and *breakdancing* are among the most similar words for "dancing" when using dependency-based embeddings, as opposed to topically related words surfaced by regular linear context embeddings, such as "dancer", "dance", and "dances." We adapt the former model to focus on specific types of dependencies that encode aspects, distinguishing between the different functional uses of a word. For example, we can find roles that are most relevant to a given aspect, rather than the words that are generally related either by domain or by function.

3 Collecting a Cross-Cultural Data Set of Social Roles

The perception of a social role can be characterized by the descriptors or actions that people associate with it. We created a data set by surveying a large and demographically diverse audience on Amazon Mechanical Turk (AMT) about the aspects they associate with different roles. Our survey task is similar to that of gathering word associations, where survey participants are provided with a list of *stimulus words* and are asked to provide the first word that comes to their mind [21,27,33]. However, rather than asking for free-form associations, as done before, we added structure to our prompts to induce responses that correspond to descriptive aspects. Specifically, we asked survey participants to provide actions and descriptors for each stimulus role, given prompts such as *What is a friend like?* and *What does a friend do?*

Selecting Social Roles. Language abounds with the names of the many social roles that people partake in, from common names (like mother or teacher) to less common ones (like debtor or occultist). Here, we aim to curate a set of social roles for annotation that meet three criteria: (1) occur with high frequency in text, (2) appear in daily life, and (3) have relatively unambiguous words associated with them. We detail the selection process next.

A large set of candidate social roles were selected using WordNet [31], a large lexical database for English. WordNet provides an ontological organization of a word's meanings and contains a semantic network of how these meanings (i.e., *senses*) relate to one another. In particular, WordNet specifies the hyponymy relationship between senses that allows us to identify more specific meanings of people; for example, *mother* and *father* are both hyponyms of *parent*. To get all potential social roles, we collected the 8,654 words that are children of *person* in the hyponymy tree.

As WordNet contains many infrequent words, we extracted frequency counts for each role from a large collection of blog data from India and the US, described in detail in Sect. 5.1. We tagged each blog sentence with part-of-speech information, and then counted the frequency of each candidate role occurring as a noun.

Finally, we analyzed the most frequently occurring candidate roles and identified roles that occurred in blogs from both countries, that are generally unambiguous, and are likely to be encountered in day-to-day life. For instance, we did not include *queen* because most people are unlikely to interact with queens, and therefore descriptors and actions are unlikely to reflect personal experiences. We also excluded ambiguous roles such as *official* or *director*, since their attributes can change depending on the context. Ultimately, the selection process resulted in a set of 49 social roles.

Crowdsourcing Setup. The descriptors and actions for each social role were collected through AMT English surveys[1], targeted to individuals in India and the US. We chose countries that were likely to differ in terms of cultural and societal norms, but still have many English speakers to bypass translation issues. Each participant was presented with five social roles and asked to provide three actions and three descriptors for each role. Participants were also asked to indicate how often they interact with the role and how positively they view those interactions. A demographic questionnaire was included at the end of the each survey containing questions about the respondent's gender, age, level of education, ethnicity, and nationality. Responses were collected from 200 participants from each country for each role. This resulted in 600 actions and 600 descriptors collected for each social role, for each country.

To ensure answer quality, we included a spam-check question that asked for the answer to an earlier question. This filtered out participants that responded without reading the prompts. Built-in form restrictions prevented the submission of answers that were given as examples, or empty answers. As a final check, we manually spot-checked responses before accepting them, to make sure participants did not fill in random words. We lemmatized all of the responses and for each given social role we kept those responses that occurred five times or more as culturally-salient aspects of the role.

Previous studies [6,13] have shown that while Turkers tend to be younger and more educated, it is possible for the data they supply to reflect aspects of the population at large, such as ideology. The data we gathered serves as an

---

[1] English is one of the official languages of India and the second most-spoken language behind Hindi.

Table 1. Top survey responses for societal role words.

Role word	Actions		Descriptors	
	US	India	US	India
Mother	Care, love, cook	care, love, cook	Loving, caring, nurturing	Caring, lovable, loving
Baby	Cry, sleep, eat	Cry, play, smile	Loving, sweet, kind	Cute, innocent, chubby
Doctor	Diagnose, prescribe, examine	Treat, care, cure	Smart, intelligent, helpful	Caring, god, helpful
Policeman	Protect, arrest, serve	Arrest, protect, help	Strong, brave, helpful	Strict, brave, strong
Student	Study, learn, read, write, work	Study, play, learn, read, write	Studious, smart, young	Obedient, intelligent, studious
Politician	Lie, campaign, speak, talk, cheat	Speak, vote, lead, promise, rule	Dishonest, greedy, corrupt	Powerful, honest, influential

additional resource to complement existing cross-cultural resources, providing insight into cultural differences pertaining to how social roles are perceived. Despite the potential skew in demographics, we still find differences between the two countries, as detailed in later sections.

Table 1 shows the top responses for a sample set of social roles.

4   Demographic Variations in Social Roles

The characteristics associated with social roles in different countries can reveal cultural similarities and differences. Many aspects are associated with a role regardless of the underlying culture, such as a *mother* being *caring* and a *policeman* being *brave*. On the other hand, *doctors* are more associated with preliminary actions in the treatment process such as *examine*, *diagnose* and *prescribe* in the US, while in India they are more associated with treatment results, such as *treat* and *cure*. Also, Indian descriptors show a stronger perception of doctors as being *caring*, versus *smart* and *intelligent* in the US. Additionally, US participants associate many negative aspects with *politician*, reflecting the current political climate, while in India, the actions are mostly associated with positive aspects.

Intra-group and Inter-group Similarities. We measure the agreement between respondents within and across cultural groups. Given the set of response words for a social role from a single held-out respondent, we determine whether any of these responses match the most frequent response or any of the top 25 responses of the remaining respondents in the group. If so, then we consider this respondent in agreement with the group. We define the agreement score as the ratio of participants whose responses are in agreement with the group. Similarly, we measure the agreement between each survey respondent in one group with the most frequent or top 25 most frequent responses from the other group.

The intra-group and inter-group analyses are shown in Table 2. From the intra-group similarities, we can see that there is high agreement among both the top and top 25 responses given by participants from the same country, with the US having higher agreement in general than India. Overall, action responses are more cohesive across the two countries compared to descriptor answers; we noted earlier that there is more variation and subjectivity in regards to descriptors.

Table 2. Left: intra-group similarities (higher similarity indicates a more cohesive group). Right: inter-group similarities (higher similarity indicates a less distinct group).

Intra-group similarity			Inter-group similarity		
Demographic	Primary	Top 25	Demographic	Primary	Top 25
US-US (Descriptors)	0.33	0.89	US-India (Descriptors)	0.19	0.78
India-India (Descriptors)	0.24	0.76	India-US (Descriptors)	0.15	0.61
US-US (Actions)	0.40	0.93	US-India (Actions)	0.35	0.90
India-India (Actions)	0.40	0.89	India-US (Actions)	0.32	0.85

When we look at how much participants from one country agree with participants from *the other country*, we find a much lower agreement for descriptors, both in terms of primary response and the top 25 responses. For example, the similarity drops by 0.08 (from 0.40 to 0.32) between India-India and India-US for the most frequent response for actions. We see the agreement drop in all cases when comparing intra- versus inter-group similarity. We conclude that the agreement for actions between the countries is comparable to the agreement within countries, implying that the actions attributed to roles are more objective and universal.

Levels of Social Role Similarity Across Cultures. We closely examine how various roles are perceived differently across countries. To measure how similar a role is between India and the US, we compute the cosine similarity between the frequencies pertaining to the set of aspects resulting from the union of the responses for that role for each country. Table 3 shows a sample of roles that display various levels of similarity ranging from high to low in regards to their associated actions or descriptors across the countries in question. We notice that *soldier* exhibits the highest similarity level both for actions (*fight, protect*) and descriptors (*brave, strong*). *Actor*, on the other hand, showcases a medium action-based similarity, as actors in India regularly engage in dancing, unlike their US counterparts. Interestingly, *friend*, despite its ubiquitousness as a social role, displays among the lowest scoring action-based similarity. We note that in the US, *friend* is more associated with communication-focused actions such as *listen*, *talk*, *laugh*, while in India, given the more collectivist culture, people primarily think of friends in the context of being *helpful* and *caring*.

Levels of Aspect Similarity Across Cultures. We further analyze the frequency of aspect usage across roles to identify how predictive a given aspect is of a social role. Table 4 aggregates the responses at the aspect level. We see that some actions are highly predictive of a role. For instance, *arrest* occurs with *police* and *vote* appears with *citizen, politician* roles in both countries. However, *sacrifice* occurs in the action-focused answers for *soldier* in the US, while in India, *mother* and *father* also trigger this response. *Counsel* also displays a divergent usage, in the US being associated with *lawyer*, while in India, with *priest*. Similarly, descriptors also show variations in their associations with roles. These range from a high similarity of 1 for *religious* (which always appears in the context of *priest*), to mid-range (0.46) for *obedient* (which in the US caries a stronger meaning of loyal, and applies to a hierarchical organization, e.g. army for *soldier* or country for *citizen*, while in India it is more indicative of filial piety and the need to listen to one's elders, whether as a *student, son*, or *daughter*), to low (0) for *committed* (which in the US occurs in prompts for *wife* and *husband*, while in India it appears in prompts for *farmer*).

Sentiment and Emotion in Social Role Perceptions. Social roles can evoke a variety of emotional responses, such as feelings of authority, love, or even fear. Viewed in aggregate, the aspects used to describe roles can potentially reveal which emotional aspects of social roles are most important to a culture. Therefore, we perform two analyses where we convert the actions and descriptions for each role into their sentiment and emotion associations. For sentiment, we map each word to its mean score in SentiWordNet [19] and then average across all the words for each aspect of a role for its estimated sentiment score. For emotion, we repeat a similar process with the NRC Emotion Lexicon [32]. This lexicon maps individual words to a binary indicator of whether they have an association with each of the eight Plutchik emotions [36]. Here, we compute the probability that an aspect word for a role has an association with each emotion. We then average the sentiment and emotion-association probabilities across all roles.

For sentiment, Fig. 1 shows clear differences between India and the US responses, with AMT workers from India using significantly more positive descriptors about roles. No significant difference is seen for actions, though this is expected, as adjectives (descriptors) typically carry more sentiment than verbs (actions); for example, common sentiment lexicons like SentiWordNet [19] and OpinionFinder [47] contain more adjectives than verbs, and adjectives have been shown to outperform verbs as features in sentiment classification [48]. Examining AMT workers' explicit sentiment ratings for roles, we see that their ratings have high correlation with the inferred sentiment, with Pearson's r ranging from 0.51 to 0.61. This result suggests that the inferred ratings are capturing representative attitudes but, crucially, that roles' aspect words convey more than the workers' sentiment about the role.

Table 3. Social roles exhibiting different levels of similarity (H(igh), M(edium), L(ow)) between the US and India based on the differences between the top 20 responses.

Similarity	Role	Score	Top US aspects	Top IN aspects
Actions				
H	Soldier	0.94	Fight, protect, defend	Fight, protect, shoot
	Professor	0.91	Teach, grade, lecture	Teach, guide, educate
	Mother	0.89	Care, love, cook	Care, love, cook
M	Girlfriend	0.77	Love, kiss, listen	Love, care, help
	Policeman	0.77	Protect, arrest, serve	Arrest, protect, help
	Actor	0.71	Act, perform, pretend	Act, dance, perform
L	Doctor	0.66	Diagnose, prescribe, examine	Treat, care, cure
	Politician	0.59	Lie, campaign, speak	Speak, vote, lead
	Friend	0.58	Listen, talk, laugh	Help, care, play
Descriptors				
H	Soldier	0.89	Brave, strong, loyal	Brave, strong, patriotic
	Writer	0.88	Creative, imaginative, smart	Creative, imaginative, good
	Mother	0.72	Caring, loving, nurturing	Caring, lovable, kind
M	Researcher	0.62	Smart, intelligent, curious	Intelligent, knowledgeable, brilliant
	Prisoner	0.60	Angry, sad, guilty	Bad, criminal, guilty
	Friend	0.59	Fun, loyal, funny	Helpful, caring, honest
L	Farmer	0.44	Strong, hardworking, diligent	Hardworking, poor, helpless
	Judge	0.38	Fair, powerful, smart	Honest, intelligent, knowledgeable
	Politician	0.17	Dishonest, greedy, corrupt	Powerful, honest, influential

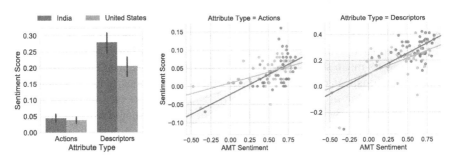

Fig. 1. India and the US differ significantly in the sentiments of roles attributes (left); indeed, AMT workers' explicit sentiment ratings for each role were highly correlated with inferred sentiments of their descriptors and actions (right). Bars and shaded regions show 95% confidence intervals.

The emotion trends, shown in Fig. 2, reveal a more complex picture with Indian respondents being more likely to use emotionally-associated language than their US counterparts. This heightened emotionality occurs both for positive emotions like trust, surprise, and anticipation, as well as negative emotions like disgust and sadness. However, US respondents are more likely to evoke anger or fear; yet, these emotions are the two least-frequently used in our data. While cross-cultural studies of emotion have shown differences between India and the

Table 4. Aspects exhibiting different levels of similarity (H(igh), M(edium), L(ow)) between the US and India based on the differences between the top 20 responses.

Similarity	Aspect	Score	Top US roles	Top IN roles
Actions				
H	Arrest	1.0	Police	Police
	Vote	0.99	Citizen, politician	Citizen, politician
	kiss	0.93	Girlfriend, boyfriend, mother	Girlfriend, boyfriend, husband
M	Medicate	0.71	Nurse	Doctor, nurse
	Sacrifice	0.61	Soldier	Father, mother, soldier
	Forgive	0.51	Priest	Friend, priest, mother
L	Invent	0.15	Engineer, chef, writer	Scientist, researcher, engineer
	Meditate	0.0	—	Priest
	Counsel	0.0	Lawyer	Priest
Descriptors				
H	Religious	1.0	Priest	Priest
	Loving	0.96	Mother, husband, wife	Mother, husband, sister
	Curious	0.91	Tourist, researcher, journalist	Journalist, tourist, researcher
M	wise	0.71	Father, priest, professor	Professor, teacher, judge
	Loyal	0.65	Friend, husband, wife	Friend, citizen, soldier
	Obedient	0.46	Son, soldier, citizen	Student, son, daughter
L	Faithful	0.15	Wife, husband	Priest, secretary, chef
	Jovial	0.0	—	Politician
	Committed	0.0	Wife, husband	Farmer

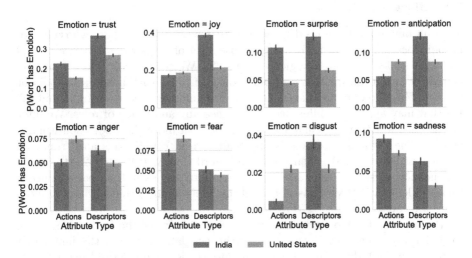

Fig. 2. AMT answers' emotions. The emotionality of actions and descriptors across social roles shows clear cultural differences in how each is conceived; plots show the probability of an action or descriptor using a word associated with each emotion in the NRC Emotion Lexicon, with bars showing 95% confidence intervals of mean probability.

US [15,37,40], these studies have typically looked at specific settings such as childhood development, rather than general attitudes; our data set provides a valuable new source of comparison.

5   Pilot Evaluation

We conduct two initial experiments to gauge how demographic-aware roles can be predicted from descriptors and actions using textual data. We evaluate our models on the task of predicting the most likely social roles for a given aspect. For example, if we think of *lovely,* we want to identify the roles in each culture that are most strongly associated with this descriptor. This enables us to underscore the particularities of each culture, where some roles are associated with softer traits, while others with stronger traits.

We take the top 20 aspects for each role from the survey responses of both countries and combine them into a set of descriptors and a set of actions. Table 5 shows statistics pertaining to these aspects. For each aspect, the set of expected roles (i.e., ground truth) are the ones for which the aspect appears in the top 20 responses. Evaluations are conducted on each aspect type separately. Our models rank the roles for each aspect, which we compare with the expected roles. We report the precision and recall at 5, averaged over the aspects. We also report Pearson correlation (which is typical in word similarity tasks [11,16]), as this gauges how accurate the model is in arranging the roles in order of association with the given aspect.

5.1   Blogger Data Set

To train our models, we need to employ text written by authors whose demographic location is known. For that, we use a set of blogs written between 1999 and 2016 collected from Google Blogger [22]. We select those blogs that also contain location information and only consider those with authors in India or the US. This allows us to analyze the cultural differences between India and the US that may appear as differences in the meaning and usage of roles. We filter out sentences with more than 150 words[2] or with more than 25% non-English words[3]. The remaining sentences are cleaned from HTML tags and truncated to the first 50 words. We then use the Stanford CoreNLP library [29] to obtain dependency parses for the sentences in our data set, as well as part-of-speech tags and lemmatized versions of the tokens. Only lemmas that occur 5 or more times are considered.

Because the US blog data is roughly twice the size of the Indian blog data, we balance the data by downsampling the US data to match the number of sentences in the Indian data. Table 6 provides statistics of the resulting data set.

---

[2] Normal sentences are rarely this long, and upon manual inspection we found that these tend to be malformed sentences.

[3] https://github.com/rfk/pyenchant.

Table 5. Statistics for unique aspect words given by survey responses.

Type	US-only	India-only	Both	All
Action	126	76	199	**401**
Descriptor	154	136	156	**446**

Table 6. Blog data statistics.

	# Sentences	# Tokens
US	17,476,527	348,479,631
US (balanced)	7,394,484	146,347,629
India	7,426,583	148,710,411

5.2 Computational Models to Predict Social Roles

We propose two computational models to predict social roles. The first model focuses on corpus statistics using dependency link counts, while the second uses neural-network dependency-based word embeddings.

Dependency Link Count (DLC). We first look for the actions and descriptors that engage in a syntactic relation with a role in a sentence as a way of modeling the way people associate roles and their aspects. In order to extract role-aspect relations, we leverage dependency parsing information.

Let us consider the following example: *"The attentive policeman arrested the perpetrators."* The dependency parse results in the following relations (the relations in which *policeman* appears in are italicized): *det* (policeman-3, The-1), *amod* (policeman-3, attentive-2), *nsubj* (arrested-4, policeman-3), root (ROOT-0, arrested-4), det (perpetrators-6, the-5), dobj (arrested-4, perpetrators-6).

The first three relations showcase scenarios where words appear with our target role *policeman*. Since we are interested in finding descriptors for the target role, we focus on the *AMOD* relationship (or adjectival modifier) where the role appears in the source position in the dependency relation; to identify associated actions for the target role, we utilize the *NSUBJ* relations (or nominal subject) where the role appears in the target position in the dependency relation. Consequently, *attentive* is marked as participating in an AMOD relation, while arrested participates in a NSUBJ relation, corresponding to descriptors and actions, respectively.

Word co-occurrence is used extensively to model relationships between words [8,9,17]. Therefore, we rank the roles for an aspect according to how frequently they co-occur in the link type corresponding to the aspect type.

Dependency Aspect Embedding (DAE). Neural word embeddings have proven useful for a large variety of tasks [14,45,49]. Here, we make use of their representation power, but aim to capture demographic-focused embeddings for social role aspects in particular. Previous work has shown that dependency-based word embeddings induce different word similarities [28], yielding more functional similarities, rather than topical similarities.

Rather than training our embedding models on all dependency links, we consider only the links that correspond to descriptors and actions. We train separate models for the two different link types for each of the two countries. This yields four models for: actions in the US, descriptors in the US, actions in India, and descriptors in India. We use the Python *Gensim* Word2Vec library and use 300 latent dimensions with negative sampling.

Table 7. Role prediction results for *actions* (left) and *descriptors* (right). Metrics: precision at 5, recall at 5 and Pearson correlation.

Model		Actions US P@5	R@5	Corr.	Actions India P@5	R@5	Corr.	Descriptors US P@5	R@5	Corr.	Descriptors India P@5	R@5	Corr.
DLC	US	**0.13**	**0.26**	**0.15**	**0.10**	**0.19**	**0.11**	**0.12**	**0.20**	**0.13**	0.09	0.14	0.07
	India	0.12	0.24	0.14	**0.10**	0.18	**0.11**	0.11	**0.20**	0.11	**0.10**	**0.16**	**0.09**
DAE	US	**0.12**	**0.28**	**0.14**	**0.11**	0.24	0.12	**0.09**	**0.19**	**0.09**	0.08	**0.18**	0.08
	India	0.11	0.25	0.12	**0.11**	**0.25**	**0.13**	**0.09**	0.17	**0.09**	**0.09**	**0.18**	**0.09**

For a given aspect (a descriptor or action), we compute the cosine similarity between the embedding pertaining to the aspect and the embedding pertaining to each of the social roles. The roles are then ranked according to their cosine similarity, where higher values imply a greater likelihood that the aspect is associated with the role.

5.3   Evaluations and Discussions

Our experiments analyze models that are widely assumed to capture social information [23] and we test the degree to which they are able to do so on a data set designed with this information in mind. The results for the role prediction task are provided in Table 7[4]. The columns represent the source countries of the survey responses, used as the gold standard data for evaluation, while the rows indicate the country of the blogs on which the models were trained. Bold values represent the best performance, when comparing between model countries, for a given combination of model type and gold standard evaluation.

The DAE model is able to achieve a higher recall for actions than the DLC model, but otherwise the two perform comparably. Notably, these two models achieve equal or better performance when the country of the gold standard responses matches the one on which the model was trained. This implies that these models are picking up the distinctive cultural features of the countries.

The gap between identical models trained on different countries is more pronounced when evaluating on the gold standard US responses than on the Indian responses. As English is not the primary language used by Indians, online users may implicitly be conforming to Western societal norms.

We also noticed that implicit or common sense aspect assumptions, while appearing in primary positions in AMT responses, were less likely to appear in the blog data, and sometime did not occur at all. For instance, *faithful* is a top AMT descriptor for *wife* and *husband*, but occurs very infrequently in the blog text. We also see this for *educated* with *professor* and *creative* with *musician*. Blog data often contained aspects that were actually antonyms of the actions

---

[4] Results for word association tasks are traditionally low, and our results are within the same range as previous word association research [21].

and descriptors provided as answers by the respondents. For example, *corrupt* is among the most frequent descriptors linked to *policeman*, as is *estranged* with *wife* and *unwed* with *mother*. This shows that commonsense knowledge is often not expressed in text, as humans tend not to state the obvious. Consequently, in the blog genre, one tends to express anomalous behavior as it pertains to roles.

6 Conclusion

In this paper we introduced a new data set of social roles and the associations they trigger in terms of actions and descriptors in two cultures (US and India). We showed that there are differences in the perceptions associated with the roles, with actions showcasing less variability and descriptors exhibiting a wider variation. Furthermore we analyzed the way roles are associated with various sentiment and emotional dimensions. We further used the data set we collected to conduct pilot evaluations focused on predicting social roles. Both our corpus-statistics and embedding dependency-based models show a stronger predictive ability when the train and test set culture match, indicating that there are indeed cultural differences that can be automatically accounted for in our models. In the future, we aim to devise more refined predictive models that could be used in a variety of settings, from predicting roles, to predicting aspects, to ultimately tackling model bias. The dataset introduced in this paper is publicly available at http://lit.eecs.umich.edu/downloads.html.

Acknowledgments. This material is based in part upon work supported by the Michigan Institute for Data Science, by the National Science Foundation (grant #1815291), and by the John Templeton Foundation (grant #61156). Any opinions, findings, and conclusions or recommendations expressed in this material are those of the author and do not necessarily reflect the views of the Michigan Institute for Data Science, the National Science Foundation, or the John Templeton Foundation.

References

1. Andrews, M., Vigliocco, G., Vinson, D.: Integrating experiential and distributional data to learn semantic representations. Psychol. Rev. **116**(3), 463 (2009)
2. Ashforth, B.E., Kreiner, G.E., Fugate, M.: All in a day's work: boundaries and micro role transitions. Acad. Manag. Rev. **25**(3), 472–491 (2000)
3. Bamman, D., Dyer, C., Smith, N.A.: Distributed representations of geographically situated language. In: Proceedings of the 52nd Annual Meeting of the Association for Computational Linguistics (Volume 2: Short Papers), pp. 828–834 (2014). http://www.aclweb.org/anthology/P/P14/P14-2134
4. Bamman, D., O'Connor, B., Smith, N.A.: Learning latent personas of film characters, pp. 352–361. http://www.aclweb.org/anthology/P13-1035
5. Bengio, Y., Ducharme, R., Vincent, P., Jauvin, C.: A neural probabilistic language model. J. Mach. Learn. Res. **3**(Feb), 1137–1155 (2003)
6. Berinsky, A.J., Huber, G.A., Lenz, G.S.: Evaluating online labor markets for experimental research: Amazon.com's mechanical turk. Political Anal. **20**(3), 351–368 (2012)

7. Biddle, B.J.: Recent developments in role theory. Ann. Rev. Sociol. **12**(1), 67–92 (1986)
8. Blei, D.M., Ng, A.Y., Jordan, M.I.: Latent Dirichlet allocation. J. Mach. Learn. Res. **3**, 993–1022 (2003)
9. Brown, P.F., Desouza, P.V., Mercer, R.L., Pietra, V.J.D., Lai, J.C.: Class-based n-gram models of natural language. Computat. Linguist. **18**(4), 467–479 (1992)
10. Bruni, E., Boleda, G., Baroni, M., Tran, N.K.: Distributional semantics in technicolor. In: Proceedings of the 50th Annual Meeting of the Association for Computational Linguistics: Long Papers-Volume 1, pp. 136–145. Association for Computational Linguistics (2012)
11. Chaudhari, D.L., Damani, O.P., Laxman, S.: Lexical co-occurrence, statistical significance, and word association. In: Proceedings of the Conference on Empirical Methods in Natural Language Processing, pp. 1058–1068. Association for Computational Linguistics (2011)
12. Cialdini, R.B., Kallgren, C.A., Reno, R.R.: A focus theory of normative conduct: a theoretical refinement and reevaluation of the role of norms in human behavior (1991)
13. Clifford, S., Jewell, R.M., Waggoner, P.D.: Are samples drawn from mechanical turk valid for research on political ideology? Res. Polit. **2**(4), 2053168015622072 (2015)
14. Collobert, R., Weston, J.: A unified architecture for natural language processing: deep neural networks with multitask learning. In: Proceedings of the 25th International Conference on Machine Learning, pp. 160–167. ACM (2008)
15. Daga, S.S., Raval, V.V., Raj, S.P.: Maternal meta-emotion and child socioemotional functioning in immigrant Indian and white American families. Asian Am. J. Psychol. **6**(3), 233 (2015)
16. De Deyne, S., Navarro, D.J., Storms, G.: Better explanations of lexical and semantic cognition using networks derived from continued rather than single-word associations. Behav. Res. Methods **45**(2), 480–498 (2013)
17. Deerwester, S., Dumais, S.T., Furnas, G.W., Landauer, T.K., Harshman, R.: Indexing by latent semantic analysis. J. Am. Soc. Inf. Sci. **41**(6), 391–407 (1990)
18. Eagly, A.H., Karau, S.J.: Role congruity theory of prejudice toward female leaders. Psychol. Rev. **109**(3), 573 (2002)
19. Esuli, A., Sebastiani, F.: SentiWordNet: a publicly available lexical resource for opinion mining. In: Proceedings of the 5th Conference on Language Resources and Evaluation (LREC 2006), Genova, IT (2006)
20. Feng, Y., Lapata, M.: Visual information in semantic representation. In: Human Language Technologies: The 2010 Annual Conference of the North American Chapter of the Association for Computational Linguistics, pp. 91–99. Association for Computational Linguistics (2010)
21. Garimella, A., Banea, C., Mihalcea, R.: Demographic-aware word associations. In: Proceedings of the International Conference on Empirical Methods in Natural Language Processing (EMNLP 2017), Copenhagen, Denmark (2017)
22. Garimella, A., Mihalcea, R., Pennebaker, J.: Identifying cross-cultural differences in word usage. In: Proceedings of the International Conference on Computational Linguistics (COLING 2016), Japan (2016)
23. Gupta, A., Boleda, G., Baroni, M., Padó, S.: Distributional vectors encode referential attributes. In: Proceedings of the 2015 Conference on Empirical Methods in Natural Language Processing, pp. 12–21. Association for Computational Linguistics, Lisbon, September 2015. https://doi.org/10.18653/v1/D15-1002. https://www.aclweb.org/anthology/D15-1002

24. Hovy, D., Purschke, C.: Capturing regional variation with distributed place representations and geographic retrofitting. In: Proceedings of the 2018 Conference on Empirical Methods in Natural Language Processing, pp. 4383–4394 (2018)

25. Jurgens, D., Tsvetkov, Y., Jurafsky, D.: Writer profiling without the writer's text. In: Ciampaglia, G.L., Mashhadi, A., Yasseri, T. (eds.) SocInfo 2017. LNCS, vol. 10540, pp. 537–558. Springer, Cham (2017). https://doi.org/10.1007/978-3-319-67256-4_43

26. Katz, D., Kahn, R.L.: The Social Psychology of Organizations, vol. 2. Wiley, New York (1978)

27. Kent, G.H., Rosanoff, A.J.: A study of association in insanity. Am. J. Psychiatry 67(1), 37–96 (1910)

28. Levy, O., Goldberg, Y.: Dependency-based word embeddings, pp. 302–308 (2014). http://www.aclweb.org/anthology/P14-2050

29. Manning, C.D., Surdeanu, M., Bauer, J., Finkel, J., Bethard, S.J., McClosky, D.: The Stanford CoreNLP natural language processing toolkit. In: Association for Computational Linguistics (ACL) System Demonstrations, pp. 55–60 (2014). http://www.aclweb.org/anthology/P/P14/P14-5010

30. Mikolov, T., Yih, W., Zweig, G.: Linguistic regularities in continuous space word representations. In: NAACL HLT, Atlanta, GA, USA, pp. 746–751 (2013)

31. Miller, G.A.: WordNet: a lexical database for English. Commun. Assoc. Comput. Mach. 38(11), 39–41 (1995)

32. Mohammad, S.M., Turney, P.D.: Crowdsourcing a word-emotion association lexicon. Comput. Intell. 29(3), 436–465 (2013)

33. Nelson, D.L., McEvoy, C.L., Schreiber, T.A.: The university of South Florida free association, rhyme, and word fragment norms. Behav. Res. Methods Instrum. Comput. 36(3), 402–407 (2004)

34. Paul, M., Girju, R.: Cross-cultural analysis of blogs and forums with mixed-collection topic models. In: Proceedings of the 2009 Conference on Empirical Methods in Natural Language Processing, Singapore, pp. 1408–1417, August 2009. http://www.aclweb.org/anthology/D/D09/D09-1146

35. Pennington, J., Socher, R., Manning, C.: Glove: global vectors for word representation. In: Proceedings of the 2014 Conference on Empirical Methods in Natural Language Processing (EMNLP), pp. 1532–1543 (2014)

36. Plutchik, R.: The Emotions. Random House, New York (1962)

37. Raval, V.V., Raval, P.H., Salvina, J.M., Wilson, S.L., Writer, S.: Mothers' socialization of children's emotion in india and the usa: a cross-and within-culture comparison. Soc. Dev. 22(3), 467–484 (2013)

38. Ritzer, G., et al.: The McDonaldization of Society. Pine Forge Press, Newbury Park (1992)

39. Rogers, A., Hosur Ananthakrishna, S., Rumshisky, A.: What's in your embedding, and how it predicts task performance. In: Proceedings of the 27th International Conference on Computational Linguistics, Santa Fe, NM, USA, pp. 2690–2703, August 2018

40. Roseman, I.J., Dhawan, N., Rettek, S.I., Naidu, R., Thapa, K.: Cultural differences and cross-cultural similarities in appraisals and emotional responses. J. Cross Cult. Psychol. 26(1), 23–38 (1995)

41. Salton, G., Lesk, M.: Computer evaluation of indexing and text processing. J. ACM 15(1), 8–36 (1968). https://doi.org/10.1145/321439.321441. http://portal.acm.org/citation.cfm?doid=321439.321441

42. Shweder, R.A.: Thinking Through Cultures: Expeditions in Cultural Psychology. Harvard University Press, Cambridge (1991)

43. Sunstein, C.R.: Social norms and social roles. Columbia Law Rev. **96**(4), 903–968 (1996)
44. Triandis, H.C., Marin, G., Hui, C.H., Lisansky, J., Ottati, V.: Role perceptions of hispanic young adults. J. Cross Cult. Psychol. **15**(3), 297–320 (1984)
45. Turian, J., Ratinov, L., Bengio, Y.: Word representations: a simple and general method for semi-supervised learning. In: Proceedings of the 48th Annual Meeting of the Association for Computational Linguistics, pp. 384–394. Association for Computational Linguistics (2010)
46. Wang, S., Manning, C.D.: Baselines and bigrams: simple, good sentiment and topic classification. In: Proceedings of the 50th Annual Meeting of the Association for Computational Linguistics: Short Papers, vol. 2, pp. 90–94 (2012). http://dl.acm.org/citation.cfm?id=2390688
47. Wilson, T., et al.: OpinionFinder: a system for subjectivity analysis. In: Proceedings of HLT/EMNLP 2005 Interactive Demonstrations (2005)
48. Zafar, L., Afzal, M.T., Ahmed, U.: Exploiting polarity features for developing sentiment analysis tool. In: EMSASW@ ESWC (2017)
49. Zou, W.Y., Socher, R., Cer, D., Manning, C.D.: Bilingual word embeddings for phrase-based machine translation. In: Proceedings of the 2013 Conference on Empirical Methods in Natural Language Processing, pp. 1393–1398 (2013)

Predicting Audience Engagement Across Social Media Platforms in the News Domain

Kholoud Khalil Aldous[1(✉)], Jisun An[2], and Bernard J. Jansen[2]

[1] College of Science and Engineering, Hamad Bin Khalifa University, Doha, Qatar
kaldous@mail.hbku.edu.qa
[2] Qatar Computing Research Institute, Hamad Bin Khalifa University, Doha, Qatar
{jisun.an,jjansen}@acm.org

Abstract. We analyze cross-platform factors for posts on both single and multiple social media platforms for numerous news outlets to better predict audience engagement, precisely the number of likes and comments. We collect 676,779 social media posts from 53 news outlets during eight months on four social media platforms (Facebook, Instagram, Twitter, and YouTube), along with the associated comments (more than 31 million) and the number of likes (more than 840 million). We develop a framework for predicting the audience engagement based on both linguistic features of the post and social media platform factors. Among other findings, results show that content with high engagement on one platform does not guarantee high engagement on another platform, even when news outlets use similar cross-platform posts; however, for some content, cross-sharing posts on a platform will increase overall audience engagement on another platform. As one of the few multiple social media platform studies, the findings have implications for the news domain, as well as other fields that distribute online content via social media.

Keywords: Audience engagement · News outlets · Social media

1 Introduction

News outlets that produce digital content rely on social media platforms for dissemination [34]. Nearly all news outlets engage in online content dissemination [13,26], that almost all have accounts on multiple social media platforms [37], and 67% of news readers get their news, at least in part, from social media platforms [35]. Given the importance of social media for reaching audiences, news outlets are interested in measuring and evaluating performance via these channels. As such, there are various audience engagement metrics with many of these metrics being platform-specific, such as the number of likes, and comments, which we frame into four levels, from private to public expressiveness of user engagement [3]. Additionally, there has been prior work that investigates audience engagement on various social media platforms from the perspective of the news outlet [5,25], the audience of a news outlet [38], or both [3].

© Springer Nature Switzerland AG 2019
I. Weber et al. (Eds.): SocInfo 2019, LNCS 11864, pp. 173–187, 2019.
https://doi.org/10.1007/978-3-030-34971-4_12

Although impactful, much of this prior work focused on single news outlets (e.g., The New York Times, Al Jazeera), single topics (e.g., disasters, sporting events), or single platforms (e.g., Twitter, YouTube). There is a critical need for an analysis of multiple news outlets across multiple social media platforms unconstrained by topic. It is obvious that news outlets do not operate in a vacuum and that many times, they are competing with other news and other content creation outlets across multiple online platforms for audience numbers or are sharing an audience with other content organizations (i.e., a reader engaging with the same content from multiple news sources). Therefore, to truly investigate audience engagement effects, one should not limit the investigation to a single news outlet or a single social media platform; the investigation requires multiple news outlets posting content across multiple social media platforms. Although there has been some prior work looking into multiple news outlets [5,38], this work does not focus on audience engagement. There is also a general scarcity of cross-platform social media studies, especially in the news domain. Although a few prior works have focused on more than one platform [7,11,27], little has focused on the news industry. This lack of cross-platform analysis is a particularly notable shortcoming, as studies highlight that people generally have multiple social media accounts and get their news from multiple sources [38].

Gottfried [16] reports that 34% of users access multiple social media accounts to consume news, and some of these social media platforms attract millions of users (i.e., audience members of the news outlets) in a given day with the largest social media platforms used by news outlet being Facebook, Twitter, Instagram, and YouTube [37]. Understanding platforms differences and audience preferences across platforms are two main challenges for creating engaging content [2]. Given that news outlets are employing multiple social media platforms to distribute content [37] and the audience they are attempting to engage with are interacting with multiple social media platforms and multiple news outlets [16,33], it seems reasonable that there may be interaction effects as news outlets attempt to engage with their audience across these platforms. However, given the lack of prior work with both multiple organizations and platforms, there are several open questions. *Does audience engagement differ across platforms? Are there different audience behaviors for a news outlet on different platforms? Is news content transferable across platforms with similar engagement?* These are some of the questions that motivate our research.

To address a portion of these questions, we analyze social media posts from 53 worldwide news outlets across four major social media platforms during a continuous 8-month period. The contributions of this research are, first, an inclusive social media analysis of audience engagement for multiple major news outlets rather than an investigation of a single news source. Second, an analysis of these news outlets across multiple social media platforms, which allows for both single and cross-platform effects. Finally, the research examines potential audience engagement differences across platforms by analyzing news content posted on multiple platforms, shedding light on possible audience engagement strategies for these news outlets as they operate in a competitive online environment.

Our research differs from the existing work in that we perform a cross-platform study for four of the most active social media platforms in the news domain. Second, we predict audience engagement (high or low) for a social media post before it is published by employing linguistic features of the posts and cross-platform engagement feature. Lastly, for researchers and practitioners, this research offers insights regarding how to conduct multi-platform studies and the relationship between platforms' affordances and audience engagement.

2 Research Objectives

We aim to understand what are the similarities and differences in news outlets posting behavior and the effect of cross-sharing engagement factors for improving the prediction of user engagement. Our results can assist news outlets when using multiple social media platforms for distributing content. Focusing on the linguistic and cross-sharing aspects of the social media posts, we formulate the following research questions (RQ):

RQ1: Do news outlets tailor content when posting the same story on multiple platforms?

RQ2: Does cross-platform posting contribute to higher audience engagement?

To answer the first question, we extract the content that news outlets posted to more than one social media platform, called *cross-shared posts*. Then, we use similarity metrics to analyze the wording differences of posts across platforms. In addressing the second research question, we use *cross-shared posts*, to investigate audience engagement (likes and comments). We build a model that predicts the level of audience engagement given to a post for each platform. We use two different feature sets: (1) language features as Term Frequency-Inverse Document Frequency (TF-IDF) matrix, and (2) the level of audience engagement on another platform (called cross-platform engagement feature). By comparing the two sets of features for these multiple platform content, findings shed light on the effects of platforms impacting audience engagement.

3 Related Work

3.1 Audience Engagement in the News Domains

Audience engagement is a broad concept that encompasses a variety of phenomenon, including exposure, attention, interaction, and involvement [21,30]. At its base, engagement begins with exposure, but it constitutes additional psychological and behavioral experiences [12,30] that can be viewed from the perspective of the user, the medium, or both [32]. However, research on audience engagement typically focuses on producing, consuming, interacting with, or disseminating information, and collecting metrics to measure these engagement types [22]. This implies that the audience takes some action with the content as a fundamental component of engagement. It is these actions that news outlets are interested in measuring on social media platforms. The expected benefits for news outlets from a high level of audience engagement are superior outcomes, including popularity growth, cost reduction, and brand referrals [29]. Research on news consumption has relied on measuring user behaviors, such as page views and likes, as a composite of various metrics of both exposure and engagement behaviors [18]. One of the reasons that news outlets are interested in distributing content via social media platforms is that, in addition to the massive potential for exposure, online delivery of media via these platforms permits measurement at the individual story level. Additionally, audiences that satisfied with how they used a social media platform continually used the platform. Social media platforms also provide rather precise ways to measure whether and how a specific piece of content was consumed and, to some degree, a level of audience engagement; although, there may be news outlet differences on attracting audience [20].

3.2   Cross-Platform Analysis of Audience Engagement

While there are some studies using datasets from multiple platforms [3, 6, 7], there has been little large-scale cross-platform social media analysis in any domain. Studies have mainly focused on user behaviors and user interests on different platforms [23, 24, 39]. Additionally, there have been some studies in the news domain [10, 15, 17, 36]; however, they are small-scale studies. Research has examined cross-posting activity on multiple platforms on a larger scale, but it did not look at audience engagement [14]. Prior work [11] has shown that it is possible to accurately model overall traffic by observing the first few minutes of social media reactions. In [27], researchers report that the volume and attitude of social media posts have a significant causality relationship to the amount of web searching and that they have interaction effects on social media traffic [28], although, the focus of these studies was not specific to the news domain.

4   Data Collection and Methodology

To investigate our research questions, we develop a list (a) of news outlets and (b) the social media platforms on which these news outlets posted content. We then collect the content that these news outlets posted to the social media platforms, along with audience engagement numbers for each post. We describe our data collection methodology here.

4.1   Selection of News Outlets and Social Media Platforms

We identify English news outlets with popular online presences using different ranking sources of news sources, including PewResearch [1] and Wallethub [31]. After examining the social media presence of different news outlets, we keep those outlets that are active across different social media platforms. This process results in 53 news outlets (see Appendix A).

For this cross-social media platform research, we select the four most popular social media platforms used most by news outlet based on eBizMBA rank [19], which are Facebook, Twitter, Instagram, and YouTube. We then identify the verified social media profiles for each news outlet on each of these platforms. For each news outlet, we select one social media account per platform that has worldwide English news and not specialized for a topic (e.g., sports).

4.2 Data Collection

In creating our dataset, we target the 53 news outlets' social media accounts on each of the four platforms for an eight months data collection period, January through August 2017, inclusive. We report the total number of collected posts with the total associated engagement metrics (likes and comments) in Table 1. In YouTube, two news outlets were not active, and two others have disabled the commenting feature.

Facebook (FB): For collecting Facebook posts from the news outlet' pages, We build a web crawler via the Facebook API. Each collected post is associated with audience engagement metrics (e.g., number of likes and comments).

Instagram (IG): Using the profile name of each news outlet, we implement a crawler that retrieves all Instagram posts, with associated engagement metrics, that are publicly available online in their profile. Then, for only retaining the eight months posts, we filter them by posting time.

Twitter (TW): To overcome the limitations of Twitter's maximum number of posts that can be collected, from an account, we use a web scraper to collect all publicly available posts. We collect each news outlet's tweets IDs using the eight months time filter. Using the IDs of the tweets, we collect the content of the tweets with associated audience engagement metrics through Twitter API.

YouTube (YT): The search function of YouTube Data API takes the news outlet channel name as input and return the publicly available YouTube posts information of that news outlet. Using this function, we collect all videos posts information including title, description, and engagement metrics.

4.3 Engagement Metrics

We use two engagement metrics: (a) likes ratio (LR) and (b) comments ratio (CR), as 'likes' and 'comments' are common and measurable across all the four

Table 1. Count of social media posts, comments, and likes by platform and totals.

	Posts	Comments	Likes
FB	27,117	984,266	70,557,281
IG	35,289	11,732,837	723,493,279
TW	571,270	14,426,570	13,604,785
YT	43,103	4,674,630	33,265,610
Total	676,779	31,818,303	840,920,955

social platforms. We also considered share ratio (e.g., shares on FB or retweets on TW), but we found it highly correlated with LR (Pearson correlation of 0.83), so we do not report it in this work. Instead, we focus on analyzing user engagement at the post-level, using likes and comments.

Likes Ratio (LR): The number of likes is a common engagement metric for a post on many platforms. Our dataset contains posts that received thousands of likes; however, plenty of posts also received zero likes. In order to deal with the huge difference between the number of likes for different posts, we apply a log function. Furthermore, posts tend to receive likes over a specific period; to accommodate this effect, we divide the number of likes by duration in days for normalization. The duration is the number of days from posting time to the day we collected the data. Normalizing by the maximum number of likes is required for the news media of which the content is posted, as each news media has its maximum value. We consider this value as an estimation for the audience volume.

A limitation for this method is that some posts that are very close to the collection period can get more credit compared to the posts of the first day of the collection time, as some posts do keep getting likes and comments for a more extended period than others. However, this way of normalization helps on standardizing the measure across platforms. Throughout the paper, we use likes ratio to represent the log-normalized values for the number of likes. The equation used for calculating LR for a post i is the following: $LR_i = \log_2(\frac{L_i+1}{T_i+M_i})$, where L_i is the number of likes of the post i, and T_i is the number of days from the posting day till the collection day, inclusive. M_i is the maximum number of likes for the news outlet that posted the content.

Comments Ratio (CR): Similar to the likes ratio, we use the log-normalization approach to calculate the comments ratio using the posts' number of comments. The equation used for calculating CR for a post i is: $CR_i = \log_2(\frac{C_i+1}{T_i+M_i})$, where C_i is the number of comments and T_i is the number of days from the posting day till the collection day, inclusive. M_i is the maximum number of comments for the news outlet that posted the content.

4.4   Extracting Cross-Shared Post

We extract cross-shared posts, which is the content that news outlets have posted on more than one social media platform. To determine cross-shared posts, we pair posts from each platform with posts on the other three platforms for each news outlet within three days. For all potential post pairs, we adopt a content-based matching method used in prior work for finding the same user across social media platforms with a 94.5% accuracy [4] and an approach shown sufficient for news article [9]. In our case, we aim to find similar news posts across social media platforms. URLs matching is another possible way for finding cross-shared posts; however, URLs are not commonly used in Instagram and YouTube posts. Also, when expanding Twitter URLs, we found many invalid links, or they relate back to the homepage of the news outlet website and not to the specific news article.

Table 2. Number of cross-shared posts for platform pairs,with results of manual validation of 100 postings

Platform	#Pairs	Matched
FB-TW	5600	94%
FB-IG	3174	37%
FB-YT	5327	53%
IG-TW	10527	83%
IG-YT	8942	37%
TW-YT	2449	77%

To this end, we represent each post in a TF-IDF vector and then examine whether the two posts are similar or not by computing cosine similarity. We first apply tokenization and then construct a TF-IDF matrix for each posts pair. Once having the TF-IDF matrix, we compute the cosine similarity between two posts. We use a cosine similarity threshold of 0.3, eliminating all post pairs less than the threshold[1]. The result of this process is a set of post pairs for the six different platform pairs that are (a) Facebook-Twitter (FB-TW), (b) Facebook-Instagram (FB-IG), (c) Facebook-YouTube (FB-YT), (d) Instagram-YouTube (IG-YT), (e) Instagram-Twitter (IG-TW), (f) Twitter-YouTube (TW-YT). The number of pairs (#pairs) for each platform pair is shown in Table 2.

In order to validate the cross-shared posts for each platform pair, we manually labeled a random sample of 100 post pairs from each of the platform pairs. One of the authors performed the labeling–a pair of posts is labeled one (1) if they refer to the same story (cross-shared) and zero (0) otherwise. The findings from the manual validation match (matched) are shown in Table 2. We observe that the three pairs, including Twitter, FB-TW, IG-TW, and TW-YT, have high matching rates while the other three pairs have low matching rates. This result is in line with findings by [24], where Twitter was found to be the dominant destination for 54% of cross-sharing activities. One reason is that the cross-sharing support and usability within Instagram and YouTube use Twitter as a destination. Hence, the functional aspects of social platforms strongly affect the cross-sharing behavior. Based on the results, we use FB-TW, IG-TW, and TW-YT for our cross-shared posts analysis.

4.5 Building Models for Predicting Audience Engagement

We build a model that predicts audience engagement level of posts for each platform. We set our prediction task as a binary classification–the model predicts whether a given post will have high or low audience engagement on a platform, building separate models for each platform. We take the top and bottom 33% of

---

[1] The threshold was chosen based on our manual inspection of 600 randomly selected pairs.

the data and consider the top 33% as posts with high engagement and the bottom 33% as posts with low engagement. We use this method to distinguish highly engaging content from low engaging content and to make it clearer for the model for understanding the features differences. Another reason is to overcome the class imbalance problem, as having the top and bottom percentage equal (33%), the number of posts within each class is almost equal, and thus, the random baseline of our classifier is 0.5. Since each news media source has a different distribution for their LR and CR, we added news outlet as a categorical input feature to the model. Hence, we use different 0.33 and 0.66 percentile values across individual news media depending on their posts' engagement metrics. For example, on Twitter, the MSNBC news comments ratio top 33% is equal to 0.21 (0.66 percentile), and the bottom 33% value is -1.16 (0.33 percentile), so all posts with a comments ratio greater than 0.21 are labeled 1 (2,436 posts) and posts with comments ratio less than -1.16 are labeled 0 (2,348 posts). Posts in between are not considered in this analysis, and we reserve them for future research.

We use three different feature sets: (1) language features as a proxy of the topic of the content; (2) the level of audience engagement on another platform; and (3) news outlet as a categorical feature. To construct the language features for each platform, we take the text of all posts, and we remove punctuation and stop words, then we apply tokenization and stemming. Once we have cleaned the posts, we construct a TF-IDF matrix with setting three parameters: maximum IDF of 0.8, minimum IDF of 0.001, and the maximum number of features (i.e., words) of 2,000. The third feature is only available for cross-shared posts. Thus, we use this feature for examining audience engagement interaction among cross-shared posts. We use the news outlet categorical feature for building all models to address the effect of the actual news outlets.

To measure the prediction results, we use F1-score, Precision, Recall, and Area Under the Curve (AUC) using 10-fold cross-validation. We only report the F1 score, as results for all measures were positively correlated. We test several classification algorithms, including AdaBoost, Decision Tree, Logistic Regression, and Random Forest.

5   Results and Discussion

We aim to unveil whether knowing the level of audience engagement for a post on one platform can predict the audience engagement for the post on another platform. For this, we will use cross-shared posts (i.e., those posts a news outlet shares on more than one platform). We first explore the similarities between cross-shared posts.

5.1   Similarities of Cross-Shared Posts

For addressing the first research question (RQ1), we average three text similarity measures for the cross-shared posts, which are: Jaro distance, Levenshtein

Table 3. Average text similarity between cross-shared posts using three measures Jaro distance, Levenshtein distance, and cosine similarity. The last two columns show the average number of words per post for paired platforms (P1 and P2).

P1-P2	Jaro	Levenshtein	Cosine	Words (P1)	Words (P2)
TW-FB	0.75	81.00	0.52	116.00	135.66
TW-IG	0.71	227.69	0.51	108.39	284.60
TW-YT	0.59	601.23	0.38	119.72	681.20

distance, and cosine similarity of two posts. Jaro distance value range from 0 to 1, where the higher the Jaro distance for two posts is, the more similar the posts are. Levenshtein distance is the minimum number of single-character edits that are necessary to modify one post to obtain another post, hence the lower is the distance, the higher is the similarity between the two posts. Cosine similarity measures how similar the two posts are likely to be in terms of their subject matter, where a value of 1 means exact match and 0 means dissimilar. Table 3 shows the average similarities with the average number of words per post for both paired platforms posts. News outlets posting to TW and FB are the most similar with 0.75 similarity using Jaro distance. Then, TW and IG postings are less similar with Jaro distance of 0.71, which is related more to the extended size of IG posts, which is on average 284 word per post. The cross-shared posts between TW-YT are less similar with 0.59 Jaro and 601 Levenshtein distance.

Generally, news outlets tend to make posts different from each other when cross-posted on multiple platforms. It appears that some news outlets are making an effort to tailor their posts to each platform, even if the original article is the same. News outlets do tailor their posts to individual social media platforms, with varying degrees of similarity between platforms, which addresses the first research question.

5.2 Predicting Audience Engagement for All Posts

As explained in the methods section, we first predict the level of audience engagement for a given post for each platform using linguistic features. Table 4 presents the F1-scores of 10-fold cross-validation using AdaBoost, Decision Tree, Logistic Regression, and Random Forest on each platform. The best performing algorithm in this experiment is logistic regression for both LR and CR. The best F1 score is 0.69, which is the YouTube prediction model for CR using linguistic features (L). We can observe from this experiment that audience engagement can be predicted with F1 scores ranging from 0.62 to 69 across all platforms using logistic regression.

5.3 Predicting Audience Engagement for Cross-Shared Posts

Cross-shared posts provide a unique opportunity to understand how news outlet are leveraging multiple social media platforms in their audience engagement

Table 4. F1-scores of the four algorithms predicting engagement for a post on each platform using linguistic features (L).

	FB		IG		TW		YT	
	LR	CR	LR	CR	LR	CR	LR	CR
AdaBoost	0.45	0.54	0.66	0.49	0.52	0.59	0.56	0.61
Decision tree	0.59	0.62	0.63	0.60	0.62	0.65	0.61	0.61
Logistic regression	**0.62**	**0.64**	**0.68**	**0.66**	**0.65**	**0.68**	**0.67**	**0.69**
Random forest	0.60	**0.64**	0.63	0.61	**0.65**	0.67	0.61	0.63

strategies. We exploit the level of audience engagement on one platform in order to predict audience engagement on another platform. As mentioned in the methods section, we examined how many posts were cross-shared on two platforms (Table 2). We use the three pairs (FB-TW, IG-TW, and YT-TW), as they have the highest percentage of cross-shared posts (>75%).

Table 5 reports the Pearson's correlation coefficients for testing whether the level of audience engagement (either LR or CR) in two paired platforms are similar or not for those cross-shared posts. Facebook and Instagram have a positive correlation with Twitter for both LR and CR, indicating that a post having high LR/CR on Twitter is more likely to have high LR/CR on Facebook or Instagram, and vice versa. YouTube LR (CR) has a positive (negative) correlation with Twitter LR, but there is no significant relation between Twitter CR and YT. Overall, the results indicate that a post can be popular on different platforms, which could be the result of different factors, including posts' linguistic features or platforms' audience differences.

We build an audience engagement prediction model with the cross-shared posts for each of the platform pairs. A separate model for each platform, and thus, for example, the FB-TW pair results in two prediction models: (1) predicting audience engagement on FB using TW information and (2) predicting audience engagement on TW using FB information. Across all models, we use four algorithms (AdaBoost, Decision Tree, Logistic Regression, and Random Forest) and employ 10-fold cross-validation. Table 6 shows the results of predicting audience engagement on TW based on FB, IG, and YT information (LR or CR). We compare the model using linguistic features (L) to a model with an addi-

Table 5. The Pearson correlation between engagement metrics of cross-shared content based on cosine similarity.

		FB		IG		YT	
		LR	CR	LR	CR	LR	CR
TW	LR	0.27**	0.28**	0.52**	0.25**	0.36**	−0.23**
	CR	0.24**	0.19**	0.05**	0.18**	0.05*	0.01

Significant level codes: * $p < 0.05$, ** $p < 0.001$

Table 6. F1-scores of the four algorithms predicting engagement based on cross-shared posts on Twitter using other platforms information. Using linguistic features (L) and cross-platform information (C) with linguistic features (L+C).

			FB		IG		YT	
			L	L+C	L	L+C	L	L+C
TW	AdaBoost	LR	0.55	0.73	0.65	0.72	0.59	0.68
		CR	0.58	0.72	0.53	0.76	0.66	0.73
	Decision tree	LR	0.65	**0.74**	0.69	**0.75**	**0.71**	**0.71**
		CR	**0.68**	**0.74**	**0.70**	**0.77**	**0.73**	**0.77**
	Logistic regression	LR	**0.66**	0.70	**0.70**	**0.75**	0.69	0.69
		CR	**0.67**	0.69	**0.70**	0.74	0.72	0.72
	Random forest	LR	0.53	0.66	0.55	0.63	0.52	0.58
		CR	0.48	0.67	0.46	0.75	0.51	0.54

Table 7. F1-scores of the four algorithms for predicting engagement on the three platforms using Twitter information of cross-shared posts.

			FB		IG		YT	
			L	L+C	L	L+C	L	L+C
TW	AdaBoost	LR	0.48	0.73	0.70	0.72	0.59	0.64
		CR	0.63	0.73	0.65	0.75	0.65	0.67
	Decision tree	LR	**0.70**	**0.75**	**0.73**	**0.77**	**0.70**	**0.71**
		CR	**0.72**	**0.75**	**0.75**	**0.79**	**0.73**	0.71
	Logistic regression	LR	0.66	0.69	0.70	0.74	0.67	0.68
		CR	0.70	**0.75**	0.70	0.78	0.72	**0.72**
	Random forest	LR	0.52	0.66	0.67	0.69	0.54	0.58
		CR	0.54	0.67	0.62	0.73	0.53	0.56

tional feature of cross-platform engagement (C), i.e., the LR or CR on another platform. We denote this full model as L+C. On all platforms, using the cross-platform engagement feature significantly improves the F1-score by 7–23% for AdaBoost and 3–29% for Random Forest. Using logistic regression, LR and CR improve across FB and IG but not YT. Decision Tree shows the best F1-scores with an improvement of 6–9% when using L+C for both FB and IG, but shows slight improvement for YT CR and no effect using YT LR. Generally, there is certainly a cross-platform effect occurring, where the effect is more pronounced with FB and IG.

Table 7 shows the results of audience engagement prediction on the three platforms: FB, IG, and YT based on information from TW. FB achieves 25% and 10% improvement using AdaBoost for LR and CR, respectively. IG, taking similar advantage of TW information, has a 4% improvement using Decision Tree for LR and CR. Twitter information has slightly less effect on the prediction results of YT, with LR (5%) and CR (1%) using AdaBoost. However, using TW engagement feature to predict YT engagement with Decision Tree shows a slight improvement on LR and negative effect on CR.

Overall, for answering RQ2, we observe that using the cross-platform information can improve audience engagement prediction by 1–25%. The cross-shared effect is less between TW and YT in relative to TW and the other platforms. One reason could be that audience base or their preferences for the content of the two platforms are too different, or the technology affordance differences of the platforms do not lend themselves to shared content.

5.4   Implications for News Outlets

Our research findings using cross-shared posts provide new insights for using multiple social media platforms in the news domain, with possible implications for other domains and online user measurement [8]. First, content with high engagement on one platform does not guarantee success on another platform, even when news outlets use similar posts across platforms. Secondly, there is significant, notable engagement improvement for content that is shared cross-platform among Facebook, YouTube, and Instagram interacting with Twitter, indicating that Twitter may be a bridge platform to audience segments on these other platforms. However, there seems to be a reciprocal effect with cross-shared posts, also boosting engagement on Twitter. Finding cross-shared posts between platforms (e.g., FB-IG) other than Twitter is needed, which can be done through a crowdsourcing labeling task. The trend might differ by domains, and conducting similar experiments using datasets of other domains is needed. For instance, this "bridging" can potentially help in the marketing domain to define which platform best fits a marketing campaign and whether cross-sharing the campaign content onto other platforms generates more audience engagement.

6   Conclusions and Future Research

Prior understanding of audience engagement factors across social media platforms for a given domain was based on a patchwork of different studies, done across individual platforms, and focusing on one to a small number of news outlets, often with small datasets. In our research, we use a large number of news outlets with a large number of posts and analyze audience engagement across multiple platforms in order to study the cross-platform engagement effect. From our findings, we presented both theoretical and practical implications that further academic research and provides actionable advice for content producers. As such, the research presented here expands the prior work on engagement by focusing on multiple news outlets within a single domain and content from these news outlets in a cross-platform perspective.

In term of limitations, we highlight two confounding factors that could influence study findings, which are promoted or boosted posts. For promoted posts, since promotion works only on one platform, one could imagine that social media managers may boost different posts on different platforms according to different strategies which could throw off the observed values of engagement. Although we attempted to control the audience differences between outlets, many other user factors can influence the results. Different user features (e.g., demographics) and the overlapping percentage between platforms might affect the results. Also, the quality of matching cross-shared posts needs to be improved through manual labeling of all posts and not only a sample of 100, as done in this study. Finally, there is a need to validate whether or not CR and LR are good metrics compared to other metrics, such as impressions or reach.

A   The list of news outlets

The list of the 53 news outlets is shown in Table 8:

Table 8. List of 53 online news organizations

ABC News	Los Angeles Times	The New York Times
AlJazeera	Mail Online	The Verge
BBC News	Mic	The Wall Street Journal
Bleacher Report	MSNBC	The Washington Post
Bloomberg	National Public Radio	The Week
Boston.com	NBC News	The Blaze
Breitbart News Network	NDTV	TIME
Business Insider	New York Post	U.S. News & World Report
BuzzFeed	Newsweek	Upworthy
CBS News	NY Daily News	USA Today
Chicago Tribune	Qatar Tribune	VICE
CNBC	Salon	Vox
CNN	Slate	Xinhua News Agency
CNN digital Network	The Associated Press	
Examiner.com	The Atlantic Magazine	
Financial Times	The Boston Globe	
Forbes	The Daily Beast	
Fortune	The Economist	
Fox News	The Guardian	
Huffington Post	The Hill	

References

1. The Top 25 (2011). https://www.journalism.org/2011/05/09/top-25/. Accessed 15 Apr 2019
2. Aldous, K.K., An, J., Jansen, B.J.: The challenges of creating engaging content : results from a focus group study of a popular news media organization. In: ACM CHI (2019)

3. Aldous, K.K., An, J., Jansen, B.J.: View, like, comment, post: analyzing user engagement by topic at 4 levels across 5 social media platforms for 53 news organizations. In: ICWSM (2019)

4. Alvarez, J.J., Mendoza, F.A., Labrador, M.: An accurate way to cross reference users across social networks. In: SoutheastCon. IEEE (2017)

5. An, J., Cha, M., Gummadi, P.K., Crowcroft, J.: Media landscape in Twitter: a world of new conventions and political diversity. In: ICWSM (2011)

6. An, J., Quercia, D., Crowcroft, J.: Partisan sharing: Facebook evidence and societal consequences. In: COSN. ACM (2014)

7. An, J., Weber, I.: Diversity in online advertising: a case study of 69 brands on social media. In: Staab, S., Koltsova, O., Ignatov, D.I. (eds.) SocInfo 2018. LNCS, vol. 11185, pp. 38–53. Springer, Cham (2018). https://doi.org/10.1007/978-3-030-01129-1_3

8. Balbi, S., Misuraca, M., Scepi, G.: Combining different evaluation systems on social media for measuring user satisfaction. Inf. Process. Manag. **54**(4), 674–685 (2018)

9. Barrón-Cedeo, A., Jaradat, I., Martino, G.D.S., Nakov, P.: Proppy: organizing the news based on their propagandistic content. Inf. Process. Manag. **56**(5), 1849–1864 (2019)

10. Brems, C., Temmerman, M., Graham, T., Broersma, M.: Personal branding on Twitter. Digit. J. **5**(4), 443–459 (2017)

11. Castillo, C., El-Haddad, M., Pfeffer, J., Stempeck, M.: Characterizing the life cycle of online news stories using social media reactions. In: CSCW. ACM (2014)

12. Constantinides, M., Dowell, J.: A framework for interaction-driven user modeling of mobile news reading behaviour. In: UMAP. ACM (2018)

13. Dragoni, M., Federici, M., Rexha, A.: An unsupervised aspect extraction strategy for monitoring real-time reviews stream. Inf. Process. Manag. **56**(3), 1103–1118 (2019)

14. Farahbakhsh, R., Cuevas, A., Crespi, N.: Characterization of cross-posting activity for professional users across Facebook, Twitter and Google+. Soc. Netw. Anal. Min. **6**(1), 33 (2016)

15. Fletcher, R., Nielsen, R.K.: Are people incidentally exposed to news on social media? a comparative analysis. New Media Soc. **20**(7), 2450–2468 (2018)

16. Gottfried, J., Sheare, E.: News use across social media platforms 2016. State of the News Media, pp. 1–20 (2016)

17. Hladk, R., Štětka, V.: The powers that tweet. J. Stud. **18**(2), 154–174 (2017)

18. Hussein, R., Hassan, S.: Customer engagement on social media: how to enhance continuation of use. Online Inf. Rev. **41**(7), 1006–1028 (2017)

19. Kallas, P.: Top 15 most popular social networking sites, July 2017 (2017). http://www.ebizmba.com/articles/social-networking-websites. Accessed 19 Aug 2018

20. Kim, S.M., et al.: Twitter content eliciting user engagement: a case study on Australian organisations. In: WWW. ACM (2017)

21. Ksiazek, T.B., Peer, L., Lessard, K.: User engagement with online news: conceptualizing interactivity and exploring the relationship between online news videos and user comments. New Media Soc. **18**(3), 502–520 (2016)

22. Lalmas, M., O'Brien, H., Yom-Tov, E.: Measuring user engagement. Synth. Lect. Inf. Concepts, Retrieval Serv. **6**(4), 1–132 (2014)

23. Lee, R.K.W., Hoang, T.A., Lim, E.P.: On analyzing user topic-specific platform preferences across multiple social media sites. In: WWW (2017)

24. Lim, B.H., Lu, D., Chen, T., Kan, M.Y.: # mytweet via instagram: exploring user behaviour across multiple social networks. In: ASONAM. ACM (2015)

25. Mele, I., Bahrainian, S.A., Crestani, F.: Event mining and timeliness analysis from heterogeneous news streams. Inf. Process. Manag. **56**(3), 969–993 (2019)

26. Mitchell, A., Holcomb, J., Weisel, R.: Data and trends about key sectors in the U.S. news media industry. State of the News Media, pp. 1–118 (2016)

27. Mukherjee, P., Jansen, B.J.: Conversing and searching: the causal relationship between social media and web search. Internet Res. **27**(5), 1209–1226 (2017)

28. Mukherjee, P., Jansen, B.J.: Information sharing by viewers via second screens for in-real-life events. Trans. Web **11**(1), 1:1–1:24 (2017)

29. Muñoz Expósito, M., Oviedo-García, M., Castellanos-Verdugo, M.: How to measure engagement in Twitter: advancing a metric. Internet Res. **27**, 1122–1148 (2017)

30. Napoli, P.M.: Audience Evolution: New Technologies and the Transformation of Media Audiences. Columbia University Press, New York (2011)

31. Nicolae, M.: 2016's best news sites (2016). https://wallethub.com/blog/best-news-sites/21699/. Accessed 15 Apr 2019

32. O'Brien, H.L., Toms, E.G.: What is user engagement? a conceptual framework for defining user engagement with technology. Am. Soc. Inf. Sci. Technol. **59**(6), 938–955 (2008)

33. Picone, I., Courtois, C., Paulussen, S.: When news is everywhere: understanding participation, cross-mediality and mobility in journalism from a radical user perspective. J. Pract. **9**(1), 35–49 (2015)

34. Schlagwein, D., Hu, M.: How and why organisations use social media: five use types and their relation to absorptive capacity. J. Inf. Technol. **32**(2), 194–209 (2017)

35. Shearer, E., Gottfried, J.: News use across social media platforms 2017. Pew Research Center (2017)

36. Smith, A.N., Fischer, E., Yongjian, C.: How does brand-related user-generated content differ across Youtube, Facebook, and Twitter? J. Interact. Mark. **26**(2), 102–113 (2012)

37. Stocking, G.: Digital news fact sheet. State of the News Media, pp. 1–2 (2017)

38. Swart, J., Peters, C., Broersma, M.: Navigating cross-media news use: media repertoires and the value of news in everyday life. J. Stud. **18**(11), 1343–1362 (2017)

39. Zhong, C., Chan, H.w., Karamshuk, D., Lee, D., Sastry, N.: Wearing many (social) hats: how different are your different social network personae? In: ICWSM (2017)

Quantifying Polarization on Twitter: The Kavanaugh Nomination

Kareem Darwish[(✉)]

Qatar Computing Research Institute, HBKU, Doha, Qatar
kdarwish@hbku.edu.qa

Abstract. This paper addresses polarization quantification, particularly as it pertains to the nomination of Brett Kavanaugh to the US Supreme Court and his subsequent confirmation with the narrowest margin since 1881. Republican (GOP) and Democratic (DNC) senators voted overwhelmingly along party lines. In this paper, we examine political polarization concerning the nomination among Twitter users. To do so, we accurately identify the stance of more than 128 thousand Twitter users towards Kavanaugh's nomination using both semi-supervised and supervised classification. Next, we quantify the polarization between the different groups in terms of who they retweet and which hashtags they use. We modify existing polarization quantification measures to make them more efficient and more effective. We also characterize the polarization between users who supported and opposed the nomination.

Keywords: Political polarization · Polarization quantification · Stance detection

1 Introduction

On October 6, 2018, the US senate confirmed Brett Kavanaugh (BK) to become a justice on the US Supreme Court with a 50 to 48 vote that was mostly along party lines. This was the closest successful confirmation to the court since the Stanley Matthews confirmation in 1881[1]. Political polarization was clearly evident in the US Senate between Republicans, who overwhelmingly voted for Kavanaugh, and Democrats, who overwhelmingly voted against him. In this paper, we wanted to quantify the political polarization between Twitter users, who voiced their opinion about the nomination. Quantification involved: (a) collecting topically relevant tweets; (b) ascertaining the stances of users; and (c) properly quantifying polarization. For data collection, we collected more than 23 million tweets related to BK's nomination, and we semi-automatically tagged more than 128 thousand Twitter users as supporting or opposing his confirmation. We initially manually tagged a small set of active users, then performed label propagation based on which tweets they retweet, and lastly used supervised classification to

---

[1] https://www.senate.gov/pagelayout/reference/nominations/Nominations.htm.

© Springer Nature Switzerland AG 2019
I. Weber et al. (Eds.): SocInfo 2019, LNCS 11864, pp. 188–201, 2019.
https://doi.org/10.1007/978-3-030-34971-4_13

tag a greater number of users based on the accounts they retweeted. As for quantification, we modified two existing polarization quantification measures, namely Random Walk Controversy (RWC) and Embedding Controversy (EC) measures that were shown to be indicative of polarization [6]. Given a graph of connected users, where users are the nodes and the weights of the edges are the similarities between users, RWC is computed based on the likelihood that a shorter graph traversal can be made from a random user to a prominent user with the same stance or to a prominent user with a different stance. EC maps users into a lower dimensional space and then computes a ratio of distances between users with similar stances and users with different stances. Due to the high computational complexity of the measures, we use user samples, and we estimate the stability of the measures across: multiple samples and different sample sizes. Further, we modify the original measures reported in the literature to make them more robust. We apply the modified measures on the Twitter users who actively discussed BK's nomination. We show strong polarization between both camps particularly in terms of the accounts that users retweet.

Next, we highlight polarization by bucketing hashtags, retweeted accounts, and cited websites according to how strongly they are associated with those who supported or opposed the nomination. We show that the polarization of Twitter users caused them to retweet different accounts, cite different media sources, and use different hashtags. In doing so, we highlight some of the main differences between both groups. The contributions of the paper are:

- We showcase effective semi-supervised user labeling that combines both multiple label propagation iterations and supervised classification. We show the effectiveness of this combination in tagging more than 128 thousand users using a very small initial set of manually tagged users.
- We experimented with two reportedly effective polarization quantification measures, namely EC and RWC, elucidate their shortcomings on our dataset, and propose modifications to make them more robust.
- We analyze users who were vocal on Twitter concerning the BK nomination. We characterize them in terms of the hashtags they use, the accounts they retweet, and the media sources that they cite.

2 Background

2.1 Stance Detection

Given the ubiquity of social media use, stance detection, which involves identifying the position of a user towards an entity or a person, is emerging as a problem of increasing interest in the literature. We are specifically interested in stance detection on Twitter. Stance detection can be performed at user-level or at statement-level. For either case, classification can be performed using a variety of features such as textual features (e.g. words or hashtags), interaction-level features, (e.g. relationships and retweeted accounts), and profile-level features (e.g. user location and name) [1,10,11,14]. Typically, interaction-level features yield better results [10]. In a supervised setting, an initial set of statements and/or users are tagged with their stance, which is used to train a classifier [1,10]. This is appropriate for user-level and statement-level classification [12]. Alternatively, so-called label propagation is used to propagate labels in a network based on interactions between users such as follow or retweet relationships [1] or the retweeting of identical tweets [9,10]. Label propagation has been shown to produce highly accurate results. In this work, we manually tag an initial set of users, employ label propagation, and then use the output labels from label propagation to perform supervised classification. More recent work has focused on unsupervised stance detection that involves creating a user-similarity network based on interaction-level features, and then combines dimensionality reduction, such as Uniform Manifold Approximation and Projection (UMAP) or force-directed (FD) graph placement, with clustering, such as mean shift, to identify users who are strongly associated with specific stances [5].

2.2   Quantifying Polarization

Quantifying polarization can help ascertain the degree to which users are separable based on their stances and how far apart they are. Though multiple measures have been suggested for quantifying polarization, research on establishing widely accepted effective measures is still work in progress. Guerra et al. [7] introduced a polarization measure that relies on identifying popular nodes that lie at the boundary between different communities, where strong polarization is indicated by the absence of such nodes. Morales et al. [13] proposed a metric that measures the relative sizes of groups with opposing views and the distance between their "centers of gravity". Garimella et al. explored a variety of controversy quantification measures to ascertain their efficacy [6]. The measures rely on random graph walks, network betweenness, and distances in embedding spaces. Given their reported success, we employ so-called Random Walk Controversy (RWC) and Embeddings Controversy (EC) measures [6] in this paper. Given the most connected nodes in a graph, RWC uses the maximum likelihood estimates that a random element in one class would reach one of the most connected nodes in its class first or one of the most connected nodes in the other class first. EC maps users into a lower dimensional space and then computes a ratio of the inter- and intra-class distances between users. We propose modifications to both measures to make them more computationally efficient and more robust. As we show in the paper, aside from direct measures of polarization, the effects of polarization can be observed in data [1,2,13,14]. For example, projecting users who engage in discussing a polarized topic on to a lower dimensional space can help visualize such polarization and improve subsequent clustering [5,6]. Further, polarized groups tend to share content from different media sources and influencers on social media, and often use different words and hashtags.

2.3 Topic Timeline

On July 9, 2018, Brett Kavanaugh (BK), a US federal judge, was nominated by the US president Donald Trump to serve as a justice on the US supreme court to replace outgoing Justice Anthony Kennedy[2]. His nomination was marred by controversy with Democrats complaining that the White House withheld documents pertaining to BK's record and later a few women including a University of California professor accused him of sexual assault[3]. The accusations of sexual misconduct led to a public congressional hearing on September 27, 2018 and a subsequent investigation by the Federal Bureau of Investigation (FBI). The US Senate voted to confirm BK to a seat on the Supreme Court on October 6 with a 50–48 vote, which mostly aligned with party loyalties. BK was sworn in later the same day.

3 Data Collection

We collected tweets pertaining to the nomination of BK in two different time epochs, namely September 28–30, which were the three days following the congressional hearing concerning the sexual assault allegation against BK, and October 6-9, which included the day the Senate voted to confirm BK and the subsequent three days. We collected tweets using the twarc toolkit[4], where we used both the search and filtering interfaces to find tweets related to the nomination. The keywords we used included BK's name (*Kavanaugh*), his main accuser (*Ford*), the names of the members of the Senate's Judiciary Committee (*Blasey, Grassley, Hatch, Graham, Cornyn, Lee, Cruz, Sasse, Flake, Crapo, Tillis, Kennedy, Feinstein, Leahy, Durbin, Klobuchar, Coons, Blumenthal, Hirono, Booker,* and *Harris*), and the words *Supreme, judiciary, Whitehouse*. Though some of these terms are slightly more general (e.g. Ford or Whitehouse), potentially leading to non-relevant tweets, the public focus on the nomination during the collection period would have minimized such an effect. The per day breakdown of the collected tweets is as follows:

28-Sep	29-Sep	30-Sep	6-Oct	7-Oct	8-Oct	9-Oct	Total
5,961,549	4,815,160	1,590,522	2,952,581	3,448,315	2,761,036	1,687,433	23,216,596

In all, we collected 23 million tweets that were authored by 687,194 users. Our first step was to accurately label as many users as possible by their stance as supporting (SUPP) or opposing (OPP) BK's confirmation. The labeling process was done in three steps, namely:

1. **Manual labeling of users.** We manually labeled 43 users who had the most number of tweets in our collection. The labeling was performed by one annotator who is well-versed in American politics. Of them, the SUPP users

---

[2] https://en.wikipedia.org/wiki/Brett_Kavanaugh.

[3] https://www.nytimes.com/2018/09/26/us/politics/brett-kavanaugh-accusers-women.html.

[4] https://github.com/edsu/twarc.

were 29 compared to 12 OPP users. As for the two remaining users, one was neutral and the other was a spammers.

2. **Label propagation.** Label propagation automatically labels users based on their retweet behavior [3,9,10]. The intuition behind this method is that users that retweet the same tweets on a topic most likely share the same stance. Given that many of the tweets in our collection were actually retweets or duplicates of other tweets, we labeled users who retweeted 15 or more tweets that were authored or retweeted by the SUPP group or 7 or more times by OPP group and no retweets from the other side as SUPP or OPP respectively. We elected to increase the minimum number for the SUPP group as they were over represented in the initial manually labeled set. Such manual tweaking is one of the drawbacks of label propagation [5]. We iteratively performed such label propagation 4 times, which is when label propagation stopped labeling new accounts. After the last iteration, we were able to label 65,917 users of which 26,812 were SUPP and 39,105 were OPP. Since we don't have golden labels to compare against, we opted to spot check the results. Thus, we randomly selected 10 automatically labeled accounts, and all of them were labeled correctly. We do more thorough checks later. This labeling methodology naturally favors users who are more opinionated and vocal about a topic and hence hold strong views.

3. **Retweet-based classification.** We used the labeled users to train a classification model to guess the stances of users who retweeted at least 20 different accounts, which were users who were actively tweeting about the topic. For classification, we used the FastText classification toolkit, which is an efficient deep neural network classifier that has been shown to be effective for text classification [8]. We used the Twitter handles of the accounts that each user retweeted as features. Strictly using the retweeted accounts has been shown to be effective for stance classification [10]. To keep precision high, we only trusted the classification of users where the classifier was more than 90% confident. In doing so, we increased the number of labeled users to 128,096, where 57,118 belonged to the SUPP group and 70,978 belonged to the OPP group. We manually and independently labeled 100 random users, 50 from each class, who were automatically tagged, and manual and automatic labeling agreed for 96 of them. It is noteworthy that the relative number of SUPP to OPP users in not necessarily representative of real life.

4   Quantifying Polarization

Given the labeled users, we attempted to quantify the polarization between users given the aforementioned EC and RWC measures. Both measures range between 0 (no polarization) and 1 (extreme polarization). Due to the computational complexity of both measure, we resorted to computing the measures on random samples of users. We wanted to ascertain: a) the sensitivity of the measures to the size of the samples; and b) to the stability of the measure across different samples.

Given a graph of users, as nodes, and edges between them, weighted by the similarity between users, RWC is based on the maximum likelihood estimates that a random element in one class would reach via a graph random walk one of the most connected nodes in its class first or one of the most connected nodes in the other class. The formulation of the score is: $RWC = P_{AA}P_{BB} - P_{AB}P_{BA}$, where A and B are different classes and P_{XY} is the probability that a random node in X would reach a highly connected node in Y. We selected the top most connected users in each class and an equal number of random users from each. To compute cosine similarity, each user was represented by a vector of all the hashtags that they have used (H) or all the accounts that they have retweeted (R). We modified the method of computing RWC in one important way, compared to what is described in [6]. Namely, instead of relying on the minimum number of hops, traversed edges, required to link two users, for which we would have needed to ascertain a minimum threshold for a link, we opted to use the minimum product of the weights of the edges to be traversed to link two users. This is akin to computing the shortest path in a graph, and relieves us from trying to determine appropriate thresholds and, as we show later, leads to more consistent results. We computed the score of a full path as the product of cosine similarities along all the edges between the random node and one of the highly connected nodes.

EC on the other hand relies on projecting nodes based on their similarity into a lower dimensional space, and then computing the average distances between members of the same class (inter-class) or members of different classes (intra-class). EC is computed as: $EC = 1 - \frac{d_A + d_B}{2d_{AB}}$, where d_A and d_B are the average inter-class distances and d_{AB} is the average intra-class distance. In the work of [6], they used force directed graph (FD) placement to perform dimensionality reduction. In this work, we use both FD as well as UMAP, which is more aggressive than FD in projecting similar users closer together while pushing dissimilar users further apart. Once users are projected and hopefully separated in the lower dimensional space, we used Euclidean distance between them to measure average inter- and intra-class distances. Due to the large number of users, it was computationally prohibitive to project all users based on their similarity. To overcome the computational issue, we opted to use a sample of users to compute EC. However, we wanted to ascertain the sensitivity of EC to sample size and its sensitivity to random user selection. Thus, for every sample size, we sampled users 5 times and we computed the average EC and standard deviation across all samples. Table 1 lists the parameters we used for both RWC and EC. For sample sizes per class, we experimented with 500, 1,000, 2,610, and 5,000. Given the size of our set of labeled users, roughly 128k, 2,610 is the size of a representative random sample of users with 99% confidence and a margin of error $= \pm2.5$.[5] We compared two sets of labeled users, namely after label propagation alone and after both label propagation and supervised classification.

---

[5] Calculated using https://surveysystem.com/sscalc.htm.

Table 1. Parameters used to for polarization quantification measures.

RWC	
Parameter	Values
Top connected accounts per class	20
Sample size per class	500, 1,000, 2,650, 5,000
Similarity feature	Hashtags (H), Retweets (R)
EC	
Parameter	Values
Sample size per class	500, 1,000, 2,610, 5,000
Dimentionality reduction method	UMAP, FD
Similarity feature	Hashtags (H), Retweets (R)

Figures 1 and 2 show the values of RWC and EC using different parameters respectively. As the graphs show, unlike EC, RWC values were fairly stable across different samples sizes and the standard deviation across multiple samples decreased as sample sizes increased. For RWC and EC and regardless of parameters, users showed higher polarization when we used retweeted accounts to compute similarity compared to when we used hashtags. This is consistent with prior research which showed that retweets were more indicative of stance than hashtags [10]. Using labels from label propagation only led to higher values for both RWC and EC. This could be attributed to the tendency of label propagation to identify users with more pronounced views. As for EC, UMAP generally led to higher polarization scores compared to FD. This is an artifact of the algorithm as it attempts to push dissimilar nodes further apart. Figure 3 illustrates this difference in projecting an identical sets of 5,000 users using FD and UMAP. The figure also shows how users are more separable when computing their similarity using retweets as opposed to hashtags. Further, different samples often led to large standard deviation values for EC. This indicates that using a single sample to compute EC might not be sufficient.

To compare RWC without modification (using similarities above a threshold to constitute a link between users) to our modified version, Table 2 compares the unmodified version of RWC at different thresholds with our modified version using a sample of 5,000 users and all user labels for both Retweets and Hashtags. As the results in the table show, minor modification to the threshold can dramatically change the value of RWC, which is undesirable. Given all our analysis, RWC seems to be a more consistent than EC, and when using EC, it is important to compute an average score across multiple user samples.

Lastly, as Figs. 1 and 2 show for our BK dataset, users exhibit strong polarization particularly as characterized by the accounts that they retweet (RWC > 0.96 and EC (with UMAP) > 0.62 when using all labeled users). Users' polarization is less pronounced when characterizing them using the hashtag they use (RWC > 0.86 and EC with UMAP > 0.6 when using all labeled users).

Table 2. Comparing original RWC to modified RWC

Threshold	R	H
0.001	0.400	0.583
0.002	0.401	0.736
0.003	0.687	0.896
0.004	0.994	0.986
Modified RWC	0.967	0.878

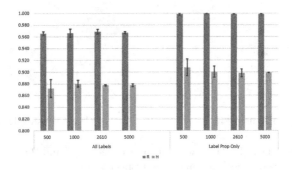

Fig. 1. Comparing different setups for RWC with error bars representing standard deviation – y-axis is the average RWC across 5 different samples.

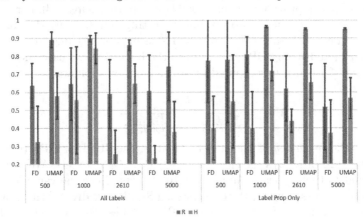

Fig. 2. Comparing different setups for EC with error bars representing standard deviation – y-axis is the average EC across 5 different samples.

5 Comparing SUPP and OPP Groups

After quantifying polarization, we analyzed the data to ascertain the effect of polarization in terms of the differences in interests and focus between both groups as expressed using three elements, namely the hashtags that they use, the accounts they retweet, and the media sources that they cite (share content

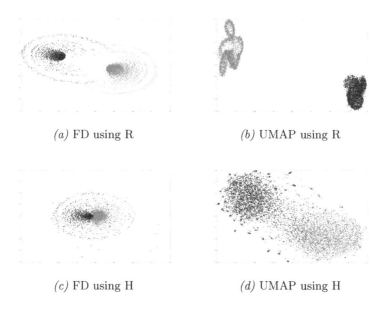

(a) FD using R   *(b)* UMAP using R

(c) FD using H   *(d)* UMAP using H

Fig. 3. Comparing FD and UMAP when using Retweets (R) and Hashtags (H). SUPP and OPP users are coded with red and blue respectively.

from). Doing so can provide valuable insights into both groups [3,4]. For all three elements, we bucketed them into five bins reflecting how strongly they are associated with the SUPP and OPP groups. These bins are: strong SUPP, SUPP, Neutral, OPP, and strong OPP. To perform the bucketing, we used the so-called valence score [2], which is computed for an element e as follows:

$$V(e) = 2\frac{\frac{tf_{SUPP}}{total_{SUPP}}}{\frac{tf_{SUPP}}{total_{SUPP}} + \frac{tf_{OPP}}{total_{OPP}}} - 1 \tag{1}$$

where tf is the *frequency* of the element in either the SUPP or OPP tweets and *total* is the sum of all tfs for either the SUPP or OPP tweets. We accounted for all elements that appeared in at least 100 tweets. Since the value of valence varies between -1 (strong OPP) to $+1$ (strong SUPP), we divided the range into 5 equal bins: strong OPP $[-1.0{-}{-}0.6)$, OPP $[-0.6{-}{-}0.2)$, Neutral $[-0.2{-}0.2)$, SUPP $[0.2{-}0.6)$, and strong SUPP $[0.6{-}1.0]$.

Figures 4(a), (b) and (c) respectively provide the number of different hashtags, retweeted accounts, and cited websites that appear for all five bins along with the number of tweets in which they are used. As the figures show, there is strong polarization between both camps. Polarization is most evident in the accounts that they retweet and the websites that they share content from, where "strong SUPP" and "strong OPP" groups dominate in terms of the number of elements and their frequency. This is consistent with the higher values we computed earlier for RWC and EC when using hashtags compared to retweets. If polarization was low, more neutral sources may have been cited more. Tables 3

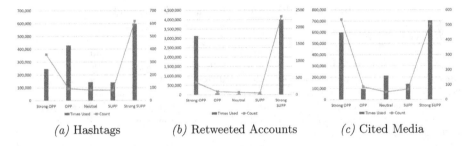

(a) Hashtags   (b) Retweeted Accounts   (c) Cited Media

Fig. 4. Count of elements and the number of times they are used for different valence bins

shows the 10 most commonly used hashtags, retweeted accounts, and most cited websites for each of the valence bands. Since the "Strong SUPP" and "strong OPP" groups are most dominant, we focus here on their main characteristics.

For the **"Strong SUPP"** group, the hashtags can be split into the following topics (in order of importance as determined by frequency):

- **Trump related:** #MAGA (Make America Great Again), #Winning.
- **Pro BK confirmation:** #ConfirmKavanaugh, #ConfirmKavanaughNow, #JusticeKavanaugh.
- **Anti-DNC:** #walkAway (from liberalism), #Democrats, #Feinstein
- **Conspiracy theories:** #QAnon (an alleged Trump administration leaker), #WWG1WGA (Where We Go One We Go All)
- **Midterm elections:** #TXSen (Texas republican senator Ted Cruz), #Midterms, #VoteRed2018 (vote Republican)
- **Conservative media:** #FoxNews, #LDTPoll (Lou Dobbs (FoxNews) on Twitter poll)

It is interesting to see hashtags expressing support for Trump (#MAGA and #Wining) feature more prominently than those that indicate support for BK. Retweeted accounts for the same group reflect a similar trend:

- **Trump related:** realDonaldTrump, mitchellvii (Bill Mitchell: social media personality who staunchly supports Trump), RealJack (Jack Murphy: co-owner of ILoveMyFreedom.org (pro-Trump website)), DineshDSouza (Dinesh D'Souza: commentator and film maker)
- **Conservative media:** dbongino (Dan Bongino: author with podcast), FoxNews, FoxAndFriends (Fox News), JackPosobiec (Jack Posobiec: One America News Network), IngrahamAngle (Laura Ingraham: Fox News)
- **Conservative/GOP personalities:** charliekirk11 (Charlie Kirk: founder of Turning Point USA), AnnCoulter (Ann Coulter: author and commentator), Thomas1774Paine (Thomas Paine: author), paulsperry_ (Paul Sperry: author and media personality), RealCandaceO (Candace Owens: Turning Point USA), McAllisterDen (D. C. McAllister: commentator)

Table 3. Top 10 elements for each valence band

Top 10 retweeted hashtags

Strong SUPP	SUPP	Neutral	OPP	Strong OPP
MAGA	SCOTUS	KavanaughHearings	Kavanaugh	DelayTheVote
Winning	ChristineBlaseyFord	KavanaughVote	MeToo	StopKavanaugh
ConfirmKavanaugh	kavanaughconfirmation	Breaking	BrettKavanaugh	GOP
ConfirmKavanaughNow	Ford	FBI	Trump	BelieveSurvivors
walkaway	kavanaughconfirmed	flake	republican	SNLPremiere
JusticeKavanaugh	SaturdayMorning	JeffFlake	DrFord	SNL
QAnon	TedCruz	SupremeCourt	KavanaghHearing	TheResistance
Democrats	FridayFeeling	Grassley	BelieveWomen	Resist
TXSen	HimToo	LindseyGraham	Republicans	Voteno
Midterms	TCOT	KavanaughHearing	RT	SusanCollins

Top 10 retweeted accounts

Strong SUPP	SUPP	Neutral	OPP	Strong OPP
realDonaldTrump	PollingAmerica	RiegerReport	AP	krassenstein
mitchellvii	cspan	lachlan	CBSNews	kylegriffin1
dbongino	JenniferJJacobs	Sen_JoeManchin	Reuters	KamalaHarris
charliekirk11	JerryDunleavy	AaronBlake	USATODAY	SenFeinstein
FoxNews	JulianSvendsen	WSJ	Phil_Mattingly	EdKrassen
RealJack	jamiedupree	markknoller	dangercart	thehill
DineshDSouza	CNNSotu	Bencjacobs	WalshFreedom	MichaelAvenatti
Thomas1774Paine	AlBoeNEWS	lawrencehurley	4YrsToday	SethAbramson
AnnCoulter	elainaplott	AureUnnie	byrdinator	funder
foxandfriends	AlanDersh	choi_bts2	MittRomney	Lawrence

Top 10 media sources (T stands for twitter.com)

Strong SUPP	SUPP	Neutral	OPP	Strong OPP
thegatewaypundit.com	usatoday.com	dr.ford	nytimes.com	hill.cm
foxnews.com	mediaite.com	T/michaelavenatti/	T/thehill/	washingtonpost.com
dailycaller.com	T/realdonaldtrump/	dailym.ai	thehill.com	rawstory.com
breitbart.com	theweek.com	lawandcrime.com	politi.co	vox.com
thefederalist.com	T/lindseygrahamsc/	nypost.com	abcn.ws	huffingtonpost.com
westernjournal.com	nyp.st	T/donaldjtrumpjr/	usat.ly	nyti.ms
politico.com	T/senfeinstein/	T/senjudiciary/	axios.com	nbcnews.com
ilovemyfreedom.org	T/kamalaharris/	T/mediaite/	politico.com	CNN.com
chicksonright.com	T/newsweek/	c-span.org	reut.rs	apple.news
hannity.com	T/natesilver538/	T/gop/	po.st	dailykos.com

The list above show that specifically pro-Trump accounts featured even more prominently than conservative accounts. Table 4 lists cited media for the "Strong SUPP" group. The media were generally right-leaning, with some of them being far-right and most of them having mixed credibility.

For the **"strong OPP"**, the top hashtags can be topically grouped as:

- **Anti-BK:** #DelayTheVote, #StopKavanaugh, #KavaNo (BK no), #voteNo.
- **Republican Party related:** #GOP, #SusanCollins (GOP senator voting for BK).
- **Sexual assault related:** #BelieveSurvivors, #JulieSwetnick (BK accuser).

Table 4. Top cited media for SUPP and OPP groups. Bias and credibility are determined by `MediaBiasFactCheck.com`.

Strong SUPP			Strong OPP		
Source	Bias	Cred	Source	Bias	Cred
theGatewayPundit.com	far right	low	theHill.com	left-center	high
FoxNews.com	right	mixed	WashingtonPost.com	left-center	high
DailyCaller.com	right	mixed	RawStory.com	left	mixed
breitbart.com	far right	low	Vox.com	left	high
theFederalist.com	right	high	HuffingtonPost.com	left	high
WesternJournal.com	right	mixed	NYTimes	left-center	high
Politico.com	left-center	high	NBCNews.com	left-center	high
ILoveMyFreedom.org	far right	low	CNN.com	left	mixed
ChicksOnRight.com	–	–	apple.news	–	–
Hannity.com (FoxNews)	–	–	dailykos.com	left	mixed

- **Media related:** #SNLPremiere (satirical show), #SNL, #SmartNews (anti-Trump/GOP news)
- **Anti Trump:** #TheResistance, #Resist
- **Midterms:** #vote, #voteBlue (vote democratic)

As the list shows, the most prominent hashtags were related to opposition to the confirmation of BK. Opposition to the Republican Party (#GOP) and Trump (#TheResistance) may indicate polarization.

As for their retweeted accounts, media related accounts dominated the list. The remaining accounts belonged to prominent Democratic Party officials and anti-Trump accounts. The details are as follows (in order of importance):

- **Media related:** krassenstein (Brian Krassenstein: `HillReporter.com`), kylegriffin1 (Kyle Griffin: MSNBC producer), theHill, EdKrassen (Ed Krassenstein: `HillReporter.com`), funder (Scott Dworkin: Dworkin Report and Democratic Coallition), Lawrence (Lawrence O'Donnell: MSNBC), MSNBC, JoyceWhiteVance (Joyce Alene: professor and MSNBC contributor), Amy_Siskind (Amy Siskind: The Weekly List)
- **DNC:** KamalaHarris (Senator), SenFeinstein (Senator Dianne Feinstein), TedLieu (Representative)
- **Anti Kavanaugh:** MichaelAvenatti (lawyer of BK accuser)
- **Anti Trump:** SethAbramson (author of "Proof of Collusion"), tribelaw (Laurence Tribe: Harvard Professor and author of "To End a Presidency")

Concerning the cited media shown in Table 4, they were mostly left or left-of-center leaning sources. The credibility of the sources were generally higher than those for the "strong SUPP" group.

6   Conclusion

In this paper, we characterized the political polarization on Twitter concerning the nomination of judge Brett Kavanaugh to the US Supreme Court. We used the automatically tagged set of more than 128 thousand Twitter users to ascertain the robustness of two different measures of polarization quantification. We proposed changes to both measures to make them more efficient and more effective. We showed that those who support and oppose the confirmation of Kavanaugh were generally using divergent hashtags and were following different Twitter accounts and media sources. For future work, we plan to look at different topics with varying levels of polarization, as the Kavanaugh nomination was a strongly polarizing topic.

References

1. Borge-Holthoefer, J., Magdy, W., Darwish, K., Weber, I.: Content and network dynamics behind Egyptian political polarization on twitter. In: Proceedings of the 18th ACM Conference on Computer Supported Cooperative Work & Social Computing, pp. 700–711. ACM (2015)
2. Conover, M., Ratkiewicz, J., Francisco, M.R., Gonçalves, B., Menczer, F., Flammini, A.: Political polarization on twitter. In: ICWSM, vol. 133, pp. 89–96 (2011)
3. Darwish, K., Magdy, W., Rahimi, A., Baldwin, T., Abokhodair, N.: Predicting online islamophopic behavior after# parisattacks. J. Web Sci. **3**(1), 34–52 (2017)
4. Darwish, K., Magdy, W., Zanouda, T.: Trump vs. Hillary: what went viral during the 2016 US presidential election. In: Ciampaglia, G.L., Mashhadi, A., Yasseri, T. (eds.) SocInfo 2017. LNCS, vol. 10539, pp. 143–161. Springer, Cham (2017). https://doi.org/10.1007/978-3-319-67217-5_10
5. Darwish, K., Stefanov, P., Aupetit, M.J., Nakov, P.: Unsupervised user stance detection on twitter. arXiv preprint arXiv:1904.02000 (2019)
6. Garimella, K., Morales, G.D.F., Gionis, A., Mathioudakis, M.: Quantifying controversy on social media. ACM Trans. Soc. Comput. **1**(1), 3 (2018)
7. Guerra, P.C., Meira Jr., W., Cardie, C., Kleinberg, R.: A measure of polarization on social media networks based on community boundaries. In: Seventh International AAAI Conference on Weblogs and Social Media (2013)
8. Joulin, A., Grave, E., Bojanowski, P., Mikolov, T.: Bag of tricks for efficient text classification. arXiv preprint arXiv:1607.01759 (2016)
9. Kutlu, M., Darwish, K., Elsayed, T.: Devam vs. Tamam: 2018 Turkish elections. arXiv preprint arXiv:1807.06655 (2018)
10. Magdy, W., Darwish, K., Abokhodair, N., Rahimi, A., Baldwin, T.: # isisisnotislam or# deportallmuslims?: Predicting unspoken views. In: Proceedings of the 8th ACM Conference on Web Science, pp. 95–106. ACM (2016)
11. Magdy, W., Darwish, K., Weber, I.: # failedrevolutions: Using twitter to study the antecedents of ISIS support. First Monday **21**(2) (2016)
12. Mohtarami, M., Baly, R., Glass, J., Nakov, P., Màrquez, L., Moschitti, A.: Automatic stance detection using end-to-end memory networks. In: Proceedings of the 2018 Conference of the North American Chapter of the Association for Computational Linguistics: Human Language Technologies, vol. 1 (Long Papers), pp. 767–776 (2018)

13. Morales, A., Borondo, J., Losada, J.C., Benito, R.M.: Measuring political polarization: twitter shows the two sides of Venezuela. Chaos Interdisc. J. Nonlinear Sci. **25**(3), 033114 (2015)
14. Weber, I., Garimella, V.R.K., Batayneh, A.: Secular vs. Islamist polarization in Egypt on twitter. In: Proceedings of the 2013 IEEE/ACM International Conference on Advances in Social Networks Analysis and Mining, pp. 290–297. ACM (2013)

Understanding Gray Networks Using Social Media Trace Data

Megan Squire$^{(\boxtimes)}$ (iD)

Elon University, Elon, NC 27244, USA
msquire@elon.edu

Abstract. In contrast to dark (illegal, covert, illicit) or bright (legal, overt, above-ground) networks, gray networks conduct a mixture of legal and illegal activities and have an organizational structure that may be only partially known. The goal of this research is to demonstrate techniques for using trace data from Venmo, a payment network, and Facebook, a social networking site, to understand the organizational structure of one particular gray network: a membership organization of self-described "Western chauvinists" called Proud Boys. Using publicly-available data from the Facebook API and from the Venmo web site, this research reveals the underlying organizational structure for this group as it grew and matured from October 2016–March 2019. The payment network is modeled as a one-mode directed network of payers and payees conducting transactions such as dues payments and activity fees. A two-mode network of the Venmo users and their memberships in Proud Boys groups on Facebook further illuminates the structure of the organization. Supplementary data from news reports and arrest records is used to confirm the findings from this network analysis. Results will be useful for understanding the extent to which trace data from online activities can expose the offline organizational structure of semi-clandestine groups.

Keywords: Social media data · Venmo · Facebook · Proud boys · Dark network · Gray network · Clandestine network

1 Introduction

Founded by far-right political commentator and media personality Gavin McInnes in September 2016, "Proud Boys" is a membership organization describing itself as "proud Western chauvinists who refuse to apologize for creating the modern world" [1]. Claiming chapters in 38 states in the US and internationally [2], membership in the group is "limited to persons who were born male, who currently identify as male" according to their bylaws [3]. The bylaws also state that the group does not consider itself a gang, and its website explains that Proud Boys is "a bona fide men's club with rituals, traditions, and even its own in-house court called 'The Sharia'" [4]. On its home page, the group describes itself as a place for men who have "tried being ashamed of themselves and accepting blame for slavery, the wage gap, ableism, and some fag-bashing that went on two generations ago" and are now "completely finished" with being "politically correct" and with "apology culture" [4].

© Springer Nature Switzerland AG 2019
I. Weber et al. (Eds.): SocInfo 2019, LNCS 11864, pp. 202–217, 2019.
https://doi.org/10.1007/978-3-030-34971-4_14

Proud Boys have captured the attention of law enforcement, media, and extremist monitoring groups for their anti-Muslim, misogynist rhetoric and for their embrace of street fighting and politically-motivated violence [5]. They have sponsored harassment of the Muslim town of Islamberg, New York [6]. They affiliated with a right-wing street fighting group called the "Alt-Knights" [7]. Their members have been arrested for violent street brawling in Oregon [8] and convicted of assaults in New York [9]. Their former lawyer was disbarred in Texas [10], and they have been banned from Twitter [11], Facebook, and Instagram [12].

Although extolling one's public allegiance to Proud Boys on social media is a requirement for achieving the first degree of initiation [3], many members use aliases online and in person [13, 14]. The group is also reticent about sharing details of its leadership structure. For example, when its bylaws were re-written and re-published in November of 2018 following the supposed departure of McInnes from the group [15], the names of the new leaders (called "Elders" [16]) were intended to have been redacted from the document [17]. However, in the initial release of the bylaws the redaction was unsuccessful, and the names of the Elders were in fact visible by using a computer mouse to highlight the redacted text [18, 19].

Thus, we posit that Proud Boys are a "gray" network: a semi-clandestine group with characteristics of both dark (covert, illegal) and bright (overt, legal) networks [31, 32]. For example, when allowed, Proud Boys will use above-ground social media sites to recruit, fundraise, and organize. However, they also use aliases, have secretive vetting procedures for new members, and engage in street-fighting and violence. They have even developed their own specialized jargon that has evolved to assist in their member acculturation and in-group identity. Phrases like POYB ("proud of your boy") and CUAWF ("see you at WestFest") are used to identify members, while phrases like FAFO ("fuck around and find out") and "helicopter rides for commies" are used to intimidate people they identify as enemies.

The purpose of this research is to use social network analysis and publicly available data to understand more about the activities and organizational structure of the Proud Boys as a gray network. To map the financial organization and fundraising activities of the group, we collected 461 transactions between 179 Proud Boys using Venmo, a social payments network, to conduct group business during the period October 2016–March 2019. To understand more about the social structure of the Proud Boys, we use data collected about the membership of 7920 Facebook users in 157 Proud Boys-affiliated Facebook groups during the period June 2017–March 2018. We use social network analysis techniques to demonstrate that trace data from these social media sites can indeed reveal pieces of a "gray" network's geographic organization, leadership hierarchy, and activity calendar.

Section 2 reviews the literature on the characteristics of dark and clandestine social networks and specifies how this work adds to that literature. Section 3 describes how the data used in this project was collected from Venmo and Facebook. Section 4 presents the method for and results of social network analysis on this data. Section 5 reviews some of the limitations of this approach, suggests avenues for future work with this data, and presents a brief conclusion.

2 Background and Prior Work

Dark networks come in many shapes and sizes. Much prior research on covert networks comes out of a desire to understand how to deploy effective disruption strategies [20, 21] for terrorist organizations, criminal gangs, and drug traffickers.

Dark networks can be modeled as collections of nodes, usually people, who may all be members of the network being studied or who may be co-conspirators or associates. These nodes are connected by edges representing some relationship: financial, familial, social, and so on. Edges usually comprise a single type of relationship but if there are multiple ties between people, it is possible to build a multi-graph where multiple edges between nodes is expressed as a vector of possible actions, for example in the work of Shetty and Adibi on the Enron email dataset [22].

Because a key differentiator for dark networks is that they operate under risk, the literature on dark network topologies focuses on whether the network exhibits the signs of a tradeoff between maintaining secrecy and ease-of-communication [23, 24]. Networks with high requirements for secrecy will sacrifice efficient communication by distributing it through a less centralized network, thus insulating leaders and avoiding single points of failure. Krebs [25] demonstrates this by measuring the average path length through the network and distances between the 19 hijacker nodes in the 9/11 terrorist network, concluding that the network has a "serpent" shape.

Morselli et al. [26] agree that terrorist networks and criminal enterprises have different shapes (terrorist networks lack a single core, for instance), but they assert that different "times to task" drive the shape of the network. Being financially motivated, criminal networks have a shorter "time to task" and may therefore prioritize communication efficiency over secrecy. In doing so, [26] finds that criminal networks adopt a more hierarchical, clustered structure with identifiable hubs. Terrorist networks on the other hand, are motivated by ideology, and will wait for an optimal time to act. They can therefore tolerate a network structure and communication flow that are more dispersed. By way of example, when 18 co-conspirator nodes are added to the 9/11 terror network, [26] shows that the path lengths and network distance are decreased (i.e. communication flow is improved) but secrecy is jeopardized.

Similarly, Xu and Chen [27] find that dark networks with "small world" properties – those in which nodes that are not neighbors can still reach other nodes in a relatively low number of hops – lead to efficient communication paths even in a sparse network. In such networks, the hub nodes are less vulnerable than in a hierarchical or highly clustered network, and instead it is the bridge nodes connecting multiple sub-communities together that are the most vulnerable. Morselli [28] points out that locating key players in a dark network can be more difficult than simply looking for nodes with high centrality measures, however, since higher-status individuals may purposely insulate themselves from more vulnerable positions in the network. Depending on what relationship is being used to create the ties between nodes, high-status individuals may not appear on the network at all.

Magouirk et al. [29] additionally provide evidence that dark networks change over time and will change shape based on responses to unplanned events, such as the departure of a key leader or the intermarrying of families involved in the network. Kalm

[30] summarizes structural characteristics of four different types of dark networks (traditional criminal, cybercriminal, ideologically motivated, and state-sponsored) and compares similarities and differences between types, with special attention to the network's ability to resist disruption.

Millward and Raab [31, 32] concede that many "dark" networks are not entirely dark, but have elements common to legal, visible/overt networks as well. They term these "gray" networks and describe the various circumstances that can put a network into a legal or visibility gray area. For example, an organization may have multiple layers to it, with some of its actors conducting business below-ground (dark) and some above-ground (bright). Or, an organization might be conducting business that is legal (bright) in one jurisdiction but illegal (dark) in another.

While a few examples of gray networks are listed in these papers, to our knowledge no prior work specifically studies a gray network. Both [31] and [29] stress that classifying a network as "bright" or "dark" or "gray" is less about strict definitions and more about empirical observation of the data driving the network. Thus, our project is data-driven, and advances this prior work in two ways. First, we intentionally investigate a gray network, a typology which is understudied in the literature. Second, we collect data from publicly-available sources on two different types of relationships – financial and social – to learn about the Proud Boys gray network as it changes over time.

3   Data Collection

The data for this work is comprised of three main subsets: (1) data collected from the public ledger of Venmo, a payment social network; (2) data collected from the Facebook public group API; (3) data collected from arrest records, news articles, and from the Proud Boys own media channels. In this section, we will describe how the data was collected, stored, and cleaned.

3.1   Venmo Data

Venmo is a social network and payment system. Users can request and send monetary payments to one another using the platform, and users can also add people as their "friends" on the platform. Friends can be added from a phone contact list or from an existing Facebook account. Users who request or send money are encouraged to add a comment to each transaction. Venmo user accounts and transactions are "public by default" [33]. A 2018 Federal Trade Commission complaint about Paypal, Venmo's parent company, describes Venmo privacy this way:

"By default, all peer-to-peer transactions on Venmo are displayed on the Venmo social news feed. On this news feed, Respondent displays the names of the payer and recipient, the date of the transaction, and a message written by the user that initiated the transaction, to anyone using Respondent's service. In addition, each Venmo user has a profile page on Respondent's website that lists the user's Venmo transactions. A user's five most recent public Venmo transactions are visible, by default, to anyone who views the user's Venmo web page, including to visitors who do not have a Venmo account." [34, p.4]

For this project, a list of 193 Proud Boys with public Venmo accounts was compiled manually. Accounts were initially discovered using names of 15 known Proud Boys who have appeared in news media accounts of their activities [e.g. 19, 35] or in feature stories in the Proud Boys Magazine [36]. From these 15 accounts, viewing public Venmo transactions and friends lists yielded additional Proud Boy members or close affiliates. Each person was only added to the list if one or more of the following conditions were met:

- Person had same name, same photo, and similar friends as a confirmed Proud Boy who was openly in Proud Boys groups on other social media; or
- Person used Proud Boys, PB, POYB or other Proud Boys slogans in their comments on transactions (e.g. "January dues POYB"), or
- Person was wearing Proud Boys apparel in their Venmo photo or had some Proud Boys signifier in their Venmo name.

Of these 193 accounts, 179 accounts had publicly viewable transactions for which the comments indicated Proud Boys business was being conducted. We define Proud Boys business as:

- Paying dues to or collecting dues from another known Proud Boy; or
- Contributing money to or collecting money for a Proud Boys sponsored event such as travel to a rally; or
- Buying or selling goods (e.g. shirts, alcohol, food) for a Proud Boys sponsored social event; or
- Buying or selling tickets to Proud Boys sponsored events (e.g. WestFest or TexFest).

In all, 461 transactions were collected between the 179 different user accounts. In Venmo it is not possible for a third party to see the amount of a transaction between two parties, however most of the payments in this data set included very clear language like "dues" or "tickets." However, humorous comments, emojis, and jokes between Venmo users are common [37]. We collected transactions of this nature only if they were between two known Proud Boys.

3.2   Facebook Data

For this portion of the project, we collected data about members and administrators of Proud Boys groups on Facebook. On Facebook, groups can be set up as one of three types [38]: Public, Closed or Secret. Membership lists are visible for Public groups, and until June 15, 2018 Closed group membership lists were also viewable by any Facebook user [39]. In all, 157 Proud Boys groups were located on Facebook.

Then, the public Facebook Graph API version 2.10 was used to collect the group membership rosters from all 157 Proud Boys groups. The membership roster for each group included the group name, each member's name, and the member's role in the group (e.g. member, administrator). Until April 4, 2018, these membership rosters were available via the Facebook developer API to anyone with a valid authentication token [39]. All of the data for this portion of the project was collected using the Facebook API between June 20, 2017 and March 31, 2018. Many of these Proud Boys and

Alt-Knights groups were reported to have been removed by Facebook as of October 2018 [40], however numerous groups and brand pages for both organizations still remain active on Facebook as of this writing.

In all, 7920 different Facebook user accounts were collected from the 157 groups. Within these groups, 152 of them were "Closed" and 5 were "Public". 287 different user accounts served as administrators for at least one of the 157 groups.

3.3   Other Data

In this section we describe additional data sources to confirm offline participation and geographical location for discovered members, and to construct a timeline of events to help explain the growth of the group. We prioritized primary source documents such as the Proud Boys' own bylaws [3, 19] and the web-based Proud Boys magazine [36]. Newspaper articles with interviews and arrest reports were also helpful to this project. The tasks of geolocating as many members as possible and constructing a timeline of events was made much easier by newspaper accounts of arrests and interviews at rallies and events. Table 1 shows the timeline of key events that helped to inform the network analyses in Sect. 4.

Table 1. Timeline of key Proud Boys events

Year	Month	Event
2016	Spring	Proud Boys Facebook page launched (now banned) [41]
2016	Jul	First official Proud Boys meeting in New York City; media coverage of Proud Boys begins [41]
2017	Feb	Proud Boys arrested after fight at McInnes event in NYC [42]
2017	Spring	Kyle "Based Stickman" Chapman founds Fraternal Order of Alt-Knights as paramilitary wing of Proud Boys following violence and arrests at rallies in Berkeley, California [7]
2017	July	McInnes prohibits Proud Boys from attending August 12 *Unite the Right* event in Charlottesville, Virginia [43]; Proud Boys harass residents of Islamberg, New York [7, 44]
2017	Aug	Proud Boys, including 2019 chairman Enrique "Henry" Tarrio, attended Unite the Right event [35]
2017	Sep	First WestFest held in Las Vegas [45]
2018	Mar	First TexFest event held in Austin [46]
2018	Sep	Second WestFest event [45]
2018	Oct	McInnes speaks at Metropolitan Republican Club in New York City, 10 Proud Boys arrested [47]
2018	Nov	21st: McInnes announces he is disassociating himself from Proud Boys [48]; 28th: Texas lawyer Jason Lee Van Dyke is announced as new Proud Boys leader; eight other "Elders" are announced as part of leadership team [19]; 29th: Elders remove Van Dyke as leader, promote Enrique "Henry" Tarrio as leader [49]
2019	Feb	Arrest warrants issued for two Proud Boys in Oregon [8, 50]
2019	Mar	Second TexFest event held in Texas

4   Data Analysis

In this section we use the data collected from Venmo, Facebook, and the events timeline to understand more about the structure of the Proud Boys as a gray network.

4.1   Venmo Network

The first Venmo transaction in our data set was from October 11, 2016 and the final was from March 24, 2019. Figure 1 shows the number of transactions per quarter. The most noticeable large jump between 3rd (July-September) quarter and 4th quarter (October-December) 2017 follows the first annual WestFest event, held in Las Vegas on September 8-10, 2017. On October 2, 2017, a large chapter in the Northeast region of the United States began using Venmo to take dues.

Fig. 1. Count of Proud Boys transactions on Venmo, per quarter.

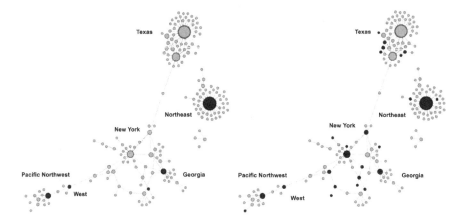

Fig. 2. Proud Boys Venmo users and transactions. Left: elders shown in black, members in gray. Right: Proud Boys facebook group administrators shown in black.

Figure 2 shows a directed network in which the 179 Venmo user accounts are nodes and the payer-payee transactions are directed edges. This graph was generated in Gephi [51] using the Yifan Hu layout [52] with node size scaled for degree.

Edges are left unweighted for visibility reasons, but labels have been added to show geographically-related Venmo users. Regular member and affiliate nodes are shown in gray. The graph reveals a large component subgraph and two smaller, self-contained subgraphs representing the Northeast chapter and a smaller Florida chapter. Both of the large Texas nodes are alias accounts set up to take payments for TexFest.

The left graph shows in black each of the five "Elders" who has an account on Venmo. These five represented geographically distinct areas: Northeast, Georgia, Midwest, West, and Pacific Northwest. The three remaining Elders hailed from Canada, Florida, and Texas but were – to our knowledge – not Venmo users.

Our social network analysis of Venmo payments shows that the Elders seem to be geographically dispersed, however nothing in the bylaws indicates that geography is a criterion for being chosen as an Elder. The lack of an Elder from the New York City cluster is surprising, but since New York is the home of Founder Gavin McInnes, this may have played a role in whether to appoint an Elder from this area.

The right graph in Fig. 2 shows in black the 26 Venmo Proud Boys who were also the administrator of at least one Facebook group. All eight Elders administered at least one Facebook group. The administrators of the Facebook groups are geographically dispersed and not limited to Elders or high-Venmo-degree individuals.

Next, to learn how the network grew and changed over time, Fig. 3 (next page) shows the social network evolving across 10 quarters. To make this graph, the first three quarters were combined since they are relatively small and self-similar. The next seven quarters show periods of great activity. Table 2 describes each frame.

Table 2. Explanation of Venmo network activity shown in Fig. 3

Frame	Quarter	Explanation
1	4Q16–2Q17	All nodes are geographically located in New York
2	3Q 2017	A small group is added from California and the mountain West. WestFest is held in Las Vegas
3	4Q 2017	A large group of members from the Northeast states (Rhode Island, Massachusetts, Connecticut) has joined and are paying dues to a central leader. Eight smaller cells form, shown in the lower left, including a four-member Florida cell
4	1Q 2018	Texas cell emerges, sending payments for 2018 TexFest. Three of the smaller cells merge into the main subgraph
5	2Q 2018	Georgia/Carolinas nodes merge into main subgraph. Florida, Texas and Northeast are still separate
6	3Q 2018	The Pacific Northwest strand is expanded as its smaller cells are completely absorbed into main subgraph. Only Florida, Texas, and Northeast remain as separate cells
7	4Q 2018	New nodes are added to main network, Texas, and Northeast
8	1Q 2019	Texas is absorbed into main network; second Texas cell emerges as 2019 TexFest tickets are sold

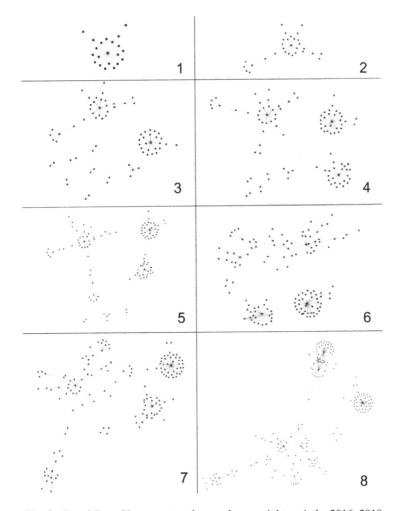

Fig. 3. Proud Boys Venmo network growth over eight periods, 2016–2019

4.2   Facebook Network of Venmo Users

Next we consider in more depth the network of Proud Boys who were on both Venmo and Facebook. What can we learn about the gray network from their participation on both social networks? 107 of the Venmo Proud Boys also had identifiable Facebook accounts. These users joined 118 of the 157 Facebook groups in our collection.

Figure 4 (next page) shows a two-mode network [53] in which person nodes only connect to groups, not to each other. The OpenOrd [54] layout is used to emphasize clustering between people and groups. The settings for OpenOrd were chosen to maximize cluster finding (liquid phase, 25%; expansion, 50%; cooldown, 15%; crunch, 5%; simmer, 5%). On the left graph, Facebook groups are shown in black and individual members of those groups are shown in gray. On the right graph, the five Venmo Elder nodes are shown in black, as well as a sixth (alias) account for the Northeast Elder.

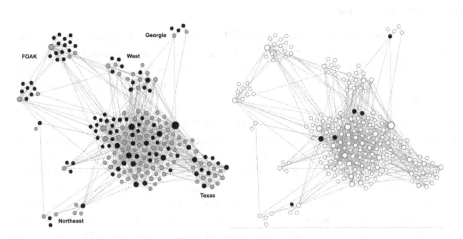

Fig. 4. Two-mode network of Venmo Proud Boys also using FB. Left: Proud Boys (gray) and FB groups (black). Right: Proud Boys elders overlaid on FB network.

As with the network of Venmo transactions shown in Fig. 3, geographic patterns emerge here as well. Texas, Northeast, Georgia, and Western region users and groups are clearly visible. Examples of geographically-named Facebook groups in this network include: East Texas Proud Boys, Los Angeles Proud Boys, Proud Boys Atlanta Vetting Page, Northeast USA Proud Boys - Vetting Group, and the like.

Despite these geographical similarities, the Facebook network shows two distinct differences from the Venmo network. First, the Pacific Northwest cell is indistinguishable. While the PNW did have some geographically-oriented Facebook pages, their members joined enough generic, non-geographic pages (e.g. Proud Boys Gear, Proud Boys Armory) that no clusters emerged as clearly as they did on the Venmo diagram.

Second, two Alt-Knights/FOAK clusters are evident on the upper left of the Facebook network, but these were not part of the Venmo network at all. The two principal leaders of these FOAK groups were present in the Venmo data set, but their impact is much greater in the Facebook network than it was on Venmo. Interestingly, following the inclusion of FOAK as a defendant in a lawsuit against leaders of the *Unite the Right* rally [55], neither of the two FOAK leaders were chosen to be Elders in the Proud Boys.

Differences between the Venmo and Facebook graphs may be due to the 10-month time span during which the Facebook data was collected, compared to the longer timespan of the Venmo data. More limitations will be addressed in Sect. 5.

4.3   Network Metrics

We have established that Proud Boys Elders and Facebook group administrators occupy geographically dispersed positions in the network, but are these leaders serving as hubs and bridges in the Venmo network? Network metrics such as degree, betweenness centrality, and the clustering coefficient can provide insight into this question.

Are the Proud Boys on Venmo a "small world" network? Literature on dark networks [31] indicates that "small world" characteristics can smooth communication even in sparse networks (such as this one, which has lots of hubs but fewer bridges). Small world networks have a higher clustering coefficient, or likelihood that clusters will form, than a random network of the same size. The clustering coefficient for the directed network is 0.042, and the clustering coefficient for the undirected version of the network is 0.216. Random networks of this size measured a clustering coefficient of between 0.001 and 0.008, with an average of 0.003. Following [31], this higher clustering coefficient indicates that the Proud Boys Venmo network does exhibit "small world" characteristics, including clusters, hubs, and bridges.

Table 3. Network metrics for leadership nodes in Proud Boys Venmo network

Position	Location	Directed			Undirected	
		In	Out	Degree	Betweenness	Role
Elder	NE	37	5	42 (1)	894 (13)	Hub
Elder	PNW	9	3	12 (5)	1469 (9)	Hub
Elder	GA	12	0	12 (6)	1408 (11)	Hub
Elder	West	5	0	5 (18)	1853 (7)	Bridge
Elder	MW	1	1	2 (41)	129 (41)	–
Leader	TF18	22	1	23 (3)	4419 (2)	Hub
Leader	TF19	37	4	41 (2)	2793 (5)	Hub
Leader	NYC1	17	1	18 (4)	4343 (3)	Hub
Leader	NYC2	5	3	8 (9)	4429 (1)	Bridge

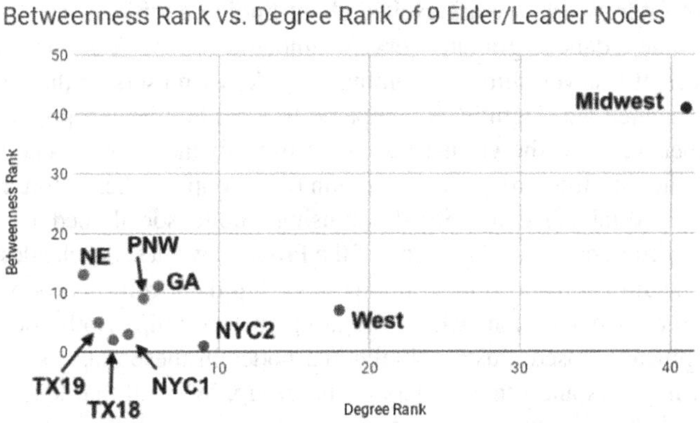

Fig. 5. Degree and betweenness ranks for elder and leader nodes. Red = bridges; blue = hubs. (Color figure online)

Are the Elders and leaders serving as hubs or bridges? Table 3 shows the network measures for five Elders and four other leader nodes, including the two TexFest ticket selling nodes (2018 and 2019) and two known NYC leaders. Ranks (1-179) for degree and betweenness are given in parentheses.

Degree is useful for finding Proud Boys that serve as hubs on Venmo. Four of the five Elders are found in the top nine highest degree nodes. The TexFest nodes and NYC leaders are also in the top nine. *Betweenness centrality* measures a node's capacity to serve as a bridge, measuring how many times the shortest path between any two nodes goes through a given node. Here we switched to an undirected network in order to more accurately reflect the two-way relationship opportunities presented by Venmo. As shown in Table 3, eight of the nine Elders and leaders are ranked in the top 13 of all nodes for betweenness.

Figure 5 shows a scatter plot of the degree ranks and the betweenness ranks for the nine Elders and leaders. Nodes are colorized red for bridges and blue for hubs. Hubs get top ranks for degree and rank lower on betweenness. Bridges have good betweenness rankings but lower degree rankings. The Midwest Elder is shown in black as neither a hub nor a bridge.

5   Limitations, Future Work, and Conclusions

There are several limitations to the way we approached understanding the Proud Boys as a gray network. First, our Facebook data set was limited to only 10 months of data, and while those months did directly overlap with the Venmo data set, the Venmo data set continued after our research access to the Facebook data had been removed. Second, not every Venmo transaction was publicly visible, due to privacy settings of each individual user. Third, the set of Proud Boys using Venmo is small, compared to number of Proud Boys on Facebook. A full analysis of the Facebook network would be a valuable addition. Finally, we are missing Venmo data from three Elders and we were also unable to determine the real names controlling the two TexFest accounts.

In terms of future work, we are excited about finding additional trace data sources that can illuminate a dark or gray network. Venmo and Facebook are just two of many possible sources. It was very time-consuming to track down users on these systems, but the insight we gained was significant compared to what had been reported previously.

In this paper we have shown that trace data from financial and social systems can help to illuminate the structure and organization of a group that heretofore has operated in shadows. We established a method for using public social media trace data to understand the structure and organization of the Proud Boys, a semi-clandestine, "gray" network. Financial data from Venmo and membership data from Facebook groups are used to construct two social networks of group membership. Both social networks reveal geographically-based clusters. Individual nodes in these clusters are then compared to known Elders and other leaders of the group. We find that leaders hold both "hub" and "bridge" positions in the network, and the network has a communication-smoothing "small world" structure. Like many criminal networks described in the literature, the Proud Boys network favors communication efficiency and leadership hierarchy.

Finally, we must point out that in the course of conducting this work, we noticed a number of Venmo transactions that were concerning. Proud Boys members and Elders conducted several transactions in which they paid each other to rent buses and otherwise prepare for rallies that included violence against their perceived "enemies." We concede that gray networks are only "gray" until their illegal activities become known, at which point they would be considered a full-fledged dark network and would likely move further underground. This work presents a method of studying such a group while it is still operating on social media, and at least partially without concealment.

References

1. Culkin, R.: Proud boys: who are they? proud boys magazine (2017). https://officialproudboys.com/proud-boys/whoaretheproudboys. Accessed 29 Mar 2019. http://archive.li/BoO1k. Accessed 9 Apr 2019
2. Proud boys chapters. http://proudboysusa.com/chapters. Accessed 29 Mar 2019. http://archive.li/Vv7iR. Accessed 9 Apr 2019
3. The constitution and bylaws of proud boys international L.L.C (2018). https://www.scribd.com/document/394310661/Proud-Boys-Redacted-Bylaws-Adopted-11–25-2018. Accessed 29 Mar 2019
4. Proud boys website. http://proudboysusa.com. Accessed 13 Apr 2019. https://archive.is/SxVq9. Accessed 8 Aug 2018
5. Coaston, J.: The Proud Boys, the bizarre far-right street fighters behind violence in New York. explained. Vox (2018). https://www.vox.com/2018/10/15/17978358/proud-boys-gavin-mcinnes-manhattan-gop-violence. Accessed 29 Mar 2019
6. Bazile, P.: How to survive driving through Islamberg with the Proud Boys. Proud Boys Magazine (2017). https://officialproudboys.com/columns/how-to-survive-driving-through-islamberg-with-the-proud-boys. Accessed 29 Mar 2019. http://archive.li/5OfCa. Accessed 9 Apr 2019

7. Feuer, A., Peters, J.W.: Fringe groups revel as protests turn violent. New York Times (2017). https://nytimes.com/2017/06/02/us/politics/white-nationalists-alt-knights-protests-colleges. html. Accessed 29 Mar 2019

8. KATU News. Judge issues arrest warrant for Proud Boys member Tusitala "Tiny" Toese (2019).   https://katu.com/news/local/judge-issues-arrest-warrant-for-proud-boys-member-tusitala-tiny-toese. Accessed 29 Mar 2019

9. Feuer, A., Winston, A.: Founder of Proud Boys says he's arranging surrender of men in brawl. New York Times (2018). https://nytimes.com/2018/10/19/nyregion/the-proud-boys-gavin-mcinnes-arrested.html. Accessed 29 Mar 2019

10. Moritz-Rabson, D.: Former Proud Boys lawyer suspended by Texas bar after series of alleged threats, slurs (2019). https://www.newsweek.com/proud-boys-lawyer-suspended-texas-bar-after-threats-1340618. Accessed 29 Mar 2019

11. Roettgers, J.: Twitter shuts down accounts of Vice co-founder Gavin McInnes, Proud Boys ahead of 'Unite the Right' rally. Variety (2018). https://variety.com/2018/digital/news/twitter-shuts-down-accounts-of-vice-co-founder-gavin-mcinnes-proud-boys-ahead-of-unite-the-right-rally-1202902397. Accessed 29 Mar 2019

12. Matthews, K.: Facebook, Instagram ban far-right Proud Boys and founder. AP News (2018). https://apnews.com/2714b6a697d34f59982c398a235858e7. Accessed 29 Mar 2019

13. Wilson, J.: Who are the Proud Boys, 'western chauvinists' involved in political violence? The Guardian (2018). https://www.theguardian.com/world/2018/jul/14/proud-boys-far-right-portland-oregon. Accessed 29 Mar 2019

14. Barrouquere, B.: Skinhead 'Irv' among five charged in Proud Boys' New York City assault. Southern Poverty Law Center (2018). https://www.splcenter.org/hatewatch/2018/10/22/skinhead-irv-among-five-charged-proud-boys-new-york-city-assault. Accessed 29 Mar 2019

15. Sommer, W.: Proud Boys founder Gavin McInnes claims he's quitting far-right group. Daily Beast (2018). https://www.thedailybeast.com/proud-boys-founder-gavin-mcinnes-quits-far-right-group. Accessed 29 Mar 2019

16. The Elders. Official statement: We're not going anywhere. Proud Boys Magazine (2018). https://officialproudboys.com/uncategorized/official-statement-were-not-going-anywhere. Accessed 29 Mar 2019. http://archive.li/EokfM. Accessed 9 Apr 2019

17. The Elders. Announcing the new Proud Boys bylaws, and our chairman. Proud Boys Magazine (2018). https://officialproudboys.com/uncategorized/announcing-the-new-proud-boys-bylaws-and-our-chairman. Accessed 29 Mar 2019. http://archive.li/ugrdc. Accessed 9 Apr 2019

18. Langton, A.: Tweet (2018). https://twitter.com/AsherLangton/status/1067605372234551297. Accessed 29 Mar 2019. http://archive.li/phFhW. Accessed 28 Nov 2018

19. Crosbie, J.: Proud Boys failed to redact their new dumb bylaws and accidentally doxxed their 'Elders'. Splinter (2018). https://splinternews.com/proud-boys-failed-to-redact-their-new-dumb-bylaws-and-a-1830700905. Accessed 29 Mar 2019

20. Cunningham, D., Everton, S.: Murphy, P: Understanding Dark Networks. Rowman & Littlefield, Lanham (2016)

21. Roberts, N., Everton, S.F.: Strategies for combating dark networks. J. Soc. Struct. **12**(2), 1–32 (2011)

22. Shetty, J., Adibi, J.: Discovering important nodes through graph entropy: the case of the Enron email database. In: Proceedings of the Knowledge Discovery in Databases Conference (KDD), Chicago, IL, USA. ACM (2005)

23. Erickson, B.: Secret societies and social structure. Soc. Forces **60**(1), 188–210 (1981)

24. Baker, W.E., Faulkner, R.R.: The social organization of conspiracy: illegal networks in the heavy electrical equipment industry. Am. Soc. Rev. **58**, 837–860 (1993)

25. Krebs, V.E.: Mapping networks of terrorist cells. Connections **24**(3), 43–52 (2002)

26. Morselli, C., Giguère, C., Petit, K.: The efficiency/security trade-off in criminal networks. Soc. Netw. **29**(1), 143–153 (2007)
27. Xu, J., Chen, H.: The topology of dark networks. Commun. ACM **51**(16), 58–65 (2008)
28. Morselli, C.: Hells angels in springtime. Trends in Organized Crime **12**, 145–158 (2009). https://doi.org/10.1007/s12117-009-9065-1
29. Magouirk, J., Atran, S., Sageman, M.: Connecting terrorist networks. Stud. Conflict Terror. **31**, 1–16 (2008)
30. Kalm, K.: Illicit network structures in cyberspace. In: 5th International Conference on Cyber Conflict, pp. 1–13 (2013)
31. Milward, H.B., Raab, J.: Dark networks as problems revisited: adaptation and transformation of Islamic terror organizations since 9/11. In: 8th Public Management Research Conference (2005)
32. Milward, H.B., Raab, J.: Dark networks as organizational problems: Elements of a theory. Int. Public Manag. J. **9**(3), 333–360 (2006)
33. Venmo Help Center. Payment activity and privacy. https://help.venmo.com/hc/en-us/articles/210413717-Payment-Activity-Privacy. Accessed 8 Apr 2019
34. United States before the Federal Trade Commission. In the matter of PAYPAL, Inc., a corporation. 1623102. Docket C-4651. (2018). https://www.ftc.gov/system/files/documents/cases/1623102_c-4651_paypal_venmo_complaint_final.pdf. Accessed 8 Apr 2019
35. Moynihan, C., Winston, A.: Far-right Proud Boys reeling after arrests and scrutiny. New York Times (2018). https://www.nytimes.com/2018/12/23/nyregion/gavin-mcinnes-proud-boys-nypd.html. Accessed 8 Apr 2019
36. Official Proud Boys Magazine. https://officialproudboys.com. Accessed 8 Apr 2019. https://web.archive.org/web/*/officialproudboys.com. Accessed 25 Apr 2017
37. Hampton, R.: In praise of Venmo humor. Slate (2018). https://slate.com/human-interest/2018/07/venmo-transaction-humor-scrolling-through-the-emojis-and-jokes-of-the-payment-platform.html. Accessed 8 Apr 2019
38. Facebook. What are the privacy settings for groups? (n.d.) https://www.facebook.com/help/220336891328465. Accessed 8 Apr 2019
39. Facebook. An update on our plans to restrict data access (2018). https://newsroom.fb.com/news/2018/04/restricting-data-access. Accessed 8 Apr 2019
40. Hatmaker, T.: Facebook bans the Proud Boys, cutting the group off from its main recruitment platform. TechCrunch (2018). https://techcrunch.com/2018/10/30/facebook-proud-boys-mcinnes-kicked-off. Accessed 8 Apr 2019
41. Disser, N.: Gavin McInnes and his Proud Boys want to make men great again. Bedford + Bowery (2016). http://bedfordandbowery.com/2016/07/gavin-mcinnes-and-his-proud-boys-want-to-make-white-men-great-again. Accessed 9 Apr 2019
42. Offenhartz, J.: Anti-Fascist protesters clash with 'Proud Boys' as Gavin McInnes speaks at NYU. Gothamist (2017). http://gothamist.com/2017/02/03/nyu_proud_boy_protest.php. Accessed 9 Apr 2019. https://web.archive.org/web/20170320150155/. Accessed 20 Mar 2017
43. Barnes, L.: Proud Boys founder disavows violence at Charlottesville but one of its members organized the event. Think Progress (2017). https://thinkprogress.org/proud-boys-founder-tries-and-fails-to-distance-itself-from-charlottesville-6862fb8b3ae9. Accessed 13 Apr 2019
44. Obeidallah, D.: Trump-supporting bigots to target upstate New York Muslims. The Daily Beast (2017). https://www.thedailybeast.com/trump-supporting-bigots-to-target-upstate-new-york-muslims. Accessed 9 Apr 2019
45. WestFest. Official Proud Boys Magazine. https://officialproudboys.com/tag/westfest. Accessed 9 Apr 2019. http://archive.is/LKasN. Accessed 9 Apr 2019

46. Biggs, J.: "There's a shit ton of proud boys in downtown Austin tonight and they have taken over. (This is a pic of one view. There are many more)". Twitter (2018). Original Twitter URL: https://twitter.com/rambobiggs/status/977388616161943553. Accessed 9 Apr 2019. http://archive.li/uxKmj. Accessed 9 Apr 2019
47. Madani, D.: Two Proud Boys members plead guilty in New York City brawl case. NBC News (2019). https://www.nbcnews.com/news/us-news/two-proud-boys-members-plead-guilty-new-york-city-brawl-n978481. Accessed 9 Apr 2019
48. Wilson, J.: Proud Boys founder Gavin McInnes quits 'extremist' far-right group. The Guardian (2018). https://www.theguardian.com/world/2018/nov/22/proud-boys-founder-gavin-mcinnes-quits-far-right-group. Accessed 9 Apr 2019
49. The Elders. RELEASE: Proud Boys statement on J.L. Van Dyke. Proud Boys Magazine (2018). https://officialproudboys.com/uncategorized/release-proud-boys-statement-on-j-l-van-dyke. Accessed 9 Apr 2019. http://archive.li/JBCjd. Accessed 2 Dec 2018
50. Zielinski, A.: Proud Boy arrested in Multnomah County for June assault. Portland Mercury (2019). https://www.portlandmercury.com/blogtown/2019/03/12/26142565/proud-boy-arrested-in-multnomah-county-for-June-assaul. Accessed 9 Apr 2019
51. Gephi. https://gephi.org
52. Hu, Y.: Efficient, high-quality force directed graph drawing. Math. J. **10**(1), 37–71 (2005)
53. Borgatti, S.P.: 2-Mode concepts in social network analysis. Encycl. Complex. Syst. Sci. **6**, 8279–8291 (2009)
54. Martin, S., Brown, W.M., Klavans, R., Boyack, K.W.: OpenOrd: an open-source toolbox for large graph layout. Vis. Data Anal. **7868**, 786806 (2011)
55. Kessler, S.V., et al.: United States District Court for the Western District of Virginia. https://www.integrityfirstforamerica.org/sites/default/files/Complaint.pdf

Using Simulated Reproductive History Data to Re-think the Relationship Between Education and Fertility

Daniel Ciganda$^{(\boxtimes)}$ and Angelo Lorenti

Max Planck Institute for Demographic Research, Rostock, Germany
{ciganda,lorenti}@demogr.mpg.de

Abstract. The weakening negative educational gradient of fertility is usually interpreted as the expression of changes in the way education shapes reproductive decisions across cohorts. We argue, however, that the reversal of the statistical association does not imply a reversal in the underlying mechanisms that connect education and fertility. Instead, we believe the reversal in the statistical association emerges as a result of the convergence of the life-course of individuals with different educational attainment levels across two dimensions: the ability to control the reproductive process and the desire for a given family size. In order to show this we reproduce the results reported in previous studies by using simulated reproductive trajectories, generated from a model that assumes no change in the way education shapes reproductive intentions over time. Beyond our substantive focus, we intend to show how our understanding of key demographic processes could change if we were able to incorporate in our modeling difficult or impossible to observe quantities.

Keywords: Computational modelling · Education · Fertility

1 Introduction

Education has been considered one of the main drivers of fertility decline since the earliest versions of the demographic transition theory [37]. By the 1970' the negative association between educational attainment and fertility seemed one of the most established regularities in the social sciences, supported by evidence from a variety of contexts and time periods [13].

This notion persisted in the following decades, supported by analysis that focused on education and contraceptive use in developing countries [12,14], but also on education and postponement of parenthood in richer countries [25,41].

Perceptions of the relationship between education and fertility started to change in the late 1980's after a series of studies suggested the emergence of a positive effect of education on the transition to higher order births [22,26]. Although follow-up studies revealed the existence of significant selection effects [27–29], fertility scholars started paying more attention to the changing educational gradient of reproduction. A number of studies argued that the negative effect of

© Springer Nature Switzerland AG 2019
I. Weber et al. (Eds.): SocInfo 2019, LNCS 11864, pp. 218–238, 2019.
https://doi.org/10.1007/978-3-030-34971-4_15

educational attainment on fertility outcomes was weakening (or reversing in the case of men) [8,15,28], but also that in a number of countries fertility intentions were higher among highly educated women [15,44].

These individual-level findings were in line with those reported at the macro level, which showed a recuperation of period fertility after countries exceeded a certain level of economic and social development [30,36]. The observation of these *reversals* in long-established patterns of association suggested a fundamental change in the mechanisms involved in the family formation process across cohorts. One popular interpretation suggests that these changes are driven by the redefinition of gender roles, assumed to have predominantly affected women with higher education levels [18].

We aim to show, however, that the reversal of the *statistical association* between education and fertility does not necessarily imply a reversal in the *mechanisms* behind this association. Instead, we believe that the narrowing educational gradient of fertility is primarily driven by compositional changes in two different dimensions. First, the change in the composition of births, as the share of unplanned births decreases over time transforming the meaning of the indicators commonly used to measure fertility. Second, the steadily increasing proportions of *working* women, which has make women with different education levels more similar with respect to their desired family size.

The implication here is that given better information, that would allow, for example, to distinguish planned from unplanned births, a different relationship will be observed between increased ability and fertility outcomes. This was, in fact, the main argument in Gary Becker's seminal paper providing an economic analysis of fertility [1]. Unfortunately this initial interpretation was overshadowed by the attention devoted to the formal analysis of the quantity/quality trade-off in the discussion that followed [16].

In this paper we intend to work around the limitations posed by missing information by using a simulation approach. We employ a computational model of reproductive decision-making to simulate birth histories of several cohorts of women, making an explicit distinction between planned and unplanned births and working and non-working women. We later model the relationship between education and fertility in our simulated data using event-history analysis techniques typically found in the literature. This approach allows us to control the data generating process and show the effects of incorporating difficult-to-obtain information on the estimates of the association between educational attainment and fertility over time.

We believe the mechanisms explored here can explain a substantial part of the statistical reversals associated to the family formation process, while at the same time addressing the puzzle created by the discrepancy between the effects of education on fertility *outcomes* and fertility *intentions*. We also intend to show how individual-level computational models can be combined with more traditional approaches to improve our understanding of the behavioral mechanisms behind statistical correlations.

2   Increased Resources and Fertility: Theory

Educational attainment measures are often easier to obtain than reliable estimates of income or wealth, therefore they are widely used in empirical studies as a way of classifying individuals with respect to the resources and ability. In this sense, the discussion surrounding the relationship between education and fertility overlaps to a great extent with the discussion surrounding the relationship between income and fertility.

One of the reasons these relationships have received so much attention is the long-run negative association between increased resources and fertility outcomes. From a theoretical point of view this is an unexpected, puzzling observation and researchers have tackled this problem from different approaches. At the beginning of the 60's Gary Becker introduced the foundations of what would become one of the most popular explanations of the secular decline of fertility rates by establishing a distinction between the elasticity of child quality and the elasticity of child quantity with respect to income [1]. In his original study, the relationship between quality and quantity was not presented as a trade-off, both effects were assumed to be positive, although it was also assumed that an increase in resources would lead to a greater increase in child quality than in child quantity. This distinction represented a novelty but it was still not enough to explain the observed negative relationship between increasing development and fertility. Becker found the missing link in the differential spread of contraceptive knowledge across social classes and went on to show how the relationship between resources and fertility reversed when information about family planning was used.

> An increase in income or a decline in the cost of children would affect both the quantity and quality of children, usually increasing both. An increase in contraceptive knowledge would also affect both but would increase quality while decreasing quantity. [...] Differential knowledge of contraception does convert a positive relation between income and *desired* fertility into a negative relation between income and *actual* fertility [1][1].

The discussion that followed pushed the attention away from the distinction between desired and realized fertility and focused it on the more theoretically appealing quantity/quality distinction. Later refinements of the theory introduced the idea of a trade-off through the increase in the price of child quantity as quality increased, which implied that a negative relationship between income and fertility could be generated without considering differential contraceptive knowledge and the associated difficulties in measuring unplanned fertility [2,3].

In the real world, however, the distinction between desired (or planned) and unplanned fertility is still key, because the behavioral mechanisms that generate these two quantities are qualitatively different. A planned/wanted birth is the result of a goal-seeking behavior, therefore the risk of observing such a birth will be positively associated to higher ability and resources. An unplanned birth, on

---

[1] Italics in the original.

the other hand, results from the inability to control the reproductive process therefore it will be negatively associated with the skills acquired through formal schooling and with the individual and family resources that usually contribute to the achievement of higher education levels. Failing to establish this distinction will likely bias any estimates expressing the influence of a given attribute on a given measure of fertility quantum as we will try to show in the following sections.

3   Unplanned Fertility

Although analysis of the first demographic transition paid considerable attention to fertility control, specially those looking at the supply side [17], the discussion of fertility trends in the post-war era was completely dominated by social and economic arguments. In the report of the IUSSP meeting discussing low fertility in Europe in 1981, [47] notes: "The practice of contraception [..] is barely mentioned in the course of the population policy debate currently being waged in Europe".

In one notable exception, Murphy [35] showed the key role played by the use of the contraceptive pill in the fertility decline of the 1960s and 1970s in Britain. The overwhelming majority of demographic analyses of unplanned fertility, however, have focused on developing countries [4–6] and to a lesser extent in the US, where high teenage pregnancy rates have long been a pressing public health issue [21]. The scarcity of data from unplanned pregnancies and births in Europe is likely a combination of difficulties in measuring the unintended fraction of births and the belief that the control over the reproductive process is nearly perfect, or at least moving in that direction [23].

The few available estimates, however, contradict these assumptions. Half of the decline of fertility in the 1970s in France, for example, has been attributed to the drop in unplanned births [40], while 25% of the births of women born around 1950 in Italy has been estimated to be unplanned [9]. If we consider that these cohorts reached their peak reproductive years during the 1970's and 1980's, after the diffusion of effective contraceptive methods, it seem reasonable to assume that a larger fraction of births were unplanned among women from earlier cohorts.

Even if we assume a decreasing trend in the proportions of unplanned births to the extent that they do not longer represent a relevant dimension of the experience of recent cohorts in rich countries, any cross-cohort comparison would likely be affected by this change in the relative fractions of planned and unplanned births that comprise total fertility.

4   Education and Fertility: Empirical Approaches

As mentioned earlier, efforts to identify a positive association between educational attainment and fertility outcomes go back to the 1980s. The typical approach to address this question relies on the estimation of educational gradients across cohorts using hazard regression models for the transition to second and third births. A study using Swedish data, for example, found a higher relative risks for the transition to second and third births for women with higher education when age at first birth and employment status were controlled for [22], while others reported a positive relationship between education and third birth rates for married Norwegian women [26].

These findings were interpreted as the results of the prevalence of income effects, an unprecedented result in the case of women although theoretically plausible in the Scandinavian context where full-time day care, job-protection for mothers and a relatively high involvement of fathers in housework promoted the compatibility of childcare and employment. But similar results were repeatedly found for West Germany (Huinink, 1989, 1995, 2001 in [29], which prompted a closer examination of the problem.

This positive effect of education on the transition to higher order parities, however, turned negative when the transitions to different parities were modeled jointly and a parameter to capture unobserved heterogeneity was included in the regression models [26,29]. These models intend to control for heterogeneity with respect to family-formation preferences (family proneness) that can bias the estimates when women that had a previous child *at the same age* but belong to different educational groups are compared.

The problem with this comparison is that, given a certain age, women from the lower education group will tend to be behind schedule for the experience of that particular parity transition with respect to other women in the same educational category, while women in the higher education group will tend to be ahead of their group. The assumption here is that the relative positions of these women with respect to their reference groups is indicative of different inclinations towards family life.

Revisiting the problem years later Kravdal and Rindfuss [28] showed how the negative effect of education on higher order births disappears for recent cohorts of women in Norway even after controlling for selection effects. This study is still today one of the central references in the literature therefore we take it as a reference point to develop our argument. In Fig. 4 we present coefficients from hazard regression models of the risk of having a second birth by educational attainment and cohort as reported in [28] (Fig. 1).

Both panels show a convergence between educational groups i.e. a reduction of the negative effect of education for women with higher education as their relative risk approaches the risk of the group of women with less education (approaches 1 in the y axis). Our first objective is to replicate this results using simulated data generated by a known set of behavioral mechanisms. Before proceeding, however, in the next section we describe our simulation model, followed by a brief description of the statistical models applied to our simulated data in the attempt to replicate the results introduced in this section.

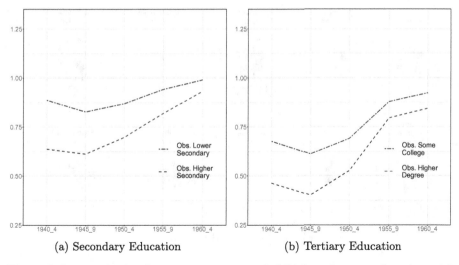

Fig. 1. Relative risks for the transition to second child by cohort en education, with lowest education as the reference | Women, Norway

5 Simulation Model

We use a discrete-event simulation model that generates synthetic life courses for the birth cohorts of women from 1925 to 2016 in a theoretical population (see Sect. 7). These simulated trajectories are structured around six main events: Leaving the education system, searching and finding a partner, getting into a cohabiting union, trying to have a child, having a/an additional child, dying.

Figure 2 shows the basic operation of the model through an example. It depicts a hypothetical life trajectory of a woman that is born during the simulation. The level of education that she will achieve and whether she will participate in the labor market or not are obtained from observed cohort data as discussed in Sect. 7. At birth she is at risk of three competing events: Finishing her education ($_ET$), finding a partner ($_pT$) or dying ($_DT$). The event with the shortest waiting time is realized, in our example, she completes her education at age 22 and later she finds a partner at age 24. At this moment she develops an intention to get into a union ($_UI$) which is affected by the economic situation at the time but also by the share of people in her age group that is already living with a partner. This intention is associated to a waiting time to the formation of the union ($_UT$), if the intention is high the waiting time to the event is short and vice-versa.

If the waiting time is shorter than 12 months, then at the end of this time a union will be formed, if not, at the end of the twelve months the couple will update their intention ($_UI^*$) and repeat the process. The woman in our example starts a cohabiting union at age 26. At this moment the couple develops their desired family size (D) that is associated with their short-term fertility intentions ($_BI$). As in the case of the formation of a union, the intention to have a child

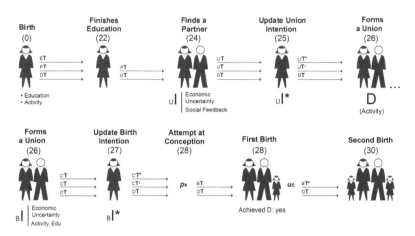

Fig. 2. A simulated trajectory.

determines when the couple will start *trying* to have a child. This intention is updated every year until the waiting time is shorter than twelve months. The couple might or might not be successful in their attempt depending on the probability p_x, which depends on her age. In our example the attempt is successful and, after a gestation period $(_BT)$ they have their first child. Even though their objective was to have a single child $(D = 1)$, when she is 30 they have a second, unplanned birth.

The model, then, allows to distinguish between planned and unplanned births. Planned births are those that are a intentional, i.e., within the fertility goals of a woman/couple. Unplanned births are those that occur after the desired family size has been already achieved, therefore they have no relation with intentions and the effects that shape them.

For each woman in the simulated population we collect information on the total number of births, the type and age at each birth, her education level and her labor force participation status (working vs. non working). Using these simulated reproductive histories we intend to reproduce the results reported in previous studies which show the convergence in the risks of higher order parities for women with different educational attainment (see Sect. 4).

5.1 Simulating the Weakening Educational Gradient of Fertility

In our model an increase in education can have both positive and negative effects on fertility outcomes. The negative effects are indirect: First, through the postponement of the age at which couples marry/start cohabiting. Second, through a better use and faster adoption of contraceptive methods, which results in a reduced probability of unplanned births. Finally, more educated women are also more likely to work, which is in turn associated with a smaller desired family size.

The positive effect, on the other hand, is directly expressed at the level of the intention and is based on empirical evidence showing how in many countries fertility intentions are actually higher among highly educated women [15, 44]. Some studies have explained this result as an expression of women's increased bargaining power, which can help establish a more gender egalitarian arrangement with their partners regarding housework [31, 32], in addition to an increased probability to meet partners who are willing to assume a larger share of unpaid work in the first place [18, 43]. Additionally, and as long as higher education leads to a more advantaged position in the labor market, women with higher educational attainment should benefit from more flexible working hours and less constraints to organize the daily routine as well as an increased capacity to outsource housework and childrearing activities.

All these mechanisms, however, are assumed to be constant across cohorts. This implies that the convergence of the risks of transitioning to higher order parities between women of different education levels is not driven, in our model, by changes in the mechanisms through which education shapes fertility outcomes. This convergence is driven instead, by a combination of two processes: the generalization of labor force participation among women and the diffusion of contraceptive methods and ideas.

Figure 3 shows the cohort trends in educational attainment and labor force participation by education of women that are used in the simulation. A description of how this data is obtained is provided in Sect. 7. When we consider these two processes together, it can be seen how the experience of women of different education levels has become more similar with respect to paid work.

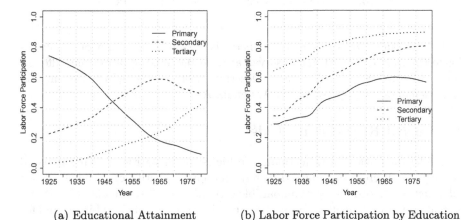

(a) Educational Attainment   (b) Labor Force Participation by Education

Fig. 3. Educational attainment and labor force participation of women by education level | Cohorts

Women's lives have also become more similar with respect to their ability to control their reproductive process. Figure 4 shows the way this movement is represented in our model. Following the diffusion of effective contraceptive methods and ideas, the probability of having an unplanned birth experiences a sharp decline. The adoption of these methods across the board reduces the distance between women with different education levels that existed before the transition.

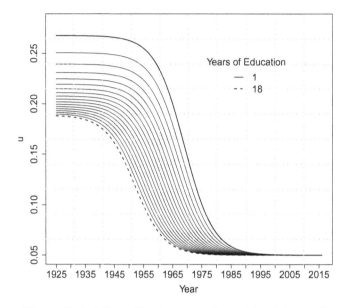

Fig. 4. Probability of having an unplanned birth | Period

The parametrization employed here is based on a previous calibration/estimation exercise using observed age-specific fertility rates from different European countries [10]. A detailed description of each model component and its implementation is presented in Appendix A.

6 Hazard Regression Models

We model the hazard of transitioning to higher order parities in our simulated data using a discrete-time hazard regression approach with Complementary Log link function. In order to get comparable estimates to those presented in [28] we estimate separate models for each transition, i.e. second and third births, and for each five-year birth cohort from 1940 to 1964. We also follow the approach in [28] by modelling the baseline duration using linear splines, with one knot at age 35 in the case of age, and four knots at 2, 4, 6 and 8 years in the case of time since previous birth. Educational attainment in the simulated data is represented by three categories (primary, secondary and tertiary) while in the reference study there are five categories (compulsory, lower secondary, higher secondary, some college, higher degree).

After comparing the results from the model described above with those presented in Sect. 4 we compare different specifications of the model applied to our simulated data. In the second specification we add a binary predictor with information about long-term labor force status. As described earlier, labor force participation is linked in our simulation both to education and fertility goals, with more educated women being more likely to work and working women usually preferring smaller families than non working women. Therefore including this information should account for the variation related to desired family sizes and reduce the gap between levels of educational attainment.

The third model we specify keeps the same structure of the previous one but instead of considering all births in the reproductive histories, we only consider those births that are planned, in other words, we remove those births that occurred after a given individual reached their desired family size. As argued earlier, removing unplanned fertility and controlling for labor force status should result in estimates that reflect a positive association between educational attainment and the transition to higher order parities.

7 Data

The information on educational attainment and labor force participation by birth cohorts from 1925 to 1980[2] comes from Census data available at IPUMS [33]. To get the distributions of education by cohort and the joint distribution of education and labor force participation by cohort we pooled all available Census rounds for the European countries that provided this information to IPUMS: France, Spain, Greece, Hungary, Ireland, Italy, The Netherlands, Poland, Portugal and Switzerland.

To obtain the labor market participation figures we selected women aged 30 to 55 in the pooled set and obtain the proportions active (employed + unemployed) and inactive by birth cohort, observations of the same women in more than one census round were treated as independent observations.

For the initial population we use the age structure of the Population of France in 1925 available at the National Institute of Statistics and Economic Studies (INSEE).

To get a series of unemployment spanning the entire simulation window we use information of the unemployment rate in the European Union from 1998 to 2016 and the average of the unemployment rate in Spain and France for the earlier period. The series for France and Spain were obtained from [45] and [38] respectively.

8 Results

Figure 5 presents aggregate fertility indicators computed from the simulated reproductive histories. The four indicators presented here show trajectories that

---

[2] For the cohorts born after 1980 we extrapolate linearly from previous trends.

resemble the general patterns observed in different European countries, which suggests the model is generating feasible reproductive trajectories.

In the case of the Total Fertility Rate Fig. 5 shows a sharp decline since the mid 1960s followed by stabilization and small increase since the 2000s that comes to an end with the economic recession of 2008.

Cohort fertility shows a steady decline for the cohorts that went through their peak reproductive years during the 1970's and 1980's. For the most recent cohorts observed there seems to be an incipient deceleration of the downward trend. The decline of cohort fertility coincides with a re-increase in the proportion childless (Fig. 5c).

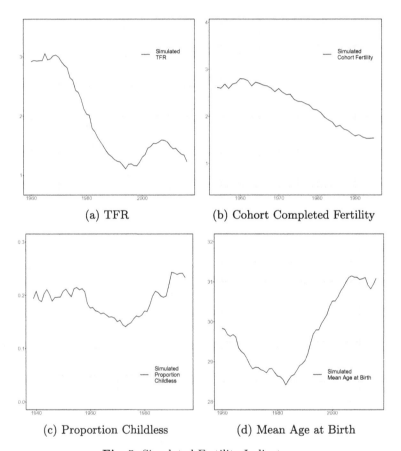

(a) TFR

(b) Cohort Completed Fertility

(c) Proportion Childless

(d) Mean Age at Birth

Fig. 5. Simulated Fertility Indicators.

The mean age at birth (Fig. 5d) shows a downward trend until the mid 1980's and then a rapid and sustained increase that stabilizes by the end of the period.

Moving to the results of the hazard regression models, Fig. 6 compares the estimates for the transition to a second child obtained from the simulated data

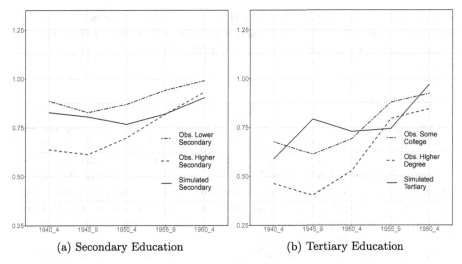

Fig. 6. Relative Risks for the Transition to Second Child by Cohort en Education with Lowest Education as the Reference | Women, Simulated vs. Observed Results.

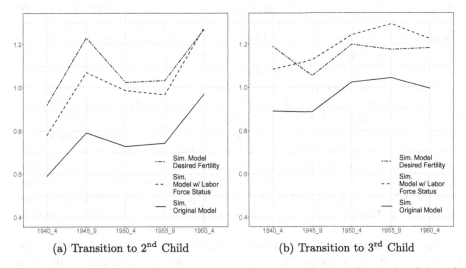

Fig. 7. Relative Risks for the Transition to Second and Third Births by Cohort | Women with Tertiary Education, Comparison of Model Specifications.

with those reported in [28]. The simulated results follow closely the observed ones, both showing a convergence trend between women with different educational attainment levels.

Figure 7 compares relative hazards for women with tertiary education from different model specifications. As explained in Sect. 6 the first modification of the original model consist in introducing the labor force participation status as a covariate, in order to account for differences in desired family size. The third model considers only desired fertility, that is, excludes unplanned births. For both the transition to the second and third child, the estimates from the two alternative specifications show either no educational gradient or a higher risk for more educated women.

9 Discussion

Our main objective was to contribute to our understanding of the changing relationship between educational attainment and fertility. The reversal of the sign of the statistical association between education and fertility is usually interpreted as a reversal of the behavioral mechanisms behind the association. We showed, however, that some of the key empirical results that support the notion of the reversal can be reproduced using simulated data from a known set of mechanisms that do not include a change over time in the way educational attainment affects fertility intentions at the micro level.

Instead, we explain the decreasing negative association between education and fertility and its potential reversal over time as a result of two main transformations that have progressively made the life courses of women with different education levels more alike. The first one is related to the erosion of the male-breadwinner model and the massive entry of women to the labor market. As a result of this movement the competition between different life goals has become part of the experience of most women in recent cohorts, reducing the gap with respect to the notion of what constitutes an *ideal* family.

The second process is related to the diffusion of effective contraceptive methods, which has made women's life-courses more similar with respect to the number of unplanned births they experience throughout their reproductive life.

In fact, we showed how when differences with respect to ideal family size were taken into account and only planned births were considered, more educated women in our simulation showed a higher risk of transitioning to higher order parities. When working with observed data, however, it is often not possible to make the distinction between planned and unplanned fertility and correctly identify the different mechanisms through which education shapes fertility outcomes.

The explanation we proposed here reconciles two empirical puzzles in contemporary fertility research: First, the fact that women with higher education have higher intentions but lower achieved fertility. Second, and beyond educational gradients, the fact that social and economic development can in a first stage contribute to the secular decline in fertility but also to its recuperation later on. In fact, our argument implies that this turning point depends heavily on the stage of the contraceptive transition and the transition of women into the labor market. After both transitions are completed and the mechanisms through which education negatively affects fertility outcomes become negligible, additional gains in the educational attainment of the population can positively affect fertility levels. Still, the positive influence of an increasingly educated population also has limits, as a longer period of enrollment continues to reduce the amount of time couples are exposed to the risk of having a child [10].

A   Appendix

A.1   Detailed Model Description

We use a discrete-event simulation approach in which time advances with the realization of each event. As shown in the pseudocode in Appendix A, at each iteration the algorithm realizes the event with the shortest waiting time from a list of all possible events for the entire population of agents. After the realization of each event the system is updated and the simulation continues to the next run.

We refer to the time between events as process (or duration) time t, which is expressed in seconds. Process time can be related to calendar time c which, as mentioned before, runs from the beginning of 1925 until the end of 2016. The third relevant duration in our model is Age x, which goes from 0 to 51, age at which our simulated individuals are removed from the population.

Desire Family Size: Known as the demand for children, the Desired Family Size (D) is the central quantity in classic microeconomic models of fertility, from the New Home Economics approach to Coale's Ready Willing and Able framework, Easterlin's supply-demand framework and its applications to developing countries [7].

In our model D does not represent an ideal number, but the answer a simulated woman would give to the question *How many children do you want to have?*.

Most explanations of the fertility transitions of the 1960s and 1970s in Europe have focused on the reduction of the demand for children as a consequence of the erosion of the conditions that led to the baby-boom, in particular the dominance of the male bread-winner paradigm following the rapid increase of women's participation in the labor market [35]. In our model we try to capture this movement defining D as:

$$D_i \sim \Gamma_{a \leq D_i \leq b}(_0D + \alpha - \beta^{A_i}, 1) \tag{1}$$

where $A_i \in \{0, 1\}$, is the labor force participation status of agent i (obtained from census data as explained in Sect. 7). Our computations based on the Integrated Value Surveys Database (not shown) confirmed our expectation that the distribution of family size preferences is positively skewed and justifies the choice of a Gamma distribution. The limits of the distribution a and b are the minimum and maximum number of desired children and the shape parameter is a function of $_0D$ (an initial value of D to be estimated) and parameters α & β, which define the distance between the distributions of D for active and inactive women. This distance expresses different preferences regarding the distribution of time between childrearing and other activities, but also the difficulties women expect to find when combining work and family.

Intentions: In our model the number of *planned* children people end up having is closely connected to their short term fertility intentions. Although there is a lengthy list of factors that could affect fertility intentions, here we necessarily have to focus on those most relevant to the context and periods we analyze, i.e., school enrollment status, perceived economic uncertainty, labor force participation status and educational attainment. Formally, the intention to have a child $_BI$ is defined as:

$$_BI_{i,x} = {_B}\rho_i - \varepsilon_{i,x} - R_c - \upsilon_i \tag{2}$$

where ρ is the baseline intention which can be interpreted as the intention, free of constraints, to have a child for those agents who have the desire to have children ($D > 0$). We assume that ρ comes from a truncated normal distribution, which allows us to introduce some variation in fertility intentions that is not directly related to the set of factors listed above.

$E_i \in \{0,1\}$ is the enrollment status of agent i and ε expresses the strength of the negative effect than being in the education system has over short-term fertility intentions.

R represents the perceived resources to afford a/an additional child and is given by a smoothed series of the unemployment rate, which we use to approximate the perception of agents regarding the economic situation at time c.

The last mechanism in 2 expresses the effect of education among working women and is defined as:

$$\upsilon_i = \eta/(1 + exp(\delta \cdot (Y_i - Y^*))) + (1 - \eta) \tag{3}$$

The mechanism is represented as a logistic function that moves from $1-\eta$ to 1 as the number of years of education Y approaches the threshold Y^*. The central idea here is that educational attainment helps to reduce the gap between working and non-working women with respect to short-term intentions as explained in Sect. 5.1.

From Intentions to Births: To connect intentions to births we assume that waiting times to the attempt to conceive are exponentially distributed with a rate proportional to the intention $_BI$.

This allows us to draw a waiting time for each woman with a partner who still has not achieved her desired family size. If the resulting waiting time is shorter than one year, at the end of that time our simulated couple will attempt to have a child, if it is longer they will update their intention after one year and reconsider whether or not to have a child within the next twelve months. These formulation allows us to introduce period effects in a discrete-event context that is in general better suited for the analysis of cohort processes.

We define the event as the *attempt* to conceive in order to be able to represent the decline in the probability to experience a pregnancy with age. This probability is defined as:

$$p_x = 1/1 + \exp(\theta(x - \omega)) \tag{4}$$

where ω controls the age at which the probability starts decreasing and it is assumed to be fixed for all agents.

If the couple fail to conceive, they will try again in a period of one to four months (draw from a truncated normal distribution with mean 1.5), until they reach a predefined limit for failed attempts. If they succeed, a waiting time equal 270 days is created which represents the duration of the pregnancy. After conception, if they still have not reached D they will go back to updating their intention/evaluating whether to try and have a new child after a period of ten to eighteen months (also drawn from a truncated normal distribution).

Unplanned Births: In our model, a couple that had already achieved their desired family size (including $D = 0$) still has a probability u to have an unplanned birth defined as:

$$u_{i,c} = \frac{\phi/(Y_i^\kappa)}{1 + e^{\iota \cdot (c - (c_0 - Y_i))}} \tag{5}$$

The use of a logistic function follows the representation of the adoption of contraception as a diffusion process [42]. As contraceptive methods become more effective the probability to have an unplanned birth declines. Parameters ι and ψ control the pace of the decline and its inflection point. Besides, as the diffusion process is usually led by more educated women we also make u dependent on an agent's educational attainment and let κ control the differences in the probability by years of education (Y).

Education Completion: The time agents take to complete their education depends on their level of education, which is determined by drawing a random number from 1 to 3 (representing the three educational levels considered) with probability equal to the observed proportions in each level by birth cohort.

After an education level is assigned the number of years Y_i agents will remain in the education system is obtained from a truncated normal distribution:

$$Y_i \sim N_{c \le Y_i \le d}(\mu, 3) \tag{6}$$

where $c = 0$ and $d = 6$ for those with *primary* education or less; $c = 6$ and $d = 12$ for those with *secondary* education; $c = 12$ and $d = 24$ for those with *tertiary* education. The mean of the distribution μ increases linearly throughout the period from 3 to 6, 8 to 12 and 16 to 22 years, for primary, secondary and tertiary education respectively. The waiting time to education $_E T_i$ is then obtained by expressing Y_i in seconds.

Union Formation: The process that leads to the formation of a cohabiting union begins with the search for a partner. To define the dynamics of the search we adapt some ideas from previous marriage markets models [19,20]. Women start searching for a partner around the time they complete their education. Once the time to select a partner arrives they choose among the pool of potential partners (composed by all men in the population born ten years before and three years after their own birth year) with a probability proportional to:

$$v_{ij} = \left(\frac{S_{max} - |s_i - s_j|}{S_{max}} \right) \cdot W_j \tag{7}$$

where s_i represents her level of education and s_j his. Besides preferring partners that have similar levels of instruction we assume that women prefer partners that work over partners that do not. Therefore we define W as:

$$W_j = \begin{cases} 1, & \text{if } A_j = 1 \\ 1/\tau, & \text{if } A_j = 0 \end{cases} \tag{8}$$

After a woman chooses a partner they start a relationship and she develops an intention to form a union which is defined as:

$$_U I_{i,x} = {}_U \rho_i - \varepsilon^{E_{i,x}} - R_c - U_x \tag{9}$$

where U_x is a function of the proportion of a woman's birth cohort that is already married at the time of updating $_U I$. The negative effect of U_x decreases as the proportion of married women increases, capturing the effects of social pressure. This mechanism generates a feedback that amplifies the effects of economic uncertainty and prolonged enrollment on the postponement of the age at union formation. It has been shown that these social multiplier effects are central to understand several sociodemographic processes like the spread of contraceptive use [34] and the postponement transition [11,24].

As in the decision to have a child, $_U I$ is updated on a yearly basis until the simulated couple moves in together or one of them leaves the population.

Death. The waiting time to death $_D T_i$ is sampled using the inverse distribution function method [46] where the distribution of waiting times to death is reconstructed using age-specific cohort mortality rates from the Human Mortality Database. For the ages/years where information is not available we use the latest available figures. Missing data corresponds essentially to the most recent decades, when mortality of females under 50 years of age is low.

A.2   Model Pseudo-Code

Function

> **Read Input Data:**
> Age Structure
> Initial Education Structure
> Educational Attainment Data
> Labor Force Participation Data
>
> ---
>
> **Initialization:**
> Define Beginning and End Times
> Define Initial Population Size
> Define Attributes Init. Pop:
> Age, Edu., Nr. Kids, Waiting Times, etc.
>
> ---
>
> **Start Simulation:**
>
> **while** $time < end\ time$ **do**
>
> > Define List of Events and Waiting Times
> > Choose Next Event $\rightarrow nEvent$
> > Update Clock, Ages and Waiting Times
> >
> > **if** $nEvent = Complete\ Education$ **then**
> > | Update Attributes and Waiting Times
> > **end**
> > **if** $nEvent = Birth$ **then**
> > > Decide whether male of female
> > > Assign attributes and waiting times to new agent
> > > Update attributes of mother
> > > Record parity and age in reproductive history
> > > Update waiting times of mother
> >
> > **end**
> > ...
> >
> > **if** $nEvent = Death$ **then**
> > | Update Attributes and Waiting Times
> > **end**
> >
> > Remove individuals older than $maxAge$
> >
> > **if** $End\ of\ Current\ Year$ **then**
> > | Compute and Store Aggregate Indicators
> > **end**
>
> **end**
>
> ---
>
> **Result**:
> Collect Output in List for Analysis

end

References

1. Becker, G.S.: An economic analysis of fertility. In: Demographic and Economic Change in Developed Countries, pp. 209–240. Columbia University Press (1960)
2. Becker, G.S., Lewis, H.G.: On the interaction between the quantity and quality of children. J. Polit. Econ. **81**(2, Part 2), S279–S288 (1973)
3. Becker, G.S., Tomes, N.: Child endowments and the quantity and quality of children. J. Polit. Econ. **84**(4, Part 2), S143–S162 (1976)
4. Bongaarts, J.: The measurement of wanted fertility. Population Dev. Rev. **16**, 487–506 (1990)
5. Bongaarts, J.: Trends in unwanted childbearing in the developing world. Stud. Fam. Planning **28**, 267–277 (1997)
6. Bongaarts, J.: Fertility and reproductive preferences in post-transitional societies. Population Dev. Rev. **27**, 260–281 (2001)
7. Bulatao, R.A., Lee, R.D., Hollerbach, P., Bongaarts, J.: Determinants of fertility in developing countries (1983)
8. Caltabiano, M., Castiglioni, M., Rosina, A., et al.: Lowest-low fertility: signs of a recovery in Italy. Demographic Res. **21**(23), 681–718 (2009)
9. Castiglioni, M., Dalla Zuanna, G., Loghi, M.: Planned and unplanned births and conceptions in Italy, 1970–1995. Euro. J. Population/Rev. Européenne de Démographie **17**(3), 207–233 (2001)
10. Ciganda, D., Todd, N.: Micro-level dynamics behind the recuperation of fertility at higher development levels. Max Planck Institute for Demographic Research Working Paper (2019)
11. Ciganda, D., Villavicencio, F.: Feedback mechanisms in the postponement of fertility in Spain. In: Grow, A., Van Bavel, J. (eds.) Agent-Based Modelling in Population Studies. TSSDMPA, vol. 41, pp. 405–435. Springer, Cham (2017). https://doi.org/10.1007/978-3-319-32283-4_14
12. Cleland, J.: Marital fertility decline in developing countries: theories and the evidence (1985)
13. Cochrane, S.H.: Fertility and education: what do we really know? (1979)
14. Cochrane, S.H.: Effects of education and urbanization on fertility (1983)
15. De Wachter, D., Neels, K.: Educational differentials in fertility intentions and outcomes: family formation in flanders in the early 1990s. Vienna Yearb. Population Res. **9**, 227–258 (2011)
16. Doepke, M.: Gary becker on the quantity and quality of children. J. Demographic Econ. **81**(1), 59–66 (2015)
17. Easterlin, R.A., Crimmins, E.M.: The Fertility Revolution: A Supply-Demand Analysis. University of Chicago Press (1985)
18. Esping-Andersen, G.: Incomplete Revolution: Adapting Welfare States to Women's New Roles. Polity, Cambridge (2009)
19. Grow, A., Schnor, C., Van Bavel, J.: The reversal of the gender gap in education and relative divorce risks: a matter of alternatives in partner choice? Population Stud. **71**(Suppl. 1), 15–34 (2017)
20. Grow, A., Van Bavel, J.: Assortative mating and the reversal of gender inequality in education in Europe: an agent-based model. PloS One **10**(6), e0127806 (2015)
21. Henshaw, S.K.: Unintended pregnancy in the united states. Fam. Plann. Perspect. **30**, 24–46 (1998)
22. Hoem, B., Hoem, J.M.: The impact of women's employment on second and third births in modern sweden. Population Stud. **43**(1), 47–67 (1989)

23. Klijzing, E.: Are there unmet family planning needs in Europe? Fam. Plann. Perspect. **32**, 74–88 (2000)
24. Kohler, H.P.: Fertility and Social Interaction: An Economic Perspective. Oxford University Press, Oxford (2001)
25. Kohler, H.P., Billari, F.C., Ortega, J.A.: The emergence of lowest-low fertility in Europe during the 1990s. Population Dev. Rev. **28**(4), 641–680 (2002)
26. Kravdal, Ø.: The emergence of a positive relation between education and third birth rates in Norway with supportive evidence from the united states. Population Stud. **46**(3), 459–475 (1992)
27. Kravdal, Ø.: The high fertility of college educated women in Norway: an artefact of the separate modelling of each parity transition. Demographic Res. **5**, 187–216 (2001)
28. Kravdal, Ø., Rindfuss, R.R.: Changing relationships between education and fertility: a study of women and men born 1940 to 1964. Am. Sociol. Rev. **73**(5), 854–873 (2008)
29. Kreyenfeld, M.: Time-squeeze, partner effect or self-selection? An investigation into the positive effect of women's education on second birth risks in west Germany. Demographic Res. **7**, 15–48 (2002)
30. Luci-Greulich, A., Thévenon, O.: Does economic advancement 'Cause'a re-increase in fertility? An empirical analysis for OECD countries (1960–2007). Eur. J. Population **30**(2), 187–221 (2014)
31. Mencarini, L., Tanturri, M.L.: Time use, family role-set and childbearing among Italian working women. Genus **60**, 111–137 (2004)
32. Mills, M., Mencarini, L., Tanturri, M.L., Begall, K.: Gender equity and fertility intentions in Italy and The Netherlands. Demographic Res. **18**, 1–26 (2008)
33. Minnesota Population Center: Integrated public use microdata series, international: Version 7.0 (2018)
34. Montgomery, M.R., Casterline, J.B.: The diffusion of fertility control in Taiwan: evidence from pooled cross-section time-series models. Population Stud. **47**(3), 457–479 (1993)
35. Murphy, M.: The contraceptive pill and women's employment as factors in fertility change in britain 1963–1980: a challenge to the conventional view. Population Stud. **47**(2), 221–243 (1993)
36. Myrskylä, M., Kohler, H.P., Billari, F.C.: Advances in development reverse fertility declines. Nature **460**(7256), 741–743 (2009)
37. Notestein, F.W.: Economic Problems of Population Change. Oxford University Press, London (1953)
38. Carreras de Odriozola, A., Tafunell Sambola, X.: Estadísticas históricas de España, siglos XIX-XX. Fundacion BBVA/BBVA Foundation (2006)
39. R Core Team: R: A Language and Environment for Statistical Computing. R Foundation for Statistical Computing, Vienna, Austria (2015). http://www.r-project.org
40. Régnier-Loilier, A., Leridon, H., Cahen, F., et al.: Four decades of legalized contraception in France: an unfinished revolution? Technical report, Institut National d'Études Démographiques (INED) (2007)
41. Rindfuss, R.R., Bumpass, L., John, C.: Education and fertility: implications for the roles women occupy. Am. Sociol. Rev. **45**(3), 431–447 (1980)
42. Rosero-Bixby, L., Casterline, J.B.: Modelling diffusion effects in fertility transition. Population Stud. **47**(1), 147–167 (1993)

43. Sullivan, O., Billari, F.C., Altintas, E.: Fathers' changing contributions to child care and domestic work in very low-fertility countries: the effect of education. J. Fam. Issues **35**(8), 1048–1065 (2014)
44. Testa, M.R.: On the positive correlation between education and fertility intentions in Europe: individual-and country-level evidence. Adv. Life Course Res. **21**, 28–42 (2014)
45. Villa, P.: Séries macro-économiques historiques: méthodologie et analyse économique. Institut National de la Statistique et des Etudes Economiques (1997)
46. Willekens, F.: Continuous-time microsimulation in longitudinal analysis. In: New frontiers in microsimulation modelling, pp. 353–376 (2009)
47. Wulf, D.: Low fertility in Europe: a report from the 1981 IUSSP meeting. Fam. Plann. Perspect. **14**(5), 264–270 (1982)

A Voice for Education: A Digital Analysis of Sheikha Moza's Public Statements, 2009–2018

Dina Sawaly[1], Wajdi Zaghouani[1]([⊠]) [iD], and David Kaufer[2]

[1] Hamad Bin Khalifa University, Doha, Qatar
dsawaly@mail.hbku.edu.qa, wzaghouani@hbku.edu.qa
[2] Carnegie Mellon University, Pittsburgh, PA, USA
kaufer@andrew.cmu.edu

Abstract. Women in politics have been subject to extensive research, and their speeches examined from different gender and discourse analysis perspectives; however, little has been written on female political participation in the Arab world. This paper examines how Sheikha Moza's public statements have evolved from 2009 to 2018 in terms of linguistic features and content. The method used is both qualitative and quantitative. Unlike previous digital studies to date, this research employs two different digital tools: DocuScope and AntConc. DocuScope was used to trace statistically significant changes and to identify the variables that have changed over time. To complement these results, AntConc was employed in order to analyze unique word choices. Results suggest that there were significant differences between Sheikha Moza's public statements over the period in question, specifically between the years 2009 and 2018. These were examined and compared here as being predominantly "ceremonial" vs. "realistic". Thus, in 2009 she adopted a more ceremonial, positive, academic and institutional-idealist stance on education. In comparison, in 2018, she focuses on major international tribulations; her statements contain more narrative, character, negative and descriptive clusters as per DocuScope's analysis. In particular, in her statements, she makes striking references to human suffering and comes to an understanding that education depends on cultural, political, and economic tranquility. Her language in 2018 becomes much idealist-nationalist and much more realist about the savagery that conflict and war can exact on educational opportunity.

Keywords: DocuScope · Education · Language · Qatar · Speech · Sheikha Moza Bint Nasser Al-Missned

1 Introduction

Traditional research into textual analysis in general, and public speaking in particular, can be significantly advanced and refined with the help of digital tools. These tools make it possible to capture the patterns and varied content within a large corpus without losing valuable information. Various tools efficiently and reliably identify patterns and unique words, providing useful insights into intentions, attitudes, style and

© Springer Nature Switzerland AG 2019
I. Weber et al. (Eds.): SocInfo 2019, LNCS 11864, pp. 239–252, 2019.
https://doi.org/10.1007/978-3-030-34971-4_16

approach. As a result, thousands of influential texts and transcripts can be examined to reveal further the complexity and nature of our society and culture. Inspired by the immense potential of applying digital tools in the field of humanities and social sciences, this research employs tools such as DocuScope[1] and AntConc[2] to examine linguistic features and content of Sheikha Moza's public statements delivered in English between 2009 and 2018. This examination aims to enhance the experience of exploring and navigating the text of her public statements, which have not been to date subjected to this type of academic analysis. The research focus on the public statements delivered by Sheikha Moza bint Nasser Al-Missned (b. 1959), stems from her remarkable contribution to women empowerment and equality both nationally and globally. Further, due to the fact that she is one of the very few in the region who have played a major role in education in Qatar and around the world.

This study utilizes DocuScope and AntConc to examine linguistic features and content of Sheikha Moza's public statements delivered between 2009 and 2018. This examination of the corpus of 77 transcripts focuses on identifying patterns and tracing the evolution of Sheikha Moza's stance on education and its expression. The employment of two different text-processing technologies takes this research beyond the traditional paradigm of speech analysis. To the best of our knowledge, no research to date has looked in detail into the rhetoric of the Qatari female leaders, who successfully operate *within* the framework of a traditional society, not *against* it, unlike many western female leaders. Public statements have been studied from different perspectives, for example, discourse analysis or gender. However, there have been limited studies that have been devoted to Sheikha Moza. This research offers one of the first analyses of Sheikha Moza's public statements, using two different digital tools and existing academic approaches to public speaking.

2 Related Work

Political discourse analysis refers to the examination of speeches by politicians. Language use in both text and speech represents a person's perception of the social setup. Rhetoric analysis checks the appropriateness and effectiveness of a speech for a given occasion; the eloquence and the cues in its presentation; and the effective use of language to pass the message persuasively. Political discourse analysis is regarded as a subset of Critical Discourse Analysis (CDA), which deals with rhetoric and the use of language for communication in political speeches. CDA analyzes the context of language use to obtain an in-depth perspective of political discourse and it questions the structure and distribution of power as evidenced in texts. A register is the context-specific style used which determines how one's speech is to be understood, whether political, economic, or social (Van Dijk, 2001). Additionally, grammar and the lexical use of words affects the reception of speech. Van Dijk (2001) explored the various structures that are typical to political speeches and found that: topics, textual structures,

---

[1] https://www.cmu.edu/dietrich/english/research/docuscope.html.

[2] https://www.laurenceanthony.net/software/antconc/.

local semantics, syntaxes, lexicons, expression structures, rhetoric, speech acts, and interactions are the key identifiers. Political speeches vary according to the context, but conform to a predetermined discourse structure. The consistency in the structure is attributed to the fact that all political speeches exhibit some common underlying structure that makes them classifiable as "political". Similarly, other discourse types have their own unique criteria for classification.

In a study by Rajakumar (2014), that assesses the feminist rhetoric of Sheikha Moza, where the researcher examined her rhetorical style through her speeches. For example, she examined Sheikha Moza's speech in 2009 where she acknowledged other universities along with the ones in Education City. According to Rajakumar (2014), this "public pairing" of universities demonstrates part of Sheikha Moza's constituency and highlights the loyalty in a close-knit society. Other researchers conduct discourse analysis from the perspective of systemic functional grammar proposed by Halliday. These researchers use concepts of ideational, interpersonal, and textual structure as a means for comparative analysis. The research by Wang (2010) analyzed Obama's speeches during his presidency using the Systematic Functional Linguistics (SFL) framework.

There have been substantial studies using DocuScope as a tool to analyze text. For instance, Pessoa, Miller and Kaufer (2014) used DocuScope in order to detect the development and challenges of student's literacy skills in their shift to university. The researchers conducted interviews to find out student's difficulties in the first semester for example, difficulties in reading comprehension as a result of their limited knowledge of vocabulary or background information. Other studies analyze text using AntConc; for instance, Al-Rawi (2017) used AntConc in order to identify keywords and explore what they tell about the Victorian novel "A tale of two cities".

3   Methodology

The aim of this research is to interpret and classify Sheikha Moza's public statements, as well as to demonstrate the essential linguistic elements and features of this interpretation. Hence, the methods of this research are observation, description, identification and classification. This research is a corpus analysis of 77 public statements – speeches, interviews and articles published by Sheikha Moza during the period 2009–2018. These are all of the statements made by Sheikha Moza in the given period. The data was downloaded manually from Sheikha Moza's website (https://www.mozabintnasser.qa/en) and then converted to ".txt" files.

We used quantitative and qualitative methods. Tracing the evolution of the rhetoric employed in Sheikha Moza's statements requires their thorough examination within the broader context of her views. The distribution of themes and language will be examined here through DocuScope, in order to identify language patterns within these texts. Digital corpus analysis enables access to and examination of linguistic phenomena (from simple to complex, frequent to rare words, see Hasko, 2012); it identifies patterns as well as the frequency of recurring phrases in the corpus. Drawing on these results, the study will identify liminal points, major trends and shifts in the rhetoric Sheikha Moza employed to advance her educational projects. To conduct this analysis, we relied on two tools: DocuScope the rhetorical analysis tool and AntConc the corpus analysis toolkit.

3.1 DocuScope

DocuScope is a text analysis tool with an interactive visualization element, which relies on corpus-based analysis. This program began in 1998 between David Kaufer and Suguru Ishizaki at Carnegie Mellon University. DocuScope originally embedded the Knuth-Morris-Pratt (KMP) algorithm for fast pattern matching in strings (Knuth, Morris, and Pratt, 1977). The innovation of the algorithm was, from any starting point in a text, the algorithm would search for the longest match available. Once that match was found, the algorithm would set the current destination to the new starting point. In this way, the algorithm could tag a text without having to backtrack. With innovations in the Python language, the functionality of this algorithm was made available in Pythons standard natural language processing libraries. A dictionary was created which consists of more than 40 million linguistic patterns of English over 20,000 categories of rhetorical effects. Their theoretical framework and the overview of the generic dictionary is in the book *Power of Words: Unveiling the speaker's and writer's hidden craft* (Kaufer, Ishizaki, Butler and Collins, Routledge, 2004).

The theoretical framework of the book is based on what the authors call "rhetorical primary theory". This theory assumes that readers learn to extract meaning from text by associating patterns of text with a repertoire of higher-level semantic representations. The patterns, in essence "prime" readers to build these representations. For example, the pattern "I was" or "I used to be", which matches a scheme of first person + past tense primes readers to believe that a speaker or writer is writing autobiographically. A pattern like "she used to…" primes narrative biography. In sum, the theory behind DocuScope is that micro-patterns of language prime higher-level semantic representations. When these patterns of statistically aggregated, it is possible to see priming agents in texts help build a semantics of whole texts and even text collections.

DocuScope was used in this research in order to tag the text by semantic category and turn word counts into frequencies in order to find measures of the linguistic features in Sheikha Moza's public presentations. DocuScope searches a text for strings of characters and then matches to those stored in its memory. Each string is allocated to a linguistic- rhetorical category, called "Language Action Type" (LAT). Each LAT captures a set of words, which were built into DocuScope by the designers. After counting the strings, the frequencies get extracted as a CSV (comma separated variable) file, which can then be exported to a statistical package, such as Minitab. The Minitab data was then statistically analyzed through a tool called factor analysis. Factor analysis works in two stages. First, it builds a correlation matrix of the frequencies of all the variables DocuScope recognized. Next it uses linear algebra to look for linear combinations of highly positively correlated and highly negatively correlated variables, called factors. In the statements, We analyzed factor analysis recommended a two-factor solution, with the one pole interpretable through variables like academic, public, and positive, which We interpreted to mean "ceremonial". The other pole contained variables such as narrative and negative, which We interpreted to mean "realism". These poles separated Sheika Moza's speeches between 2008 and 2011 on the one hand and between 2015 and 2018 on the other. To better understand the relationship between the language variables in the corpus, various visualizations used to clarify the relationships among variables, can be extracted both from the DocuScope platform and from various statistic applications within Minitab. This is very important; DocuScope processes thousands of variables of raw natural language data, which would be overwhelming to analyze by the naked eye or close reading.

DocuScope provides an overview and reveals statistically significant changes and their underlying variables. We began by importing the corpus on DocuScope, and then extracting the frequencies of the cluster variables for the analysis on Minitab. As a matter of DocuScope background, the clusters break down into 25 variables, supported by over 500 lower-level variables, in turn supported by over 20,000 language relevant variables. This research only deals with the top 25 level variables. The lower-level variables are designed only to ensure maximal precision of the cluster variables. Then the cluster frequencies were imported on Minitab to run three different analyses: factor analysis, One-Way ANOVA, and a Tukey Pairwise Comparison. By using these three statistics using the statistical package on Minitab, We were able to identify which variables to focus on using DocuScope to determine the characteristics of Sheikha Moza's public statements.

3.2 Factor Analysis

This section discusses factor analysis in more detail. Factor analysis is a standard multivariate technique used for data reduction when researchers are working with many variables and need to reduce the data to a very few super-dimensions or "factors." A factor is essentially a linear combination of variables extracted from the correlation matrix containing the pairwise comparisons of all the raw variables. The researcher began the analysis by applying the Factor Analysis statistic which first assesses the structure of the data by evaluating the correlations between variables (Kachigan, 1986). After assessing the correlations, the Factor Analysis statistic applies well-known procedures of linear algebra to extract combinations of variables whose correlational structure is highly correlated or highly inversely correlated. The researcher must input into the Factor Analysis statistic the number of factors to be extracted. To determine this number, the researcher ran a Scree Plot, which visualizes the strength of the factors that can be extracted through a unit called eigenvalue. The scree plot identifies the clusters of correlated variables (called factors) and their relative strength in descending order. Strength is measured in terms of units called "eigenvalues", which measures the strength of the correlations. As one can see from the Fig. 1 above, the first factor (x-axis) has an eigenvalue above 4 (y-axis) while the second factor drops to an eigenvalue of 2. An eigenvalue of 4 indicates that the factor has the explanatory power of 4 variables. An eigenvalue of 2 means that the factor has the explanatory power of 2 variables. In natural language work using DocuScope, it is customary to choose factors with an eigenvalue of 2 or greater. As one can see from the Boxplot below (Fig. 2), We found two factors that met this condition. Consequently, the researcher sought a two-factor solution from the data.

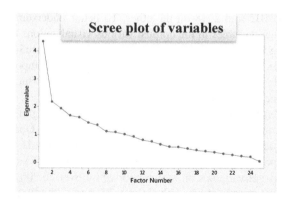

Fig. 1. Scree Plot showing clusters of variables and their strength

Running one-way MANOVA, We discovered that the first factor was highly statistically significant (F (76, 2) = 6.05; p = 0.004) but the second factor was not. We thus mapped the first factor on the x-axis to understand where the differences were. This resulted in Fig. 2 below. ANOVA allowed us to test for the quality of means and assess the difference existing between pairs of means. This will allow us to determine the following: (1) which factor is significant; (2) what each factor represents; and (3) how we can interpret the variables within each factor. As shown below, there is a significant difference (or spatial displacement) between the presentations of 2009 (blue circles) on the far left of the x-axis and 2018 (purple triangles) to the extreme right of the x-axis After close reading the speeches of these book end years, We determined that the blue circles indicate "ceremonial" discourse on the x-axis, where Sheikha Moza spoke mostly ceremoniously, with great optimism about education and the role it can play in changing the world. In this sense, it does not imply that Sheikha Moza's statements were frivolous, however, it implies the way in which Sheikha Moza talked mostly ceremoniously, with great optimism about education and the role it can play in changing the world. By 2018, her public statements dominate the right side of the x-axis where she has become dominantly "realist". Classifying Sheikha Moza's statements as "realism" does not imply that has become cynical or that she has given up on education, rather it indicates the growing traces of a realist position that education is depended on and interacted with many other factors and could not be treated as an isolated reason for society's challenges. These results reveal a significant difference between the statements delivered in the years 2009 and 2018. However, this software does not identify unique word choices. For this reason, We will use AntConc in order to see the same story that DocuScope told but in the context of unique words chosen. Hence, We will then complement the initial findings by way of using AntConc, an analysis toolkit designed by Laurence Anthony.

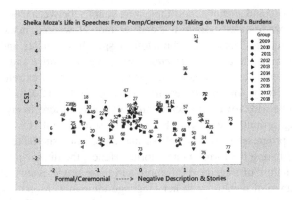

Fig. 2. Differences in public statements in terms of variables (Color figure online)

3.3 AntConc

AntConc is a widely used software program for analyzing digital transcripts. It has many functions such as Word List, Keyword list, Concordance and Collocates. Using the Word list, the researcher can create an ordered list of the occurring words in the text file. The Keyword tool is also very helpful as it identifies words that are infrequent but have a significant role in the given text. They indicate what the text is about and gives insight to the content of the selected transcript compared to the whole or standard text. Moreover, the Concordance tool enables the researcher to view a selected word in its immediate context along with its neighboring words. It searches the corpus for every instance of the chosen word and presents each one along with its context. This can be very beneficial to find collocations or patterns and to see different examples of the same word at the same time. Furthermore, the Collocates tool generates a list of collocations and words that most likely occur with a specific term or pattern. This examination reveals the patterns that are linked to a word.

4 Results and Discussion

In this section, we will present the research findings and discussion in the following three sections: (a) DocuScope Analysis; (b) AntConc Analysis; (c) post-hoc analysis using AntConc.

4.1 DocuScope Analysis

The results above show that there has been a significant change between Sheikha Moza's public statements which were ranked at the bottom of the factor analysis which highlight "ceremonial" and between the ones ranked at the top of the factor analysis which emphasize "realism". The application of one-way ANOVA found that the polarities of "ceremonial" and "realism" distinguished Sheikha Moza's early (2009–2011) and her later speeches (2017–2018) with high statistical significance $F(76, 2) = 6.05, p = .004$. Hence, when she was ceremonial, she was high in the variables: *public, academic, syntactic complexity* and *positive*, and they were mainly between 2009–2011. In that sense, Sheikha Moza sounded more formal and ceremonial, whereas in the texts that were embodying realism, they were a combination of speeches, articles and an interview, which were high in the variables: *character, description, narrative* and *negative*.

By looking deeper, and comparing her style between both extremes, it becomes clear that comparatively, she talks differently between 2009 and 2018. Towards 2018, it seems that Sheikha Moza was less ceremonial and talked more freely while tackling issues happening around the world. For that reason, overall levels of negativity increased as she progressed, so do levels of narrative, since she talked about "issues" around the world taking the form of dark stories. Hence, the diminishing positivity can be linked to the nature of tragedy. With more and more tragic events taking place, the more the percentage of negativity in her language increased. Moreover, her tone was distinctly emotional; she expressed gratitude and thanked others. The overall structure of the text was almost deductive; and Sheikha Moza spent a lot of time discussing her experiences and stories of different people.

The analysis in the previous section indicates her willingness to take unilateral action in solving these problems, as opposed to her earlier public statements, which emphasized listening and collaboration. Her style and structure were more encompassing, as she made broader statements and decisions about the cause and solution of poverty and terrorism for instance. Her more expansive language implied that she had the authority and power to make these observations, and she had the power to actually deliver on them. Furthermore, towards 2018, she talked about her personal experience, and appeals to children and women, unity and collectivism. By contrast, when she was more ceremonial, she seemed to be swinging between embodying the tough, empowered idealistic woman that is often projected onto her. However, towards 2018 when she became leaning towards "realism" she drops the ceremonial and formal in favor of a more realistic and nuts-and-bolts problem-solver.

Therefore, we can say that in 2018, Sheikha Moza's shift to a higher frequency of *character, description, negative* and *narrative* are linked together as she talked about people (Character) and events (narrative) in detail (Description) happening around the world which are mostly problems (negative).

4.2 AntConc Analysis

This section is an understanding of DocuScope findings through the selection of unique words. Hence, We run two separate sets of public statements on AntConc; seven transcripts embodying "ceremonial" and eight transcripts embodying "realism". For each, word list, key word list, and collocates were extracted then compared. Word lists is an ordered list of the occurring words in the transcript classified based on high frequency. To illustrate the comparison between the "ceremonial" and "realist" ends of the factor, we tracked the same word and its frequency across both poles. We selected words that appear much more frequently at one end of the factor more than another.

The results are presented in the Table 1 (Appendix A). Table 1 sheds more light on the shift in Sheikha Moza's public statements. Her ceremonial speeches paint a picture of "education city" being built in order to get "Research", "scientific" and "development" into Qatar in order to advance the nation. In abstract, it is all about giving knowledge and scientific research as a strategy to a country to unleash human potential and advance human rights. However, in Sheikha Moza's turn to "realism", scientific research recedes and terms like "poverty", "war" and "refugees" are introduced to replace it. Sheikha Moza has moved from a telescopic lens of aspiration to a microscopic of journalist. From a local-national focus on Qatar or the Arab region, she begins to focus on international countries. Notice how the terms "Qatar" and "Arab" have decreased in Table 1. Mentions of "Qatar" dropped from 38 to 14 and mentions of "Arab" dropped from 15 to 1. At the same time, "world" doubled in mentions from 21 in ceremonial statements to 44 in realist statements. Most importantly, "children" increased drastically, from ceremonial statements, which was at a frequency of 1 to realism with a frequency of 109.

Sheikha Moza talked about children in many different aspects. For instance "we need to do more to inoculate our children against extremism", "the benefit of their education to their own children", "I was struck by the strength of these children", "out-of-school children" and "10 million children." Hence, children were one of Sheikha Moza's main foci in her realist speeches. This is roughly proportional to other aspects of her realism, such as narrative and negative. The more Sheikha Moza spoke about the darker stories that are happening in the world, the more she references children. For that reason, the frequency of children increased with the frequency of dark stories. It could be true that referencing children can create a sense of sympathy among the audience, hence generating a higher effect and immediate action. Similarly, the term "women" did not appear in the ceremonial transcripts but appeared nine times in the realism transcripts. Although the number is not big, the shift is noticeable as Sheikha Moza starts to frame women, and starts to show a willingness to make "gender" a category in her realist presentational that she was less willing to do in her "ceremonial" presentations, in a way she was not willing to do previously in her speaking career. However in this stage of her career, she takes pains to draw special consideration to women. For instance in her realist presentations, she says "Women are no longer silent"; "not just women, children and all vulnerable people are affected"; "women in the most disadvantaged communities"; "women in these situations have no other choice" and "most influential women on the international stage". In this sense, she is talking about the women as marginalized and other women who are empowered and confident.

Keyword analysis can be used to identify the "trademark" words of a given corpus of interest (in this case Sheikha Moza's public statements) by comparing the occurrence of words in this corpus with a typically much larger reference corpus of random English. It is important to note that keywords are not the same as frequency lists generated for a single corpus. Keywords are not the most frequent words. They are a comparative calculation, a calculation of the ratio between how often a word occurs in the target corpus (for example, Sheikha Moza's transcripts) versus how often it occurs in a larger typically randomized corpus of English (for example, the Brown and Frieberg-Brown Corpus of Written English).

As seen in Table 2 (Appendix A), Sheikha Moza's own country (Qatar) is more a trademark reference of her ceremonial phrase of language than her realist phrase. In her ceremonial phase, she is more a nationalist. In her realist phase, as we will see, she speaks more as an internationalist. She mentions "Qatar" 38 times in her ceremonial phase but less than half of that (14 times) in her realist phase. Curiously, the term "challenges" was one of the highest rankings in ceremonial but ranked much less under realism. This might be due to the fact that Sheikha Moza used the word "challenges" in her ceremonial speeches when she was not interested in naming or getting too specific about challenges. She just "telescoped" these challenges as abstractions out there to be dealt with. However, towards 2018 when a more realist woman is starting to tackle minute issues through a microscopic lens, her use of "challenges" as a faraway abstraction almost disappears.

Another future-oriented abstraction that meets near extinction when she turns realistic is "education". This term was ranked 62 in her ceremonial phase and increased to 3 when her public statements turn to realism. In fact, it was the highest word in the realism which leaves a trademark in all of her transcripts as it plays a special role since she gave more emphasis on education and quality education towards 2018. The term "world" and "international" both were ranked high in realism but low in ceremonial; this reflects that Sheikha Moza's outlook seemed to become more internationalist as she moved toward 2018. Other words such as "conflict", "war", "terrorism", "marginalized" and "refugee" were highly ranked in realism, but never appeared as keywords for ceremonial. Conversely, words like "scientific", "language", "national", "strategy" and "vision" that were high in "ceremonial", were not generated in the "realism" keyword analysis. This shows that in the ceremonial framing, the context and focus of the texts were telescopic, national based, academic and strategic, focusing on Qatar's national vision, while in the realist framing, the context or the trademark of the texts were microscopic, focusing on the whole world close up, and illuminating education, narrative and negative.

4.3 Post-hoc Analysis

Based on the word lists previously generated, education was one of the significant changes. Since Sheikha Moza's main motive is education, this word was chosen in order to identify how she spoke about education differently and in what context. In order to conduct this analysis, We will rely on the collocates tool in AntConc to identify various collocates that could be of relevance to the theme at hand. Primarily, we looked at the collocate frequency of each of the transcripts (ceremonial and realism) and where are they situated in the concordance analysis to understand whether the collocates chosen would have relevance to the topic at hand as observed in Table 3 (Appendix A).

From a frequency perspective, the term "education" appeared 12 times in the ceremonial transcript and 120 times in the realism transcript. In the ceremonial transcript, education was mostly linked with scientific research; which is why the collocates listed above are mostly associated with the notion of keeping pace with education and research. In that era, Sheikha Moza was focusing solely on the advancement of education and promoting the continuous growth of scientific research meeting the requirements of the society. On the contrary, the realism column projects completely different collocations; for instance, education became associated with words that describe the current situation in countries affected by terrorism or poverty. For instance, words like "zone" with reference to conflict zones, and "suffer" and "struggle" are all descriptions related to war and highlights the necessity in having education in safer places. Further, the collocates "virus" and "viscous" were noted as trademarks as they was very strong in context when she said "And in communities of the marginalized and disadvantaged, terrorism can spread like a virus. Education is the world's vaccine against terrorism" and "vicious circle of poverty that this so often engenders". Here there is a direct statement, which implies that education can help stop terrorism especially in developing countries. For that reason, Sheikha Moza argued strongly on the notion that education should be considered as a basic human need, exactly like "food, water and shelter."

Hence, Sheikha Moza has indeed changed the way in which education is projected, focusing more on figuring out ways in which education can be delivered to people around the world. Throughout her speeches towards 2018, she was calling upon other countries by scaling up model of education delivery from community level to global programs. Hence, the context of education has changed drastically in Sheikha Moza's public statements throughout the years, from a telescopic to a microscopic view, from focusing on education and research in Qatar, to expanding the vision of education all around the world especially in conflict zones stressing on the notion that education offers people resilience and the critical skills needed to condemn terrorism and violence.

4.4   Main Findings

The above discussion of the results of the DocuScope and AntConc analysis suggests the following observations:

- Digital tools analysis identifies a shift in the language and style of Sheikha Moza's public statements delivered over the period between 2009 and 2018.
- The DocuScope's analysis shows that the most significant changes can be traced to 2009–2011 and 2017–2018.
- Most of Sheikha Moza's public statements delivered in 2009–2011 were higher in terms of *Academic, Syntactic Complexity, Public* and *Positive* variables. Her statements were more ceremonial, assumed telescopic stance, and promoted human potential. The importance of education was associated with advancing research and knowledge.
- Towards 2017–2018, her public statements tend to espouse *Character, Description, Negative* and *Narrative* variables. The focus shifts to realistic, microscopic referencing when discussing international issues. Education is now discussed within the context of poverty, unemployment and military conflict.

5   Conclusion

This study has examined Sheikha Moza's public statements delivered at different points between 2009 and 2018 in order to identify if there is a statistically significant difference between their content and language. These differences were analyzed to argue that Sheikha Moza's views on education and their expression in her public statements undergo a significant development over this period.

A significant difference was found between the presentations of 2009–11 and 2017–2018. In 2009–11, Sheikha Moza spoke mostly ceremoniously, with great optimism about education and the role it can play in changing the world. Between the years 2010 and 2017, her presentations begin to fluctuate between the unconditional optimism of 2009 and the increasing realistic stance on the factors preventing many people from accessing education. She admits that education couldn't be treated as an isolated factor of society's challenges. By 2018, her public presentations became predominantly realistic. Education is no longer a silver lining; its challenges reflect severe challenges faced by the world: poverty, unemployment, war and terrorism, which counter and undermine the positive effect of education.

Major distinctions that reveal this shift in her stance were discussed in terms of opposites: telescopic vs. microscopic, clarity vs. passion, ceremonial vs. realism, idealistic politics vs. real world, public vs. private, positive vs. negative, institutional vs. problem solving, informing vs. narrating. The analysis above compares an earlier period in the performance of a public figure (ceremonial, representing an optimistic power), with her later stance, when she can talk from her heart, from years of experience, and from her established reputation as a successful humanitarian.

Appendix A

See Tables 1, 2 and 3.

Table 1. Head-to-head word list comparison

	Ceremonial	Realism
Children	1	109
Education	12	120
I	30	94
You	28	41
We	95	146
Research	91	1
Scientific	64	0
Educate	0	26
Conflict	0	23
Quality	6	17
Refugee	0	14
War	0	13
Women	0	9
Poverty	0	7
Qatar	38	14
Development	30	7
National	27	1
World	21	44
Arab	15	1
Health	14	1
Society	1	12
International	8	16

Table 2. Head-to-head ranking comparisons

	Ranking	
Word	Ceremonial	Realism
Qatar	3	11
Challenges	9	48
Doha	16	30
Education	62	3
World	76	18
International	126	28

Table 3. Collocates of "Education" in "Ceremonial" & "Realism"

Ceremonial	Realism
Scientific	Prevent
Research	Zone
City	Youths
Quality	Virus
Unique	Vicious
Technology	Universal
Systematic	Transforms
Resources	Transformative
Keeping	Transformational
Higher	Suffer
Achievement	Struggle

References

Al-Rawi, M.: Using AntConc: a corpus-based tool, to investigate and analyse the keywords in Dickens' novel 'A Tale of Two Cities'. Int. J. Adv. Res. **5**(2), 366–372 (2017). https://doi.org/10.21474/ijar01/3158

Clark, R.P.: Why it worked: a rhetorical analysis of Obama's speech on race (2017). Retrieved from https://www.poynter.org/reporting-editing/2017/why-it-worked-a-rhetorical-analysis-of-obamas-speech-on-race-2/

Donald, K., Morris, D., James, H., Vaughan, P.: Fast pattern matching in strings. SIAM J. Comput. **6**(2), 323–350 (1977). https://doi.org/10.1137/0206024

Kachigan, S.K.: Statistical Analysis: an Interdisciplinary Introduction to Univariate & Multivariate Methods. Radius Press, Santa Fe (1986)

Kulo, L.: Linguistic features in political speeches: how language can be used to impose certain moral or ethical values on people (Dissertation) (2009). Retrieved from http://urn.kb.se/resolve?urn=urn:nbn:se:ltu:diva-55589

Kaufer, D.S., Ishizaki, S., Butler, B.S., Collins, J.: The Power of Words: Unveiling the Speaker and Writer's Hidden Craft. Routledge, New York (2004)

Pessoa, S., Miller, R.T., Kaufer, D.: Students' challenges and development in the transition to academic writing at an English-medium university in Qatar. Int. Rev. Appl. Linguist. Lang. Teach. **52**(2), 127–156 (2014)

Rajakumar, M.: Assessing the Rhetoric of Sheikha Moza. Glob. Women Leaders Stud. Feminist Political Rhetoric 127–137 (2014)

Sunderland, J.: Gendered Discourses. Palgrave Macmillan, Basingstoke (2004)

Ishizaki, S., Kaufer, D.: Computer-aided rhetorical analysis. In: McCarthy, P., Boonthum, C. (eds.) Applied Natural Language Processing and Content Analysis: Identification, Investigation, and Resolution, pp. 276–296 (2011)

Van Dijk, T.A.: 18 critical discourse analysis. In: Schiffrin, D., Hamilton, H., Tannen, D. (eds.) The Handbook of Discourse Analysis, pp. 349–371. Blackwell Publishing, Malden (2001)

Wang, J.: A critical discourse analysis of Barack Obama's speeches. J. Lang. Teach. Res. **1**(3), 254–261 (2010). https://doi.org/10.4304/jltr.1.3.254-261

You Can't See What You Can't See: Experimental Evidence for How Much Relevant Information May Be Missed Due to Google's Web Search Personalisation

Cameron Lai and Markus Luczak-Roesch$^{(\boxtimes)}$ (iD)

School of Information Management, Victoria University of Wellington,
Wellington, New Zealand
Markus.Luczak-Roesch@vuw.ac.nz
https://www.victoria.ac.nz/sim

Abstract. The influence of Web search personalisation on professional knowledge work is an understudied area. Here we investigate how public sector officials self-assess their dependency on the Google Web search engine, whether they are aware of the potential impact of algorithmic biases on their ability to retrieve all relevant information, and how much relevant information may actually be missed due to Web search personalisation. We find that the majority of participants in our experimental study are neither aware that there is a potential problem nor do they have a strategy to mitigate the risk of missing relevant information when performing online searches. Most significantly, we provide empirical evidence that up to 20% of relevant information may be missed due to Web search personalisation. This work has significant implications for Web research by public sector professionals, who should be provided with training about the potential algorithmic biases that may affect their judgments and decision making, as well as clear guidelines how to minimise the risk of missing relevant information.

Keywords: Web search · Personalisation · Human-computer interaction · Social informatics

1 Introduction

The challenges of technology and the public sector are well documented [15]. Many of these challenges such as investment/maintenance costs, and change resistance are well founded in both private and public organisations, and have been grouped into governance, organizational/managerial, and general IT barriers. [6,13,26]. However, challenges unique to the public sector – such as the digital divide, citizen participation, and policy cycle management – present considerations that constitute greater change resistance as opposed to their private counterparts. Even though the challenges are well known and extensively

© Springer Nature Switzerland AG 2019
I. Weber et al. (Eds.): SocInfo 2019, LNCS 11864, pp. 253–266, 2019.
https://doi.org/10.1007/978-3-030-34971-4_17

researched, the public sector is still positioned as a uniquely interesting case given the importance of the value that it provides to the general public [26]. We can therefore expect that any shortcomings in the quality of information utilised by the public sector will have considerable impact on this value.

Because the inner workings of the ranking and personalisation algorithms utilised by modern Web search engines such as Google are likely to remain corporate secrets [19], a general and important issue exists with public sector officials' work that involves the use of such digital services provided by global IT companies. Some of the questions in this problem domain, which we suggest is as an understudied area that requires timely and deeper investigation, are: What is the impact of search engine personalisation on the work of public sector officials? Which technical features of search engine personalisations impact public sector officials' work? Is it possible for public sector officials to prevent being affected by search engine personalisation with respect to their work?

Here we contribute to this line of scientific inquiry by performing an experiment involving public sector professionals from a range of governmental agencies in New Zealand. In order to understand the impact of Google's search result personalisation on knowledge work in the public sector, we address the following questions: (RQ1) How reliant are public sector officials on the use of Google search? (RQ2) Is there a difference between personalised and un-personalised Google search for queries in different public sector agencies? (RQ3) How does the personalisation of search results affect the perceived relevance of search results for public sector officials with respect to their work?

By answering these questions we make the following contributions: First, we show how highly public sector officials self-assess their dependency on Google Web search and provide evidence for a lack of awareness that Google search personalisation may have an impact on knowledge work in professional contexts. Second, we quantify the amount of relevant information that may be missed due to Web search personalisation. Third, we provide insight into how alternative search practices may help to overcome this issue.

The remainder of this paper is structured as follows: We begin with a description of the foundations of Web search and Web search personalisation, followed by a review of related studies that looked into quantifying the impact of Web search personalisation. Informed by the related studies, we describe the research design and subsequent results. We then discuss the implications of the results for research and practice.

2 Preliminaries and Related Work

2.1 A Brief History of Web Search

Yahoo, AltaVista, Lycos and Fireball were among the first search engines to emerge when the World Wide Web was established [14,16]. While using traditional cataloging, indexing and keyword matching techniques initially was sufficient for basic information retrieval on the Web, it was soon regarded to be a poor way to return search results when focusing on the commercialisation of

Web content and search [20]. With the entry of Google into the search engine market began the era of algorithms that take "advantage of the graph structure of the Web" to determine the popularity of Web content [3] in order to produce better, more relevant search results. Over time Google outperformed other search engine providers to become the market leading search engine, now with a market share of just over 74% in 2017, getting as high as 90% for mobile users thanks to the Chrome application that is embedded into the Android operating system for mobile devices[1]. It is due to this widespread use of Google that the search engine is likely to play a role not only in people's private life but also impacts their behaviour when they are at work.

2.2   Search Results Personalisation

Personalisation, regarded as a process that "tailors certain offerings (such as content, services, product recommendations, communications, and e-commerce interactions) by providers (such as e-commerce Web sites) to consumers (such as customers and visitors) based on knowledge about them, with certain goal(s) in mind" [1] was introduced to Web search by Google in 2005 as a means of getting better at providing the most relevant results [8,18]. From the perspective of the search engine provider this was necessary since the vast (and continuously growing) amount of information available on the Web meant that more effective information retrieval systems were required in order to provide users the most relevant items according to their query [2]. While Google's personalisation process is not fully transparent [19], it is known to include a plethora of behavioral signals captured from search engine users, such as past search results a user has clicked through, geographic location or visited Web sites, for example [18,24].

Such search result personalisation has led to concerns about what has been coined the *filter bubble*, i.e. the idea that people only read news that they are directly interested in and agree with, resulting in less familiarity with new or opposing ideas [7,22]. However, there is still no academic consensus about whether the filter bubble actually does exist at all, or whether it is an overstated phenomenon [5,7,10]. Hence, research such as the one described here is still required to bring clarity to the current ambiguity about that matter.

2.3   Related Studies on Search Result Comparison

In [4] a heavy reliance on search engines by academic users was found. This brought personalisation into the focus of research, prompting Salehi et al.'s [25] research into personalisation of search results in academia. Using alternative search setups involving Startpage and Tor to depersonalize search results and comparing the rank order of different search results using the percentage of result overlap and Hamming distance [25], it was found that on average only 53% of search results appear in both personalised and unpersonalised search.

---

[1] Numbers for market share as per 2018 market research reported in https://www.smartinsights.com/search-engine-marketing/search-engine-statistics/.

The work by Hannak et al. [11] introduced a different approach for measuring personalisation of search results. They compared search results of a query performed by a participant (personalized) with the same query performed on a 'fresh' Google account (control) with no history. Comparison between the two sets is done using the Jaccard Index and Damerau-Levenshtein distance as well as Kendall's Tau to understand the difference in the rank order between two search results. They observed measurable personalisation when conducting search when signed into a Google account, and location personalisation from the use of the IP address. Ultimately, they observed that 11.7% of search results were different due to personalisation.

In their audit of the personalisation and composition of politically related search result pages, Robertson et al. [23] found, while relatively low, a higher level of personalisation for participants who were signed into their Google account and/or regularly used Alphabet products. In order to account for the behavioral pattern of search engine users to stronger focus on top results [17] they used Rank-Biased Overlap [27] to compare search results.

Overall, these previous studies confirm corporate statements by Google regarding the use of location data and the profile of the user conducting the search [8,18] for the tailoring of search results. Our work benefits from the continuous improvement of the methodologies used for search result comparison and transfers such a study setup into the public sector to shed light on the impact of personalisation of professional knowledge work.

3   Research Design and Data

We based the research design of our experiment on the previous studies that sought to investigate search result personalisation in an academic search context [4,25] and the quantification of search result personalisation [11,23]. Additionally, we introduce search result relevance as an additional dimension. The idea of self-assessed relevance has been explored perhaps most notably in [21]. In this work we will investigate the relevance of the results that appear in personalised and unpersonalised search.

3.1   Study Participants

We recruited 30 volunteer participants from the public sector following the typical procedure of convenience sampling (21 self-identified as female and 9 as male). Of these participants, 5 were at managerial level or higher. The results are slightly skewed towards one public sector organisation, with over half of the participants (16) from that particular organization, but participants were chosen randomly. Most participants are experienced, indicating they have been in their current industry for 10 years or more.

3.2 Survey

To gauge how 'important' the use of Google search was to public sector officials we performed a pre-experiment survey. The survey design was informed by two of the studies mentioned earlier of how academic researchers sought information by Du and Evans [4], and personalisation in academic search by Salehi et al. [25]. Due to time constraints, the survey remained pre-qualifying, we did not perform a follow-up survey or interview. In order to determine the importance of Google and search engines, questions were directed at how important the participants believed that Google was to their work functions. For example, the survey included questions that seek to determine the extent of a participant's self-assessed reliance on Google and how often they used Google as part of their work routines.

3.3 Experiment

Following completion of the survey, we asked participants to perform two Google searches on their work computers, to simulate a "normal" search query that they might perform in the course of their everyday work duties. For each query that was performed, we performed the same search queries at the same time under two different conditions, both designed to obfuscate Google's knowledge of who performed the search. For the first query (Query 1), participants were asked to search something that they had actually searched before. For the second query (Query 2), participants were asked to search something that they would potentially search in the course of their work duties, but to the best of their knowledge had not searched before. This results in two queries being performed under 3 different search conditions. The queries were limited to two as we balanced time constraints with our participants, and capturing the amount of information required for robustness.

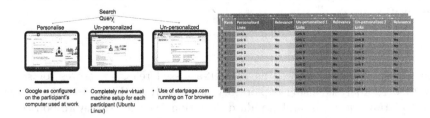

Fig. 1. Overview of the study setup and the three search result sets generated per query and participant.

Personalized Search: Participants performed the search for both queries at work on their work computers to simulate search performed during the course of their normal working day.

Unpersonalised Search 1: This condition attempted to depersonalise search query results through the use of a virtual machine running Mozilla Firefox on Linux's Ubuntu Operating System. A virtual machine allows for a virtual computer to be created within a computer. By using a virtual machine, it is less likely that a person's real identity will be left, unless they did something that allowed for their identity to be linked to the virtual machine [12]. The identity of whoever is performing the Google search should be tied to the virtual machine. Since each virtual machine was created for the purpose of this experiment, there is no history of any past searches that could influence the output of the search results, nor any identity to link to. A test run of this condition found that location personalisation was present, but only to the extent that the country from which the search was performed could be identified. It is believed that this is the extent of personalisation for this condition.

Unpersonalised Search 2: This second condition attempted to completely depersonalise search query results through the use of the Startpage search engine running on Tor, and is borrowed directly from Salehi et al. [25]. Startpage is a search engine that gathers the best Google results, but does not reveal or store any personal information of the user. It has also been awarded a European Privacy Seal [25]. Tor is essentially a modified Mozilla Firefox Browser with additional proxy applications and extensions that hides any identifying information by 'fragmenting' the links between the client and server by redirecting the traffic through thousands of relays [12].

After each search result was retrieved, we asked the participants to rate the relevance of each of the top 10 search result items on a three-point Likert scale (relevant, maybe relevant, not relevant). This three-point scale was chosen to reduce potential ambiguity of more nuanced levels on any larger scale with respect to the rating of the relevancy of search results. When using larger scales we experienced higher variance in how study participants interpret the different levels which would lead to undesired limitations for the study of the result relevancy.

3.4   Data Analysis

The survey responses as well as the self-assessed relevance scores for search results were analysed using exploratory data analysis (EDA) techniques such as calculating the mean and standard deviation (SD) for survey responses. To compare the rank of any pair of ordered sets of Uniform Resource Identifiers (URIs) A and B we use the Rank-Biased Overlap (RBO) measure as justified in [23]. RBO provides a rank similarity measure that takes top-weightedness (stronger penalties for differences at the top of a list) and incompleteness (lists with different items) into account. In our study setup we only compare sets of equal size limited to the top 10 results retrieved under the three aforementioned query conditions.

The RBO measure contains the parameter $\Psi \in [0, 1]$, which represents the degree to which a fictive user is focused on top ranked results, with smaller values of Ψ reflecting stronger focus on top results. RBO is a common measure for this kind of analysis and outperforms other measures to assess the similarity or distance of vectors of strings (e.g. hamming distance) due to the possibility to factor in the focus on top results.

For each unpersonalised result set (i.e. unpersonalised search 1 and unpersonalised search 2), we computed the proportion of URIs self-assessed as relevant that were not in the respective personalised search result set. This provides us with an understanding how much relevant information is missed in the personalised search.

We also computed six sets of URIs that were common between pairs of result sets (leading to three such sets per query) but that were rated differently in terms of their relevance in order to find out whether participants were consistent with their relevance assessment. To investigate deeper whether the rank order may add bias to the participants' self-assessment of the search result relevance, we also analysed the rank change for URIs within those sets (i.e. whether a URI that was assessed differently moved up or down in the ranking).

Finally, we derived the sets of URIs that are deemed relevant in any of the unpersonalised result sets but that were not present in a respective personalised search result. To understand whether there is any bias in the participant's assessment of the relevancy (e.g. implicit assumption that highly ranked results in search must be relevant) we then computed the distribution of the ranks of those URIs in the four respective unpersonalised search result sets.

4   Findings

4.1   Trust in and Reliance on Google in the Public Sector

As presented in Table 1 the majority of participants indicated that they use Google every day for both work and non-work purposes. Furthermore, most participants said that Google is their first point of enquiry as opposed to other sources such as asking co-workers. Participants also indicated that they do not compare the results of their Google searches with other search engines. These responses indicate a high level of trust and reliance on Google in the public sector. The responses to questions asking about the quality of people's work if they were not able to use Google further confirms this reliance. Participants indicated that they generally believed that their work would become of worse quality if they could not use Google, even if they could use other sources of information.

Table 1. Mean and standard deviation for the survey responses related to the use and trust in Google as a first and single point of online research.

Survey item	Mean response (SD)
Frequency of use	4 (0.92)
As the first point of enquiry	4 (0.91)
Search engine comparison frequency	2 (1.05)
Impact on quality of work	4 (0.90)

That the overwhelming majority of participants use Google as their first point of enquiry at work draws comparisons with studies that found that around 80% of Internet users in an academic context used Google search as their first point of enquiry [4,25]. The participants in the study by Du et al. [4] indicated that this was because they found Google easy to use, and that it had become a habit to use Google as the first option when they needed to search for information. While participants in our study were not explicitly asked why they used Google as their first point of enquiry, other factors such as the fact that they did indicate that they do not compare results with other search engines' results point into the direction that Google plays a similar role in the public sector.

4.2 Variance in Personalised and Unpersonalised Search Results

Figure 2 shows the results of our analysis of the RBO. We plotted a smoothed line graph for 21 RBO scores for Ψ in the range from 0 to 1.0 (increased in steps of 0.05). Since smaller Ψ values indicate stronger focus on top ranks in search results, the shape of these graphs shows that the similarity of search results is consistently lower for top ranked search results and increases as lower ranks are taken into account. The similarity of search results is consistently the highest for personalised and unpersonalised search 1, reaching an RBO of almost 0.8 when focusing on low-ranked results and a lower bound of around 0.4 when relaxing the Ψ parameter to focus on the top results only. Any comparison with unpersonalised search 2 does not even reach an RBO of 0.4 even when focusing on low-ranked results.

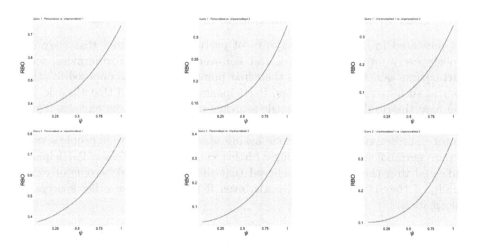

Fig. 2. Rank-Biased Overlap analysis with variable Ψ threshold from 0 to 1 (in steps of 0.05) for both queries performed by the study participants under all three experimental conditions.

While this result supports the recommendations to use advanced measures to compare search result rankings [23,27], we suggest that it is a call for deeper investigations into the role higher and lower ranks of search results play when quantifying and qualifying the information professional knowledge workers would miss out on if they focus on top ranked search results.

4.3   Result Relevance in Personalised and Unpersonalised Search

With respect to the search result relevance assessment we find that between half and two-thirds of the search results have been assessed as relevant by the study participants. However, the mean number of maybe responses for query 2 result sets is about 50% smaller than that of query 1, which means participants were making more certain assessments whether a result is relevant or not for the second query they performed during the experiment.

Table 2. Means for the yes, no and maybe responses of the relevance assessment.

		Yes (SD)	No (SD)	Maybe (SD)
Query 1	Personalised	6 (2.6)	2.6 (2.5)	1.3 (1.7)
	Unpersonalised 1	6 (2.7)	2.9 (2.7)	1.1 (1.7)
	Unpersonalised 2	5 (2.8)	3.8 (2.9)	1.2 (1.6)
Query 2	Personalised	6.6 (2.1)	2.8 (2.2)	0.6 (1.3)
	Unpersonalised 1	6.3 (2.5)	3.1 (2.5)	0.5 (1.1)
	Unpersonalised 2	6.2 (2.5)	3.3 (2.6)	0.5 (1.4)

The proportion of URIs that are found in different result sets for the same participant but that this participant rated differently ranges from 15.7% up to 19.7% of all URIs in the intersection of pairs of result sets as shown in Table 3. We also highlight that this relevance assessment inconsistency is higher for query 1, which is the query that the participant did perform before as part of her work.

Table 3. Proportion of inconsistently rated URIs.

Query 1	Personalised vs. unpersonalised 1	19.7%
	Personalised vs. unpersonalised 2	19.7%
	Unpersonalised 1 vs. unpersonalised 2	19.3%
Query 2	Personalised vs. unpersonalised 1	18%
	Personalised vs. unpersonalised 2	16.3%
	Unpersonalised 1 vs. unpersonalised 2	15.7%

The results of our deeper investigation of whether unique URIs for which the participants' assessment varied between the different conditions are depicted in Fig. 3. The graphs show that macroscopically there is no tendency towards URIs that are ranked higher or lower to be assessed inconsistently.

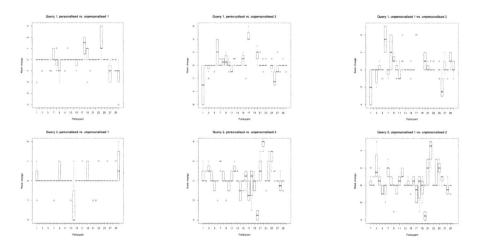

Fig. 3. Change in rank of unique URIs for which the users' relevance assessment varied between the three experimental conditions.

Further to the results shown in Fig. 3 we also investigated whether there is any trend towards higher or lower ranking of inconsistently assessed URIs specifically for those URIs for which the assessment increased (e.g. assessment of maybe to yes), decreased (e.g. assessment from yes to no) or remained the same. As Fig. 4 shows, there is if at all a moderate tendency that URIs are ranked higher if the perception changed but that it has no influence whether the perception increased or decreased.

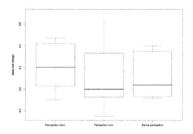

Fig. 4. Change in rank of unique URIs for which the users' relevance assessment increased, decreased or remained the same.

All these results related to the relevance assessment can be interpreted that the self-assessment of search result relevance is either a task prone to human error or that the participants are impacted by an unobserved factor in the experimental setup that causes this behavior. The former would be again in-line with previous studies with regards to Internet search behaviour and people's ability to assess search result relevance [21], while the latter means we additionally suggest that there is potentially a cognitive bias at work impacting the participants' assessment. In other words, the observation that the relevance assessment inconsistency is higher for query 1, which is the query that the participant did perform before as part of her work, allows to question whether the links in the query 1 result sets were more tricky to assess consistently because of the fact that this was a query they performed before so had more detailed knowledge about the topic leading to more nuanced opinions, or whether the participants just became more certain in how to rate relevance as the experiment progressed because of a training effect kicking in.

Missing Relevant Results. Table 4 shows the proportion of unique URLs that were exclusively found in unpersonalised search result sets but considered relevant as per participants' assessment. The numbers show that in both, unpersonalised search 1 and unpersonalised search 2, there is a significant amount of relevant information to be found. Most significantly, the depersonalised search setup using Tor and startpage.com allowed to retrieve up to 20.3% of relevant information that were not found under personalised search conditions in our experiment. While previous studies also found that people may miss information due to search engine personalisation [11], our unique experiment using the two different unpersonalised search settings allows to further detail how one may circumvent this filter bubble effect and also quantifies the difference this may make.

Table 4. Overall proportion of unique URLs that are not found in personalised search but in one of the unpersonalised searches and that are assessed as relevant.

Query 1	Unpersonalised 1	7.3%
	Unpersonalised 2	16.7%
Query 2	Unpersonalised 1	6%
	Unpersonalised 2	20.3%

Figure 5 shows the rank order distribution of those relevant results that are missing from personalised search. The distributions show a weak tendency that those missing but contain relevant information are found in the lower ranks of search results. In the light of multiple previous studies that found that search engine users focus substantially on top ranked results [9,21] this is important because it means finding all relevant information is not just a challenge to be solved by either removing or circumventing personalisation algorithms but also a user interface (UI) and user experience (UX) design issue.

5   Limitations

Similar to previous work [11,25] our research was limited due to the small sample size. This was a practical constraint due to the way the experiment was designed

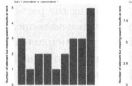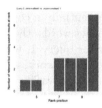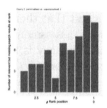

Fig. 5. Rank order distribution of links that are missing from personalised but are deemed relevant in any of the unpersonalised search result sets.

and can only be avoided when either accepting uncertainty about whether the participants are actually public sector workers (e.g. by running it as a self-administered online experiment) or by running it over a much longer period of time. We consider the latter for our future research combined with an extension to cover alternative search engines and performing the experiment in multiple countries to also account for localisation. Future research should also expand the investigation of relevance of search results and in particular the properties and implications of self-assessment of relevance. Relevance is a subjective matter, and how the participants rated relevance in our experiments differed between each participant. Pan et al. [21] were able to take this subjectivity into account through an objective third party evaluation, which we did not do, because our participants were the subject matter experts for the queries that they performed in a work context.

6   Conclusion

We investigated not only how important public sector workers perceive Google Web search to be for fulfilling their information needs, but also whether Google's personalisation means they may miss relevant information. We find that the majority of participants in our experimental study are neither aware that there is a potential problem nor do they have a strategy to mitigate the risk of missing relevant information when performing online searches. Most significantly, we provide empirical evidence that up to 20% of relevant information may be missed due to Web search personalisation.

The fact that personalisation has an impact on search results was not surprising, particularly in the light of previous studies focused on academic Web search [11,25]. However, our work provides new empirical evidence for this phenomenon in the public sector. Therefore, our research has significant implications for public sector professionals, who should be provided with training about the potential algorithmic and human biases that may affect their judgments and decision making, as well as clear guidelines how to minimise the risk of missing relevant information. This does not just involve comparing search results using different search engines and to actively look further down the ranks for relevant search results, and maybe even that public sector agencies provide dedicated infrastructure to obfuscate the users' identities to circumvent personalisation.

References

1. Adomavicius, G., Tuzhilin, A.: Personalization technologies: a process-oriented perspective. Commun. ACM **48**(10), 83–90 (2005)
2. Brin, S., Page, L.: Reprint of: the anatomy of a large-scale hypertextual web search engine. Comput. Netw. **56**(18), 3825–3833 (2012)
3. Broder, A., et al.: Graph structure in the web. Comput. Netw. **33**(1–6), 309–320 (2000)
4. Du, J.T., Evans, N.: Academic users' information searching on research topics: characteristics of research tasks and search strategies. J. Acad. Libr. **37**(4), 299–306 (2011)
5. Dutton, W.H., Reisdorf, B., Dubois, E., Blank, G.: Search and politics: the uses and impacts of search in Britain, France, Germany, Italy, Poland, Spain, and the United States (2017)
6. Ebrahim, Z., Irani, Z.: E-government adoption: architecture and barriers. Bus. Process. Manag. J. **11**(5), 589–611 (2005)
7. Foster, R.: News plurality in a digital world. Reuters Institute for the Study of Journalism Oxford (2012)
8. Google news blog: personalized search graduates from Google labs (2005). https://googlepress.blogspot.com/2005/11/personalized-search-graduates-from_10.html. Accessed 27 Apr 2019
9. Granka, L.A., Joachims, T., Gay, G.: Eye-tracking analysis of user behavior in WWW search. In: Proceedings of the 27th Annual International ACM SIGIR Conference on Research and Development in Information Retrieval, pp. 478–479. ACM (2004)
10. Haim, M., Graefe, A., Brosius, H.B.: Burst of the filter bubble? Effects of personalization on the diversity of Google news. Digital J. **6**(3), 330–343 (2018)
11. Hannak, A., et al.: Measuring personalization of web search. In: Proceedings of the 22nd International Conference on World Wide Web, pp. 527–538. ACM (2013)
12. van Hardeveld, G.J., Webber, C., O'Hara, K.: Deviating from the cybercriminal script: exploring tools of anonymity (Mis) used by carders on cryptomarkets. Am. Behav. Sci. **61**(11), 1244–1266 (2017)
13. Henningsson, S., van Veenstra, A.F.: Barriers to it-driven governmental transformation. In: ECIS, p. 113 (2010)
14. Hölscher, C., Strube, G.: Web search behavior of internet experts and newbies. Comput. Netw. **33**(1–6), 337–346 (2000)
15. Lan, Z., Cayer, N.J.: The challenges of teaching information technology use and management in a time of information revolution. Am. Rev. Public Adm. **24**(2), 207–222 (1994)
16. Lewandowski, D.: Evaluating the retrieval effectiveness of web search engines using a representative query sample. J. Assoc. Inf. Sci. Technol. **66**(9), 1763–1775 (2015)
17. Lu, X., Moffat, A., Culpepper, J.S.: The effect of pooling and evaluation depth on IR metrics. Inf. Retr. J. **19**(4), 416–445 (2016)
18. Official Google blog: Personalized search for everyone (2009). https://googleblog.blogspot.com/2009/12/personalized-search-for-everyone.html. Accessed 27 Apr 2019
19. Ørmen, J.: Googling the news: opportunities and challenges in studying news events through Google Search. Digital J. **4**(1), 107–124 (2016)
20. Page, L., Brin, S., Motwani, R., Winograd, T.: The PageRank citation ranking: bringing order to the web. Technical report, Stanford InfoLab (1999)

21. Pan, B., Hembrooke, H., Joachims, T., Lorigo, L., Gay, G., Granka, L.: In google we trust: Users' decisions on rank, position, and relevance. J. Comput.-Mediat. Commun. **12**(3), 801–823 (2007)

22. Pariser, E.: The filter bubble: what the Internet is hiding from you, Penguin, UK (2011)

23. Robertson, R.E., Lazer, D., Wilson, C.: Auditing the personalization and composition of politically-related search engine results pages. In: Proceedings of the 2018 World Wide Web Conference on World Wide Web, pp. 955–965. International World Wide Web Conferences Steering Committee (2018)

24. Roesner, F., Kohno, T., Wetherall, D.: Detecting and defending against third-party tracking on the web. In: Proceedings of the 9th USENIX Conference on Networked Systems Design and Implementation, p. 12. USENIX Association (2012)

25. Salehi, S., Du, J.T., Ashman, H.: Examining personalization in academic web search. In: Proceedings of the 26th ACM Conference on Hypertext & Social Media, pp. 103–111. ACM (2015)

26. Savoldelli, A., Codagnone, C., Misuraca, G.: Understanding the e-government paradox: learning from literature and practice on barriers to adoption. Gov. Inf. Q. **31**, S63–S71 (2014)

27. Webber, W., Moffat, A., Zobel, J.: A similarity measure for indefinite rankings. ACM Trans. Inf. Syst. (TOIS) **28**(4), 20 (2010)

Short Papers

Arabic Offensive Language Classification on Twitter

Hamdy Mubarak and Kareem Darwish[✉]

Qatar Computing Research Institute, HBKU, Doha, Qatar
{hmubarak,kdarwish}@hbku.edu.qa

Abstract. Social media users often employ offensive language in their communication. Detecting offensive language on Twitter has many applications ranging from detecting/predicting conflict to measuring polarization. In this paper, we focus on building effective offensive tweet detection. We show that we can rapidly build a training set using a seed list of offensive words. Given the automatically created dataset, we trained a character n-gram based deep learning classifier that can effectively classify tweets with F1 score of 90%. We also show that we can expand our offensive word list by contrasting offensive and non-offensive tweets.

Keywords: Offensive language · Obscenities · Text classification

1 Introduction

Social media platforms provide a medium for individual or group expression, often with limited inhibitions. Hence, social media users may use vulgar, pornographic, or hateful language [13]. The detection of such language is essential for many application such as: (1) creating adult content filters; (2) quantifying the intensity of polarization [6,8]; (3) classifying trolls and propaganda accounts that often use offensive language [9]; (4) identifying hate speech that may correlate with hate crimes [21]; and (5) detecting signals of conflict, which are often preceded by verbal hostility [7]. One way to detect such language involves building a list of offensive words and then filtering text based on these words. This approach is problematic for two main reasons. First, offensive words are ever evolving with new words continuously emerging, complicating the maintenance of such lists. Second, the offensiveness of certain words is highly context and genre dependent. In this work we introduce a method for accurately identifying offensive tweets using character-level deep leaning based text classification, which could enable building and expanding an offensive word list from tweets. The method is based on the intuition that tweets containing offensive words are likely to contain other offensive words. Thus, if we tag a large number of tweets based on a seed list of offensive words, then we can discover other offensive words by contrasting such tweets with other random tweets. The automatically tagged set can be used to train a classifier that outperforms the use of a word lists, particularly in terms of recall. Coupling our intuition with supervised classification, we are able to:

© Springer Nature Switzerland AG 2019
I. Weber et al. (Eds.): SocInfo 2019, LNCS 11864, pp. 269–276, 2019.
https://doi.org/10.1007/978-3-030-34971-4_18

perform highly accurate classification of tweet offensiveness and build a large offensive word list from an initial seed list. We focus in this paper on vulgar and pornographic language in Arabic tweets. Even though social media use is ubiquitous in the Arab World, work on Arabic offensive language detection is fairly nascent, with preliminary results appearing in the past two years [1,3,4,19]. Arabic poses interesting challenges such as complex derivational morphology and the existence of multiple dialects that lack well accepted spelling conventions, and that differ in lexical selection, syntax, and morphology. We overcome some of these issues by employing a character n-gram model that can work at sub-word level alleviating the need for proper segmentation and overcoming spelling variations. The contributions of this paper are:

- We introduce a method for building a large training corpus for detecting offensive language based on a seed word list of offensive words.
- We employ a character n-gram deep learning model to build a robust offensive language classifier for Arabic tweets. Our classifier is able to overcome some of the peculiarities of Arabic, such as morphology, and tweets, such as ubiquitous misspellings, while capturing word context.
- We implement a method for expanding the list of offensive words by contrasting sets of offensive and non-offensive tweets. We intrinsically and extrinsically compare this method on sets of tweets that were classified using word matching and supervised classification.

2   Related Work

Multiple studies have been conducted concerning the detection of offensive language, particularly hate speech in English [2,5,10,11,16,17,20,23]. Jay et al. [13] identified three categories of offensive speech, namely: **Vulgar**, which include explicit and rude sexual references, **Pornographic**, and **Hateful**, which includes offensive remarks concerning people's race, religion, country, etc. Most of these studies used supervised classification at either word level [16], character sequence level [17], and word embeddings [11]. The studies used different classification techniques including using Naïve Bayes [16], support vector machines [17], and deep learning [2,5,20] classification. The accuracy of the aforementioned system ranged between 76% and 90%. Earlier work looked at the use of sentiment words as features as well as contextual features [23].

The work on Arabic offensive language detection is relatively nascent [1,3, 4,19]. Mubarak et al. [19] suggested that certain users are more likely to use offensive languages than others, and they used this insight to build a list of offensive Arabic words and they constructed a labeled set of 1,100 tweets. We use their test set in our experiments. Abozinadah et al. [1] used supervised classification based on a variety of features including user profile features, textual features, and network features. They reported an accuracy of nearly 90%. Alakrot et al. [3] used supervised classification based on word unigrams and n-grams to detect offensive language in YouTube comments. They employed stemming to improve classification, and they achieved a precision of 88%. Unfortunately, we don't have access to the datasets of Abozinadah et al. [1] and Alakrot et al. [3]. Albadi et al. [4] focused on detecting religious hate speech using a recurrent neural network. In our work, we use fastText, which is an effective deep learning text classifier. The focus in this work on vulgar and pornographic speech in Arabic social media.

Fig. 1. Tweet has multiple offensive words: Meaning: "God damn you and your father. O dog, O son of a dog ... "

3 Experimental Setup

As mentioned earlier, we have two main goals, namely building a robust classifier of Arabic offensive language for tweets, and building and expanding a large word lists of offensive words. Our main intuition is that a tweet that contains one offensive word is likely to contain other offensive words. Figure 1 shows such an example. Thus, given a seed list of offensive words, we can readily create a training set for offensive language detection by automatically labeling tweets that contain any of the words on the list as offensive and a random set of tweets not containing any of the words as non-offensive. This labeled dataset can then be used to train a classifier directly. Using a word based classifier would likely yield sub-optimal classification results for three main reasons. First, spelling mistakes and creative spellings are ubiquitous in tweets. Thus, rare misspellings appearing the tweets that are automatically labeled as offensive might be misconstrued by the classifier as offensive. Conversely, slight variations of offensive words might not be learned by the classifier. Second, the offensiveness of words is often highly context dependent. Thus, using a bag-of-words classifier may not capture local context that is necessary for proper classification. Third, Arabic is a morphologically rich language where prefixes and suffixes are attached to words, and many dialectal varieties of Arabic with varying morphological patterns are prevalent in Arabic social media. We overcome these problems by using a bag of variable length character n-grams in conjunction with deep neural network based classification. Using variable length character n-grams allows the classifier to capture sub-word features that may help overcome spelling errors and morphological complexities of Arabic, and longer character n-grams can cross word boundaries capturing local context. Using a deep neural network classifier

Table 1. Comparing the classification using word-list matching and classification.

	Prec	Recall	F1
Word-list (baseline)	**97%**	43%	59%
SVM	95%	48%	64%
fastText	90%	**90%**	**90%**

can produce latent representations of the input and can capture interactions between different features. We use the fastText classifier, which is a deep learning based text classifier that can be configured to use variable length n-grams and has been shown to be effective for text classification [15].

For the seed list of offensive words, we used a publicly available list containing 415 words and phrases [19]. Though the list was created in a semi-automated manner, it was manually verified. We also used their freely available test set of 1,100 tweets that were tagged for offensiveness using crowdsourcing [19]. To expand the lexicon of offensive words, we experimented with two setups. Both involved using an automatically tagged set of tweets to ascertain which terms are most discriminating between the offensive and non-offensive tweets. In the first setup, we used a tweet set that was automatically tagged using a list of offensive words. In the second setup, we used a tweet set that was tagged using our character n-gram based deep learning classifier. Given a set of labeled tweets as offensive or not offensive, we found discriminating terms by computing the so-called valence score for every word [8], which is computed as follows:

$$V(t) = 2\frac{\frac{tf_{set_0}}{total_{set_0}}}{\frac{tf_{set_0}}{total_{set_0}} + \frac{tf_{set_1}}{total_{set_1}}} - 1 \tag{1}$$

where set_0 and set_1 refers to the two corpora (offensive and non-offensive), tf is the frequency of a term in either set and $total$ is the sum of all tfs for either set. For each word, this equation gives a valence score between $+1$ (highly offensive) and -1 (highly non-offensive). Though there are other scoring function such as using mutual information or log odds ratio [12], the valence score has strong discriminatory power and it is simple and efficient to compute [8,22].

4   Data and Experiments

To establish a baseline, we used the seed list of offensive words containing 415 words to classify the test set of 1,100 tweets [19]. Classification simply means that we consider a tweet containing a word or phrase in the list as offensive and non-offensive otherwise. Baseline results were 97%, 43%, and 59% for precision, recall, and F1 measure respectively. Next, we automatically tagged a set of 175M Arabic tweets that we collected in March 2014. We extracted 3.3M tweets that had one or more offensive words from the word list, which is roughly 1.9% of all the tweets. To contrast offensive tweets with non-offensive ones, we randomly picked 33.3M tweets (10 times larger than the set of offensive tweets) from the dataset that did not match any of our offensive words. Our intuition is that most tweets don't contain offensive language, and thus the overwhelming majority of random tweets are not offensive. In all, we used 36.6M automatically tagged tweets to train a fastText classifier using character n-grams ranging length between 3 and 6 characters. We used 100 dimension feature vectors, a learning rate of 0.05, and ran 50 training epochs. We compared this setup to another supervised learning setup, where we used a Support Vector Machine (SVM) classifier that is trained at word level, which is different in the learning algorithm and features (words vs. character sequences). SVMs have been shown to be highly effective for text classification [14]. We used the trained classifiers to tag the test set. It is noteworthy that we used the SVM^{light} implementation[1], and the classifier took over 3 days to finish training on a Linux machine with an i7 processor and 32MB of RAM. For comparison, fastText required less than 4 hours to train. Table 1 summarizes the classification results. Using the SVM classifier led to slightly lower precision compared to using word-list matching, but with greater recall. Using our proposed approach led to identical precision, recall, and F1 measure of 90%. The results show the validity of our intuition that offensive tweets may have multiple offensive words, enabling us to automatically build an automatic offensive language training set and to achieve solid results that surpass the use of word matching and word-based SVM classification, particularly for recall. Next, we wanted to expand the list of offensive words using valence score to identify terms that discriminate between offensive and non-offensive tweets. In the first setup (Word-List Setup), we computed the valence score for all the words in our automatically tagged set of 36.6M tweets. In the other two setups (Classifier:fastText & Classifier:SVM Setups), we obtained 100M tweets that we collected in April 2016. We automatically tagged these tweets using our previously trained fastText and SVM classifiers. FastText tagged 177k tweets as offensive (1.3% of the tweets) and the remaining tweets as non-offensive. On the other hand, the SVM classifier tagged 5.92M tweets as offensive (5.86% of the tweets). We computed the valence scores of all words for all three setups. We filtered words to retain those with valence scores higher than 0.8 and with frequency greater than or equal to 20 in the tweets. We set high thresholds to ensure high precision. In doing so, we identified 17.2k, 8.3k, and 30.2k words for the Word-List, Classifier:fastText, and Classifier:SVM setups respectively. We excluded words that were in our initial set of offensive words. To assess the identified words, we conducted an intrinsic and extrinsic evaluation of the offensiveness of the words. For intrinsic evaluation, we manually tagged a random set of 200 terms from each as offensive or not and computed the accuracy of each word list. When manually annotating the words, many words seemed innocuous. Thus, we checked how they were typically used in tweets to determine their offensiveness. For example, the word "AlmHArm" (a woman's next of kin) is a

---

[1] http://svmlight.joachims.org/.

normal word, but we found that it was overwhelmingly used as part of the bigram "znA AlmHArm" meaning "incest" and tweets were typically pornographic in nature. The identified offensive words were mainly new words that did not exist in the original seed list or morphological expansions of seed words with variations in prefixes and suffixes. For example, the word "msAj" (massage) which didn't appear in the seed words was tagged as offensive because it appeared 15k times in offensive tweets and 5k times in non-offensive tweets (valence score = 0.95), and generally tweets having it tend to be pornographic advertisements.

Table 2 lists the percentage of words that were actually offensive in the 200 word sample for each setup. As the results show, using the Word-List setup yielded the highest accuracy. Though using the Classifier:SVM setup yielded the largest number of candidate offensive words, it had the lowest accuracy of the three setups. This is somewhat surprising given the effectiveness of classification setups. For extrinsic evaluation, we tagged the 1,100 tweet test set using the lists we obtained using the different setups and then computed precision, recall, and F1 measure. Table 2 summarizes the results for both lists. As the results show, identifying discriminating terms using the Classifier:fastText Setup was far superior compared to the Word-List Setup, which in turn was more accurate than the Classifier:SVM setup. Precision of the word list obtained from Classifier:fastText was 76% higher than Word-List without loss in recall.

Errors in classification can be attributed to a few reasons. First, complexities of Arabic language (dialectal variations, creative ways of expressing offensiveness, figurative language, metaphors, etc.). Second, the seed list of offensive words that was used in extracting offensive tweets was rather small, composed of a few hundred word unigrams. More advanced techniques, such as using multi-word patterns, could be applied to expand the seed list. Finally, the test set is small (1,100 tweets) and written in only one dialect (Egyptian dialect). Meanwhile, the majority of Arabic tweets come from the Gulf region [18], which causes language mismatches between tweets used in data collection for training and the test set. We plan to create a multi-dialectal test set with good representation from the major dialectal groups: Gulf, Egyptian, Levantine, Iraqi, and Maghrebi.

Table 2. Evaluation of automatically created offensive word lists.

Setup	List size	Evaluation	
		Intrinsic	Extrinsic
		Accuracy	P/R/F1
Word-List	17.2k	32%	38/61/46
Classifier:fastText	8.3k	25%	67/61/64
Classifier:SVM	30.2k	13%	18/65/28

5 Conclusion

In this paper we present a method for rapidly creating a training set for identifying offensive tweets using a seed list of offensive words. The intuition for this is that a tweet containing an offensive word is likely to have other offensive words. We show that the newly created training set can be used to train a highly effective offensive tweets deep-learning based classifier using variable length character n-gram as features. Using character n-grams can help overcome the morphological complexities of Arabic and the ubiquity of spelling mistakes and creative spellings in tweets.

References

1. Abozinadah, E.: Detecting abusive arabic language twitter accounts using a multidimensional analysis model. Ph.D. thesis, George Mason University (2017)
2. Agrawal, S., Awekar, A.: Deep learning for detecting cyberbullying across multiple social media platforms. In: Pasi, G., Piwowarski, B., Azzopardi, L., Hanbury, A. (eds.) ECIR 2018. LNCS, vol. 10772, pp. 141–153. Springer, Cham (2018). https://doi.org/10.1007/978-3-319-76941-7_11
3. Alakrot, A., Murray, L., Nikolov, N.S.: Towards accurate detection of offensive language in online communication in arabic. Procedia Comput. Sci. **142**, 315–320 (2018)
4. Albadi, N., Kurdi, M., Mishra, S.: Are they our brothers? analysis and detection of religious hate speech in the arabic twittersphere. In: 2018 IEEE/ACM International Conference on Advances in Social Networks Analysis and Mining (ASONAM), pp. 69–76. IEEE (2018)
5. Badjatiya, P., Gupta, S., Gupta, M., Varma, V.: Deep learning for hate speech detection in tweets. In: Proceedings of the 26th International Conference on World Wide Web Companion, pp. 759–760. International World Wide Web Conferences Steering Committee (2017)
6. Barberá, P., Sood, G.: Follow your ideology: measuring media ideology on social networks. In: Annual Meeting of the European Political Science Association, Vienna, Austria (2015). http://www.gsood.com/research/papers/mediabias.pdf
7. Chadefaux, T.: Early warning signals for war in the news. J. Peace Res. **51**(1), 5–18 (2014)
8. Conover, M., Ratkiewicz, J., Francisco, M.R., Gonçalves, B., Menczer, F., Flammini, A.: Political polarization on twitter. In: ICWSM, vol. 133, pp. 89–96 (2011)
9. Darwish, K., Alexandrov, D., Nakov, P., Mejova, Y.: Seminar users in the arabic twitter sphere. In: Ciampaglia, G.L., Mashhadi, A., Yasseri, T. (eds.) SocInfo 2017. LNCS, vol. 10539, pp. 91–108. Springer, Cham (2017). https://doi.org/10.1007/978-3-319-67217-5_7
10. Davidson, T., Warmsley, D., Macy, M., Weber, I.: Automated hate speech detection and the problem of offensive language. In: Eleventh International Conference on Web and Social Media (ICWSM), pp. 512–515 (2017)
11. Djuric, N., Zhou, J., Morris, R., Grbovic, M., Radosavljevic, V., Bhamidipati, N.: Hate speech detection with comment embeddings. In: Proceedings of the 24th international conference on world wide web, pp. 29–30. ACM (2015)
12. Forman, G.: An extensive empirical study of feature selection metrics for text classification. J. Mach. Learn. Res. **3**(Mar), 1289–1305 (2003)

13. Jay, T., Janschewitz, K.: The pragmatics of swearing. J. Politeness Res. Lang. Behav. Cult. **4**(2), 267–288 (2008)
14. Joachims, T.: A statistical learning model of text classification with support vector machines. In: ACM SIGIR Conference on Research and Development in Information Retrieval (SIGIR), pp. 128–136 (2001)
15. Joulin, A., Grave, E., Bojanowski, P., Mikolov, T.: Bag of tricks for efficient text classification. arXiv preprint arXiv:1607.01759 (2016)
16. Kwok, I., Wang, Y.: Locate the hate: detecting tweets against blacks. In: Twenty-seventh AAAI Conference on Artificial Intelligence (2013)
17. Malmasi, S., Zampieri, M.: Detecting hate speech in social media. arXiv preprint arXiv:1712.06427 (2017)
18. Mubarak, H., Darwish, K.: Using twitter to collect a multi-dialectal corpus of arabic. In: Proceedings of the EMNLP 2014 Workshop on Arabic Natural Language Processing (ANLP), pp. 1–7 (2014)
19. Mubarak, H., Darwish, K., Magdy, W.: Abusive language detection on arabic social media. In: Proceedings of the First Workshop on Abusive Language Online, pp. 52–56 (2017)
20. Nobata, C., Tetreault, J., Thomas, A., Mehdad, Y., Chang, Y.: Abusive language detection in online user content. In: Proceedings of the 25th international conference on world wide web, pp. 145–153. International World Wide Web Conferences Steering Committee (2016)
21. Waseem, Z., Hovy, D.: Hateful symbols or hateful people? predictive features for hate speech detection on twitter. In: Proceedings of the NAACL student research workshop, pp. 88–93 (2016)
22. Weber, I., Garimella, V.R.K., Batayneh, A.: Secular vs. islamist polarization in Egypt on twitter. In: Proceedings of the 2013 IEEE/ACM International Conference on Advances in Social Networks Analysis and Mining, pp. 290–297. ACM (2013)
23. Yin, D., Xue, Z., Hong, L., Davison, B.D., Kontostathis, A., Edwards, L.: Detection of harassment on web 2.0. Proc. Content Anal. WEB **2**, 1–7 (2009)

Assessing Sentiment of the Expressed Stance on Social Media

Abeer Aldayel[(✉)] and Walid Magdy

School of Informatics, The University of Edinburgh, Edinburgh, UK
a.aldayel@ed.ac.uk, wmagdy@inf.ed.ac.uk

Abstract. Stance detection is the task of inferring viewpoint towards a given topic or entity either being supportive or opposing. One may express a viewpoint towards a topic by using positive or negative language. This paper examines how the stance is being expressed in social media according to the sentiment polarity. There has been a noticeable misconception of the similarity between the stance and sentiment when it comes to viewpoint discovery, where negative sentiment is assumed to mean against stance, and positive sentiment means in-favour stance. To analyze the relation between stance and sentiment, we construct a new dataset with four topics and examine how people express their viewpoint with regards these topics. We validate our results by carrying a further analysis of the popular stance benchmark SemEval stance dataset. Our analyses reveal that sentiment and stance are not highly aligned, and hence the simple sentiment polarity cannot be used solely to denote a stance toward a given topic.

Keywords: Stance detection · Sentiment analysis · Public opinion · Event analysis · Social media

1 Introduction

The stance can be defined as the expression of the individual's standpoint toward a proposition [4]. Detecting the stance towards an event is a sophisticated process where various factors play a role in discovering the viewpoint, including personal and social aspects. Most of the studies in this area have focused on using the textual elements of user's posts such as sentiment of the text to infer the stance [6,7,21]. While the goal of the stance detection is to determine the favorability towards a given entity or topic [16], sentiment analysis aims to determine whether the emotional state of a given text is positive, negative, or neutral [14]. There is a rich body of research where the sentiment has been used solely to discover the viewpoints towards an event [13,17,23,24]. These studies expected that the sentiment polarity could indicate the stance. However, another line of research develops a stance specific model to infer the viewpoints where sentiment is being neglected [5,11,22]. As the dependence on sentiment as a sole factor for the stance prediction has been found to be suboptimal, which might indicate a weak relation between sentiment and stance [7,16].

© Springer Nature Switzerland AG 2019
I. Weber et al. (Eds.): SocInfo 2019, LNCS 11864, pp. 277–286, 2019.
https://doi.org/10.1007/978-3-030-34971-4_19

Accordingly, it becomes important to examine the relation between the sentiment and the stance for viewpoint discovery toward an event. This leads us to pose the following research questions:

– RQ1: Can sentiment polarity be used to capture the stance towards an event?
– RQ2: How does sentiment align with stance? When does positive/negative sentiment indicate support/against stance?

These questions aim to identify whether the sentiment can substitute the stance by studying the polarity nature of the expressed stance. In other words, this study examines whether the supporting/opposing stances can be identified with positive/negative sentiment. To answer these questions, we used the SemEval stance dataset [15], the popular stance dataset that contains sentiment and stance labels. To further validate the results, we constructed a new stance detection dataset that has about 6000 tweets towards four topics and annotated with gold labels for sentiment and stance. This dataset contains the parent tweets along with reply tweets, which provides contextualized information for the annotator and helps in judging the sentiment and stance of the reply tweets. After that, we analyze the datasets to determine the degree of the correlation between sentiment polarity and the gold label stance.

2   Related Work

In the literature, sentiment has been widely used either to infer the public opinion or as a factor to help in detecting the stance towards an event. The next sections illustrate these cases with a focus on studying the stance towards an event where the simple sentiment has been used either by using a sentiment lexicon or the textual polarity of the text.

2.1   Sentiment as Stance

Sentiment has been used interchangeably with stance to indicate the viewpoint detection [2,9,13,18,19,23,24]. In these studies the sentiment polarity has been used purely as the only factor to detect the viewpoint towards various events in social media. For instance, the work of [19] used sentiment to investigate the opinion towards the terrorist attack in Paris, during November 2015. They used annotators from Crowdflower to label the sentiment (negative, positive or neutral) as expressed in the tweet and used these labels as a way to analyse the public reaction toward Paris attack in 2015. In a study done by [18], they used the sentiment to discover the political leaning of the commenter on news articles. In their study, a sentiment profile constructed for each commenter to help in tracking their polarity toward a political party. For instance, a liberal commenter uses negative comments in conservative articles and positive comments to liberal articles.

A more recent study by [13] used the sentiment to examine the opinions following the release of James Comey's letter to Congress before the 2016 US presidential election day. The previous study categorized 25 most common hashtags with sentiment polarity towards Hillary Clinton and Trump. Furthermore, the work of [24] used sentiment to analyze the political preferences of the users for the 2013 Australian federal election event. For the sentiment they recruited three annotators to label the tweet with a polarity score (positive, negative or neutral). In their study they used aspect-level sentiment for predicting user's political preference and they overlooked the cases where the sentiment is negative and the stance is expressing a support viewpoint.

Another study [23] developed an opinion score equation based on sentiment lexicon and frequency of a term to infer the users' opinions towards events as they extracted from the timeline. In addition, the work of [9] designed topic-sentiment matrix to infer the crowd's opinion. Another recent study by [2] used AFINN-111 dictionary for sentiment analysis and used sentiment polarity as an indication of the opinion towards Brexit. All of the above studies treated sentiment as the indicator of the stance toward the event of the analysis.

2.2 Sentiment as Proxy for Stance

Another line of research used sentiment as a feature to predict the stance [6,7,16,21]. In the popular SemEval stance dataset [15], the tweets are labeled with sentiment and stance to provide a public benchmark to evaluate the stance detection systems. In their work, they showed that using sentiment features are useful for stance classification when they combined with other features and not used alone. The work of [6] used an undirected graphical model that leverages interactions between sentiment and the target of stance to predict the stance. Also, the work of [21] developed a stance classifier that used sentiment and arguing expressions by using sentiment lexicon along with arguing lexicon which outperforms Uni-gram features system. In [10] they used SentiWordNet to produce sentiment for each word and use the sentiment value along with other features to predict the stance in SemEval stance dataset and compared with CNN stance model. They found that feature based model performed better in detecting stance. The work of [12] used surface-level, sentiment and domain-specific features to predict the stance on SemEval stance dataset. Overall, the use of sentiment in conjunction with other features helps in predicting the stance but not as the only dependent feature.

The work of [16,20] studied the extent to which the sentiment is correlated with the stance in the sense of enhancing stance classifier. The main focus of the previous study was to investigate the best features for the stance classification model. In their work, they concluded that sentiment might be beneficial for stance classification, but when it is combined with other factors.

This study investigates another dimensionality of the sentiment-stance relation with focus on gauging the alignment between sentiment and stance by analysing in depth the relation of how the stance is being expressed in conjunction with the sentiment.

Table 1. Number of tweets for each topic.

SemEval stance	#	CD stance	#
Atheism (A)	733	Antisemitic (AS)	1050
Climate Change is Concern (CC)	564	Gender (G)	1050
Feminist Movement (FM)	949	Immigration (I)	3174
Hillary Clinton (HC)	934	LGBTQ (L)	1050
Legalization of Abortion (LA)	883		
Total	4063	Total	6324

3 Data Collection

We study the sentiment nature in the expressed stance. To accomplish this, we used SemEval stance dataset which contains about 4000 tweets on five topics, including Atheism (A), Climate Change (CC), the Feminist Movement (FM), Hillary Clinton (HC) and the Legalisation of Abortion (LA). Furthermore, we designed a context-dependent (CD) stance dataset that contains 6324 reply tweets covering four controversial topics: Antisemitic (AS), Gender (G), Immigration (I), LGBTQ (L). Table 1 shows the distribution of the tweets with respect to each topic. In this dataset, each tweet has been annotated by five annotators using Figure-eight platform[1], and the label with a majority vote is assigned. We used the same annotations guideline of SemEval stance dataset [15]. Since CD dataset is all reply tweets, the parent tweet along with reply tweet has been provided to the annotators to understand the context of the conversation to better judge the sentiment and stance.

4 Methodology

4.1 Analysis of the Correlation Patterns

To get a good insight of how the stance is being expressed, we first analyze the distribution of stance and sentiment on the topic level. Figures 1 a and b, illustrate the stance and sentiment distribution in the SemEval stance dataset and CD stance dataset, respectively. Overall the negative sentiment constitutes the major polarity of the most topics. This reveals the tendency of using negative sentiments to express a viewpoint in a controversial topic. It can be observed that for the climate change the supporting stance constitutes about 59%; however the overall tweets with negative sentiment constitute 50%. Furthermore, 30% of the LGBTQ tweets show negative sentiment, while only 7% of the tweets express the opposing stance. From these numbers, it is clear that sentiment does not simply represent stance.

---

[1] https://figure-eight.com/.

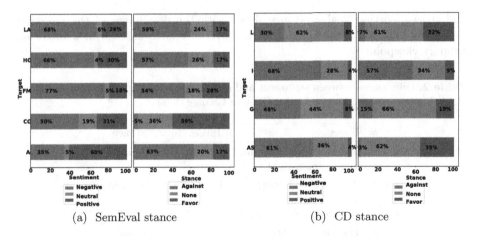

(a) SemEval stance   (b) CD stance

Fig. 1. The distribution of sentiment and stance with respect to each topic.

Figure 2 illustrates the sentiment distribution over the stance in the two datasets. The graphs show that the negative sentiment constitutes the major polarity over the Favor and Against stances. As the negative sentiment represents over 56% and 54% of the supporting stance in the SemEval and CD stance datasets, respectively. These results reveal the tendency of using negative sentiments to express a viewpoint towards a controversial topic.

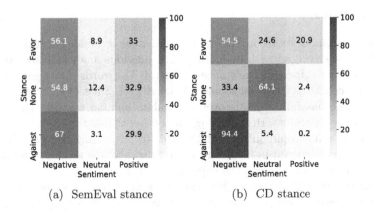

(a) SemEval stance   (b) CD stance

Fig. 2. Distribution of sentiment per a given stance.

Table 2 shows some examples where the sentiment does not reflect the stance. Examples 1 and 2 show tweets with an opposing viewpoint to targets, while using positive sentiment. Examples 3 and 4 show the opposite situation, where the expressed stance is supporting, while the sentiment is negative.

These results show that sentiment fails to detect the real stance toward a topic. There is a clear mismatching between the negative/positive sentiment and the supporting/against stance. Even with the dominance of the negative sentiment in most of the topics, yet the overall stance has shown a mixer of support viewpoint.

Table 2. Differences between sentiment and stance. Targets: Legalization of Abortion (LA), Immigration (I), Atheism (A), Climate Change (CC).

#	Tweet	Target	Sent.	Stance
1	Life is our first and most basic human right	LA	+	Against
2	@realDonaldTrump Thank you for protecting our border	I	+	Against
3	The biggest terror threat in the World is climate change #drought #floods	CC	−	Favor
4	In the big picture, religion is bad for society because it blunts reason. #freethinker	A	−	Favor

5   Discussion

Our first research question concerns with whether the sentiment captures the real stance, can be answered with dissenting. The previous analysis shows that the sentiment cannot substitute the stance in general. The words choice gap exists for in-favor stance and positive sentiment (Appendix A). Subsequently, We noticed that sentiment has failed to discover the public opinion towards most of the topics in the two datasets. Hence, using the sentiment polarity as the only factor to predict the public opinion potentially leads to misleading results. The result of the mismatch between in-favor and positive stance was sizable. The positive sentiment failed to distinguish the supporter viewpoints.

As for the overall alignment between the sentiment and stance, there is a noticeable disparity between sentiment and stance for a given topic. In general, the sentiment tends to be negative in the expressed stance as a way to rebuttal or defend the viewpoint and show support or opposing stance. The negative sentiment could help in discovering some of the against stances, but it will be mixed with a proportion of the supporter viewpoints.

In summary, our analysis in this paper illustrates the sophisticated nature of stance detection and that it cannot be simply captured using the sentiment polarity. This finding is crucial, especially when assessing the credibility of results in studies that used sentiment to measure public support of a given topic on social media.

6   Conclusion

In this paper, we study the relation between the sentiment and the stance. To gauge the extent of this relation, we constructed a new stance dataset with gold sentiment and stance labels. Then we conducted a textual and quantitative analysis of the expressed stance with respect to the sentiment polarity. Our study provides evidence that sentiment cannot substitute the stance. As a final consideration, researcher should be more cautious when it comes to identifying the viewpoints toward an event and to take into account the clear difference between the sentiment and the stance. As using sentiment purely overshadows the real stance and leads to truncated results.

A   Analysis of the Textual Patterns

To gauge the similarity between the vocabulary choice that has been used to express the sentiment and stance we analyzed the tweets in the two datasets using Jaccard similarity. We used Jaccard coefficient the widely adopted measure to capture the overlap between two sets [1,3,8]. In this analysis, for each sentiment and stance gold labels we combine all tweets and use Term Frequency-Inverse Document (TF-IDF), to find important words in each type of sentiment and stance. In order to compute the TF-IDF on tweet level we consider each tweet as document. Using TF-IDF helps in filtering out less significant words. The Jaccard similarity between the set of sentiment and stance words defined as following:

$$Jaccard(W_{sentiment}, W_{stance}) = \frac{W_{sentiment} \cap W_{stance}}{W_{sentiment} \cup W_{stance}} \tag{1}$$

where $W_{sentiment}$ and W_{stance} denote the list of top N words by TF-IDF value for the tweets with specific sentiment and stance type.

Figure 3 shows that the similarity between the words that have been used to express favor stance has less than 20% of similarity with tweets that has a positive sentiment. That means users tend to express their Favor stance without using positive sentiment words. In contrast, the common words for against stance have the most significant similarity with against sentiment words. The Jacquard similarity become stable with growing N. As Fig. 4 shows that the overall agreement between the sentiment and the stance is minuscule in general. The tweets that have against-negative labels constitutes less than 33%. Similarly less than 8% of the data has positive sentiment and favor stance. This shows that in general negative words tend to be similar to the against words while the matching cases are minuscule. On the other-hand, the matching cases where the tweet express favor and positive sentiment constitute about 8.9% and 4% of the overall data of SemEval stance and CD stance dataset.

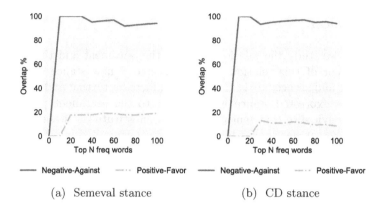

(a) Semeval stance   (b) CD stance

Fig. 3. Jaccard similarity of the top N-most frequent words between sentiment and stance.

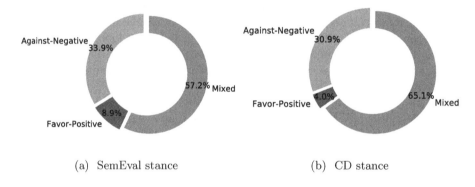

(a) SemEval stance   (b) CD stance

Fig. 4. Tweets with matching and mixed stance and sentiment.

References

1. Achananuparp, P., Hu, X., Shen, X.: The evaluation of sentence similarity measures. In: Song, I.-Y., Eder, J., Nguyen, T.M. (eds.) DaWaK 2008. LNCS, vol. 5182, pp. 305–316. Springer, Heidelberg (2008). https://doi.org/10.1007/978-3-540-85836-2_29
2. Agarwal, A., Singh, R., Toshniwal, D.: Geospatial sentiment analysis using twitter data for UK-EU referendum. J. Inf. Optim. Sci. **39**(1), 303–317 (2018)
3. An, J., Kwak, H., Posegga, O., Jungherr, A.: Political discussions in homogeneous and cross-cutting communication spaces (2019)
4. Biber, D., Finegan, E.: Adverbial stance types in English. Discourse Process. **11**(1), 1–34 (1988)
5. Darwish, K., Magdy, W., Zanouda, T.: Improved stance prediction in a user similarity feature space. In: ASONAM 2017 (2017)
6. Ebrahimi, J., Dou, D., Lowd, D.: A joint sentiment-target-stance model for stance classification in tweets. In: COLING, pp. 2656–2665 (2016)

7. Elfardy, H., Diab, M.: CU-GWU perspective at SemEval-2016 task 6: ideological stance detection in informal text. In: Proceedings of the 10th International Workshop on Semantic Evaluation (SemEval-2016), pp. 434–439 (2016)

8. Gomaa, W.H., Fahmy, A.A.: A survey of text similarity approaches. Int. J. Comput. Appl. **68**(13), 13–18 (2013)

9. Hu, Y., Wang, F., Kambhampati, S.: Listening to the crowd: automated analysis of events via aggregated twitter sentiment. In: Twenty-Third International Joint Conference on Artificial Intelligence (2013)

10. Igarashi, Y., Komatsu, H., Kobayashi, S., Okazaki, N., Inui, K.: Tohoku at SemEval-2016 Task 6: feature-based model versus convolutional neural network for stance detection. In: SemEval@ NAACL-HLT, pp. 401–407 (2016)

11. Kareem, D., Peter, S., Aupetit, M.J., Preslav, N.: Unsupervised user stance detection on Twitter. arXiv preprint arXiv:1904.02000 (2019)

12. Krejzl, P., Steinberger, J.: UWB at SemEval-2016 Task 6: stance detection. In: SemEval@ NAACL-HLT, pp. 408–412 (2016)

13. Lee, H.W.: Using Twitter Hashtags to gauge real-time changes in public opinion: an examination of the 2016 US presidential election. In: Staab, S., Koltsova, O., Ignatov, D.I. (eds.) SocInfo 2018. LNCS, vol. 11186, pp. 168–175. Springer, Cham (2018). https://doi.org/10.1007/978-3-030-01159-8_16

14. Liu, B., et al.: Sentiment analysis and subjectivity. Handb. Nat. Lang. Process. **2**(2010), 627–666 (2010)

15. Mohammad, S., Kiritchenko, S., Sobhani, P., Zhu, X.D., Cherry, C.: SemEval-2016 task 6: detecting stance in tweets. In: SemEval@ NAACL-HLT, pp. 31–41 (2016)

16. Mohammad, S.M., Sobhani, P., Kiritchenko, S.: Stance and sentiment in tweets. ACM Trans. Internet Technol. (TOIT) **17**(3), 26 (2017)

17. Overbey, L.A., Batson, S.C., Lyle, J., Williams, C., Regal, R., Williams, L.: Linking Twitter sentiment and event data to monitor public opinion of geopolitical developments and trends. In: Lee, D., Lin, Y.-R., Osgood, N., Thomson, R. (eds.) SBP-BRiMS 2017. LNCS, vol. 10354, pp. 223–229. Springer, Cham (2017). https://doi.org/10.1007/978-3-319-60240-0_26

18. Park, S., Ko, M., Kim, J., Liu, Y., Song, J.: The politics of comments: predicting political orientation of news stories with commenters' sentiment patterns. In: Proceedings of the ACM 2011 Conference on Computer Supported Cooperative Work, pp. 113–122. ACM (2011)

19. Smith, K.S., McCreadie, R., Macdonald, C., Ounis, I.: Analyzing disproportionate reaction via comparative multilingual targeted sentiment in Twitter. In: Proceedings of the 2017 IEEE/ACM International Conference on Advances in Social Networks Analysis and Mining 2017, pp. 317–320. ACM (2017)

20. Sobhani, P., Mohammad, S., Kiritchenko, S.: Detecting stance in tweets and analyzing its interaction with sentiment. In: Proceedings of the Fifth Joint Conference on Lexical and Computational Semantics, pp. 159–169 (2016)

21. Somasundaran, S., Wiebe, J.: Recognizing stances in ideological on-line debates. In: Proceedings of the NAACL HLT 2010 Workshop on Computational Approaches to Analysis and Generation of Emotion in Text, pp. 116–124. Association for Computational Linguistics (2010)

22. Trabelsi, A., Zaiane, O.R.: Unsupervised model for topic viewpoint discovery in online debates leveraging author interactions. In: Twelfth International AAAI Conference on Web and Social Media (2018)

23. Tsolmon, B., Kwon, A.-R., Lee, K.-S.: Extracting social events based on time-line and sentiment analysis in Twitter corpus. In: Bouma, G., Ittoo, A., Métais, E., Wortmann, H. (eds.) NLDB 2012. LNCS, vol. 7337, pp. 265–270. Springer, Heidelberg (2012). https://doi.org/10.1007/978-3-642-31178-9_32
24. Unankard, S., Li, X., Sharaf, M., Zhong, J., Li, X.: Predicting Elections from social networks based on sub-event detection and sentiment analysis. In: Benatallah, B., Bestavros, A., Manolopoulos, Y., Vakali, A., Zhang, Y. (eds.) WISE 2014. LNCS, vol. 8787, pp. 1–16. Springer, Cham (2014). https://doi.org/10.1007/978-3-319-11746-1_1

Do Events Change Opinions on Social Media? Studying the 2016 US Presidential Debates

Sopan Khosla[1], Niyati Chhaya[1(✉)], Shivam Jindal[2], Oindrila Saha[3], and Milind Srivastava[4]

[1] Big Data Experience Lab, Adobe Research, Bangalore, India
{skhosla,nchhaya}@adobe.com
[2] Indian Institute of Technology, Roorkee, Roorkee, India
[3] Indian Institute of Technology, Kharagpur, Kharagpur, India
[4] Indian Institute of Technology, Madras, Chennai, India

Abstract. Social media is the primary platform for discussions and reactions during various social events. Studies in this space focus on the aggregate opinion and sentiment analysis but fail to analyze the micro-dynamics. In this work, we present a case study of the 2016 US Presidential Debates, analyzing the user opinion micro-dynamics across the timeline. We present an opinion variation analysis coupled with micro and macro level user analysis in order to explain opinion change. We also identify and characterize varied user-groups derived through this analyses. We discover that aggregate change in opinion is better explained by the differential influx of polarized population rather than the change in individual's stance or opinion.

1 Introduction

Twitter is the most common social platform for political discussions. A number of studies [3,4,7,9,18,20] attempt political insights such as candidate popularity, user inclination, and election results prediction using this data. These studies are limited to the study of aggregate opinion during specific events. [2] suggests many existing approaches which attempt to infer trends in social and behavioral data overlook the micro-dynamics that may reflect a different view of the event (e.g. biases due to Simpson's Paradox [1,5,19]). Processes such as the change in tweet patterns or change in the active user population that lead to a change in aggregate opinion are usually ignored. We present the first comparative study to analyze the three Presidential Debates during the 2016 US Presidential Elections and explain the resulting shifts in aggregate user opinion on Twitter towards the candidates, 'Donald Trump' and 'Hillary Clinton'.

We use *stance* towards these candidates to score target-specific opinion as Favor or Agains. *Stance* and *opinion* are used interchangeably through rest of this paper. The SemEval 2016 Task 6 [15] is a shared task on detecting stance from tweets. The size of the dataset (approx. 4000 examples only), limits the

© Springer Nature Switzerland AG 2019
I. Weber et al. (Eds.): SocInfo 2019, LNCS 11864, pp. 287–297, 2019.
https://doi.org/10.1007/978-3-030-34971-4_20

generalizability of models [8,13,16,20] to other domains. Stance is subjective, crowd sourcing for ground truth data hence yields ambiguous results. We overcome this limitation by using target-specific (targets include *hillary* or *trump*) hashtags as pseudo-positive and pseudo-negative stance labels. A large number of users do not use polarized hashtags in their tweets, we leverage a CNN to model a prediction task to label users, in turn achieving a larger labeled dataset.

Stance in social media is not only driven by the topics but is also influenced by user behavior. We group users based on their tweet behavior overlayed with the stance to characterize the influence of user dynamics on aggregate opinion. This analysis not only leads insights about causes of aggregate stance but also reveals distinguishing language preferences across different user groups.

The contributions of this work include **(1) an analysis of the aggregate opinion shift in Twitter during the 2016 US Presidential debates; and (2) a study of user-segments based on their stance and tweet patterns during this period.** We compare the user groups based on their content characteristics and discover distinguishable patterns among the users who are active (tweet continuously) vs the ones who are not. Analysis around aggregate opinion shift along with the user-segment definitions are discussed in Sect. 3. Section 4 studies the platform activity and content characteristics (topics, hashtags, and psycholinguistic traits) across these groups.

1.1 Data

The Harvard Dataverse 2016 United States Presidential Election Tweet Ids Dataset [12] is used here. The dataset contains 280 million tweet IDs. We focus on the activity around the 3 US Presidential debates in 2016 (dated 26th Sept, 9th Oct and 19th Oct) in this work. Hence we extract tweets and replies during the time period from September 15, 2016 to October 24, 2016. Retweets and quotes are ignored for this analysis.

Annotation and Pre-processing: Bovet et al. [7] use a co-occurrence based label expansion method [14] to create a list of hashtags used in favor of and against the Presidential Elections candidates. We use these hashtags as distant supervision for stance detection in this paper. The list is further refined, by considering 1000 random tweets per hashtag, with the aim of removing ambiguous tags that are extensively used in tweets to convey both positive as well as negative stance towards a given candidate. We also remove tweets (and associated users) that contain (1) hashtags with negative stance towards both candidates (e.g. *Lets not go red or blue #nevertrumporhillary*); or (2) one or more hashtags against both candidate (e.g. *These are my options? WTF... #crooked-hillary #nevertrump*). This refined hashtag list[1] is used for proxy annotation of the dataset resulting in around 3.8 million labeled tweets (Favor of Hillary: 1,474,316, Trump: 2,299,072).

---

[1] Refer to Appendix A for the refined Hashtag list.

2   Model

For dataset expansion, we use the annotated tweets extracted to train a CNN for stance detection on the complete Harvard Dataverse dataset. The model is inspired from Kim et al. [10][2]. We initialize the embeddings layer with pre-trained Google word2vec vectors and train the model for 200 epochs. The input the tweet text and the output is the predicted stance label.

Results: Logistic Regression and XGBoost based on features inspired from Lai et al. [11] are used as baselines. The dataset is randomly split into 80:10:10 for training, validation, and testing respectively. The CNN outperforms other models with a test accuracy (average across 10 independent runs) of 92.45%[3], followed by XGBoost (88.34%) and Logistic Regression (82.10%).

Limitations: On error analysis, we notice the ambiguous use of few more hashtags. For example, *Judging by #ImWithHer hashtag in your bio, I'm going to assume you're just stupid. So bye.* This tweet uses *#ImWithHer*, a positive hashtag towards Hillary in the text, but the overall tone is against her. This results in an inevitable noise in the training set not explicitly handled in this paper.

3   Analyzing Opinion Dynamics

We present an analysis of opinion dynamics on Twitter towards Hillary Clinton (*hillary*) and Donald Trump (*trump*). We start by looking at how the debates affect opinion of the population at an aggregate and then break up the population based on their stance and tweet behavior to analyze the micro-dynamics. Tweets categorized by our model as positive towards a presidential candidate (*c*) are referred to as T(+, C:c) and users with positive stance towards the candidate as U(+,C:c), where tweets or users against hillary are considered to be in favor of trump (-, C:hillary) ≡ (+, C:trump) and vice-versa.

3.1   Did 2016 Presidential Debates Affect Opinion ?

Aggregate Analysis: We plot aggregate user stance (User Polarity) in Fig. 1. User polarity is defined as (T(+,C:c) - T(-,C:c))/(T(+,C:c) + T(-,C:c)) The aggregate opinion graphs reveal significant differences before and after the Debates but the effects are only visible for 2 to 3 days post debate. Debate 1 and 3 witness a substantial jump in *hillary's* image, whereas the changes due to Debate 2 were overshadowed by the Vice Presidential Debate (4th Oct) and the news of 'Leaked Tapes' against *trump* and Wikileaks against *hillary* (7th Oct), shown as *light blue* vertical lines in Fig. 1.

---

[2] https://github.com/dennybritz/cnn-text-classification-tf.
[3] Refer to Appendix B for results of CNN model on SemEval 2016 Task 6 test-set.

Table 1. Break-up of **Aggregates** into micro-dynamics (**Volubles** and **Passivists**). **Steady** supporters did not change their polarity after the debate as against **Swing** who shifted allegiance, i.e. (+, hillary) during e_t^- and (+, trump) during e_t^+ or vice-versa. **Joinees** depicts users with no activity during e_t^-; and **Dropouts** are those who remained dormant during e_t^+.

U(+,C:c) (T(+,C:c))	Debate 1				Debate 2				Debate 3			
	Hillary		Trump		Hillary		Trump		Hillary		Trump	
	Before	After	Before	After	Before	After	Before	After	Before	After	Before	After
Aggregate	93472	246999	150664	318303	205363	204970	251530	266411	180433	225214	299355	264979
	(287635)	(601127)	(474876)	(799811)	(631658)	(457959)	(872368)	(608676)	(582506)	(537644)	(1045533)	(686611)
Volubles (Users active during both e_t^- and e_t^+)												
Steady	22364	22364	45592	45592	42015	42015	61583	61583	39176	39176	74001	74001
	(135980)	(168766)	(271215)	(308475)	(312446)	(191886)	(503535)	(294957)	(303457)	(219031)	(624232)	(372414)
Swing	13464	16346	16346	13464	22045	20494	20494	22045	18353	25450	25450	18353
	(31112)	(56136)	(45426)	(39228)	(71891)	(45288)	(64697)	(48688)	(54257)	(70374)	(89263)	(39531)
Passivists (Users active either during e_t^- or e_t^+ but not both)												
Dropouts	53084		83044		141303		169453		122904		199904	
	(73380)		(114826)		(221747)		(274959)		(188386)		(311352)	
Joinees		205363		251530		143090		182885		159628		174200
		(321327)		(387835)		(206138)		(252024)		(236670)		(250155)

3.2 Explaining the Aggregate Opinion Change

We study the underlying processes to explain the aggregate variations in opinion around the presidential debates.

Did Users Change their Stance Towards the Candidate After the Debates? We check if the change in aggregate opinion originates from individual-level shifts in stance towards the candidate. We posit that user's stance/opinion has changed, after the external event e_t, if $UserPolarity(e_t^-) * UserPolarity(e_t^+) < 0$, where e_t^- is user's stance between beginning of the debate and 48 hours (0 to -2 days) pre-debate and e_t^+ denotes the stance from debate to 48 hours post event. As shown in Table 1, about 35% of the aggregate users show online tweet activity both before and after the debates (**Volubles**), 1/3rd of which changed their stance around the debates (**Swing**). Figure 1 shows the stance plots after removal of Swing users (dashed lines). We observe that even after excluding these users, the time-series portrays similar trends to the aggregate stance suggesting that **the individual-level changes in stance do not completely explain the aggregate shifts**.

Change in User Population: Did Some Users Leave/Join the Discussion Before/After the Debates? The intersection between people participating in online discussion before and after the debates is low. More than 65% of the users who were active during e_t^- are absent post-debate (e_t^+) (**Dropouts**) (Table 1). We also observe a large number of new active users during e_t^+ (**Joinees**). This shows that the changes in aggregate opinion around the debates were more due to an efflux/influx of users rather than a change in individual's stance towards the candidates - in accordance with previous work [6].

Did the Frequency of Tweets of Users Change After the Debates?
We study how the tweet frequency changed for users who were active during both e_t^- and e_t^+ and were predicted by our model to have the same stance throughout (**Steady**). We observe that the number of tweets posted by this audience increased after Debate 1. An opposite trend is noticed for Debates 2 and 3.

4   Analyzing User Segments

This section presents an analysis of the various user segments introduced in Table 1. We show how **Passivists** (=**Dropouts** + **Joinees**) differ from **Volubles** (= **Steady** + **Swing**). We combine Steady and Swing users into Volubles for this analysis to show how users who were active both before and after the debate differ from the ones who either left or joined the conversation after/before the debates. Furthermore, tweets written by Volubles before/after the debates are referred to as **Volubles_b/Volubles_a** respectively.

Platform Activity: We study users' activity in terms of *#tweets, followers* and *following*. Steady and Swing users tweet significantly more[4] (hillary: $\mu =$ 46118.67 and $\mu =$ 38037.49 respectively; $p < 0.001$) than Dropouts (hillary: $\mu = 18841.03$) and Joinees (hillary: $\mu = 15595.33$). A similar trend is evident for *#followers* and *#following* across all presidential debates.

Popular Topics and Hashtags: Discussion on varied topics ranging from 'same-sex marriage' to 'gun control' was observed. To understand the inherent

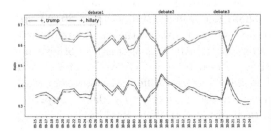

Fig. 1. Day wise aggregate user stance (ratio) towards *hillary* and *trump* between Sept 15, 2016 and Oct 25, 2016. Dashed lines (-.-) represent ratios after excluding users who changed their opinion after the debates. The yellow vertical lines depict the three presidential debates. (Color figure online)

Table 2. % Tweets with atleast one popular election topics & (hashtags). **Volubles_b (Volubles_a)** refers to tweets written by Volubles before (after) the debate.

Tweets (%)	Debate 1		Debate 2		Debate 3	
Topics (Hashtags)	Hillary	Trump	Hillary	Trump	Hillary	Trump
		Before Debate				
Volubles_b	25.5 (9.5)	23.6 (7.4)	32.2 (7.3)	30.9 (8.9)	30.5 (6.9)	33.6 (8.9)
Dropouts	17.3 (4.7)	17.6 (4.3)	26.8 (4.1)	24.5 (4.1)	24.0 (3.5)	26.1 (5.2)
		After Debate				
Volubles_a	25.7 (8.2)	26.1 (7.4)	29.7 (6.2)	28.8 (7.2)	28.3 (7.3)	33.3 (8.1)
Joinees	19.9 (5.5)	21.8 (5.0)	23.1 (3.8)	21.6 (4.0)	26.8 (6.2)	25.9 (4.6)

---

[4] We use a 2-sample t-test to compare the population distributions.

differences between the usage of these policy-related terms among the different user segments we extracted 60 key terms from the debate transcripts[5]. As shown in Table 2, Volubles show a higher usage of popular topics discussed in the debates compared to Passivists (a similar trend is seen in the usage of popular hashtags [7]) suggesting that the latter's responses might be more about how they feel about the candidate, e.g. *@hillaryclinton wife of governor, wife of president - fortunate much?*, rather than her/his stance on the issues discussed in the debates. An example tweet from Volubles - *reddit: proof that trump spoke out against nafta before it was passed. report this, liars url url.*

4.1 Psycholinguistic Analysis

We use LIWC2015 [17] to analyze the tweets by users from different segments. We focus on the summary scores, cognitive processes(Cogproc), and pronoun usage for this analysis[6]. Figure 2 shows the mean scores for key LIWC dimensions. Note that we compare Dropouts against Volubles_b (tweets before debate) and Joinees against Volubles_a (after debate).

Volubles' Exhibit Higher Clout and Analytical Thinking, While Passivists' Tweets Show Higher Emotional Tone, Differentiation and Tentativeness. Figures 2a and c show the key summary language values obtained from LIWC 2015 averaged over all tweets for Volubles and Passivists. Volubles' tweets have lower mean value for analytical thinking scores ($p < 0.001$) in comparison to Joinees (hillary: $\mu = 66.17$) and Dropouts (hillary: $\mu = 75.38$). We also find that Volubles demonstrate higher clout values ($p < 0.001$). This suggests that Volubles' tweets reflect formal, logical, and high expertise whereas Passivists use more informal, personal, and an anxious style.

The tweets from Passivists show higher scores of emotional tone (Tone) indicating that Dropouts (hillary: $\mu = 32.83$) and Joinees (hillary: $\mu = 30.08$) use more positive tone in their tweets to show support towards the candidate of their choice ($p < 0.001$), while Volubles' show more bitterness against the other candidate (hillary: before debate $\mu = 21.90$, after debate $\mu = 17.68$). Figures 2b and 2d show that Passivists have a higher mean score for differentiation (words like *hasn't, but, without*) and tentativeness (*maybe, perhaps*) ($p < 0.001$) implying that they might be less confident in their arguments than Volubles.

Volubles Emphasize 'he or she' but not 'I' or 'you' Pronouns. Figures 2b and d show that Volubles use more third personal singular pronouns in their language ($p < 0.001$), e.g. *clinton baits trump into fight, and he more than counters url*, therefore being authoritative in their argument. Whereas, Passivists resort to higher usage of first and second personal singular pronouns (I/you)

---

[5] https://www.debates.org/index.php?page=debate-transcripts. Refer to Appendix C and Appendix A for the Topic and Hashtag list respectively.
[6] We refer the reader to the LIWC2015 development manual [17] for more information.

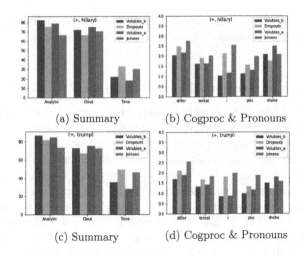

(a) Summary   (b) Cogproc & Pronouns

(c) Summary   (d) Cogproc & Pronouns

Fig. 2. Mean scores for LIWC attributes for different user-segments around Debate 1: +,Hillary (a,b) and +,Trump (c,d). Note that these trends are consistent for both candidates across all three US Presidential Debates.

$(p < 0.001)$, e.g. *trump is very entertaining. i thought i was watching a episode of comic view*, consequently showing low expertise and low confidence. Thus, highlighting differences in language and personalities of different user categories.

5 Conclusion

We present a study of micro-dynamics in Twitter during important events. The 2016 US presidential debates are analyzed with respect to users' opinions towards 'hillary' and 'trump'. This study highlights that an observed change in aggregate opinion is not due to users' changing opinions but rather due to the change in their tweet or participation behavior, in particular the influx/efflux of users in active conversations. The language analysis establishes the differences in audiences with varying tweet behavior based on the linguistics characteristics as well as their platform activities. We find that Volubles focus more on debate topics and are authoritative in their arguments, as compared to Passivists whose tweets portray high emotions and less confidence. The insights presented can be extended towards identifying triggers for users' participation behavior. We are now working towards creating computational social science for these problems.

A Hashtag list

Following hashtags were used as distant supervision to annotate 3.8 million tweets from the Harvard Dataverse 2016 United States Presidential Election Tweet Ids Dataset [12]. Hashtags in Appendix A.1 and A.2 were combined to label tweets with stance in favor of Hillary (or equivalently against Trump).

Whereas, hashtags in Appendixs A.3 and A.4 were combined to label tweets with positive stance towards Trump (or equivalently negative stance towards Hillary).

A.1   Hashtags in favor of Hillary (+, Hillary)

hillaryforpr, imwithher2016, imwithhillary, hillaryforpresident, hillaryforamerica, hereiamwithher, estoyconella, hillarysopresidential, uniteblue, hillstorm2016, bluewave2016, welovehillary, itrusther, bluewave, hrcisournominee, itrusthillary, standwithmadampotus, momsdemandhillary, madamepresident, madampresident, imwither, herstory, republicans4hillary, hillarysoqualified, werewithher, vote4hillary, strongertogether, readyforhillary, hillafornia, unitedagainsthate, votehillary, wearewithher, republicansforhillary, hrc2016, connecttheleft, yeswekaine, voteblue2016, hillary2016, sheswithus, hillyes, iamwithher, heswithher, voteblue, hillaryaprovenleader, imwiththem, bernwithher, ohhillyes, imwithher, clintonkaine2016, whyimwithher, turnncblue, hillarystrong

A.2   Hashtags against Trump (-, Trump)

nevertrumppence, lgbthatestrumpparty, boycotttrump, orangehitler, wheresyourtaxes, poordonald, losertrump, notrumpanytime, dirtydonald, drumpf, trumpsopoor, nodonaldtrump, makedonalddrumpfagain, nastywomen, defeattrump, sleazydonald, weakdonald, unfittrump, trump20never, loserdonald, trumplies, dumbdonald, trumpliesmatter, releaseyourtaxes, crybabytrump, freethedelegates, lyingtrump, nastywomenvote, trumpleaks, stupidtrump, stoptrump, trumpthefraud, racisttrump, dumpthetrump, dumptrump, anyonebuttrump, wherertrumpstaxes, crookeddonald, treasonoustrump, antitrump, nevertrump, notrump, womentrumpdonald, nevergop, donthecon, crookeddrumpf, traitortrump, showusyourtaxes, trumptrainwreck, lyingdonald, crookedtrump, lyindonald, ripgop, trumptreason, lyintrump, chickentrump

A.3   Hashtags against Hillary (-, Hillary)

hillarysolympics, hillaryforprison, hillaryforprison2016, moretrustedthanhillary, heartlesshillary, neverclinton, handcuffhillary, queenofcorrupton, crookedhillary, nomoreclintons, hillary4jail, fbimwithher, clintoncrimefamily, hillno, queenofcorruption, hillarylostme, ohhillno, billclintonisrapist, democratliesmatter, lyingcrookedhillary, hypocritehillary, crookedclintons, hillarylies, neverhilary, shelies, releasethetranscripts, stophillary2016, riskyhillary, hillaryliedpeopledied, corrupthillary, hillary4prison2016, nohillary2016, wehatehillary, whatmakeshillaryshortcircuit, crookedhillaryclinton, deletehillary, dropouthillary, lyinhillary, hillaryliesmatter, nevereverhillary, stophillary, neverhilllary, clintoncorruption, clintoncrime, notwithher, hillary2jail, imnotwithher, lockherup, corruptclintons, indicthillary, sickhillary, crookedhilary, crookedhillary, hillaryrottenclinton, theclintoncontamination, lyinghillary, clintoncollapse, clintoncrimefoundation, neverhillary, criminalhillary, crookedclinton, hillary4prison, killary, iwillneverstandwithher

A.4   Hashtags in favor of Trump (+, Trump)

trumppence2016, trumpstrong, donaldtrumpforpresident, rednationrising, depl
orablesfortrump, makeamericaworkagain, latinos4trump, trumpiswithyou, blacks
4trump, feelthetrump, votetrumppence2016, bikers4trump, votetrump2016,
votetrumppence, americafirst, trumpcares, draintheswamp, votetrumpusa, trum
ppence16, gaysfortrump, buildthewall, trump2016, trumpwon, alwaystrump,
onlytrump, maga3x, veteransfortrump, latinosfortrump, cafortrump, gays4
trump, makeamericasafeagain, latinoswithtrump, trump16, woman4trump,
womenfortrump, makeamericagreat, votegop, makeamericagreatagain, maga,
trumptrain, gotrump, bikersfortrump, votetrumppence16, feminineamer-
ica4trump, trumpwins, imwithhim, buildthatwall, babesfortrump, america1st,
securetheborder, vets4trump, democrats4trump, women4trump, trumpforpresi-
dent, magax3, blacksfortrump, heswithus, presidenttrump, votetrump

B   Evaluation on SemEval2016 Task 6 test-set

We evaluate our best performing CNN model on SemEval2016 Task 6 test-set
with target 'Hillary Clinton'. This dataset contains 295 tweets with gold labels of
'AGAINST', 'FAVOR' or 'NEUTRAL' as stance towards Hillary. Since our CNN
is trained on 'FAVOR' and 'AGAINST' stance, following the same experimental
setup, we extract tweets that are in favor (or against the target (hillary clinton).
We find that our model model performs well on the test-set with weighted F1-
score of 0.75 (See Table 3 for the confusion matrix).

Table 3. Performance of CNN on 'AGAINST'/'FAVOR' tweets in SemEval2016 Task
6 test-set (target 'Hillary Clinton')

Prediction	Gold Labels	
	−, Hillary	+, Hillary
−, Hillary	134	20
+, Hillary	38	25
Total	174	45

C   Topic list

money, japan, justice, climate change, economy, rapist, healthcare, podesta, oba-
macare, abortion, foreign, women, nato, cyber, russia, weapon, podesta email,
voter fraud, benghazi, iran, assault, email, blm, gun, tape, job, podestaemail,
middle east, police, p2, climatechange, 2ndamendment, amendment, audit, lgbt,
2nd amendment, appoint, climate, nafta, war, second amendment, black, middle
class, mosul, tax, nuke, 2a, scotus, korea, isis, iraq, haiti, putin, trade, paytoplay,
voterfraud, woman, china, law, nuclear, syria, secondamendment, rig, debt

References

1. Agarwal, T., Burghardt, K., Lerman, K.: On quitting: performance and practice in online game play. In: Eleventh International AAAI Conference on Web and Social Media (2017)
2. Alipourfard, N., Fennell, P.G., Lerman, K.: Can you trust the trend? discovering Simpson's paradoxes in social data. In: Proceedings of the Eleventh ACM International Conference on Web Search and Data Mining, pp. 19–27. ACM (2018)
3. Allcott, H., Gentzkow, M.: Social media and fake news in the 2016 election. J. Econ. Perspect. **31**(2), 211–36 (2017)
4. Anstead, N., O'Loughlin, B.: Social media analysis and public opinion: the 2010 UK general election. J. Comput.-Mediated Commun. **20**(2), 204–220 (2014)
5. Bickel, P.J., Hammel, E.A., O'Connell, J.W.: Sex bias in graduate admissions: data from Berkeley. Science **187**(4175), 398–404 (1975)
6. Borge-Holthoefer, J., Magdy, W., Darwish, K., Weber, I.: Content and network dynamics behind Egyptian political polarization on Twitter. In: Proceedings of the 18th ACM Conference on Computer Supported Cooperative Work & Social Computing, pp. 700–711. ACM (2015)
7. Bovet, A., Morone, F., Makse, H.A.: Validation of Twitter opinion trends with national polling aggregates: Hillary Clinton vs Donald Trump. Sci. Rep. **8**(1), 8673 (2018)
8. Chen, Y.C., Liu, Z.Y., Kao, H.Y.: IKM at semeval-2017 task 8: convolutional neural networks for stance detection and rumor verification. In: Proceedings of the 11th International Workshop on Semantic Evaluation (SemEval-2017), pp. 465–469 (2017)
9. Himelboim, I., Sweetser, K.D., Tinkham, S.F., Cameron, K., Danelo, M., West, K.: Valence-based homophily on twitter: network analysis of emotions and political talk in the 2012 presidential election. New Med. Soc. **18**(7), 1382–1400 (2016)
10. Kim, Y.: Convolutional neural networks for sentence classification. In: Proceedings of the 2014 Conference on Empirical Methods in Natural Language Processing (EMNLP), pp. 1746–1751 (2014)
11. Lai, M., Hernández Farías, D.I., Patti, V., Rosso, P.: Friends and enemies of Clinton and Trump: using context for detecting stance in political Tweets. In: Sidorov, G., Herrera-Alcántara, O. (eds.) MICAI 2016. LNCS (LNAI), vol. 10061, pp. 155–168. Springer, Cham (2017). https://doi.org/10.1007/978-3-319-62434-1_13
12. Littman, J., Wrubel, L., Kerchner, D.: 2016 United States presidential election Tweet ids (2016). https://doi.org/10.7910/DVN/PDI7IN
13. Liu, C., et al.: IUCL at semeval-2016 task 6: an ensemble model for stance detection in Twitter. In: Proceedings of the 10th International Workshop on Semantic Evaluation (SemEval-2016), pp. 394–400 (2016)
14. Martinez-Romo, J., Araujo, L., Borge-Holthoefer, J., Arenas, A., Capitán, J.A., Cuesta, J.A.: Disentangling categorical relationships through a graph of co-occurrences. Phys. Rev. E **84**(4), 046108 (2011)
15. Mohammad, S., Kiritchenko, S., Sobhani, P., Zhu, X., Cherry, C.: Semeval-2016 task 6: detecting stance in tweets. In: Proceedings of the 10th International Workshop on Semantic Evaluation (SemEval-2016), pp. 31–41 (2016)
16. Patra, B.G., Das, D., Bandyopadhyay, S.: JU_NLP at semeval-2016 task 6: detecting stance in Tweets using support vector machines. In: Proceedings of the 10th International Workshop on Semantic Evaluation (SemEval-2016), pp. 440–444 (2016)

17. Pennebaker, J.W., Boyd, R.L., Jordan, K., Blackburn, K.: The development and psychometric properties of LIWC2015. Technical report (2015)
18. Primario, S., Borrelli, D., Iandoli, L., Zollo, G., Lipizzi, C.: Measuring polarization in Twitter enabled in online political conversation: the case of 2016 US presidential election. In: 2017 IEEE International Conference on Information Reuse and Integration (IRI), pp. 607–613. IEEE (2017)
19. Romero, D.M., Meeder, B., Kleinberg, J.: Differences in the mechanics of information diffusion across topics: idioms, political hashtags, and complex contagion on Twitter. In: Proceedings of the 20th International Conference on World Wide Web, pp. 695–704. ACM (2011)
20. Wei, W., Zhang, X., Liu, X., Chen, W., Wang, T.: pkudblab at SemEVAL-2016 task 6: a specific convolutional neural network system for effective stance detection. In: Proceedings of the 10th International Workshop on Semantic Evaluation (SemEval-2016), pp. 384–388 (2016)

"Hashjacking" the Debate: Polarisation Strategies of Germany's Political Far-Right on Twitter

Philipp Darius[1]([⊠])(iD) and Fabian Stephany[2](iD)

[1] Hertie School of Governance, Berlin, Germany
p.darius@phd.hertie-school.org
[2] Humboldt Institute for Internet and Society, Berlin, Germany
fabian.stephany@hiig.de

Abstract. Twitter is a digital forum for political discourse. The emergence of phenomena like *fake news* and *hate speech* has shown that political discourse on micro-blogging can become strongly polarised by algorithmic enforcement of selective perception. Recent findings suggest that some political actors might employ strategies to actively facilitate polarisation on Twitter. With a network approach, we examine the case of the German far-right party *Alternative für Deutschland* (AfD) and their potential use of a *"hashjacking"* strategy (The use of someone else's hashtag in order to promote one's own social media agenda.). Our findings suggest that right-wing politicians (and their supporters/retweeters) actively and effectively polarise the discourse not just by using their own party hashtags, but also by *"hashjacking"* the political party hashtags of other established parties. The results underline the necessity to understand the success of right-wing parties, online and in elections, not entirely as a result of external effects (e.g. migration), but as a direct consequence of their digital political communication strategy.

Keywords: Hashtags · Networks · Political communication strategies

1 Introduction

In recent years many countries were facing increasingly polarised political discourses and social networking and micro-blogging sites play a crucial role in these processes. While the Internet has for long been seen to promote public sphere like spaces for democratic discourse [5], the most recent developments remind more of echo chambers, in which particularly the far-right is successful in promoting their worldview [3,9,12]. We understand right-wing politicians and parties as important actors that actively fuel and benefit from discourse polarisation online (and offline). Thus, this study investigates the use of political party hashtags in Germany, where the right-wing party AfD has not just established itself in the federal and all state parliaments, but is also highly visible on Twitter. Existing studies have underlined the importance and high publicity of the AfD

© Springer Nature Switzerland AG 2019
I. Weber et al. (Eds.): SocInfo 2019, LNCS 11864, pp. 298–308, 2019.
https://doi.org/10.1007/978-3-030-34971-4_21

in social media discourses [14], but not focused on the use of political party hashtags and communication structures. This study investigates the use of political party hashtags on Twitter with a network approach that allows analysing the underlying structures of communication on Twitter. By using community detection algorithms, we identify different clusters within hashtag discourses and are able to show with a logistic regression model that right-wing users or supporters of the AfD are much more likely to use other party hashtags as part of a strategy called "hashjacking" [2]. By using this "hashjacking" strategy official AfD accounts, that are among the most retweeted users in the sample, aim to increase the reach of individual messages and to co-opt the hashtags of other political parties.

2 Background

In political communication literature the importance of social media communication for right-wing populist parties is increasingly highlighted, because they allow right-wing parties to circumvent traditional media gatekeepers and issue messages without conforming to political norms [6,7,12,15].

As an example, before the last German federal elections in 2017 the AfD generated the highest attention on social media and the political party hashtag was much more frequently used than any other political hashtag [14]. While this itself may be seen as a success in terms of publicity, it remains unclear whether the hashtag use was in support or opposition to the party, but the authors suspect a polarised use of the hashtag. Another recent study on Twitter before and during the 2017 elections scrutinised that the AfD has by far the highest proportion of single-party followers, which indicates that among this group echo chambers are more likely to be found than among other party followers [11].

Similar studies in the US have investigated strategic expression on Twitter in a more detailed manner and underlined the importance of retweeting and so called "hashjacking" in political discourses on Twitter [2]. The term "hashjacking" (hijacking a hashtag) refers to a person's or group's strategic use of someone else's hashtag to promote their own social media page, product or agenda. Most users only retweet Tweets they politically agree with and some use hashtags of politically opposed groups to co-opt these (ibid). Respectively, Conover et al. [4] show that retweet networks using political hashtags have a highly polarised structure, in which two communities of users only propagate content within their own groups. This however, has not been investigated for political debates on German politics and could illuminate the outlier role (in terms of frequency) of the #AfD and the high media representation of the AfD on Twitter and other social media. In contrast to the US, Twitter popularity is relatively low in Germany and remains to be primarily used by politically interested citizens, media professionals and political professionals [8]. However, singular tweets and accounts are frequently cited by established media outlets and polarisation on Twitter might affect the perceived importance of certain topics, which as a result are more likely to be reported on mass media.

3   Hypotheses

This study investigates two main hypotheses based on the background literature: First, we assume that the retweet networks of German political party hashtags are polarised and moreover, we expect that the retweet network using #AfD is the most polarised of all retweet networks, for the case of German political party hashtags.

Secondly, we expect an overlap between different hashtag discourses and thus users to appear in multiple retweet networks, because they have used multiple political party hashtags during the observation period. Additionally, we expect the cluster overlaps to be asymmetrical: a certain group of users (AfD support) is more likely to use other party hashtags in opposition (indicator of "hashjacking").

4   Research Design

The study is based on Twitter data that was collected by accessing Twitter's Rest API and using political party hashtags of German parties represented in the federal parliament (#AfD, #CDU, #CSU, #FDP, #GRUENE, #LINKE, #SPD) as a macro-level selection criterion. In total this study builds on a sample (n = 173,612) of all public Tweets using one or multiple of the selected political party hashtags between May 28th 00:00:00 (CEST) and June 4th 2018 23:59:59 (CEST) on Twitter. The analysis focuses on a network approach and a visualisation of the retweet networks in Gephi using the Force2 layout algorithm [10] for each political party hashtag where retweeting creates a link (edge) between two accounts (nodes). Since the data was collected as separate streams of data pertaining to each hashtag, an account using several political hashtags during the observation period in a retweet or being retweeted, will appear in each of the respective hashtag networks.

The literature indicated that political discourses on Twitter show polarised or clustered structures due to the retweeting behaviour. Consequently, the analysis will focus on the retweeting networks of the chosen political party hashtags. In a first step of analysis the modularity (community detection) algorithm [1] assigns the nodes to different communities based on the structural properties of the network graph and the cluster membership is indicated by the colour of nodes in Fig. 1. Thereafter, the interpretability of the clustering, as being in support of or opposition to a party, is controlled with a qualitative content analysis of the 50 most retweeted accounts similar to Neuendorf et al. [13]. This pro-/contra-polarisation of each party retweet network gives an indication of groups and whether individual nodes from these clusters are likely cluster of other party hashtags.

Regarding the second hypotheses we assume that a high pro-party X & contra-party Y association indicates "hashjacking" strategies. Consequently, we use a logistic regression model to test all cluster combinations (as the likelihood to be in a contra-cluster of party Y given a node was in the pro-cluster of

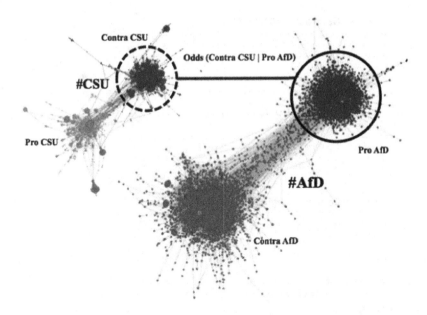

Fig. 1. Users of the political party hashtag #AfD are clearly clustered in two groups (right hand side). Users in the contra-AfD cluster have shared tweets in which #AfD had been used with negative connotations, while users in the pro-AfD cluster have predominantly shared Tweets in which #AfD had a positive connotation. All prominent political AfD accounts are located in this cluster. For the hashtags of other parties, like #CSU, similar clusters emerge (left hand side). We estimate the probability that a user retweeting the CSU-hashtag in critical tweets is also part of cluster A, the pro-AfD cluster: $Odds(X \epsilon ContraCSU | X \epsilon ProAfD)$. (Color figure online)

party X). We decide to apply a logistic model for the assessment of cross-cluster heterophily, since our dependent variable is binary (location in contra-cluster) and the resulting odds are easy to interpret. Assuming there is no group that uses other party hashtags more frequently, users from all clusters should have the same odds to appear in the other network clusters. Thus, a high affiliation

Table 1. Cluster membership proportions (in %) for all seven political party hashtags retweet clusters are clearly polarised. The majority of all users can be found in either one of the two dominant clusters.

	#AfD	#CDU	#CSU	#FDP	#SPD	#GRUENE	#LINKE
Pro-Cluster	30.23	26.71	36.38	13.84	36.66	14.62	26.20
Contra-Cluster	67.93	63.11	44.90	53.72	50.00	75.04	64.06
Neutral	01.84	10.18	18.72	32.54	13.34	10.34	09.74
Total	100	100	100	100	100	100	100

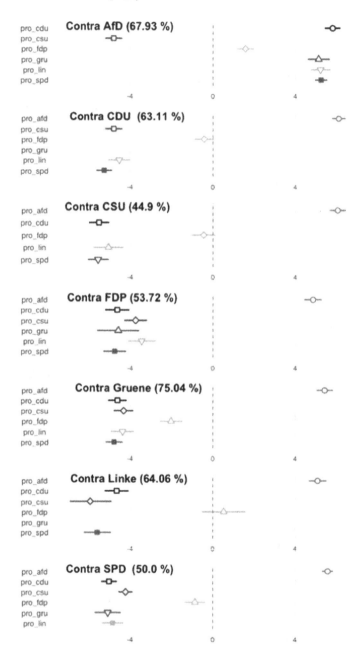

Fig. 2. Results of the logistic regression models from Tables 2, 3, 4, 5, 6, 7 and 8 (Appendix). Dots indicate odds with a 99% confidence interval, the relative size of the party contra-cluster is given in parentheses. We find remarkably high association between the pro-AfD cluster and the contra-clusters of all other parties, e.g., users in the contra-CSU cluster are six times more likely to be located in the pro-AfD cluster than users in the contra-CSU cluster on average.

between two clusters in terms of their users being more likely to appear in both of them is an indication for strategic hashtag use or "hashjacking".

5   Results

The network graphs and modularity assignments confirm the assumption that all retweet networks pertaining to the different political party hashtags are polarised or clustered (the graphs for #AfD and #CSU are shown as an example in Fig. 1). In addition, Table 1 shows the proportion of nodes assigned to the two largest clusters of all seven parties. The assumed pro-party X/contra-party Y alignment was underlined by a qualitative content analysis of the 50 most retweeted accounts in each network, that indicated a high content share of AfD politicians in the Pro-AfD and contra-party X clusters, whereas in the Contra-AfD cluster the most retweeted accounts were journalists, media accounts and outspoken opponents of the AfD (mentioning the opposition in their bio or usernames).

We consult the results of seven logistic regression models (Tables 2, 3, 4, 5, 6, 7 and 8) to assess the odds for the users in a contra-party cluster to be located in the pro-cluster of the remaining other parties. Figure 2 illustrates the coefficients (odds) of the seven regression models. The results indicate that users that were located in the pro-AfD cluster are much more likely than users of any other pro-party cluster to appear in the contra-clusters of a given party. When looking at the contra-AfD cluster, however, pro-party users are very likely to be in the contra-cluster of the AfD, which is in line with our expectation of polarised retweeting behaviour corresponding to political party hashtags.

6   Conclusion

In this study we understand discourse polarisation as a result and a strategy of far right and right-wing populist parties and are able to show, in the case of the German "Alternative für Deutschland" (AfD), how official politicians and their supporters polarise the political Twitter discourse by using hashtags strategically in a way that we call "hashjacking". The results underline the assumption of a high polarisation between the AfD and the rest of the political spectrum, whereas it needs to be noted that the FDP seems to be less affected by this polarisation or its supporters seem to restrain from "hashjacking" strategies. While, as expected, we find a high likelihood of AfD supporters to use "hashjacking", we also observe a high likelihood of other parties supporters to use the #AfD. To assess whether clusters show a high similarity in tweet content a sentiment classifier could be used to verify the structural clustering. Concluding, our study underlines the extent of online polarisation and stresses the importance of awareness for this polarisation when mapping political debates on social media.

A   Appendix

Table 2. Contra AfD

	Dependent variable:					
	con_afd					
	(1)	(2)	(3)	(4)	(5)	(6)
pro_cdu	5.803*** (0.192)					
pro_csu		4.694*** (0.190)				
pro_fdp			1.582*** (0.207)			
pro_gru				5.132*** (0.272)		
pro_lin					5.226*** (0.245)	
pro_spd						5.253*** (0.149)
Constant	−2.519*** (0.073)	−1.556*** (0.067)	−0.995*** (0.062)	−2.548*** (0.084)	−2.671*** (0.116)	−2.118*** (0.060)
Observations	3,664	2,361	1,412	2,351	1,555	4,287
Log Likelihood	−871.454	−862.020	−831.233	−610.247	−378.995	−1,236.388
Note:	*p < 0.1; **p < 0.05; ***p < 0.01					

Table 3. Contra CDU

	Dependent variable:					
	con_cdu					
	(1)	(2)	(3)	(4)	(5)	(6)
pro_afd	6.103*** (0.168)					
pro_csu		−4.782*** (0.207)				
pro_fdp			−0.425* (0.248)			
pro_gru				−6.085*** (0.516)		
pro_lin					−4.529*** (0.271)	
pro_spd						−5.244*** (0.193)
Constant	−2.462*** (0.111)	1.951*** (0.080)	0.922*** (0.065)	2.643*** (0.093)	2.490*** (0.117)	2.218*** (0.068)
Observations	3,664	1,959	1,230	1,981	1,197	3,106
Log Likelihood	−610.823	−652.277	−739.500	−470.209	−337.841	−904.649
Note:	*p < 0.1; **p < 0.05; ***p < 0.01					

Table 4. Contra CSU

	Dependent variable:					
	con_csu					
	(1)	(2)	(3)	(4)	(5)	(6)
pro_afd	6.059*** (0.205)					
pro_cdu		−5.491*** (0.249)				
pro_fdp			−0.453 (0.297)			
pro_gru				−20.634 (603.018)		
pro_lin					−5.042*** (0.371)	
pro_spd						−5.538*** (0.260)
Constant	−3.339*** (0.170)	2.102*** (0.086)	0.741*** (0.072)	2.068*** (0.099)	2.403*** (0.137)	1.999*** (0.085)
Observations	2,361	1,959	941	1,133	834	1,910
Log Likelihood	−460.732	−557.775	−594.543	−356.718	−232.964	−555.419
Note:	*p < 0.1; **p < 0.05; ***p < 0.01					

Table 5. Contra FDP

	Dependent variable:					
	con_fdp					
	(1)	(2)	(3)	(4)	(5)	(6)
pro_afd	4.867*** (0.220)					
pro_cdu		−4.624*** (0.297)				
pro_csu			−3.732*** (0.283)			
pro_gru				−4.572*** (0.518)		
pro_lin					−3.440*** (0.346)	
pro_spd						−4.750*** (0.280)
Constant	−2.639*** (0.192)	1.617*** (0.087)	1.286*** (0.088)	1.448*** (0.087)	1.664*** (0.115)	1.741*** (0.091)
Observations	1,412	1,230	941	946	641	1,264
Log Likelihood	−418.176	−480.632	−445.678	−430.810	−279.173	−458.656
Note:	*p < 0.1; **p < 0.05; ***p < 0.01					

Table 6. Contra Gruene

	Dependent variable:					
	con_gru					
	(1)	(2)	(3)	(4)	(5)	(6)
pro_afd	5.430*** (0.204)					
pro_cdu		−4.615*** (0.229)				
pro_csu			−4.316*** (0.242)			
pro_fdp				−2.025*** (0.274)		
pro_lin					−4.366*** (0.290)	
pro_spd						−4.776*** (0.212)
Constant	−1.783*** (0.146)	3.005*** (0.111)	2.802*** (0.139)	1.539*** (0.088)	2.385*** (0.115)	2.861*** (0.102)
Observations	2,351	1,981	1,133	946	1,116	2,141
Log Likelihood	−390.453	−423.606	−291.871	−453.614	−333.390	−495.157
Note:	*p < 0.1; **p < 0.05; ***p < 0.01					

Table 7. Contra Linke

	Dependent variable:					
	con_lin					
	(1)	(2)	(3)	(4)	(5)	(6)
pro_afd	5.098*** (0.221)					
pro_cdu		−4.653*** (0.298)				
pro_csu			−5.922*** (0.526)			
pro_fdp				0.532 (0.547)		
pro_gru					−6.798*** (1.009)	
pro_spd						−5.582*** (0.339)
Constant	−2.471*** (0.187)	2.224*** (0.105)	2.418*** (0.138)	1.301*** (0.099)	2.027*** (0.099)	2.279*** (0.106)
Observations	1,555	1,197	834	641	1,116	1,348
Log Likelihood	−394.553	−376.197	−215.392	−329.432	−364.283	−372.746
Note:	*p < 0.1; **p < 0.05; ***p < 0.01					

Table 8. Contra SPD

	Dependent variable:					
	con_spd					
	(1)	(2)	(3)	(4)	(5)	(6)
pro_afd	5.588*** (0.134)					
pro_cdu		−5.022*** (0.194)				
pro_csu			−4.226*** (0.181)			
pro_fdp				−0.873*** (0.256)		
pro_gru					−5.085*** (0.321)	
pro_lin						−4.852*** (0.270)
Constant	−2.726*** (0.103)	1.993*** (0.062)	1.706*** (0.075)	0.842*** (0.063)	2.313*** (0.079)	2.156*** (0.100)
Observations	4,287	3,106	1,910	1,264	2,141	1,348
Log Likelihood	−935.764	−1,018.574	−731.424	−778.571	−633.318	−423.084
Note:	*p < 0.1; **p < 0.05; ***p < 0.01					

References

1. Blondel, V.D., Guillaume, J.L., Lambiotte, R., Lefebvre, E.: Fast unfolding of communities in large networks. J. Stat. Mech: Theory Exp. **2008**(10), P10008 (2008)
2. Bode, L., Hanna, A., Yang, J., Shah, D.V.: Candidate networks, citizen clusters, and political expression: strategic hashtag use in the 2010 midterms. Ann. Am. Acad. Polit. Soc. Sci. **659**(1), 149–165 (2015). https://doi.org/10.1177/0002716214563923
3. Colleoni, E., Rozza, A., Arvidsson, A.: Echo chamber or public sphere? predicting political orientation and measuring political homophily in Twitter using big data. J. Commun. **64**(2), 317–332 (2014)
4. Conover, M.D., Ratkiewicz, J., Francisco, M., Goncalves, B., Flammini, A., Menczer, F.: Political Polarization on Twitter, p. 8 (2011)
5. Dahlgren, P.: The Internet, public spheres, and political communication: dispersion and deliberation. Polit. Commun. **22**(2), 147–162 (2005). https://doi.org/10.1080/10584600590933160
6. Engesser, S., Ernst, N., Esser, F., Büchel, F.: Populism and social media: how politicians spread a fragmented ideology. Inf. Commun. Soc. **20**(8), 1109–1126 (2017). https://doi.org/10.1080/1369118X.2016.1207697
7. Enli, G., Simonsen, C.A.: 'Social media logic' meets professional norms: Twitter hashtags usage by journalists and politicians. Inf. Commun. Soc. **21**(8), 1081–1096 (2018). https://doi.org/10.1080/1369118X.2017.1301515
8. Frees, B., Koch, W.: Internetnutzung: frequenz und vielfalt nehmen in allen altersgruppen zu. Media Perspektiven **9**(2015), 366–377 (2015)

9. Grinberg, N., Joseph, K., Friedland, L., Swire-Thompson, B., Lazer, D.: Fake news on Twitter during the 2016 U.S. presidential election. Science **363**(6425), 374–378 (2019). https://doi.org/10.1126/science.aau2706

10. Jacomy, M., Venturini, T., Heymann, S., Bastian, M.: ForceAtlas2, a continuous graph layout algorithm for handy network visualization designed for the Gephi software. PLoS ONE **9**(6), e98679 (2014)

11. Keller, T.R., Klinger, U.: Social bots in election campaigns: theoretical, empirical, and methodological implications. Polit. Commun. **36**(1), 171–189 (2019). https://doi.org/10.1080/10584609.2018.1526238

12. Krämer, B.: Populist online practices: the function of the Internet in right-wing populism. Infor. Commun. Soc. **20**(9), 1293–1309 (2017). https://doi.org/10.1080/1369118X.2017.1328520

13. Neuendorf, K.A.: The Content Analysis Guidebook. 2nd edn. SAGE, Los Angeles (2017)

14. Stier, S., et al.: Systematically Monitoring Social Media: the case of the German federal election 2017. GESIS Papers 2018/4 (2018)

15. Stier, S., Posch, L., Bleier, A., Strohmaier, M.: When populists become popular: comparing Facebook use by the right-wing movement Pegida and German political parties. Inf. Commun. Soc. **20**(9), 1365–1388 (2017). https://doi.org/10.1080/1369118X.2017.1328519

Stylistic Features Usage: Similarities and Differences Using Multiple Social Networks

Kholoud Khalil Aldous[1]($\boxtimes$), Jisun An[2], and Bernard J. Jansen[2]

[1] College of Science and Engineering, Hamad Bin Khalifa University,
Doha, Qatar
kaldous@mail.hbku.edu.qa
[2] Qatar Computing Research Institute, Hamad Bin Khalifa University,
Doha, Qatar
{jisun.an,jjansen}@acm.org

Abstract. User engagement on social networks is essential for news outlets where they often distribute online content. News outlets simultaneously leverage multiple social media platforms to reach their overall audience and to increase marketshare. In this research, we analyze ten common stylistic features indicative of user engagement for news postings on multiple social media platforms. We display the stylistic features usage differences of news posts from various news sources. Results show that there are differences in the usage of stylistic features across social media platforms (Facebook, Instagram, Twitter, and YouTube). Online news outlets can benefit from these findings in building guidelines for content editors and creators to create more users engaging postings.

Keywords: Stylistic features · User engagement · News outlets

1 Introduction

Social networks are important dissemination channels for news outlets producing digital content [18]. More than half of news readers get at least part of their news from social networks [19], with most news outlets having an online presence on multiple social networks [20]. High user engagement on social networks is an indicator of news outlet success, where employees are trained to produce more engaging content [9]. Some typical user engagement metrics are likes, comments, shares, and views [2]. One commonly studied topic concerning user engagement is stylistic features (e.g., using question marks and emojis) in social media posts [3,5,6,15]. Stylistic features of online content have been used for a variety of tasks [23] and are effective in many domains [21]. However, there is a lack of studies using both multiple social networks and numerous news outlets. The largest social networks used by news outlets are Facebook, Twitter,

© Springer Nature Switzerland AG 2019
I. Weber et al. (Eds.): SocInfo 2019, LNCS 11864, pp. 309–318, 2019.
https://doi.org/10.1007/978-3-030-34971-4_22

Instagram, and YouTube [20]. Given that news outlets use multiple social platforms, and news readers are also using multiple platforms for getting their news, there are some open questions. *Does user engagement differ across platforms? Are there different audience behaviors for a news outlet on different platforms?*. Those questions motivate our research. For addressing a portion of these questions, we focus on understanding the similarities and differences of employed stylistic features in news postings of multiple news outlets. Also, we focus on four social platforms, which are Facebook (FB), Twitter (TW), Instagram (IG), and YouTube(YT).

Our objective is to understand what are the similarities and differences in styles in news social media posts affecting user engagement across social media platforms. Our results can assist news outlets when using multiple social media platforms for distributing their content. Through, focusing on the stylistic aspects of the content, we formulate the following research question (RQ): *Is user engagement on different social media platforms affected by content stylistic factors?* To answer our research question, we select two media type features: image and video, and eight common stylistic features for social networks content from the literature which are: emojis, question mark, exclamation mark, sentiment, hashtags, post length, URLs, and mentions. For simplicity, we call all ten features stylistics features, as most of them are related to the style of the post content.

2   Related Work

User Engagement on Facebook: Banhawi and Ali [3] report that posts with images, exclamation marks receive more likes and number of comments, question marks have no effect, and length of a post has a generally negative effect. Similarly, Cvijik and Michahelles [16] reported a significant relationship between media type and post topic on user engagement (likes, comments, and shares). Yu et al. [24] reported that status and photo posts trigger more likes than links and video.

User Engagement on Instagram: Manikonda et al. [14] report that users of Instagram and Twitter are fundamentally different (or users use these platforms differently) with Twitter being more of an information platform, resulting in differences in linguistic, topical and visual aspects of posts. Researching the visual content of images and emojis, Jaakonmäki et al. [11] report that these features impact the number of likes and comments. Burney [5] found that using question marks or hashtags in Instagram posts increase the number of likes and comments; however, using an exclamation mark reduces them.

User Engagement on Twitter: Naveed et al. [15] report that tweets with hashtags, usernames, and URLs are more likely to be retweeted; exclamation marks have a negative effect; question marks have a positive impact. Hua et al. [8] claim that topic influences audience interaction, and Lotan et al. [13] report that the probability of a user clicking on social media postings can also vary by topic. Brems et al. [4] report that journalists struggle with being factual or opinionated, being personal or professional, and how to balance broadcasting their message with engagement. Hong et al. [7] report that there is a network effect of the news media and user-generated content. Tweets with negative sentiment have a positive correlation with user engagement [22].

User Engagement on YouTube: Sayre et al. [17] find that the social media posts content reflects mainstream news and also influences professional media coverage. An et al. [1] show that audience segments are clustered around video topics. Hoiles et al. [6] state that title, description, and hashtags have positive effects on videos popularity if optimized.

3   Methodology

Data Collection: For addressing our research question, we used the API of the four social networks for collecting the news posting of 53 English news outlets that have active posting activities in the four networks. We collected the news postings from 1st of January 2017 until 31st of August 2017. The total collected posts are 27,117 (Facebook), 35,289 (Instagram), 571,270 (Twitter), 43,103 (YouTube). Some of the news outlets are CNN, BBC, New York Times, Vice, Bleacher Report, Aljazeera, The Guardian, The Washington Post, Fox News, The Wall Street Journal, MSNBC, Chicago Tribune, CNBC, and TIME (see appendix for complete listing).

Engagement Metrics: The number of likes and comments are common across the four selected social media platforms, so we use both to measure the effect of the usage of the stylistic feature in improving them. For overcoming the sparsity issue of many posts with zero engagement values, we use the log-normalized values for the number of likes and comments. We call the normalized values likes ratio (LR) and comments ratio (CR) throughout the rest of the paper. The normalization function used for LR is $LR_i = \log_2(\frac{L_i+1}{T_i+M_i})$, where L_i is the number of likes of the post i, T_i is the number of days from the posting day of the post i till the collection day, inclusive, and M_i is the maximum number of likes for the news outlet that posted the content. The same function used to calculate the CR using the number of comments.

Feature Extraction: *Media Type* features are video or image contained in the post. Media-type features do not apply to YouTube since all posts are videos; however, Facebook, Instagram, and Twitter posts can have a video or an image. *Emojis* are symbols used in posts to express emotions, feelings, ideas, activities, or objects within the digital text. To extract emojis from posts, we use a Python library called "emoji", which is part of the MIT licensed library. *Sentiment* of digital content can be one of three conditions: positive, neutral, or negative. For extracting sentiment for the posts, we use VADER (Valence Aware Dictionary and sEntiment Reasoner), as it is tuned to work specifically within social networks context [10]. VADER provides a compound score representing sentiment metrics for a given post. *URLs* We extract URLs from all posts and use URLs count as the URL feature. *Other* We count the question marks (?), exclamation marks (!), mentions (@), and hashtags (#) within each post. Also, we calculate the post length using the number of characters.

3.1 Prediction Model for User Engagement

We use stylistic features to build a model that predicts user engagement. Using 2-classes prediction model, we predict whether a given post will have high or low engagement on a social network. For building a model for each social network posts and each engagement metric, we use the LR and CR to separate the posts with the top 33% of engagement value posts labeled 1 (high engagement). The bottom 33% of posts with 0 (low engagement), while 0.5 is the random baseline of our model. For each news outlet, we separate the high and low engagement posts based on engagement level, as different numbers of followers are recorded for individual news outlets. We use all news outlets posts as one input to each model and add the news outlet as a categorical feature to address the effect of the actual news outlet. In total, we have 53 features representing the news outlets vector and ten stylistic features as input to the model. It is essential to highlight that we have used only suggestive stylistic features, and one can build on top of that using other features. For measuring the performance of the prediction models, we use F1-score using 10-fold cross-validation. Other measures (Precision, Recall, and Area Under the Curve) are positively correlated with F1-score as the dataset is balanced. We test four classification algorithms: AdaBoost, Decision Tree, Logistic Regression, and Random Forest. We report results only of Logistic Regression, as it performed better than other algorithms.

4   Results and Discussion

4.1   Individual Feature Analysis

To understand how individual features are associated with user engagement, we first analyze the coefficients of those features in the Logistic Regression model, shown in Table 1. Appendix A shows a visual illustration of the logistic regression coefficients values for individual features.

Table 1. Logistic regression coefficients and P-value significance

		FB	IG	TW	YT
Intercept	LR	−0.28***	0.00	−0.22***	−0.03***
	CR	−0.47***	0.09***	0.12***	−0.06***
[H1] Has Video	LR	0.68***	−0.48***	0.99***	N/A
	CR	0.68***	0.13***	0.43***	N/A
[H2] Has Image	LR	0.61***	0.48***	0.28***	N/A
	CR	−0.09	−0.04**	0.6***	N/A
[H3] Has Emoji	LR	0.76***	0.12***	0.26***	1.16*
	CR	0.49***	−0.07*	−0.11***	0.58
[H4] Has (?)	LR	−43***	−0.15**	−0.53***	0.07*
	CR	0.11*	0.48***	0.31***	0.07*
[H5] Has (!)	LR	0.07	−0.25***	−0.07**	0.05
	CR	−0.27**	−0.35***	−0.26***	0.04
[H6] Sentiment	LR	0.28***	0.29***	0.29***	−0.01***
	CR	−0.19***	−0.25***	−0.26***	−0.39***
[H7] # Count	LR	−0.34***	0.02***	−0.05***	0.0
	CR	−0.35***	0.0	−0.34***	0.0*
[H8] characters	LR	0.0*	−0.0***	0.01***	0**
	CR	0.0*	0.0*	0.01***	0.0***
[H9] URL count	LR	−0.203***	−0.22***	−0.41***	0.0
	CR	−0.37***	0.12**	−0.79***	−0.02***
[H10] @ Count	LR	−1.57***	0.05***	−0.30***	0.02
	CR	−0.84*	−0.11***	−0.11***	0.14

Significant level codes: * p<0.05,** p<0.01, *** p<0.001

Videos on FB and TW posts significantly increase both LR and CR. Videos in IG posts significantly increase CR but decreased LR. Media type features do not apply to YT because all posts are video type. **Images** significantly increase LR for FB, IG, and TW posts, as well as increasing CR for TW posts. In contrast, images significantly decrease CR engagement with FB and IG posts. This media type feature does not apply to YT. **Emojis** increase LR for the four platforms and increase the CR for FB. There is no significant effect on CR on YT and negative effect on CR on both IG and TW. **Question marks** in YT posts increase both LR and CR engagement, and they increase CR on the other three platforms (FB, IG, TW). However, question marks decrease the LR for FB, IG, and TW posts. **Exclamation marks** harm the engagement of three platforms. Exclamation marks significantly reduce both LR and CR engagement for IG and TW posts, and CR for Facebook posts. However, they do not affect the engagement of YT posts or LR for FB posts. **Post sentiment** significantly affects user engagement on all four social networks; although, the effect differed based on the type of engagement. Regarding LR, positive sentiment does increase the LR for FB, IG, and TW posts, but it decreases LR for YT posts. On the other hand, negative sentiment increases CR for all platforms. **Hashtags** have a weak but significant positive effect on LR on IG and CR for YT posts; however, hashtags have a significant negative impact on both LR and CR in FB and TW posts. The **number of characters** has a weak but significant positive effect on both LR and CR on FB, TW, and YT. With IG, the number of characters has a slight negative but significant impact on LR and a weak, positive effect on CR. The use of a **URL** within posts has a negative correlation with engagement on FB and TW. URL use decreases both LR and CR on FB and TW, LR on IG, and CR on YT posts. **Mentions** also decreases engagement on FB and TW. The use of mentions decreases CR but increases LR on IG.

Examining the results in Table 1, the takeaways are that there are some general trends across platforms, such as (a) commonality between Facebook and Twitter and also Instagram and YouTube, (b) some features can increase both LR and CR or at least one of these metrics, and (c) there are some features to avoid when attempting to increase engagement. The stylistic features have varied impact on likes and comments with some having a positive and others a negative impact. This indicates that the audience base likely varies among platforms and that likes and comments report different forms or levels of user engagement. This context complicates user engagement efforts by news outlets, as the environment is multifaceted with no simple rules or straightforward trends.

In comparing our findings to prior work, there are similarities. For Facebook, having a video in a post increases both LR and CR engagement [16]. For Instagram, emojis increase LR engagement [11]. For Twitter, exclamation marks decrease engagement [15]. On the other hand, there are differences between our findings and prior work. The number of characters was reported to affect user engagement on Facebook negatively [3]; however, our findings show a marginal but positive correlation on CR and LR. Also, negative sentiment was reported to increase user engagement on Twitter [22]; however, our findings show that negative sentiment has a positive correlation with CR but not for LR. For Facebook, having a URL in a post reportedly increases both LR and CR engagement [24]; however, our findings show a negative correlation. Our conjecture that this difference is the result of our controlled domain of news (avoiding domain differences), a large number of news outlets (avoiding news outlets differences), and the use of multiple platforms (controlling for content differences across platforms).

As such, we believe our results are an inspiration for further and more detailed research in this area by (1) providing a holistic view of media and stylistic features across the four platforms for the news domain and (2) showing what features are commonly used across different platforms within this domain. Also, we emphasize that the stylistic differences across platforms could be a result of the network (e.g., facilities and character) or because of the content and people on that network.

4.2 Predicting User Engagement

We now explore to what extent stylistic features can predict user engagement in the news domain on each of the individual platforms. As explained in the methods section, we first predict the level of user engagement given a post for each platform. Through 10-fold cross-validation using logistic regression on each platform, stylistic features perform better than random, with the F1 scores range 0.57–0.59, inclusively; hence, stylistic features work approximately the same across all platforms. Using FB (IG) posts the F1-scores are 0.58 and 0.57 (0.59 and 0.58) for LR and CR, respectively. Moreover, using TW posts stylistic features, the model predicts LR (CR) with F1-score 0.59 (0.57) while using YT posts, the F1-score is 0.58 for both LR and CR.

5   Conclusions and Future Research

In our research, we use ten common stylistic features to understand their usage similarities and differences for a large number of news outlets and across four social networks. We compared our findings with the patchwork of different studies concerning the effect of stylistic features on user engagement. In future work, other features [12] can be studied, including the volume of the posts per news outlet and the post type (e.g., breaking news, exclusive report, opinion). The 53 news outlet considered in this study are targeting an English-speaking audience, and most news outlets are US-based. This means that our results might not be generalizable for news media with other languages. It would be interesting to conduct a similar study for news media outlets in other countries in their mother tongues to see whether the patterns we found are consistent across different cultures.

A   The Logistic Regression Coefficients graphs

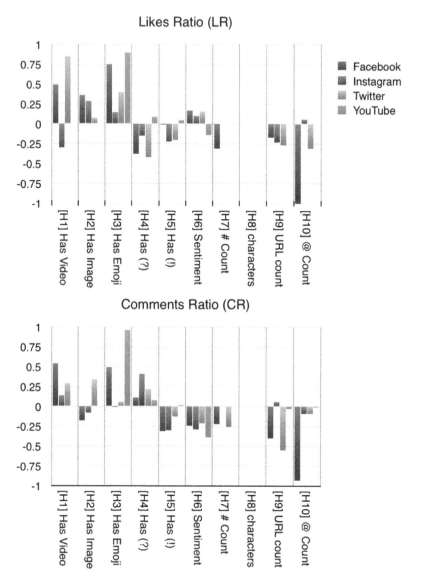

Fig. 1. The logistic regression coefficients for each stylistic feature and for each platforms

References

1. An, J., Kwak, H., Jansen, B.J.: Automatic generation of personas using youtube social media data. In: HICSS (2017)
2. Arapakis, I., Lalmas, M., Cambazoglu, B.B., Marcos, M.C., Jose, J.M.: User engagement in online news: under the scope of sentiment, interest, affect, and gaze. J. Assoc. Inf. Sci. Technol. **65**(10), 1988–2005 (2014)
3. Banhawi, F., Ali, N.M.: Measuring user engagement attributes in social networking application. In: STAIR. IEEE (2011)
4. Brems, C., Temmerman, M., Graham, T., Broersma, M.: Personal branding on twitter. Dig. J. **5**(4), 443–459 (2017)
5. Burney, K.: How to outperform fortune 500 brands on instagram (2016). http://contentmarketinginstitute.com/2016/08/outperform-brands-instagram/
6. Hoiles, W., Aprem, A., Krishnamurthy, V.: Engagement and popularity dynamics of youtube videos and sensitivity to meta-data. Trans. Knowl. Data Eng. **29**(7), 1426–1437 (2017)
7. Hong, L., Yang, W., Resnik, P., Frias-Martinez, V.: Uncovering topic dynamics of social media and news: the case of ferguson. In: Spiro, E., Ahn, Y.-Y. (eds.) SocInfo 2016. LNCS, vol. 10046, pp. 240–256. Springer, Cham (2016). https://doi.org/10.1007/978-3-319-47880-7_15
8. Hua, T., Ning, Y., Chen, F., Lu, C.T., Ramakrishnan, N.: Topical analysis of interactions between news and social media. In: AAAI (2016)
9. Huotari, L., Ulkuniemi, P., Saraniemi, S., Mäläskä, M.: Analysis of content creation in social media by B2B companies. J. Bus. Ind. Mark. **30**(6), 761–770 (2015)
10. Hutto, C.J., Gilbert, E.: Vader: A parsimonious rule-based model for sentiment analysis of social media text. In: ICWSM (2014)
11. Jaakonmäki, R., Müller, O., Vom Brocke, J.: The impact of content, context, and creator on user engagement in social media marketing. In: HICSS (2017)
12. Khatua, A., Khatua, A., Cambria, E.: A tale of two epidemics: contextual word2vec for classifying twitter streams during outbreaks. Info. Process. Manag. **56**(1), 247–257 (2019)
13. Lotan, G., Gaffney, D., Meyer, C.: Audience analysis of major news accounts on twitter. Soc. Flow **3**, 211 (2011)
14. Manikonda, L., Meduri, V.V., Kambhampati, S.: Tweeting the mind and instagramming the heart: exploring differentiated content sharing on social media. In: ICWSM (2016)
15. Naveed, N., Gottron, T., Kunegis, J., Alhadi, A.C.: Bad news travel fast: a content-based analysis of interestingness on twitter. In: WebSci. ACM (2011)
16. Pletikosa Cvijikj, I., Michahelles, F.: Online engagement factors on facebook brand pages. Soc. Netw. Anal. Min. **3**(4), 843–861 (2013)
17. Sayre, B., Bode, L., Shah, D., Wilcox, D., Shah, C.: Agenda setting in a digital age: tracking attention to california proposition 8 in social media, online news and conventional news. Pol. Internet **2**(2), 7–32 (2010)
18. Schlagwein, D., Hu, M.: How and why organisations use social media: five use types and their relation to absorptive capacity. J. Inf. Technol. **32**(2), 194–209 (2017)
19. Shearer, E., Gottfried, J.: News use across social media platforms 2017. Pew Research Center (2017)
20. Stocking, G.: Digital news fact sheet. State of the News Media, pp. 1–2 (2017)
21. Thelwall, M., Stuart, E.: She's reddit: a source of statistically significant gendered interest information? Inf. Process. Manag. **56**(4), 1543–1558 (2019)

22. Wu, B., Shen, H.: Analyzing and predicting news popularity on twitter. Int. J. Inf. Manag. **35**(6), 702–711 (2015)
23. Xing, F.Z., Pallucchini, F., Cambria, E.: Cognitive-inspired domain adaptation of sentiment lexicons. Inf. Process. Manag. **56**(3), 554–564 (2019)
24. Yu, B., Chen, M., Kwok, L.: Toward predicting popularity of social marketing messages. In: Salerno, J., Yang, S.J., Nau, D., Chai, S.-K. (eds.) SBP 2011. LNCS, vol. 6589, pp. 317–324. Springer, Heidelberg (2011). https://doi.org/10.1007/978-3-642-19656-0_44

Correction to: Measuring Personal Values in Cross-Cultural User-Generated Content

Yiting Shen, Steven R. Wilson, and Rada Mihalcea

Correction to:
Chapter "Measuring Personal Values in Cross-Cultural User-Generated Content" in: I. Weber et al. (Eds.):
***Social Informatics*, LNCS 11864,**
https://doi.org/10.1007/978-3-030-34971-4_10

The original version of this chapter was revised. A missing citation was added and the bibliography was updated accordingly.

The updated version of this chapter can be found at
https://doi.org/10.1007/978-3-030-34971-4_10

© Springer Nature Switzerland AG 2019
I. Weber et al. (Eds.): SocInfo 2019, LNCS 11864, p. C1, 2019.
https://doi.org/10.1007/978-3-030-34971-4_23

Author Index

Printed in the United States
By Bookmasters